Carola Surkamp /
Britta Viebrock (eds.)

Teaching English as a Foreign Language

An Introduction

J. B. Metzler Verlag

Die Herausgeberinnen
Carola Surkamp ist Professorin für englische Fachdidaktik an der Universität Göttingen.
Britta Viebrock ist Professorin für Didaktik der englischen Sprache und Literatur an der Universität Frankfurt.

Bibliografische Information der Deutschen Nationalbibliothek
Die Deutsche Nationalbibliothek verzeichnet diese Publikation in der Deutschen Nationalbibliografie; detaillierte bibliografische Daten sind im Internet über http://dnb.d-nb.de abrufbar.

ISBN 978-3-476-04479-2
ISBN 978-3-476-04480-8 (eBook)

J.B. Metzler ist ein Imprint der eingetragenen Gesellschaft Springer-Verlag GmbH, DE und ist Teil von Springer Nature
www.metzlerverlag.de
info@metzlerverlag.de

Einbandgestaltung: Finken & Bumiller, Stuttgart (Foto: iStock)
Satz: primustype Hurler GmbH

J.B. Metzler, Stuttgart
© Springer-Verlag GmbH Deutschland, ein Teil von Springer Nature, 2018

Contents

Contents

Foreword

The prime challenge of educating future teachers of English as a Foreign Language is to equip them with the necessary knowledge, skills and attitudes to teach to the best of their abilities and become professional practitioners with a great amount of competence, self-confidence and flexibility. At university, we strive to train experts not only with regard to the content matters of their subject, but especially with regard to pedagogical approaches and methodological principles. We try to provide profound theoretical knowledge and at the same time link this knowledge to practical issues of classroom teaching. Not only do we wish to prepare teachers for their daily practice, but also for the diverse future challenges of a vital profession. English language teachers need to become *agents of change* who actively respond to the demands posed by globalisation, multilingualism or digitalisation and use these developments for innovative teaching approaches.

The fourteen chapters of this book touch on the fundamental issues and principles of Teaching English as a Foreign Language (TEFL) in both a theoretical and a practical way. You will be able to gather insights into all competence areas important for modern foreign language teaching, its history, its framing by education policy, and most importantly, learn about the very focus point of each lesson, the students. At the same time, you will be able to reflect upon your professional development as a future teacher of English. To facilitate the acquisition of discipline-specific knowledge and professional development, each chapter contains definitions and illustrations for easy orientation, examples for practical applications and classroom use as well as occasions for the reflection of individual experiences.

In order to provide a profound knowledge base for topical discussions in introductory courses to TEFL, this book compiles a selection of up-to-date critical literature written by a young team of experts in the fields of language, literature and cultural teaching from universities and colleges all across Germany (and Austria). Upon finishing this project, we would like to thank all of the authors of this edition for their expertise and dedication. We would also like to express our gratitude to several colleagues both in Göttingen and Frankfurt without whom this project would not have been possible: Katharina Delius and Kira Sara as well as Viviane Lohe and Jan-Erik Leonhardt for critically commenting on content matters; Ina Gnauck and Jule Inken Müller for their editorial work (especially concerning the bibliographic references); and Mariella Veneziano-Osterrath for her meticulous proofreading—thank you! Ute Hechtfischer and her colleagues at Metzler Publishing House have been very enthusiastic about our project from the very beginning and maintained to show a strong sense of commitment. They have also been very helpful in providing advice on the formalities of the manuscript and supervising the production process. Finally, we would also like to thank the many students of our past introductory courses who, with their intelligent questions, ideas, and constructive feedback, have indirectly shaped the nature of this publication.

We hope that this introduction will inspire the future generations of students we had in mind when writing the chapters, but also teacher trainees, in-service teachers, and lecturers alike with new insights into Teaching English as a Foreign Language.

Carola Surkamp and Britta Viebrock

1 English Language Teaching and English Language Education — History and Methods

This chapter deals with the history of English language learning and teaching (ELT) and English language education (ELE) as an academic discipline. In the first part of this chapter, some background information will be provided with regard to the patterns that have been discovered when looking at the past centuries of language learning and teaching in Europe (and beyond). These patterns can help us to understand where we as teachers, learners and researchers of language learning and teaching come from and thus can also offer some orientation as to where we might or might not want to go with our teaching. This first part also provides some basic facts on the history of ELT in Germany since ca. 1800. The second section of this chapter zooms into the link between learning and teaching: a comprehensive discussion of ›method‹ as a flexible, multi-layered concept will be followed by an analysis of the history of selected examples of modern language teaching methods from this conceptual perspective. The third section contains an overview of how foreign language education (FLE), with a focus on ELE, evolved in Western Germany as a fairly young academic discipline with a focus on the second half of the 20th century. The chapter concludes with an outlook on the relevance for (future) language teachers to deal with the history of their profession and their discipline.

> **English Language Education (ELE)** is the academic discipline concerned with the investigation of the *what, how, why/what for* and *who* of teaching and learning English as a second/foreign language (L2). The academic discipline which looks at these phenomena from a cross-language perspective is called **Foreign Language Education (FLE)**.

Definition

1.1 | Background: milestones of ELT history in Germany and Europe since ca. 1800

Monastery tradition versus marketplace tradition: In this section, an overview of the central stages of English learning and teaching will be given, which facilitates the description and recognition of recurring patterns that have emerged in the long history of language learning and teaching. One of these patterns is the need to communicate in everyday and professional life, for example, with merchants, traders and travellers. This type of motivation and the matching ways of language learning and teaching have often been called the »marketplace tradition«. McArthur (1998, 83) sees it as complementary to the so-called »monastery tradition« in which the primary motivation for language learning is anchored in the academic field. In the latter tradition, languages are primarily seen as gatekeepers providing access to knowledge and educational institutions.

A look back over time shows that language teaching and learning have often moved between these two orientations and that in many cases teachers and learners alike have tried to strike a balance between the two poles. This conflict of interests was evident in the past centuries of the European history of language learning, teaching and (university) education and also applies to the 200-year-history of teaching/learning English in Germany since 1800. This is how long it took, in fact, until English was established as the main foreign language in society and education in Germany (cf. Doff/Klippel 2007, 17 ff.).

Self-regulated English language learning in the 18th century: The 18th century marked the beginning of a meteoric rise of the popularity of the English language. In the first two thirds of the 18th century, English was only sporadically present in schools and universities across the German countries. However, an interest in the language was continuously fed at this stage by the growing desire to read: formative works on politics, science, philosophy, theology, art and English literature attracted a large number of **educated adult readers**. In many cases, these works had to be read in the original due to a lack of translation. Therefore, reading in English was a central skill that had to be acquired individually, through home or school study. This is reflected in a number of textbooks from this period, which typically included a grammar part and additional discussions/dialogues, a dictionary, lists of key words or short reading texts. The set-up of the grammar parts of most textbooks for English was **based on Latin grammar books**. The rules and illustrations with example sentences, which often came from well-known literary works, were presented in German.

English as a school subject in the 19th century: The number of self-taught adult learners of English continued to rise in the 19th century. One of the most important new phenomena was that in this century English teaching was established **in boys' (and later on in girls') state secondary schools as a school subject** (cf. Klippel 1994; Doff 2002). This change demanded a differentiation and adaptation of content, material and methods to address the young target group adequately. Although the overall goal of teaching English was language proficiency, slightly different objectives were pursued in the different types of schools for boys and girls. There also was a growing competition between the emerging ›real‹ institutions (*Realanstalten*) in the 19th century and the traditional grammar schools (*Gymnasien*). The former put a focus on natural sciences and the practice of modern foreign languages (i. e. as part of a marketplace tradition). The latter focused on classical languages associated with a humanistic and formal education concept (rather in line with a monastery tradition).

The most ›modern‹ foreign language teaching at this stage probably took place at secondary schools for girls, where principles that are known today as ›communicative foreign language teaching‹ and ›English as a working language‹, i. e. the use of English for communicative purposes in subjects other than languages were realised (cf. Doff 2002). The different approaches led to controversial discussions about goals and methods of English language teaching as illustrated in the following quotation:

Discussions and controversies about goals and methods of English language teaching

I do not greatly value hearing a man speak perfect English, any skilled waiter can do that, babbling in institutional French is not worth much because they do not actually know why after this or that conjunction a subjunctive comes if they know the existing rule. [...] Let girls chat about the weather and walks, the educated have something else to do. [...] [H]e should penetrate the genius of languages, he should study the idea of nations, the ideas of foreigners, not master their words, he should have to study the historical background of languages and the type of languages, this method should and must come from the grammar school. The educated person from the grammar school, the only and real nursery of the educated, must be opposed to this crude language study [...]. (von Reinhardstöttner 1868, 13 f., translation SD)

Modern language reform movement: Towards the end of the 19th century, a group of modern language teachers turned against this position, a movement that spread across Europe and is now referred to as the ›(modern language) reform movement‹ (cf. Howatt/Smith 2002). The initial impetus for this movement stems from Wilhelm Viëtor's (1882) work *Der Sprachunterricht muss umkehren!* (›Language teaching must reverse!‹), originally published under the pseudonym Quousque Tandem. To put it briefly, he (and other reformers) demanded that modern languages should be taught as living languages, i. e. unlike the classical languages. For example, priority was to be given to the spoken language whereas explicit grammar knowledge should take a subservient role. Furthermore, the reformers demanded, teaching should be done in the foreign language and translation into and from the mother tongue of the learners should be reduced.

Expansion of teaching English in the 20th century: Even if the demands of the reformers did not completely dominate in the 20th century, this movement greatly influenced the academic debate in foreign language learning and teaching across Europe in the decades and century to follow. The first third of the 20th century was dominated by the question of which role the knowledge and understanding of cultural aspects should play in the teaching of foreign languages (cf. chapter 9 in this volume).

This issue formed the heart of what became known as the ***Kulturkunde-bewegung***, which gained momentum at the beginning of the 20th century. Foundations of this movement were laid in a specific memorandum, the so-called *Richert'schen Richtlinien* of 1924, where the teaching of German language, literature and culture was given a clear priority over the teaching and learning of foreign languages. This served to show the alleged ›superiority‹ of the German nation state (represented, for example, by German culture and the German language) (cf. Hüllen 2000).

This fitted in with Nazi ideology, whereby the main goal of foreign language teaching was to show the learners that their own culture should be regarded as superior to others. The Nazis extended the **dominant structural role of English as a foreign language in schools** mainly for political reasons (learning the language of the enemy). In 1937–38, the sequence of foreign languages to be taught at grammar schools was standardised to English before French. However, despite the numerous political efforts and a broad affirmative public discussion among Nazi school experts, the influence of how and what was taught in language classrooms during the time of the regime seems to have remained limited (cf. Lehberger 1986).

After 1945, there was a reverse back to the situation before 1933 in many aspects—at least initially. Pre-war methods and materials were used, partly due to the fact that there was not enough paper to print textbooks and other materials which matched the up to date requirements of school and society. One of these requirements was that foreign languages, English in particular, should be taught to all pupils, not just to grammar school students. Accordingly, in the Federal Republic of Germany the so-called *Hamburger Abkommen* (›Hamburg convention‹) in 1964 marked a milestone in the teaching of English. With this convention, English became the mandatory first foreign language at all secondary school types (including lower secondary school).

After this brief look at some key facts in the history of ELT up to the mid 1960s, the following section will offer a journey through time with a conceptual focus on ›method‹.

1.2 | Methods as an anchor of language teaching across the centuries

1.2.1 | ›Method‹ as a multidimensional concept

Definition

> Methods (from the Latin-Greek *methodus/méthodos*: ›the path towards a goal‹) are the ways a teacher proceeds to handle content in foreign language teaching and thus to achieve certain goals. To summarise, a method answers the question of how teaching and learning are organised.

In FLE, the term ›method‹ is used in different ways that are either more theory-oriented or more practice-oriented. Richards/Rodgers (2014) have structured the concept of method along a continuum of three overlapping clusters. According to them, the term method may describe

- **theoretical foundations:** i. e. scientific reasonable assumptions about the nature of language and successful language learning (APPROACH);
- **design principles:** such as objectives, syllabus, task types, role of the teacher and the learner, materials (DESIGN); or
- **practical implementations:** observable techniques, practices and behaviours when a specific approach is used (PROCEDURE).

Different
understandings
of ›method‹

While the concept of method covers the entire spectrum, not all aspects may be (completely) visible at any point of time. The question of ›best method‹ in terms of the most effective cost-benefit ratio for teachers and learners has been an everlasting question in foreign language education over the course of time. It has been answered differently depending on the era and cultural context.

Whether the application of specific methods by teachers actually leads to successful learning has been a controversial issue in more recent academic discourse, too. It is emphasised that teaching methods (or components thereof), which are often perceived as incompatible, are not usually represented as closed, logical sequences of concepts, but are in fact used parallel to one another. For instance, manifestations of the grammar-translation method often assigned to the 19th century (see below) are used in certain parts of the world to date and have remained very popular. Another example is the direct method usually anchored in the late 19th/early 20th century (see below), which continues to play quite an important role as the dominant method in the context of the Berlitz Language Institute (cf. Larsen-Freeman 2000, 177). From the 1980s, the so-called **postmethod period** has been identified, which follows this line of thought and questions the concept of method altogether (cf. Kumaravadivelu 2006a and chapter 3 in this volume).

Continuum of coexisting methodological dimensions: In addition to these considerations, methods in language teaching and learning are characterised by a coexistence of different methodological dimensions (›basic options‹ according to Pennycook 1989; cf. also Thornbury 2011, 192 f.), which have developed over time. The four general educational dimensions ›achievement‹, ›encounter‹, ›learning tool‹ and ›framing‹ (cf. illustration 1.1) can be adopted for any school subject (cf. Terhart 2005, 23 ff.). The sub-dimensions (a.1, a.2 ...) are those subject-specific concepts that need to be considered in English language teaching in particular:

Achievement accentuates method as a way to accomplish learning objectives. In the language classroom, this can mean objectives geared towards accuracy (i. e. correct use of language) or/and towards fluency, i. e. »features which give speech the qualities of being natural and normal, including native-like use of pausing, rhythm, intonation, stress, rate of speaking, and use of interjections and interruptions« (Richards et al. 1985, 108). As the name implies, process orientation focuses more explic-

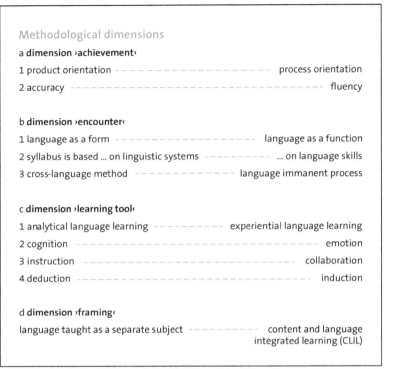

Methodological dimensions

a dimension ›achievement‹

1 product orientation – process orientation

2 accuracy – fluency

b dimension ›encounter‹

1 language as a form – – – – – – – – – – – – – – – – – – language as a function

2 syllabus is based ... on linguistic systems – – – – – – – – – ... on language skills

3 cross-language method – – – – – – – – – – – – language immanent process

c dimension ›learning tool‹

1 analytical language learning – – – – – – – – – experiential language learning

2 cognition – emotion

3 instruction – collaboration

4 deduction – induction

d dimension ›framing‹

language taught as a separate subject – – – – – – – – – content and language
integrated learning (CLIL)

Illustration 1.1:
Dimensions of
language teaching
methods (see
examples below)

itly on the learning process and less on the outcome. Conversely, product orientation focuses on a tangible final product. As in many of the sub-dimensions listed under (a)–(d), the two ends of the continuum can best be understood as complements rather than contrasts.

Encounter includes sub-dimensions which grasp ›method‹ as a combination of subject and learners, for example, a teacher's answer to the question if other languages than the language taught should be actively or passively included (b.3: cross-language) or more or less deliberately left out, i. e. language learning should be conceptualised as a language-immanent process. Likewise, an understanding of language as a formal system, which would highlight structural aspects and demand a syllabus based on the logic of linguistic systems, has different implications for teaching and learning than a functional view of language, which would highlight communicative aspects and demands a syllabus based on practicing the different language skills (listening, speaking, reading, writing and mediation; cf. chapters 6 and 7 in this volume).

Method can primarily be seen as a learning tool, i. e. as a way of producing optimum teaching and learning conditions. More often than not this optimum is seen as a balance between different ways of teaching that offer the addressees a wide choice of learning approaches, which could be more analytical, predominantly demanding mental exercise, or more experiential, predominantly demanding situations in which to experience language use (cf. Thaler 2010a). While the former most likely takes place within an instructive setting and is connected to a deductive approach, where the teacher explains the rules and the learners apply them in fairly structured exercises, the latter most likely takes place within a collaborative setting and is connected to an inductive approach, where the learners discover the rules based on their experiences. Similarly, methods can be more explicitly based on cognition, i. e. thinking and analysing, or emotion, i. e. feeling and experiencing.

Framing describes ways of institutionalising lessons in which language can be taught as a separate subject or integrated with a content-based subject, for example geography taught in English. The latter option is also referred to as Content and Language Integrated Learning (CLIL), a model that has been very successful in ELT as well as in ELE/FLE in the past decades (cf. Doff 2010; Hallet/Königs 2013; and chapter 11 in this volume).

As these explanations demonstrate, the individual sub-dimensions are not always clear-cut and often overlap. However, methods can historically be identified on account of their specific configuration of sub-dimensions. For example, within the grammar-translation method, language as form is emphasised (sub-dimension b.1), the syllabus is based on linguistic systems (b.2) and analytical language learning is usually given priority (c.1). More illustrations of the sub-dimensions and various combinations in which they have existed in the history of language teaching are provided in the next section.

1.2.2 | History and present day methods in foreign language teaching

Prototypical methods and their practical implementation: Historically, the emergence and recession of several prototypical teaching methods can be identified, which became particularly relevant in specific contexts and at specific stages in the 200-year history of teaching English as a foreign language in German classrooms. However, these highly influential methods in the history of institutionalised modern language teaching have to be understood as ideal types that were never practically implemented (›**methodology‹**) in their pure form. They were identifiable on account of typical clusters of subject-specific concepts as explained in the previous section.

Grammar-translation method: In the 19th century with the introduction of modern foreign languages in the state school system, the so-called grammar-translation method was widespread. Language was formally taught according to the teaching of classical languages; the aim was accuracy (i. e. formal correctness) in understanding and the focus was on the construction of sentences and texts. In this context, the curriculum was organised according to linguistic sub-systems—profound knowledge of words and grammar. Within the grammar-translation method great importance was placed on the written word and analytical language learning expressed in the most precise translation into or from the foreign language. The grammar-translation method was the leading method in textbooks for both French (cf. Meidinger 1811) and English (cf. Fick 1800), the two most widely learned foreign languages in the first half of the 19th century.

Direct method: With the establishment of modern languages in state schools, it became apparent in the last third of the 19th century that methods appropriate for teaching classical languages did not necessarily meet the requirements of modern language teaching. More often than not the latter focused on usability, practicality and functionality. The focus thus shifted away from the grammar-translation method towards the direct method which accentuated the characteristics of »modern« foreign language teaching, such as a focus on fluent spoken language (cf. illustration 1.1, sub-dimension a.2), as well as on language as function rather than form (b.1) and the orientation of the syllabus on language skills (b.2). This shift was supported by advocates of the modern language reform movement explained above, who also fostered inductive learning (c.4) and language-immanent learning processes (connecting to the first language of the learners, see b.3).

Audiolingual and audiovisual methods: The 1950s and 1960s brought new approaches in linguistics and educational psychology, in particular from the United States (including Lado 1967), which subsequently became very influential in Western Germany. These approaches and their impact on language teaching methods were critically discussed in academic discourse, which was characterised by a research-based reflection on language as well as processes and outcomes of language teaching and learning at the time (cf. Hüllen 2005, 142). Audiolingual and audiovisual methods, which became popular from the 1960s onwards, form the direct link between this academic discourse and the language classrooms in Western Germany.

Based on the linguistic theory of **structuralism**, these methods focused on the formal explanation of language through specific language patterns (for example in the areas of vocabulary or phonetics, which is concerned with the sound of human speech, or syntax, which is concerned with the rules for the formation of sentences). For that reason, the syllabus was organised according to linguistic systems (grammar progression; cf. illustration 1.1, sub-dimension b.2). The **audiolingual method** put the spoken (everyday) language into the foreground (a.2). Everyday language was presented in dialogues, which had to be habitually practised by way of pattern drills, i.e. a context-embedded substitution of sentence parts based on imitation and repetition. Language learning was understood as an example of experience-based behavioural change. Listening and speaking had priority over reading and writing, teaching should be carried out mainly in the foreign language (b.3), embedded in everyday situations.

The audiolingual method was further developed as the **audiovisual method** in France and in the USA. The advancement in language teaching technology, especially visuals (slides, films, transparencies) and auditory media (tapes, cassettes, language labs) supported this development. Important elements of the audiovisual method were the use of visual media as well as a situational and context-embedded language use, which included the repression of analytical and cognitive elements (c.1, c.2). Audiolingual and audiovisual teaching methods were often criticised for their neglect of conscious mental activities (cognition) and creativity.

Communicative foreign language teaching: At the beginning of the 1970s, demands for teaching methods with a different focus increased. Taking into account other influential developments such as the political theory of the Frankfurt School with Habermas' principle of communicative rationality as a key element (cf. Habermas 1981), teaching methods now should allow learners to be active and emancipated in the (foreign) language classroom and beyond, i. e. as citizens who could make their voices heard. Consequently, a key role was awarded to the process of communication in the language classroom (cf. illustration 1.1, sub-dimension a.1). Since this ›**communicative turn**‹ a pluralism of methodological characteristics can be identified under the umbrella of the so-called ›**communicative approach**‹. These characteristics all aim at the key objective of **communicative competence** (cf. Piepho 1974).

> According to Canale and Swain (1980), communicative competence can be defined in terms of the following four components:
> - grammatical competence (the ability to use correct language);
> - sociolinguistic competence (the ability to produce appropriate language);
> - discourse competence (the ability to produce cohesive and coherent language) and
> - strategic competence (the ability to use language effectively).

Definition

Initially, communicative competence meant a focus on communication (in the sense of **fluency**) while simultaneously dispensing with formal correctness (in the sense of **accuracy**). Associated with this new focus, was a move away from teaching and subject matter towards the learner. To this day, the communicative approach dominates foreign language teaching, as can be seen in task-based teaching of foreign languages (cf. chapter 11 in this volume) and intercultural pedagogy (cf. chapter 9 in this volume). Among the key features of this approach are an understanding of language as a function rather than a form (cf. b.1) and an according organisation of the syllabus (i. e. based on language skills rather than on grammatical systems, b.2).

These and related issues of (English) language learning and teaching are researched in a fairly young academic discipline, English Language Education (ELE). The next subsection deals with the emergence and subsequent development of this discipline in Germany.

1.3 | Foreign language education (FLE) and English language education (ELE) as academic disciplines in Germany

1.3.1 | Main concepts

As defined above, **Foreign Language Education (FLE)** is the academic discipline which deals with the teaching and learning of foreign/second language(s) (L2) in institutional, primarily school-based contexts. It can be seen as a connector between the specialist sub-disciplines of the individual foreign languages (for example, **English Language Education (ELE)**, Spanish language education etc.), based on their common objectives, content and methods. The genesis of these sub-disciplines (for example, English, French, Spanish, Russian or German as a Second or Foreign Language) has taken place in different ways and at different speeds.

FLE as an applied science: A key feature of FLE is that it is an applied science (comparable to, for example, medicine or engineering), »a theory of foreign language teaching reflecting the practice which is based on scientific theory, from which justified proposals and recommendations for the design [of teaching foreign languages] are derived« (Timm 1998, 3). In society, FLE, in addition to teacher education, assumes primarily the function of »representing the interests of the controlled teaching and learning of foreign languages« (Zydatiß 1988, 109) in the interplay between the real world, institutions and referential disciplines.

Core tasks of FLE include:
- the clarification of the **value** of foreign language teaching/learning in society;
- the re-enforcement of the **existence** of these subjects against other social forces;
- the participation in decision-making about the objectives and content of foreign language **curricula**, the development of target group specific methods and
- the realisation of **research** projects, which can be of empirical, hermeneutic and/or ideologically critical nature (cf. Timm 1998, 3).

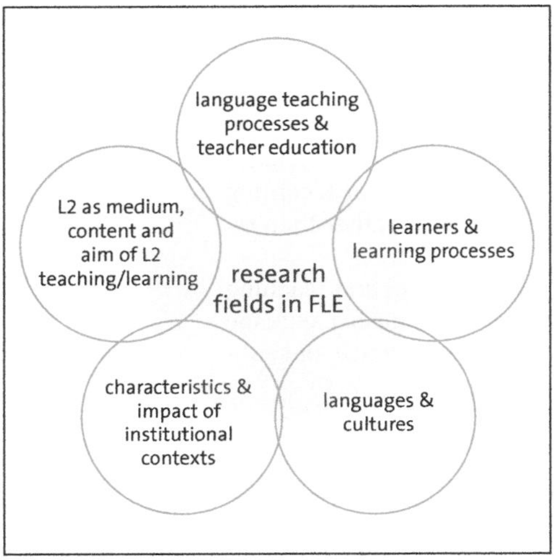

According to Christ/Hüllen (1995) five main topical areas constitute the **research fields of FLE**. The first is concerned with processes of language teaching and teacher education (e. g. aspects of teacher professionalism as discussed in chapter 3 in this volume). The second deals with learners and language learning processes (e. g. stages of language acquisition as discussed in chapter 5 in this volume or individual learner characteristics as discussed in

Illustration 1.2: Main research areas in Foreign Language Education (adapted from Christ/Hüllen 1995)

research fields in FLE

- language teaching processes & teacher education
- L2 as medium, content and aim of L2 teaching/learning
- learners & learning processes
- characteristics & impact of institutional contexts
- languages & cultures

chapter 4). The third area focuses on the interfaces of language and culture including comparisons of the foreign language with the learners' first languages (L1) as well as cultural dimensions of second or foreign language (L2) teaching and learning (cf. chapter 9 in this volume). Area 4 concentrates on the characteristics and impact of institutional contexts on L2 teaching and learning (e. g. aspects of education policy as discussed in chapter 2 or the classroom setting as discussed in chapter 13 in this volume). The last area is concerned with the foreign language as a medium of instruction as well as the overall content and objective of L2 teaching and learning.

1.3.2 | Genesis as an academic discipline

Early academic roots: In the context of learning and teaching foreign languages, the term ›didactics‹ occurred early on. **Comenius**, whose *Didactica Magna* (1657) is still the basis of some of the first known books on learning of foreign languages (so-called ›methodologies‹), demanded that the mother tongue and the other modern neighbour languages be adequately taken into account in language teaching (›lessons for all‹). In the **18th century**, this demand was only slowly realised and the classical languages were still focused on in language education. Gradually, however, modern national languages gained in significance both in literary production and in school practice. In Germany, enthusiasm for French rose during the course of the 18th century. Its distribution increased accordingly, in schools and in other educational contexts. This development also applied to English over time. In theoretical studies as well as in school education, living languages were considered alongside classical foreign languages. This meant that foreign language skills were also taught to deal with real-life issues. The notion of usefulness (as opposed to merely mental discipline) gained great importance.

In his essay on philology (1840), **Carl Mager** developed so-called school ›sciences‹, the outlines of which corresponded to today's ideas of specialist pedagogy and methodology. He even referred to the term ›didactics‹ (in the German language). Another early use of the term in the context of teaching modern foreign languages, i. e. English and French, can be found in a book title from 1895 (cf. Münch/Glauning 1895).

Constitution as an academic discipline: The beginnings of FLE as an institutionalised academic discipline lie in the second half of the **19th century** with the establishment of the first professorships for new philologies at universities as well as the founding of the first specialized academic journals and associations. The reintroduction of FLE took place **after the Second World War** (cf. Hüllen 2004) with the help of authors such as G. Hausmann, W. Klafki and P. Heimann, who often based their ideas on Comenius' *Didactica Magna*. The terms *Fachdidaktik* (subject teaching education) and *Fremdsprachendidaktik* (FLE) were implemented successively in post-WWII Western Germany but not Eastern Germany. During the 1960s, universities of education were set up as theory- and research-based educational colleges for teacher training (*Pädagogische*

Hochschulen). In this phase, which marks a fundamental reform of teacher education in Western Germany, subject-specific teaching and learning (*Fachdidaktik*) was established as an academic discipline in different domains (in addition to foreign languages there were also, for example, mathematics, geography and biology). Between the end of the 1950s and the end of the 1960s, specific subject teaching and learning education developed further based on the insight that content, goals and methods must be reflected with a distinct reference to a particular subject.

Definition

> Fremdsprachendidaktik is a term commonly used in the German language to describe the academic discipline that deals with teaching and learning foreign languages, mainly in institutional settings. In English, the term ›didactics‹ (pl.) denotes the art or science of teaching. It is not to be confused with the adjective ›didactic‹, which implies teaching or intending to teach a moral lesson, lecturing others too much or being a preachy and pedantic speaker. Other terms that are used in the English language are TEFL (teaching English as a foreign language) theory and methodology, TEFL pedagogy, or TESOL (teaching English to speakers of other languages).

First steps of institutionalisation: The immediate post-war period was marked by a strong **dogmatism** with regard to language learning processes, thus a defined set of teaching methods was firmly established (see 1.2.2 above, cf. Hüllen 2005, 145 f.). From the mid-1960s onwards, however, a continuing process of empirical substantiation and differentiation of knowledge about foreign language teaching and learning processes began. This tendency gained momentum as a result of the reorientation of the teaching content in the context of the Communicative Turn of the 1970s and its focus on spoken language and everyday communication. The first steps of the institutionalisation of FLE and ELE were influenced by general educational debates and by the important role of school language teaching in post-war Western Germany. Thus, for example, the legitimation and establishment of ELE is closely linked to the introduction of ›**English for All**‹ by the Hamburg Convention of 1964.

English Language Education as a model discipline: Since English was the most widely spread language in the field and the school curriculum, the development of ELE can be regarded as a model for similar disciplines in other languages up to the beginning of the 1980s. Over these decades the establishment of a considerable number of professorships for specialised sub-disciplines of modern language education at educational colleges and universities indicates the institutional anchoring of ELE/FLE in the Federal Republic of Germany. The integration of educational colleges (*Pädagogische Hochschulen*) into the universities (from the 1970s onwards) meant an adaptation of teacher education for grammar and non-grammar school teachers.

The main tasks of FLE, ELE and related disciplines in other modern

(Further) development of a **theory of foreign language teaching/learning** in close cooperation with **practice**.

Filter function within university teacher training courses, i.e. selection of relevant study content from the socalled ›referential disciplines‹ (for example, Linguistics, Literary and Cultural Studies, Pedagogy, Psychology) with the objective of strengthening professionalism.

Self-referential reflection on the FLE/ELE subject matter with regard to practical use, i.e. in terms of **social relevance** and common **educational requirements**.

Illustration 1.3:
Main tasks of FLE,
ELE and related
disciplines

languages were predominantly articulated within the three **target areas** (cf. Doff 2008, 198 ff.), which did not remain undisputed (see illustration 1.3).

At this early stage, the discussion of tasks and responsibilities shaped the understanding of the ELE/FLE sciences as essentially application-oriented disciplines with a **specific theory-practice-reference** (cf. Müller 1979). Also, in the middle of the 1960s the discussion of the relationship of ELE/FLE and different **referential disciplines** began. In addition to Educational Sciences (including, for example General Didactics and Pedagogy), these included especially Linguistics, Cultural and Literary Studies, but also Psychology and—more recently—Neuroscience, Sociology and Philosophy (for a more detailed overview of interdisciplinary relations in the field of language learning and teaching cf. Burwitz-Melzer et al. 2016, chap. B).

Referential disciplines

Example

- **Literary Studies** are concerned with the study of different literary genres and the interaction between author, text and reader. Models and approaches of text interpretation quite directly feed into educational considerations regarding the potential of aesthetic texts for language learning and general education.
- Moreover, insights from the field of **Linguistics**, which studies language as a system, may be helpful in understanding, teaching and learning grammatical phenomena as well as the pragmatics of language use. Especially, the findings of **Applied Linguistics** in the fields of first and second language acquisition are directly relevant for foreign language teaching.
- In a similar fashion, the learning theories derived from **Educational Sciences** and **Psychology** influence approaches to institutional (second) language learning (cf. chapter 5 in this volume).

- **Cultural Studies** as an interdisciplinary approach looks at the representation of cultural aspects and meaning-making processes in society and thus influences the choice of classroom topics. Central categories to be analysed are race, gender and class.
- **Sociology** is concerned with the empirical and theoretical study of human behaviour, also in organisations and institutions, and thus influences the field of ELE.
- The domain of **Philosophy** that is particularly relevant for ELE is epistemology, which deals with the nature and scope of knowledge and the question how it can be acquired.

Establishment, consolidation, differentiation: Since the 1980s, a phase of the establishment, consolidation and differentiation of ELE/FLE—both institutionally and conceptually—has taken place. In addition to ELE and French language education, education in teaching other foreign languages, such as Spanish, German as a Foreign Language and as a Second Language as well as Slavic languages has developed. The conceptual expansion of the field ›L2 learning and teaching‹ became visible in the emergence and consolidation of (new) related disciplines, such as Applied Linguistics, which is concerned with the systematic study of communicative aspects of language use in particular settings or social groups and second language acquisition (SLA), which is a sub-discipline of Applied Linguistics and concerned with the study of language acquisition processes. Further indicators of this establishment and consolidation are the increasing activities and number of conferences of research associations during this phase (cf. Doff 2008, 202 ff.).

| Example | **Deutsche Gesellschaft für Fremdsprachenforschung** |

The ›German Society for Foreign Language Research‹ (DGFF) was founded in the late 1980s. Today, the DGFF is an association with around 500 members worldwide that aims to bring together researchers in the fields of teaching and learning foreign languages, acquisition and use of second languages, multilingualism and intercultural learning.

Coming of age as an academic discipline: The process of the expansion and differentiation of FLE/ELE, which began in the 1970s and continues to this day, is reflected on a third level, namely that of PhD studies and further research papers related to the expansion of knowledge in the field (for a detailed discussion cf. Doff 2008, 207 f.). These include specialised bibliographies and manuals, by means of which a systematisation of the language and terminology of FLE/ELE has taken place. During the 1970s, the number of doctorates in the the field of learning and teaching foreign/ second languages grew slowly but steadily and almost quadrupled in the 1980s. In order to systematise the continually growing body of knowledge in the field, bibliographies (among others the ›Bibliography of Modern Foreign Language Teaching‹ created in 1969 by Freudenstein; cf. https://

www.uni-marburg.de/ifs/bibliographie) made an equally important contribution to relevant lexicons and reference works. The most comprehensive example is the *Handbuch Fremdsprachenunterricht* (cf. Bausch et al.
1989). The expanded and revised editions of this standard work (most
recently completely revised and extended edition 2016) show a certain
level of maturity of FLE as academic discipline, whose expansion continues up to the present day.

1.4 | Conclusion: reasons for studying ELT/ELE history

Why should you as a (future) English language teacher know (more)
about what has been discussed in this chapter and what could that mean
for your professional development? For (foreign language) teachers one of
the core questions is the choice of methods which determine their everyday practical teaching (cf. Terhart 2005, 93 ff.): Thus, the preoccupation
with and the discussion of methods and methodology are a salient issue
for all teachers as well as those involved in teacher education. A central,
yet hardly explored phenomenon in this context, is the tension of method
as a theory-based academic concept (methods) on the one hand and the
application of techniques, processes and everyday practices on the other
(methodology) (cf. Kumaravadivelu 2006a, 84; Thornbury 2011, 195 f.).

A major concern of the education of (future) foreign language teachers
is to introduce them to a range of teaching methods appropriate to the
situation and for balancing out content demands, teaching objectives and
the needs of any group of learners. A similar concern is to familiarise future teachers with the broadest possible repertoire of methods for critically reflecting on their own methodological practice (discussed as »reflective practice« in chapter 3 of this volume; cf. also Burton 2009).

Beyond these very practical considerations, a look back into the history of English language teaching and English language education has
manifold potentials (cf. Hüllen 2000; see also Doff/Klippel 2007, 15 f.)
which reach beyond the obvious, immediate practicalities and which,
unfortunately, are often overlooked. Knowledge of the past of our own
subject

- can contribute to a **deeper understanding of the present** with its
  strengths and weaknesses;
- can bring a certain **air of caution towards new fashions** and a seren-
  ity towards any kind of methodological or technical ›hype‹;
- makes it clear that language learning and teaching were and are important **culture-creating activities**;
- gives insight into the **constants of foreign language learning and
  teaching** with each era generating different solutions;
- contains interesting **individual findings**;
- offers **comparisons of past and current issues** with the potential to
  increase critical awareness and a sensitivity towards dubious concepts;
- may foster the **self-confidence of foreign language teachers** when
  they realise that they are part of a long tradition of the profession.

Historical Sources

Fick, Johann Christian (³1800): *Theoretisch-praktische Anweisung zur leichtern Erlernung der Englischen Sprache. Erster Theil: Praktische englische Sprache* [1793]. Erlangen.

Mager, Karl Wilhelm Eduard (1985): »Die moderne Philologie und die deutschen Schulen«. In: Kronen, Heinrich (ed.): *Gesammelte Werke*. Vol. 2: *Fremdsprachenunterricht* [1840]. Baltmansweiler, 84–168.

Meidinger, Johann Valentin (1811): *Practische Französische Grammatik, wodurch man diese Sprache auf eine neue und sehr leichte Art in kurzer Zeit gründlich erlernen kann*. Frankfurt a. M.

Münch, Wilhelm/Glauning, Friedrich (1895): *Didaktik und Methodik des englischen und französischen Unterrichts*. München.

Viëtor, Wilhelm (²1882) [Quousque Tandem]: *Der Sprachunterricht muss umkehren! Ein Beitrag zur Überbürdungsfrage* [1886]. Heilbronn.

von Reinhardstöttner, Carl (1868): *Über das Studium der modernen Sprachen an den bayerischen Gelehrten-Schulen*. Landshuth.

Further reading

Howatt, Antony P. R./Smith, Richard (2014): »The History of Teaching English as a Foreign Language, from a British and European Perspective«. In: *Language and History* 57/1, 75–95.

Howatt, Antony P. R./Widdowson, Henry G. (²2004): *A History of English Language Teaching* [1984]. Oxford.

Hüllen, Werner (2005): *Kleine Geschichte des Fremdsprachenlernens*. Berlin.

Müller, Richard-Matthias (1979): »Das Wissenschaftsverständnis der Fremdsprachendidaktik«. In: Heuer, Helmut/Sauer, Helmut/Kleineidam, Hartmut (eds.): *Dortmunder Diskussionen zur Fremdsprachendidaktik*. Dortmund, 132–148.

Richards, Jack C./Rodgers, Theodore S. (³2014): *Approaches and Methods in Language Teaching* [1986]. Cambridge.

Sabine Doff

2 Institutionalised Foreign Language Learning—Teaching English at Different Levels

English did not become a mandatory subject for students of all different school types in Germany until 1964. Ever since then, many changes with regard to the organisation, the objectives aspired and the corresponding teaching and learning approaches have entered the course books. Even though this chapter touches on a few methodological and intentional aspects concerning the past, it primarily focuses on the present situation of English foreign language (EFL) classrooms in Germany. It provides information on current curricular guidelines for Teaching English as a foreign language (TEFL) in primary, secondary and vocational schools and it shows how these national documents relate to the *Common European Framework of Reference for Languages* (CEFR, Council of Europe 2001; 2017). The chapter delineates which competences learners should have achieved at different levels of EFL instruction, according to the national, educational standards for the different school types. It furthermore illustrates how, according to commonly used textbooks, ministerial documents and the current literature on EFL teaching methodology, these targets should be reached. It becomes obvious that while texts and methodology change according to the learners' age and proficiency levels, the core competence areas and the main objectives stay the same. All in all, learners should be enabled to use the English language actively and respectfully in manifold discourse situations.

2.1 | The German EFL classroom as part of the European education system

Foreign language learning in Europe: In 2014, the European Commission published the results of a comparative analysis of the languages education and training profiles of 30 European countries. The report shows that within the last decade, most of the surveyed countries have taken considerable measures to improve the availability of institutionalised foreign language education. Examples include lowering the compulsory starting age for learning a first and a second foreign language as well as the introduction of specific strategies and action plans to improve the quality and availability of foreign language instruction in the public education system (cf. European Commission 2014, 14). The study also reveals that 65 % of the students in the surveyed countries learn two foreign languages (cf. ibid., 23 ff.) with an average of 42 % of those learners achieving an independent user level (B1 of the *Common European Framework of Reference for Languages*; cf. Council of Europe 2001) in the first foreign language learned.

The importance of English as a foreign language

This all, however, does not come as a surprise, as being able to communicate in at least one foreign language has become a key competence of private and professional lives in (and outside of) Europe. Especially those not being able to communicate in English, certainly have a huge disadvantage when it comes to staff appointments within the global market place. English serves as the dominant language of technology, trade and research. And even though more people in the world call Chinese or Spanish their native language, **English is** accepted as **the most common *lingua franca* worldwide,** shared by millions of speakers with different language backgrounds. Hence, profound competences in English can be recognised as high-value capital in a global world (cf. chapter 4 in this volume). According to Eurostat 2016, the clear majority (more than 90 %) of all students therefore learn English as their first language. German, French and Spanish are the most popular second foreign languages learned in school.

This important status of English translates into educational directives that oblige students to participate in a certain minimum of EFL classes during full-time compulsory education. The **average age for beginning** with learning a foreign language in Europe is **7.7 years** (cf. European Commission 2014, 27). Not only with regard to the fact that most German students start with compulsory foreign language learning when they are in year 3 of elementary school (when they are about 8 years old), but also taking into consideration that German learners usually start their foreign language career with English, mostly followed by French, Germany's foreign language education programmes have a lot in common with many others in Europe.

In German secondary schools (usually starting in year 5, with Berlin and Brandenburg as exceptions that start in year 6) two foreign languages are mandatory, one of which has to be English and continuously studied for at least 5 years in the lower tier of the tri-partite German school system (*Hauptschule*) or six years in the middle and upper tier (*Realschule* and *Gymnasium*).

2.1.1 | Overall aims of EFL

A brief look into the past: When in 1964 English became an obligatory subject for students of all school types (cf. Hüllen 2005), the overall aim of learning and teaching was to understand, speak, read and write properly in the foreign language. In addition to this, students were supposed to gain some cultural knowledge about the English-speaking world, especially Britain.

Focus on form: Teaching methods chosen to achieve these targets, mirrored the beliefs of structural linguists and behaviourist psychologists during this time: language learning was understood as a matter of **habit formation** and language itself seen as a rule-based system of symbols with underlying meanings. These views translated into teaching procedures that focused rather on linguistic correctness than on meaning. Language **practice** predominantly centred vocabulary and **grammatical rule learning**. **Pattern drills**, **imitation** and pronunciation activities as well as a lot of error correction dominated in language classrooms back then. As a result, students were able to read and write texts or speak sentences they had read or heard before, but they were hardly able to hold a spontaneous conversation with anyone.

The communicative turn: In the late 1970s these structure-based approaches were widely questioned. Educators and linguists had started to realise that language ability involved much more than merely being able to produce or understand grammatically correct sentences. As Richards (2006, 3; emphasis added) states, the

attention shifted to the knowledge and skills needed to use grammar and other aspects of language appropriately for different communicative purposes such as making requests, giving advice, making suggestions, describing wishes and needs, and so on. What was needed in order to use language communicatively was **communicative competence**.

This ›communicative turn‹ lead to completely new approaches in language classrooms. Rather than following one specific method, such as grammar-translation, the direct method, the audiolingual or the audiovisual method, the **communicative approach** followed a set of principles linked to nativist and interactionist theories about how languages are learned best (as summarised in Lightbown/Spada 2013). Learners were now held on to **actively use the foreign language in meaningful communicative situations** for a clear goal: The development of communicative competence, which according to Richards (2006, 3) includes the following aspects of language knowledge:

Communicative approach

> **Dimensions of Communicative Competence**
> - knowing how to use language for a range of different purposes and functions
> - knowing how to vary our use of language according to the setting and the participants (for example, knowing when to use formal and informal speech or when to use language appropriately for written as opposed to spoken communication
> - knowing how to produce and understand different types of texts (for example, narratives, reports, interviews, conversations)
> - knowing how to maintain communication despite having limitations in one's language knowledge (for example, through using different kinds of communication strategies)

Objectives of TEFL today:

- **Communicative competence:** the promotion of communicative competence is still one of the major aims of today's foreign language classrooms in Germany. However, the concept of communicative competence has become much more complex throughout the last twenty years, as language use, or more precisely, discourse practices have changed. Oral discourse practices are not limited to face to face conversations or disembodied communication on the telephone anymore; and the reading and writing of texts does not necessarily involve paper and pen anymore; rather these processes are connected to the use of digital tools.
- **Text and media competence:** The above explains, why recently published educational standards in Germany have integrated the development of text and media competences as an important target, especially for advanced learners (cf. e. g. KMK 2012b).
- **Intercultural competence:** Besides that, researchers working in the field of EFL pedagogy have pointed out the important interrelation of communication and culture and with this the relevance of intercultural competences, namely the knowledge and attitude about one's own and other cultures and the skills to apply cultural knowledge in intercultural encounters in a virtually and actually interconnected world (cf. e. g. Byram 1997; Volkmann 2010). Alongside the development of communicative competences, the development of inter-/transcultural competences has thus become another major objective in EFL classrooms.
- **Methodological competence:** Finally, our knowledge about how languages are learned has improved. Whereas language learning theories in the 1990s supported the separate practice of different skills, commonly accepted learning theories today suggest that languages are learned best in complex communicative situations in which a learner needs to apply a combination of different skills and knowledge (cf. e. g. Lightbown/Spada 2013). Due to this, more holistic and action-oriented approaches, such as **task-based language teaching** have become very popular (cf. e. g. Willis/Willis 2007). Such approaches move away from teacher-centred and product-oriented methods to learner-

centred and process-oriented activities. Moreover, they offer great potential for **autonomous** and more individualised **learning** (cf. e. g. Müller-Hartmann/Schocker-v. Ditfurth 2011). With this, new approaches to language learning also foster the development of methodological competences, which, in the long run, enable learners to learn languages independently.

In a nutshell, the main objective of EFL classrooms in Germany is to equip learners with competences that allow them to communicate with other speakers of the English language in a respectful manner. In addition to this, learners learn how to deal with and understand a variety of different text forms and media, and they are equipped with strategies and tools that will help them with their current and future language learning processes.

2.1.2 | Educational standards for EFL

From syllabi to educational standards: Since the mid 19th century specific syllabi (*Lehrpläne*) and guidelines (*Richtlinien*) for each school type have served as the basis for teaching and learning in EFL classrooms in each of the German states. The syllabi determined the learning objectives for each school year and listed topics and contents that had to be taught. In how far the given targets were actually reached by the majority of learners, however, was not examined on a broader level. Teachers themselves were the only ones assessing the language development of their students and judging, whether their way of implementing the topics of the syllabi in the classroom had been effective or not. The belief that the provision of learning objectives and obligatory themes would lead to comparable learning outcomes for all learners, began to totter with the results of an international reading literacy study (cf. Elley 1994). The *International Association for the Evaluation of Educational Achievement* had tested more than 210 000 students from 32 countries, including Germany, on their reading competences. The outcomes showed that the majority of the German students exposed average or below average reading skills only. Moreover, the research study displayed high variation in terms of students' performances (cf. Schwerdt 2010, 84). The overall results made obvious that the provision of input-oriented syllabi and guidelines would be no guarantee for students' achievements of certain minimal standards.

The literacy study was followed by several **large-scale assessments** (PISA, TIMMS, IGLU etc.) which, in a nutshell, uncovered that Germany's students were especially lacking problem-solving competences, transfer skills and application knowledge. Furthermore, the studies confirmed what had already been found out in the literacy study: that there was a huge variation in terms of the learners' competences. Consequently, the **Standing Conference of Ministers of Education and Cultural Affairs of the German Länder** (KMK) developed and published national educational standards for the intermediate school graduation certificate in 2003 (cf. KMK 2003).

Output-oriented foreign language teaching

In contrast to the traditional syllabi, educational standards do not specify content in form of topics and themes, but define competences which students are expected to have attained at certain stages of schooling (year 4, 9, 10, 12/13). With this, educational standards contribute to an **output-oriented education** system, whereas content-focused syllabi belong to an input-oriented form of education. National educational standards serve as the basis for comparative tests and examinations across schools and school types on regional and national levels. The results of such assessments give ground to the qualitative improvement of teaching in certain areas.

The *Common European Framework of References for Languages*: Until today, educational standards for EFL are available for all secondary school types, however, not for primary schools. Yet, all the federal states (*Länder*) have meanwhile released federal curricular standards for their different school types, including primary schools. The competence areas and the levels that need to be achieved by the students here are fortunately very comparable, as not only the KMK, but also the ministers of the federal states, used the *Common European Framework of References for Languages* (CEFR) as their primary reference source. The **CEFR** »was designed to provide a transparent, coherent and comprehensive basis for the elaboration of language syllabuses and curriculum guidelines, the design of teaching and learning materials and the assessment of foreign **language proficiency**« (Council of Europe 2017, n. p.).

CEFR proficiency levels

The CEFR describes foreign language proficiency in a global scale of six levels: A1 and A2 (Basic User), B1 and B2 (Independent User), C1 and C2 (Proficient User). It also defines three ›plus‹ levels (A2 +, B1 +, B2 +). The levels are substantiated by ›**can do**‹ **descriptors** (table 2.1) and »accompanied by a detailed analysis of communicative contexts, themes, tasks and purposes as well as scaled descriptions of the competences on which we draw when we communicate« (ibid.).

In the following, a closer look will be taken at which of these levels should be achieved at which point of schooling according to the national educational standards for the different school types. It will also be illustrated how these goals are supposed to be fulfilled according to the official documents and as mirrored in the commonly used EFL classroom materials (textbooks, literature, films) and in the secondary literature. As there are no national standards available for primary schools, the summative report of the KMK, released in 2013, will be used, which documents how EFL in primary schools is being performed in the 16 federal states, and on commonly used secondary resources for teaching EFL in primary classrooms (cf. KMK 2013).

Proficient user	C2	Can understand with ease virtually everything heard or read. Can summarise information from different spoken and written sources, reconstructing arguments and accounts in a coherent presentation. Can express him/herself spontaneously, very fluently and precisely, differentiating finer shades of meaning even in more complex situations.
	C1	Can understand a wide range of demanding, longer texts, and recognise implicit meaning. Can express him/herself fluently and spontaneously without much obvious searching for expressions. Can use language flexibly and effectively for social, academic and professional purposes. Can produce clear, well-structured, detailed text on complex subjects, showing controlled use of organisational patterns, connectors and cohesive devices.
Independent user	B2	Can understand the main ideas of complex text on both concrete and abstract topics, including technical discussions in his/her field of specialisation. Can interact with a degree of fluency and spontaneity that makes regular interaction with native speakers quite possible without strain for either party. Can produce clear, detailed text on a wide range of subjects and explain a viewpoint on a topical issue giving the advantages and disadvantages of various options.
	B1	Can understand the main points of clear standard input on familiar matters regularly encountered in work, school, leisure, etc. Can deal with most situations likely to arise whilst travelling in an area where the language is spoken. Can produce simple connected text on topics which are familiar or of personal interest. Can describe experiences and events, dreams, hopes and ambitions and briefly give reasons and explanations for opinions and plans.
Basic user	A2	Can understand sentences and frequently used expressions related to areas of most immediate relevance (e. g. very basic personal and family information, shopping, local geography, employment). Can communicate in simple and routine tasks requiring a simple and direct exchange of information on familiar and routine matters. Can describe in simple terms aspects of his/her background, immediate environment and matters in areas of immediate need.
	A1	Can understand and use familiar everyday expressions and very basic phrases aimed at the satisfaction of needs of a concrete type. Can introduce him/herself and others and can ask and answer questions about personal details such as where he/she lives, people he/she knows and things he/she has. Can interact in a simple way provided the other person talks slowly and clearly and is prepared to help.

Table 2.1:
Common reference
levels: global scale
of the CEFR

2.2 | First encounters with foreign languages— EFL in the primary classroom

Early institutional
foreign language
learning
EFL in primary schools across the federal states: Foreign language learning in the primary classroom can mean different things. In Saarland and in those areas of Baden-Württemberg and Rhineland-Palatinate that are close to the French boarder, mandatory foreign language learning means learning French. In all other federal states, early foreign language learning predominantly means learning English. However, other languages (e. g. heritage languages, Italian, French, Chinese etc.) are often offered on a voluntary basis. Whereas in six federal states foreign language learning starts in year 1, in ten federal states students do not start before year 3 (cf. KMK 2013). Foreign languages are usually taught for **2 hours per week**, some schools additionally offer **CLIL** (Content and Language Integrated Learning) programmes. In Berlin and Brandenburg, primary schools cover classes 1–6, in all other federal states primary schools end after year 4.

Even though there is a lot of variation with regard to how the states organise early language instruction, there is great consensus in terms of which competences the learners should have achieved at the end of primary education. On the one hand, this can be explained by the CEFR, which serves as a reference for all of the modern foreign language curricula. On the other hand, all federal states have to prepare their learners for the language classrooms in secondary schools and thus adjust the primary curricula according to the KMK standards for learning foreign languages at secondary I level (year 5–10) (cf. KMK 2003).

Objectives of primary foreign language instruction: The core objectives of foreign language learning in primary schools across the federal states are thus the development of intercultural and communicative competences on an **A1/A2 level of the CEFR**. This means that learners should be able to understand and produce short, simple spoken and written texts that include familiar words and very simple phrases connecting to students' lives (for more details see Elsner 2014, 46 f.). Moreover, learners are supposed to develop methodological competences, for example by observing, documenting, reflecting and assessing their own learning processes.

The following table (table 2.2) gives an overview of how early foreign language learning is organized in the 16 federal states. It is based on the summative report on English in German primary schools published by the KMK (2013).

2.2.1 | Principles of teaching and learning English in primary schools

The young language learner: Primary foreign language classrooms differ in many dimensions from secondary school language classrooms for different good reasons. From a developmental-psychology perspective, young language learners are quite different from adolescent or adult

Federal state	Languages taught	Start in class	Hours taught weekly	Graded	Aspired competence level	CLIL
Baden-Württemberg	English or French	year 1	2	yes, from year 3 on	A1	in some schools
Bavaria	English	year 3	2	no	A1	no
Berlin	English or French		year 3: 2 year 4: 3 year 5: 4 year 6: 5	yes, from year 4 on	A1	in some schools
Brandenburg	English	year 1	year 1–2: 1 year 3–4: 2 year 5–6: 3	yes, from year 3 on	A1	in some schools
Bremen	English	year 3	2	yes	A1	no
Hamburg	English	year 1	average of 2	yes, from year 4 on	A1/A2	in some schools
Hesse	English (French or Italian or Spanish possible)	year 3	2	yes	A1	in some schools
Lower Saxony	English	year 3	2	yes	A1	n.a.
Mecklenburg-Vorpommern	English	year 3	3	yes	A1	in some schools
North Rhine-Westphalia	English	year 1	2	no	A1	in some schools
Rhineland-Palatinate	1. English 2. French	both in year 1	50 min. each lang.	no	A1	in some schools
Saarland	French	1 or 3 (school choice)	2	no	A1-A2	in some schools
Saxony	English	year 3	2	yes, from year 4 on	A1	no
Saxony-Anhalt	English	year 3	2	yes	A1	in some schools
Schleswig-Holstein	English	year 3	2	yes	A1	in some schools
Thuringia	English, French, Italian, Russian (school choice)	year 3	2–4	no	A1	no

Table 2.2: Foreign language instruction in German primary schools

learners. Learners in grades 1 and 2 still have an enormous urge to move around; sitting still and concentrating for 45 minutes is almost impossible for them. They still like to play, sing and imitate, but they also get bored and distracted very easily. Young learners love roleplays, stories and competitive games. They need and want a lot of repetition, and it is important to them to frequently experience praise and success.

Visualisation and contextualisation

Moreover, learners in their first years of schooling are, for example, not able to deal with abstract grammatical rules or still have difficulties with organising vocabulary according to abstract categories, such as nouns, verbs, adjectives. In addition, it is important to consider that beginning foreign language learners in the primary classroom usually cannot read and write, which means that they cannot use the written word as a memory aid when learning first words in a foreign language. Visualisation and contextualisation are therefore very important for them. Even if the learners are already somewhat familiar with the literacy system of the school language, one needs to keep in mind that they are still in the process of learning the grammatical and orthographical rules of it. Learners will frequently compare the different languages they learn in order to make sense of them. This, however, also leads to a lot of (positive and negative) transfers from one language to the other, and the learners will work with and use the foreign language through procedures of trial and error (cf. e. g. Ringbom 1987).

Holistic learning: With regard to all of these aspects that are typical for young language learners, it becomes clear, why language learning in primary school follows a rather playful and holistic approach. Primary school curricula suggest the integration of picture storybooks or comics, action songs, games, rhymes and raps, in order to provide multisensory and active learning which are, next to repetition and learner orientation, widely accepted as core principles in early language classrooms (cf. Elsner 2014, 20 ff.). Children are supposed to practise the new language in cheerful but meaningful communicative situations, for example initiated through role plays or cooperative tasks that are related to children's real lives. The focus is clearly on oracy (speaking and listening). However, reading and writing skills are being fostered, as the visualisation of the spoken language through written texts can serve as a memory aid. Children should be offered differentiated material that caters to individual learner differences and contributes to learner autonomy, as for example learning at different stations (*Stationentraining*) or learning with varied computer programmes or apps.

2.2.2 | Textbooks, texts, technology

The role of the textbook: According to an internal statistic of one of Germany's biggest textbook publishers, *Cornelsen*, textbooks for foreign language learning are used in more than 90 % of the primary classrooms. This rather high number is due to different reasons.

First of all, many teachers who have to teach a foreign language in primary schools, still have not been trained for this subject at university.

Most primary teachers qualify for foreign language teaching by participating in further education programmes, which are usually rather short and only cover basic aspects of early foreign language instruction (cf. Enever 2011). EFL textbooks are thus a great help for unexperienced foreign language teachers with regard to course and activity design.

Yet, even for highly qualified teachers, textbooks bring many advantages, as they usually provide teachers with lesson plans and ideas that are in line with the curricular expectations and therefore help standardise instruction. The most popular textbooks that are currently used in primary classrooms consist of a **pupil's book**, a **workbook** with an integrated portfolio, an audio CD and a CDROM, a **teacher's handbook** and a teacher CD, including listening-texts spoken by native-speakers (cf. Elsner 2016). Besides these core components, additional material, such as a hand-puppet, picture or word cards, DVDs or material for the white board is offered.

Textbooks that are used in classrooms have to pass a very complex approval procedure undertaken by the education ministries. Therefore, teachers can be sure that the textbooks that they are officially allowed to use in the classroom are of high quality, based on sound learning principles and paced appropriately. Last but not least, textbooks are a great time-saver for teachers, as they provide a great variety of texts and activities. However, good language teachers will always amend the material to the individual needs of their learners. Especially with regard to the development of intercultural competences, the additional use of authentic storybooks and films is highly recommended. Furthermore, an increasing amount of computer programmes and apps for language learning is being offered, which is very useful in terms of individualised and autonomous forms of learning.

2.3 | EFL at secondary level I—preparing learners for private and professional lives

Achievable qualifications at the different school types in Germany: When students in Germany leave primary school, usually after year 4, they either attend the *Hauptschule* (lower tier), the *Realschule* (middle tier), the *Gymnasium* (upper tier) or a *Gesamtschule* (comprehensive school).

The German *Gymnasium* comprises 7 or 8 years of schooling. Years 5–10 are considered level 1 of secondary school instruction, ending with the *Mittlerer Bildungsabschluss*. Level II starts in year 11 and ends with the German *Abitur*, either after year 12 or after year 13, the diploma qualifying students for a university career. *Hauptschule* only comprises 5 obligatory years of schooling and ends after secondary I level with a diploma called *Qualifizierter Hauptschulabschluss*, which allows students to start an apprenticeship at a training company and attend vocational schools. The main aim of *Hauptschule* is to offer students with low or average educational performances a general academic education. A voluntary 6th year can be attended that leads students to the *Mittlerer Bil-*

dungsabschluss/Mittlere Reife, the diploma that students receive after having successfully completed the German *Realschule* for 6 years (grades 5–10). The diploma qualifies students either to continue their education at a vocational school that can lead to university entrance or to start an apprenticeship.

Throughout the last few years, more and more students have chosen to attend a comprehensive school (*Gesamtschule*) after finishing primary schools. Comprehensive schools offer courses for all types of learners, for those who are performing extremely well, as well as for average or weak learners. Students attending a *Gesamtschule* may usually graduate with either a *Qualifizierter Hauptschulabschluss*, the *Mittlere Reife* or the **Abitur**. Most of the comprehensive schools, however, end after secondary level I, and students striving for the *Abitur*, will be incorporated in the secondary II system of a collaborating *Gymnasium*.

2.3.1 | Curricular expectations

No matter which school-type students choose for their education, they all need to learn English and at least reach the B1 level at the end of year 10. This also explains, why the national curricula for the different school types do not differ in terms of the objectives and competence areas, determining what is taught in EFL. The following model (cf. Table 2.3), which can be found in the KMK standards for the first foreign language (available for *Hauptschulabschluss* (cf. KMK 2004) and *Mittlerer Bildungsabschluss* (cf. KMK 2003)) illustrates the main objectives of EFL at secondary I level.

Learning Expectations: Students are supposed to build on the basic **communicative, intercultural and methodological competences** that they have acquired in primary school in order to develop more independent competences that allow them to talk and write about common topics with other speakers of the English language. Students will listen to, read, discuss and mediate texts that, in their complexity, correspond to the **B1/B2 level of the CEFR**. Those texts can either be adapted for teaching purposes, for example by textbook authors, or they can be authentic texts, which have been written for native speakers with no specific educational purpose. The texts are usually accompanied by activities and tasks that support the learners in their comprehension processes, structure and assess their learning processes or serve as an initiator for oral (speaking and mediating) and written language production. Through the work with fictional and non-fictional authentic texts, learners will enlarge their vocabulary and grammatical knowledge and develop their intercultural competences further. Moreover, the work with texts and the continuation of a language portfolio, a documentation tool of student's work (cf. chapter 14 in this volume), which can be used for self-observation and the evaluation of their learning processes, contribute to students' methodological competences.

Funktionale kommunikative Kompetenzen	
Kommunikative Fertigkeiten	**Verfügung über die sprachlichen Mittel**
■ Hör- und Hör-/Sehverstehen ■ Leseverstehen ■ Sprechen ■ an Gesprächen teilnehmen ■ zusammenhängendes Sprechen ■ Schreiben ■ Sprachmittlung	■ Wortschatz ■ Grammatik ■ Aussprache und Intonation ■ Orthographie
Interkulturelle Kompetenzen	
■ Soziokulturelles Orientierungswissen ■ Verständnisvoller Umgang mit kultureller Differenz ■ Praktische Bewältigung interkultureller Begegnungssituationen	
Methodische Kompetenzen	
■ Textrezeption (Hör-, Hör-/Sehverstehen und Leseverstehen) ■ Interaktion ■ Textproduktion (Sprechen und Schreiben) ■ Lernstrategien ■ Präsentation und Mediennutzung ■ Lernbewusstheit und Lernorganisation	

Table 2.3: Objectives / competence areas at secondary I level, according to KMK standards for Hauptschule and Mittlerer Bildungsabschluss

2.3.2 | Principles of teaching and learning in secondary I

Task Based Language Teaching (TBLT): Even though the playful character of EFL will certainly decrease after primary school, teaching and learning at secondary level is still connected to meaningful and action-oriented forms of learning. One well-established approach in EFL at secondary I level is task-based language teaching (TBLT) (cf. e. g. Müller-Hartmann/Schocker-v. Ditfurth 2011). TBLT is a **learner-oriented approach** that focuses on the use of authentic language through meaningful tasks, such as making a list of food-items that need to be organised for the next classroom breakfast, calling the doctor or writing an application. Task-based learning encourages learners to use language in order to solve authentic problems, i. e. problems that they will eventually also encounter outside of school. TBLT is considered to be a very motivating approach, as learners seem to be more committed if tasks appear familiar and meaningful to them.

Scaffolding: As teachers and students should predominantly use the English language and tasks and texts in secondary schools become more challenging and abstract, teachers need to give their students a lot of support through scaffolding, which Gibbons (2009, 15) defines as follows:

This sociocultural approach to learning recognizes that with assistance, learners can reach beyond what they can do unaided, participate in new situations, and take on new roles. [...] This assisted performance is encapsulated in Vygotsky's notion of the zone of proximal development, or ZPD, which describes the ›gap‹ between what learners can do alone and what they can do with help from someone more skilled. This situated help is known as ›scaffolding‹.

When scaffolding, educators use a variety of instructional techniques to move students progressively toward stronger understanding and, ultimately, greater independence in the learning process (cf. Gibbons 2015). For example, the use of images or gestures can support vocabulary learning or explicit training of learning strategies; the information on different genre characteristics help students with their reading and listening comprehension processes (cf. chapter 6 in this volume). A systematic and detailed task description will make students' time management easier and support them at their problem-solving procedures. It becomes obvious that scaffolding techniques are supportive in two ways: they temporarily guide the learner during a certain task or activity, yet they, moreover, lay the ground for autonomous learning processes. For instance, once a learner has experienced that visuals are helpful for text comprehension or that the knowledge about a certain genre may facilitate text interpretation, he or she will hopefully apply this meta-knowledge in other tasks independently.

Learner autonomy   All in all, **the development of learner autonomy** is a major aim of secondary language classrooms, which also becomes evident in error correction and feedback procedures. When teachers correct students' written texts, for example, they should »focus on real howlers and how to avoid them« (Grimm et al. 2015, 288) instead of marking and correcting every single mistake. Error correction should be systematic and transparent to the students, and educators should provide helpful comments instead of »bleed[ing] students' papers to death« (ibid.).

Error correction: In a nutshell, English language classrooms at secondary level are all about encouraging the learners to use the language as often as possible and not to make them fear mistakes.

2.3.3 | Textbooks, texts, technology

The role of textbooks at secondary I level: Just as it is the case for primary EFL classrooms, EFL textbooks seem to be the most important medium at secondary I level. The new generation of textbooks offer a variety of different text forms and activities that aim at the integrated practice of language skills (cf. Elsner 2016). They follow the common principles of EFL teaching and learning by incorporating meaningful communicative **tasks**, catering to different learner styles and offering manifold activities for language practice. Modern textbooks for the secondary classroom embed **grammar** and **vocabulary practice** in meaningful contexts and they illustrate and explain the value of learning strategies and techniques, supporting learners in their individual learning processes. With this, textbooks are valuable timesavers in terms of teachers' preparation times and they offer a secure **learning progression** that is transparent to students, teachers and parents alike. Given the fact that there is hardly a textbook anymore that does not come with a language learning software for the computer and CDs with texts and songs spoken/sung by native speakers, textbooks are also an effective **resource for self-directed learning**.

Apart from all of these advantages, it needs to be admitted, that textbooks are no guarantee for good teaching practice. On the contrary, an uncritical and exclusive application of textbook material might even lead to a demotivation on behalf of the students. Without a doubt, textbooks are valuable tools for the EFL classroom, yet they always need to be complemented by other material, such as authentic fictional and non-fictional text, graded readers, films, music videos, language learning software for the computer and apps for mobile devices. In contrast to the primary classroom, in which students usually do not read texts on their own, but rather listen to the teacher reading rhymes or picture-storybooks to them, students in the secondary classroom start to read longer texts autonomously. Especially graphic narratives (comics and graphic novels), song lyrics and films have become very popular and especially motivational text forms used with this group of learners (cf. Elsner/Viebrock 2013).

2.4 | Preparing learners for an academic career— EFL at secondary level II

The last two, respectively three, years of schooling at secondary II level of the German *Gymnasium* comprise propaedeutics for advanced academic studies at university. In the English language classroom, but also in other subjects, current world issues as well as classical and modern literature are discussed in order to profoundly develop students' **general knowledge**. Students practise the comprehension of increasingly complex texts and topics and they are requested to write well-informed compositions and prepare oral presentations on their own. Students can choose English (or any other foreign language offered at the school) as one of their major subjects with 5 lessons per week or as a minor subject with 3 to 4 lessons per week.

2.4.1 | Curricular expectations

Learning objectives: According to the KMK standards for the German *Abitur* (cf. KMK 2012), the major aim of teaching and learning foreign languages at secondary II level is the development of discourse competences, which can be seen as the ability to actively, critically and adequately participate in oral and written communication (cf. Elsner/Viebrock 2013). Discourse competence entails intercultural and communicative competences, which are being developed through the critical examination and discussion of texts, topics and media (cf. KMK 2012b, 11) students with a major in English are expected to reach a B2/C1 level of the CEFR in reading, listening, speaking, writing and language mediation, students with a minor in English should achieve the B2 level.

Furthermore, students will develop **text and media competences** (cf. illustration 2.1), enabling them to critically analye, evaluate and create messages in and with different media and text types. Texts in this context incorporate electronic as well as paper texts or spoken language, linear

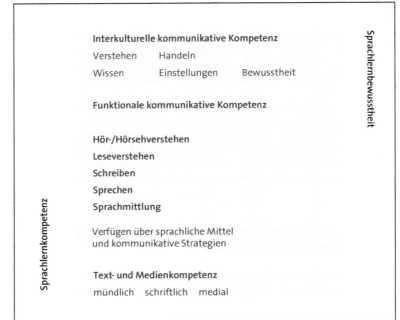

and non-linear arranged texts that may be decoded interactively, mono- or multimodally, different genres and formats (cf. Elsner/Viebrock 2013, 20).

In addition to this, students are encouraged to reflect about different languages to develop their **language awareness** (cf. KMK 2012b, 21) which is defined by Van Lier (1995, xi) as »[...] an understanding of the human faculty of language and its role in thinking, learning and social life. It includes awareness of power and control through language and the intricate relationships between language and culture«. Summing up, it can be seen that learning English in the secondary II classroom becomes more complex, abstract and literally more demanding as compared to the years before.

2.4.2 | Principles of teaching and learning

The new educational curricula for teaching and learning English at secondary II level do not give any information about how students should be taught in order to achieve the targeted competences. Yet, experts and practitioners continuously discuss different principles and approaches, that they assume to be mostly effective for teaching languages to adolescent/adult learners in their last years of schooling (cf. e. g. Thaler 2012; Grimm et al. 2015). Currently, there seems to be high consensus with regard to the following principles (cf. also chapter 3 in this volume):

> **Elements of good language teaching**
> - task-based and creative forms of learning
> - rich language input through a variety of text forms/genres
> - process-orientation rather than product-orientation
> - cooperative and collaborative forms of learning
> - increase of autonomous forms of learning
> - balanced approaches to media use (old and new/digital media)

Key points

Topics: Moreover, the local curricula published by the educational ministries of the federal states, integrate a list of topics and obligatory texts that need to be worked on in the EFL classroom. These, for example, cover topics such as global issues, the encounter of cultures, coming of age etc.

2.4.3 | Textbooks, texts, technology

Teaching and learning at secondary II level focuses on the critical and reflective work with texts of different genres, formats and modes. Texts serve as an instrument for discussion and reflection and they increasingly serve as the starting point for students' individual writing processes. As teachers are more or less free to choose how they want to approach the topics and texts set by curricular guidelines, the use of classical textbooks is not very popular at secondary II level. Yet, textbook publishers offer a great variety of digital and non-digitalised teaching material for the work with literary and non-fictional texts. Especially the work with films has become increasingly popular throughout the last years (cf. e. g. Henseler et al. 2011; Viebrock 2016) and students are more and more encouraged to produce multimodal texts (e. g. video-clips, blog-entries, digital journals etc.) on their own.

2.5 | Training on and for the job—EFL in vocational schools

Preparing students for their working lives: Germany is one of many European countries that offer a **dual education system** after general schooling. Students, who do not want to attend university or technical colleges, can decide for an **apprenticeship** in a company which is always combined with a certain amount of hours of **vocational training** in a vocational/technical school (*Berufsschule*). Lessons may have to be attended on a weekly basis or they are offered in compact classes of several weeks. The responsibility for the organization of the training part in schools lies with the school authorities of the federal states.

The role of TEFL in vocational schools: Due to the globalisation of the economic market, the educational ministers of Germany's states decided to include English as a mandatory subject in all vocational school curricula. No matter if someone will work as a hair stylist, a technician in a car company or in a bank, a basic knowledge of the English language is considered to be a highly relevant competence. The main objective of EFL classes in vocational schools is to train students for their future professions. **Communicative and intercultural competences** will be developed that are specifically necessary for certain occupations. This is done through the provision of educational tasks that correspond to real world tasks of a certain job. To be more precise: in vocational schools, for example, students training for an occupation in the service sector, will possibly practise how to talk to clients on the phone or at the front desk, how to make or take reservations etc., whereas future mechatronics will learn how to read English handbooks or communicate with other mechatronics from different countries via the Internet.

Furthermore, students in vocational schools get further training with regard to their intercultural competences (e. g. which topics/gestures/comments etc. should rather be avoided when talking to a business partner from China?) and learn how to autonomously gain **occupational specific language competences**. On a voluntary basis, students in vocational schools can decide to take a test, which—if passed—will be awarded with a special foreign language certificate named ›**KMK Fremdsprachenzertifikat Berufliche Bildung**‹ (cf. KMK n. d.).

2.6 | New paths in foreign languages education

Foreign language education programmes in Germany have changed a lot throughout the last fifty years, with regard to the aims, the content, teaching principles and methods. Changes in the education system depend on a variety of factors. First, political stakeholders, working in the educational sector of the German ministries, frequently react to the changes in our society by reorganising curricula. Second, research brings new understandings about how languages are presumably learned best in classroom situations. With regard to EFL, increasingly diverse classrooms and learner needs have led to new approaches and principles in institutional language learning and teaching.

2.6.1 | Bilingual education: CLIL and immersion

Content and Language Integrated Learning

Hamers/Blanc (2000, 321) use the term bilingual education for »any system of school education in which, at a given moment in time and for a varying amount of time simultaneously or consecutively, instruction is planned and given in at least two languages«. Bilingual education programmes such as CLIL (Content and Language Integrated Learning) and immersion have become very popular all over the world (cf. Hallet/Königs 2013). In immersion settings, most of the subjects (at least **more than 50 %,** usually up to 100 %) are taught **in the target language** in order to cater for a real ›language bath‹ as the term *immersion* suggests.

CLIL programmes, on the other hand, offer up to 50 % of the subjects in the target language (but very often less than this), while the other half or more is taught in the national language (cf. Elsner/Keßler 2013b, 2). In immersion settings, teachers are native speakers of the target language, whereas in CLIL settings for most teachers the target language is a second/foreign language. According to the current statistics of FMKS (*Verein Frühe Mehrsprachigkeit an Kitas und Schulen*), more than 1,100 schools in Germany offer such bilingual forms of learning, in which a foreign language is used as a means of instruction in different subjects (cf. FMKS n. d.). According to Eurydice (2006), bilingual education contributes specifically to:

Key points

Aims of bilingual education programmes
- preparing pupils for life in a more internationalised society and offering them better job prospects on the labour market (socio-economic objectives);
- conveying to pupils values of tolerance and respect vis-à-vis other cultures, through use of the CLIL target language (socio-cultural objectives);
- enabling pupils to develop language skills which emphasise effective communication, motivating them to learn languages by using them for real practical purposes (linguistic objectives);
- subject-related knowledge and learning ability, stimulating the assimilation of subject matter by means of a different and innovative approach (educational objectives) (cf. Eurydice 2006, 22).

Bilingual programmes at different school types: Bilingual programmes in Germany were initially only offered by German *Gymnasien* and a few primary schools. Whereas the primary schools predominantly worked according to the immersion concept, the *Gymnasien* mostly offered CLIL in one or two subjects (e. g. Bilingual History Classes) (cf. Breidbach/Viebrock 2012; Elsner/Keßler 2013a).

Meanwhile, different CLIL programmes are also offered in the other school types, bringing to light astonishing results with regard to its feasibility, students' motivation and their foreign language development (cf. Schwab et al. 2014). When it comes to the question of ›how effective‹ the different types of bilingual education are in terms of linguistic and subject-specific competencies' development, valuable answers can be found in the large pool of research outcomes arisen from studies that have been conducted in Canadian, American, European and especially in German education contexts (for detailed information see Coyle et al. 2010; Breidbach/Viebrock 2012). Many of them still focus on immersion and/or CLIL at secondary school level. However, first research results about the experiences with different approaches to bilingual learning and teaching at German primary schools have been published (for an overview cf. e. g. Burmeister/Massler 2010; Elsner/Keßler 2013a).

2.6.2 | Inclusive EFL classrooms

Inclusion Catering to individual learner needs is an educational principle that has not only become popular since the publication of the **UNESCO Policy Guidelines on Inclusion** (2009). Nevertheless, classrooms have seemingly never been as heterogeneous as today. Inclusive classrooms take into account all **dimensions of diversity**, for example gender, nationalities, socio-economic status, religions, worldviews, languages, learning preferences, abilities/disabilities etc. With regard to the selection and design of teaching materials, lesson preparation and differentiation strategies the demands of educators have definitely increased. And even if these challenges are not unique to the English language classroom, foreign language education calls for specific strategies which allow the learner to develop his/her language skills according to his/her **individual strengths** and to overcome weaknesses. Especially during teacher-centred phases in a lesson, scaffolding techniques will cater to **individual learner needs**.

Besides the frequent application of scaffolding techniques teachers should design individual education plans for students with special needs. For this they, first of all, need to be able to assess students' foreign language abilities and skills and **diagnose** students' strengths, weaknesses and needs. Specific diagnostic tools have been developed to screen EFL learners' speech samples in order to assess their language acquisition level, for example Rapid Profile (cf. Keßler 2007), or to assess their cognitive abilities (e. g. Raven's Progressive Matrices Test). Once a learner profile has been generated, individualised material can be created, varying in terms of quantity, complexity and appearance (for further information read Bongartz/Rohde 2016).

2.6.3 | Multilingual approaches to language learning

In many classrooms today, learners and teachers face the challenges and the opportunities of dealing with diverse linguistic resources and cultural experiences of learners. Not only educators and learners themselves, but also researchers and policy makers have been called upon to establish strategies and practical teaching ideas for classrooms catering to the **European tenet of a multilingual society**, in which all the languages that are being spoken by any individual are tolerated, appreciated, retained and actively promoted (cf. e. g. European Commission 2014). Against this background, a variety of multilingual approaches, have been developed, first and predominantly in the context of classrooms in which a second foreign language (e. g. French or Spanish in Germany) was/is taught. Yet, more and more ideas for the integration and **active use of different languages** have also evolved in the context of L1 (first language) and L2 (second language) instruction (for an overview see Krumm/Reich 2016); some have been tested and experimented with in a few pilot projects or in small scale studies (see Meier 2014 for an overview).

However, as Meier (2014, 137) points out, »these have remained the exception and there have been very few integrated multilingual efforts in mainstream education«. Especially for foreign language classrooms, sound suggestions for an integrative multilingual approach that makes active use of students' prior language knowledge and learning experience in order to activate language awareness and initiate multilingual learning processes, are rare to find (for an overview of different attempts see Lohe/Elsner 2014). So far, research conducted in multilingual settings such as Canada, suggests that the **appreciation and integration of pupils' first languages** supports pupils' **identity formation** (cf. e. g. Cummins et al. 2005). Research focusing on the integration of other languages as comprehension aid is still ongoing (cf. e. g. Elsner et al. 2015; Meißner 2016 for an overview).

2.7 | Conclusion

The purpose of this chapter was to give an overview of the current objectives and practices of teaching English as a foreign language in the different school types in Germany. It was shown that, even though different curricula exist for the different school types, the overall aim of teaching and learning English is to develop intercultural, communicative and methodological competences in the foreign language. With this, Germany's language curricula are comparable to those of other European countries, which is no surprise, as they all refer to the *Common European Framework of References for Languages* (Council of Europe 2001; 2017). Regarding EFL teaching practices, learner-centred, task-based, action-oriented and autonomous forms of learning are currently being considered to be more effective than teacher-centred approaches (presentation, practice and performance). Moreover, classrooms, with augmented input-opportunities, i. e. CLIL and immersion programmes, have experienced increasing demand. Last but not least, new challenges for language teachers, such as inclusive and increasingly multilingual classrooms, have emerged, making us aware of the fact that concepts for EFL classrooms always have been and always will be under way.

Further reading

Christ, Ingeborg (⁶2016): »Staatliche Regelungen für den Fremdsprachenunterricht. Curricula, Richtlinien, Lehrpläne«. In: Burwitz-Melzer, Eva/Mehlhorn, Grit/Riemer, Claudia/Bausch, Karl-Richard/Krumm, Hans-Jürgen (eds.): *Handbuch Fremdsprachenunterricht* [1989]. Tübingen, 56–59.
Elsner, Daniela (2015): *Kompetenzorientiert unterrichten. Englisch 1–4*. Berlin.
Grimm, Nancy/Meyer, Michael/Volkmann, Laurenz (2015): *Teaching English*. Tübingen.
Hallet, Wolfgang (2011): *Lernen fördern. Kompetenzorientierter Unterricht in der Sekundarstufe I*. Seelze.
Thaler, Engelbert (2016): *Standard-basierter Englischunterricht. Die neuen Abitur-Bildungsstandards in die Praxis umsetzen*. Berlin.

Daniela Elsner

3 Teachers of English as a Foreign Language—Experience and Professional Development

This little conversation between Charlie Brown and Linus van Pelt from the famous cartoon series *Peanuts* deals with what (English language) teachers do in the classroom and how they have been prepared for this. It is funny because it describes situations many of you have experienced as learners in school and, possibly, did not particularly like. At the same time, it alludes to typical tasks and assignments (future) teachers of English as a foreign language will routinely require from their learners in order to make them speak or write in the foreign language, namely report about holiday trips, family events and other personal experiences. Apart from being humorous, the cartoon instigates a number of more serious questions with regard to the English language teaching profession, which need to be addressed in teacher education:

Illustration 3.1: PEANUTS © 1965 Peanuts Worldwide LLC. Dist. By ANDREWS MCMEEL SYNDICATION. Reprint with permission. All rights reserved.

- What are appropriate tasks and who determines what a good assignment is?
- Or more generally, what is good English language teaching and who defines what this is?
- What kind of education does a foreign language teacher need to become a professional?
- What are the essential characteristics of a good language teacher?

These and other questions will be addressed in this chapter. The focus will be on the prerequisites of being a teacher of English as a foreign language. The chapter will look at the initial conditions of teacher trainees and how their experiential knowledge influences their professional development. It will then define what the necessary characteristics of a good or professional English language teacher are and how these can be acquired. To do so, it will discuss different models of teacher education and teacher professionalism. Finally, it will take into consideration current and future challenges for English language teachers, who, in a globalised world, meet increasingly heterogeneous environments in their classrooms.

3.1 | Between experiential knowledge and formal academic education: English language teachers' mind-sets

Experiential knowledge: Unlike members of other professions, teachers have accumulated a fair amount of experience in their field of work before they even start teaching. They have experienced institutional learning as a pupil for many years; they have usually done several teaching practicums during their academic training; and possibly, they have also got to know school as a parent themselves or observed the experiences of younger siblings. Consequently, they possess a lot of **autobiographically acquired** experiential knowledge (cf. Appel 2000), which influences their teaching, their thinking and their way of doing things. Experiential knowledge differs from formal and theory-driven academic knowledge in such a way that it is not necessarily objective or explicit. It may contain **personal beliefs, individual assumptions** or unjustified conclusions, which interfere with or even overlie objective formal knowledge. Despite its subjectivity, experiential knowledge is believed to provide teachers with a strong **sense of direction** and inform any of their classroom-related decisions and activities. Woods (1996, 282 f.) assumes that a steady network of beliefs, assumptions and knowledge, which he calls *BAK*, underlies »everything that the teachers did and said: as if it was through the BAK systems that the teachers structured their perceptions of the curriculum and their decision as how to implement that curriculum, from overall organisation of the units down to specific classroom activities and verbalizations.«

Structure and functions of experiential and academic knowledge: Concerning its structure and functions, experiential knowledge is very similar to formal academic knowledge. For this reason, teachers' experiential knowledge has also been called **subjective theories**, lay theories or dormant theories (cf. Viebrock 2010). Both experiential and academic knowledge rely on a **systematic and hierarchical organisation of their inventory**, for example, a categorisation of elements into main categories and sub-categories. A case in point would be the distinction between receptive and productive language skills as higher order categories with reading/listening and writing/speaking as their sub-categories (cf. also chapters 6 and 7 in this volume). Both subjective and academic theories structure their components by way of formal relations, for example, linking one element to another through if-then relations. A case in point would be the assumption that language use in the classroom is more authentic if it does not focus on formal structures. In terms of function, teachers' experiential knowledge is comparable to academic theories in the sense that both are utilised in the process of planning teaching activities and justifying decisions to this effect, either prospectively or retrospectively. They are also utilised for predicting or interpreting any classroom events.

Teachers' mind-sets: This concomitance of autobiographical, experiential knowledge and formal academic education is a distinctive feature of the teaching profession which makes for a specific mind-set of its members, as described by Lewis (1993, 32):

One of the most important factors which influence what happens in the classroom is the totality of ideas, knowledge and attitudes which represent the teacher's mind-set. This complex of ideas is partly explicit, based on information given to the teacher, formal learning and the like, but much of it is implicit, based on the teacher's self-image, value system and even prejudice.

It follows from Lewis (1993) that, by virtue of its autobiographical influences, the teacher's mind-set is extremely **stable and difficult to change**. It will usually be upheld regardless of contradictory elements or even counter evidence. In particular, its implicit elements, which the individual is not aware of and which have not been consciously reflected upon, are **prone to fossilisation**. This is to say, they will remain on a premature stage of development which precludes the advancement or innovation of teacher behaviour. However, this also means that teacher behaviour can be influenced positively, if an **awareness of its constituting elements** is raised and (future) teachers (re-)negotiate their strategies and procedures. In order to be able to continuously reflect on their mind-sets, become aware of their motives and driving forces, change well-established routines and improve their teaching behaviour, teachers need to possess certain qualities, such as openness, flexibility, self-criticism and a sense of adventurousness (cf. Bach 2013, 305 f.).

> The teacher's mind-set denotes a system of personal beliefs, assumptions, knowledge and attitudes any teacher holds on account of his previous experiences with school, teaching and learning. Its inventory is organised systematically and hierarchically, but its contents may not always be explicit or conscious. The teacher's mind-set is accessible for reflection and awareness raising. Teachers' actions and interpretations of classroom events are based on their individual mind-sets.

Definition

Individual language learning biographies: While this is true for all teachers, who need to master the transition from being a learner to becoming a professional teacher, regardless of the subject, for foreign language teachers their individual language learning biographies also plays a decisive role (cf. Dirks 2007). Whether they are bi- or multilingual speakers themselves, whether they have spent a longer period of time in an English-speaking country and have acquired the better part of their foreign language competences there or whether they have immersed themselves in a foreign educational system also influences their mind-sets and their understanding of the profession. Which specific competencies are required to become a good teacher of English as a foreign language will be discussed in the next part.

3.2 | Characteristics of the good English language teacher: reflective practice and professionalism

Good English language teachers: When thinking about good English language teachers you have encountered, how would you describe their qualities? As being passionate about their subject and their profession, as being learner-oriented, motivating and fair, as being flexible, hard-working and well-structured? Would you consider them inspiring personalities or professional teachers or both? The question which characteristics a good teacher (regardless of the subject) should possess and how these become visible in good teaching practice has occupied the academic discourse for decades (cf. e. g. Moskowitz 1976; Shulman 1986; Meyer 2004; Hallet 2010; Hattie 2011). Most of the studies come up with a list of qualities that include elements similar to the ones mentioned. Good teachers are described as »professionals who create an atmosphere of mutual respect in the classroom, the school and beyond« (Grimm et al. 2015, 21).

While these personal characteristics are considered to be prerequisites of good teaching, the more important question is how they are put into effect in the classroom situation. What does a foreign language teacher need to know and do to teach effectively? In order to answer this question, Richards (2012) resorts to a distinction between ›**competence**‹ and ›**performance**‹, which on the one hand describes each individual's cognitive, mental and emotional conditions and actually being able to put one's knowledge and qualifications into practice in specific situations on the other. The notion of competence in this understanding delineates the teacher's ›knowledge base‹ (cf. Shulman 1987, 5 ff.), i. e. their knowledge of the content, pedagogy, the curriculum, educational purposes, their learners etc. The notion of performance is concerned with the actual activity of teaching.

Good teaching practice: In a similar vein, a close connection between teacher professionalism and the quality of teaching has been established

Illustration 3.2:
Types of English
language teachers

by Helmke (2015, translation/adaptation BV), who has laid down ten characteristics of good teaching practice based on extensive empirical research:

Characteristics of good teaching practice   Key points
1. efficient time management and classroom leadership
2. a productive atmosphere
3. the implementation of versatile motivation strategies
4. structure and clarity
5. efficacy and competence orientation
6. learner orientation and support
7. the promotion of active and independent learning
8. variation in methods and social constellations
9. consolidation and intelligent practicing
10. sensitivity and adaptivity

A number of activities exemplify each of the characteristics. A promotion of active and independent learning, for example, can be achieved through the use of adequate language (vocabulary, terminology), structuring details and references (preview, summary, advance organisers), correct exemplification of the subject matter, concise language (clear diction, adequate rhetoric, correct grammar, clear sentences), adequate articulation and modulation (of voice) and loudness. Sensitivity and adaptivity include an adaptation of the level of difficulty and pace for each learning situation as well as a particular sensitivity towards heterogeneous learners concerning their social, language and cultural backgrounds and their performance levels (cf. chapter 4 in this volume).

Core dimensions of good language teaching practice: Helmke's overview of characteristics of good teaching practice is not necessarily subject-specific. Some aspects are comprehensive in nature and relate to the teacher's general pedagogical skills, for example, efficient time management or the establishment and maintenance of a productive atmosphere. Some have to be adapted and exercised in a slightly different way in each individual subject, depending on the content to be taught. The choice of adequate methods, tasks for knowledge transfer or exercises for intelligent practicing, for example, will certainly be of a different kind in mathematics, history or foreign language teaching for that matter. Concerning the field of English language teaching, Richards (2012) has suggested ten core dimensions of good language teaching practice, which partly overlap with the general characteristics described by Helmke, but overall more explicitly focus on the peculiarities of the language teaching profession. A brief overview of Richards' core dimensions is provided in table 3.1, a more comprehensive discussion will follow below.

Language proficiency: To demand a well-developed language proficiency of a teacher of English as a foreign language seems like stating the obvious. However, to define exactly how proficient a teacher needs to be in order to teach a language effectively is not a simple task. Other aspects

Dimensions	Abilities of the teacher, routines and procedures
language proficiency	<ul><li>providing good language models</li><li>maintaining use of the target language in the classroom</li><li>giving explanations and instructions in the target language</li><li>providing examples of words and grammatical structures</li><li>giving correct feedback on learner language</li><li>providing input at an appropriate level of difficulty</li><li>providing language-enrichment experiences for learners</li></ul>
content knowledge	<ul><li>understanding learners' needs</li><li>diagnosing learners' learning problems</li><li>planning suitable instructional goals for lessons</li><li>selecting and designing learning tasks</li><li>evaluating students' learning</li><li>designing and adapting tests</li><li>evaluating and choosing materials</li><li>making appropriate use of technology</li><li>reflecting on one's lessons</li></ul>
teaching skills	<ul><li>introducing and explaining tasks</li><li>setting up learning arrangements</li><li>checking students' understanding</li><li>guiding student practice</li><li>monitoring students' language use</li></ul>
contextual knowledge	<ul><li>understanding the values, norms of practice and patterns of social participation of a particular school</li><li>understanding the dynamics and relationships within the classroom</li></ul>
language teacher's identity	<ul><li>being aware of one's role as a teacher of English</li><li>enacting different social and cultural roles as a teacher of English</li></ul>
learner-focused teaching	<ul><li>being familiar with typical student behaviour</li><li>adapting one's lessons to the learners' needs and preferences</li><li>maintaining active student involvement (also in processes of planning and/or decision-making)</li><li>connecting with the learners' life experiences</li></ul>
pedagogical reasoning skills	<ul><li>analysing potential lesson content (e. g. a piece of realia, a text, an advertisement, a poem, a photo, etc.)</li><li>identifying ways in which it could be used as a teaching resource</li><li>identifying linguistic goals (e. g. in the area of speaking, vocabulary, reading, writing, etc.) that could be developed from the chosen content</li><li>anticipating problems that might occur and ways of resolving them</li><li>making appropriate decisions about time, sequencing and grouping</li></ul>
theorising from practice	<ul><li>experiential knowledge</li><li>reflecting teaching experiences in order to explain, hypothesise about or generalise aspects of foreign language teaching</li><li>evaluating one's teaching</li><li>developing principles and a personal teaching philosophy</li></ul>
membership of a community of practice	<ul><li>collaborating with fellow teachers, university colleagues or other school staff</li><li>exploring and resolving issues related to workplace practices</li><li>achieving shared goals</li></ul>
professionalism	<ul><li>becoming familiar with the standards of the profession</li><li>developing professional competence</li><li>attaining high standards</li><li>continuously and systematically reflecting one's teaching practices</li></ul>

Table 3.1: Core dimensions of good language teaching practice

of teaching may interact with one's foreign language proficiency or even compensate for possible shortcomings. In addition, more often than not English is used as an international language, which makes it difficult to determine which English to teach (cf. McKay 2012). Bach (2015, n. p.) argues that in the age of globalisation, a territorially bound, nation-oriented definition of language does no longer suffice, which in turn interferes with language teaching practices:

> For language teachers of English, this post-national perspective may have destabilizing effects. Not much longer will they be teaching what has been commonly accepted as »British English« or »American English«, since the nation-based parameters describing such variants are disappearing or, even more likely, are being rejected by those who speak it as no longer discernible or applicable to their personal situation.

This observation also touches on the question whether **non-native teachers** (or learners) of English have to acquire native-like competences and even more so whether the concept of a native speaker is still feasible (cf. Mukherjee 2005). If it proves difficult to define languages as national languages, then it is equally difficult to define who qualifies as a native speaker. In order to be able to describe or assess a foreign language speaker's competence level, the *Common European Framework of Reference for Languages* **CEFR** (cf. Council of Europe 2001; cf. chapter 2 in this volume) provides six competence levels, each of which describes the activities a speaker on that particular level needs to be able to carry out. Returning to the initial question, how proficient an English language teacher should be, Richards (2012) assumes a particular **threshold proficiency** that is needed to carry out the tasks required of a language teacher, but he does not specify what this threshold level is. In practice, most academic teacher education programmes require a C2-level of their graduates, which denotes the highest level of proficiency according to the CEFR.

The teacher's language proficiency

Content knowledge: The second element of Richards' core dimensions—content knowledge—is also difficult to define as it could either denote disciplinary knowledge, pedagogical content knowledge or even technological pedagogical content knowledge. **Disciplinary knowledge** refers to a body of knowledge that is considered to be the professional foundation in the field of TEFL (teaching English as a foreign language) as an academic discipline. It does not necessarily immediately translate into classroom practice, but rather describes specialised theoretical knowledge. In this understanding, disciplinary knowledge particularly includes insights from the field of applied linguistics (for example, language acquisition theories, the history of language teaching methods or sociolinguistics), but also from literary studies (for example, literary theories such as new criticism or reader-response-theory) or cultural studies (for example, culture theories, different international approaches to studying culture, etc.).

The term ›**pedagogical content knowledge**‹ or PCK is known as *fachdidaktisches Wissen* (cf. Baumert/Kunter 2006) in German. It was originally introduced by Shulman (1986, 1987) and is defined as »the blending of content and pedagogy into an understanding of how particular topics, problems, or issues are organised, represented, and adapted to the diverse interests and abilities of learners, and presented for instruction« (Shulman 1987, 8). As such, PCK is unique to members of the teaching profession and distinguishes them from content specialists alone. In Richards' (2012) overview, PCK is more closely connected to performance and the practical issues of language teaching as specified in the table above. It is still based on profound theoretical knowledge, but explicitly looks at the practical implications of this knowledge and its application in classroom situations.

Technological pedagogical content knowledge has been developed as a comprehensive concept by Koehler/Mishra (2009). Essentially, it emphasises the need for technical expertise and keeping up with technological developments on the part of the teacher. Not only do they have to be able to master a wide range of technology, but they also need to be able to incorporate and employ it in their teaching.

Teaching skills are even more practical in nature. They are understood as a »**repertoire of techniques and routines**« (Richards 2012, 48), which enable a teacher to navigate through a language lesson as smoothly as possible. Teaching skills are usually acquired over time. They are not exclusively theory-driven, but the outcome of a repetitive process of **action and reflection**. While teaching skills include a certain degree of automation, teaching is not simply understood as the application of a fixed set of knowledge or learned skills. Apart from certain routines, it requires a great cognitive flexibility which is needed in the complex processes of decision-making in the classroom.

Contextual knowledge: The idea of contextual knowledge is closely related to Lave and Wenger's (1991) theory of ›**situated learning**‹. It starts from the assumption that institutional learning takes place within a particular social context which needs to be taken into consideration in any reflection or analysis as the specific situation undoubtedly has an impact on the potential for learning. This becomes particularly obvious when comparing international schools and the diverse approaches to language teaching in different countries. It also becomes obvious when comparing different types of school within one country (for example, a highly heterogeneous primary school, an adult education centre or a prestigious grammar school) and the variety of educational, social, economic and cultural backgrounds of their learners. Each school has their own ›culture‹, i. e. their own way of dealing with their individual situation. A teacher has to understand **a school's norms, rules, habits and forces** that have emerged over time and in particular how these influence (language) teaching practices and **classroom dynamics**. This may include questions such as whether teachers have to adhere to a close curriculum or whether they have a relative amount of freedom in their choice of topics or whether they work solitarily, in varying co-operations or in fixed teams.

Learner-focused teaching: As the name implies, learner-focused teaching is concerned with classroom interaction from the learner's perspective. While novice teachers, quite understandably, are often concerned

Teacher's skills and knowledge

with their own performance, with the establishment of confidence and competence, more experienced teachers manage to achieve a learner-focused approach by truly involving the learners in the lessons, increasing their amount of talking time and **participation** or dealing with the content matter from the learners' perspectives and thus assuring more successful learning processes. An increase of **learner talking time** is important when taking into consideration the results of *DESI (Deutsch-Eng-lisch-Schülerleistungen-International)*, a large-scale educational achievement study, which has shown that on average teacher talking time covers the better part of a lesson, while the amount of talking time of *all* learners accounts for less than a third of the overall talking time (cf. DESI-Konsortium 2006, 47). Relating to the learners' life experiences is another way of increasing **learner involvement**. This may be done through some rather straightforward questions—as exemplified in the initial cartoon from *Peanuts*—but a comprehensive approach requires more sophisticated strategies for learner activation, such as systematically **assigning responsibilities to the learners**.

Pedagogical reasoning skills: It could be argued that pedagogical reasoning skills lie at the core of all characteristics mentioned here since they integrate and draw on many of the other dimensions. Richards' (2012) understanding of pedagogical reasoning skills is closely related to Shulman's (1987) concept of pedagogical content knowledge as explained above. Again, the term ›skills‹ hints at the fact that the performance domain is given greater priority. While Shulman is more concerned with the teachers' knowledge base, Richards focuses on the **practices of decision-making** in domains such as **lesson planning**, **material selection** or the **conduct of teaching**. What both have in common is that they look at the processes of transformation between subject-specific knowledge and its appropriations in different pedagogical contexts. *Pedagogical decision-making*

Theorising from practice: The importance of experiential knowledge has already been highlighted in the first part of this chapter, which explained the main characteristics of the language teaching profession and the mind-sets of its members (cf. Lewis 1993; Woods 1996; also Borg 2006). Theorising from practice more specifically focuses on (novice) teachers' teaching experiences and how these can be utilised for **further professional development**. One of the most influential notions in this field is that of ›**reflective practice**‹ (cf. Schön 1983), which denotes a careful consideration and critical assessment of one's professional actions. The idea of reflective practice values the importance of experiential knowledge as opposed to a rigid application of theories and technical knowledge, but accepts that experience alone (without deliberate reflection) does not necessarily trigger learning. Therefore, the reflective practitioner

allows himself to experience surprise, puzzlement, or confusion in a situation which he finds uncertain or unique. He reflects on the phenomenon before him, and on the prior understandings which have been implicit in his behaviour. He carries out an experiment which serves to generate both a new understanding of the phenomenon and a change in the situation. (Schön 1983, 68)

Schön's conceptualisation of ›practice as inquiry‹ involves two dimensions: on the one hand, the reflective practitioner engages in ›**reflection-in-action**‹, which influences the ongoing immediate and situational processes of decision-making; on the other hand, the reflective practitioner engages in ›**reflection-on-action**‹ as a retrospective activity, which describes a more profound reflective analysis of a situation already completed in order to enlarge his professional repertoire. The ideal of reflective practice is closely connected to a research-oriented attitude as, for example, represented in action research in the field of education, which is also concerned with a systematic reflection of teaching practices from the practitioner's perspective for the purpose of improving professional competences (cf. Altrichter/Posch 2007).

Definition

> In the field of teacher education, the concept of the reflective practitioner denotes a teacher with specific characteristics: On the basis of their everyday practices and their experiential knowledge as well as their academic knowledge, teachers ideally engage in meaningful reflection and awareness-raising and thus act as reflective practitioners. The pursuit of such a reflective self-development involves a research-oriented attitude, which aims at defining problems in professional practice as well as generating and assessing possible solutions.

Community of practice: While the notion of a reflective practitioner initially focuses on the individual teacher, some have argued that a solitary notion of teaching as well as teacher education is not only insufficient, but also unproductive for reflective practices (cf. Zeichner/Liston 1996). Many of the necessary processes of reflection can be exploited more effectively for the professional development of teachers if done in **cooperative settings**. Therefore, the concept of situated learning, which was explained for the English language classroom above, is also applicable to the field of teacher education and professionalism. This collective dimension of the language teaching profession is captured by the notion of a community of practice, which again relates to the theory of Lave and Wenger (1991). Being an expression of, and at the same time an extension of collegiality, a community of practice is constituted by a group of people with **common interests, values and responsibilities**, who cooperate to pursue joint goals, share knowledge, resolve workplace issues or engage in other problem-solving activities. In the context discussed here, any group of learners in the classroom, the teachers' body of a particular school, all teachers of English as a foreign language or the participants of an academic language teacher education programme could be considered communities of practice, which are also learning communities. Furthermore, communities of practice are characterised by a **functional distribution of roles** and the use of a **domain-specific language**, which is part of its members' professionalism and has to be acquired by novices in the field:

Becoming a language teacher also involves learning to »talk the talk,« that is, acquiring the specialized discourse that we use among ourselves and that helps define the subject matter of our profession. This means becoming familiar with several hundred specialized terms such as *learner centeredness, learner autonomy, self-access, alternative assessment, blended learning, task-based instruction, phoneme,* and *common European Framework* [sic] that we use on a daily basis in talking about our teaching. Being able to use the appropriate discourse (and, of course, understand what they mean) is one criteria for membership in the language teaching profession. (Richards 2010, 106f, italics in the original)

3.3 | Professional development and models of language teacher education

Teacher professionalism: The dimensions of good language teaching practice presented here culminate in the concept of teacher professionalism, which has been the subject of many considerations (cf. Hurst/Reding 2000; Richards/Thomas 2005; Bailey 2006; Bonnet/Hericks 2014). On the most basic level, the notion of professionalism involves an understanding of **English language teaching as a profession**. As such it is characterised by codified rules, for example the need to formally report on learners' achievements. A membership to the profession is based on official standards such as acknowledged academic qualifications or the acquisition of practical expertise as part of the training. Moreover, professionalism is also concerned with the question of **efficacy**. A professional teacher is understood to also be an efficient teacher who is able to create successful learning experiences for all learners. While much of this efficacy is based on the characteristics of good teaching practice described above, it cannot be achieved by skilfully executing a set of routines and procedures alone, but also requires a true sense of involvement (cf. Bach 2013, 306 f.).

To capture the different dimensions of professionalism, a helpful distinction has been proposed by Leung (2009): **prescribed professionalism** and **independent professionalism**. Prescribed professionalism as an expression of a top-down-process denotes the managerial competences needed by teachers to deal with the formal requirements and standards of regulatory bodies. As members of their profession, teachers will be held accountable for respecting the curriculum, executing final examinations or implementing new educational paradigms (such as competence-based teaching). By way of example, professional foreign language teachers would also be expected to prepare their learners for internationally acknowledged language tests, bilingual degree programmes or international certificates. In contrast, independent professionalism is an expression of a bottom-up-process triggered by the teacher's individual desire for change and improvement (cf. Viebrock 2014). It is closely related to the idea of reflective practice elaborated above and requires teachers to continuously and systematically reflect on their teaching practices and experiences as well as their values and beliefs. Richards (2010, 119) suggests a number of questions for individual reflection you may want to consider for yourself:

Key points

> **Questions for individual reflection (according to Richards 2010, 119)**
> - What kind of teacher am I?
> - What am I trying to achieve for myself and for my learners?
> - What are my strengths and limitations as a language teacher?
> - How and why do I teach the way I do?
> - How have I developed as a teacher since I started teaching?
> - What are the gaps in my knowledge?
> - What is my philosophy of teaching and how does it influence my teaching?
> - What role do I play in my school and is my role fulfilling?
> - What is my relationship with my colleagues and how productive is it?

Models of teacher education: An emphasis on experiential knowledge, reflective practice and independent professionalism as core dimensions of good language teaching is also central to teacher education (cf. Müller-Hartmann/Schocker-v. Ditfurth 2014, 12 ff.; Grimm et al. 2015, 19 ff.). Wallace (1991) distinguishes three models of teacher education having developed over time: the craft model, the applied science model and the reflective model, all of which conceptualise the relationship between theoretical academic knowledge and professional action differently.

- The **craft model** can be considered as some kind of ›training on the job‹. Professional competence is understood to evolve from observing, studying with and imitating an experienced master practitioner who serves as a role model and passes his/her expertise to the next generation. While the imitation of good practice certainly contributes to the professional development of a novice teacher, the craft model also has a number of shortcomings: it is prone to (mis-)understanding teaching as a mechanical activity employing routine motions and fails to explain how teachers can respond to unexpected situations and developments.
- The **applied science model** takes theoretical academic knowledge as a starting point, which is presented by experts through lectures and readings. Professional competence is achieved as a result of applying academic knowledge in teaching practice. Again, while nobody would seriously doubt the importance of a theoretical knowledge base for the language teaching profession, the applied science model is too unilateral. On the one hand, it disregards the impact of experiential knowledge. On the other hand, the model cannot solve any inconsistencies that might arise from conflicting knowledge in the different academic disciplines contributing to the teaching profession (cf. chapter 1 in this volume).
- The **reflective model** (cf. illustration 3.3) takes up these problems. Not only does it respect the demands of the different phases of teacher education (pre-service and in-service), but it also values teachers' prior knowledge and experiences, which are modified and refined in a circular process of practice and reflection leading to professional competence.

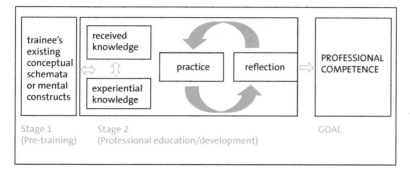

Illustration 3.3:
Reflective practice
model of profes-
sional develop-
ment
(Wallace 1991, 49)

Wallace's model is widely accepted in teacher education. It also explains why—as Charlie Brown questioned in the initial cartoon—teachers are educated at university for several years during which the acquisition of theoretical knowledge and phases of practical experimentation alternate. The formal traineeship (*Referendariat*) that teachers (in Germany) have to do as part of their professional development ties in with the model of reflective practice, too.

Standards for teacher education: On a regulatory level, standards for teacher education have been laid down in Germany by *The Standing Conference of the Ministers of Education and Cultural Affairs* (*Kultusministerkonferenz*) in the fields of **traineeship** (cf. KMK 2012a), **educational sciences** (cf. KMK 2014), **content knowledge and pedagogical content knowledge** (cf. KMK 2015). For modern languages, the aspired competence profile comprises a well-developed language proficiency, linguistic knowledge, an expertise of literary and cultural studies as well as pedagogical content knowledge. Particular emphasis is put on the fact that (future) teachers have to be able to systematically retrieve their theoretical academic knowledge and adapt it to their teaching practice in specific classroom situations.

Among many other things, they are expected to be able to analyse the potential of literary and non-literary texts and transform them into learning opportunities (cf. chapter 10 in this volume) or to be able to delineate the socio-political relevance of language teacher education and the significance of foreign language education at school (cf. KMK 2015, 39 ff.). Extending from a national perspective, a *European Profile for Language Teacher Education* has been proposed by Kelly and Grenfell (2004). Based on the examination of teacher education in 32 countries, the Profile contains a checklist of 40 items distributed over four sections (›structure‹, ›knowledge and understanding‹, ›strategies and skills‹, ›values‹), which can be used to reflect on the quality of local teacher training programmes.

3.4 | Future challenges of the English language teaching profession

An international take on teacher education, the teaching profession and foreign language teaching practice certainly belongs to the most important challenges in the future as Kumaravadivelu (2012, x) observes: »the fast evolving global society with its incessant and increased flows of peoples, goods and ideas across the world is placing huge responsibilities on the shoulders of student teachers, practising teachers and teacher educators.« Nowadays, any group of learners is characterised by a great **diversity** of socioeconomic and educational backgrounds, of languages and cultures. Schools are increasingly heterogeneous and multilingual. However, while diversity is one aspect to deal with, the **dynamics** resulting from processes of globalisation and global connectedness are probably even more difficult to handle. At a moment's notice, the social and linguistic constellation of a classroom may change and confront the teachers with unexpected challenges in view of communicative demands and processes of social interaction.

Teachers as agents of global change: Within this context, Bach (2015, n. p.) conceptualises foreign language teachers as ›agents of global change‹. He argues that the ongoing dissolution of borders and the complex processes of cultural hybridisation create highly dynamic social contexts which do »not align with any prescriptive approaches to language teaching by which insight generated by research or administrative wisdom is simply being handed down to the operational level to be implemented there by teaching professionals« (Bach 2015, n. p.). This is to say that teachers can no longer rely on clear-cut and established models of language teaching, but have to demonstrate **perceptual competences**, **context sensitivity** and a **sense of situational relevance**. As agents of global change, they will have to turn away from a top-down monolithic (›one size fits all‹) transmission approach where pre-selected and pre-sequenced sets of knowledge are passed on to the next generation of learners. Instead, teachers will have to engage in **flexible transformation-oriented pedagogical practices**, which are fuelled through **individual meaning-making processes** from bottom-up (cf. table 3.2).

The limitations of method(s): Hence, the transformation model caters for the fact that language learning and teaching situations are »unpredictably numerous« (Kumaravadivelu 2012, 10), which cannot possibly be met even by the most detailed pre-teaching plan or most intricate method: »no idealised method can visualise all the variables in advance in order to provide situation-specific suggestions that practicing teachers need to tackle the challenges they confront in the practice of their everyday teaching« (ibid.). A **critical stance on methods and methodology** certainly touches on one of the holy grails of language teaching, but there are more voices pointing at the limitations of any method within the increasingly diverse and dynamic global and local contexts of foreign language teaching (cf. Pennycook 1989; Prabhu 1990; Canagarajah 2013).

Postmethod pedagogy: This has taken Kumaravadivelu (2001, 2003) towards a postmethod perspective, where he questions the concept of

	Transmission model	Transformation model
linguistic norms	English as ›target language‹	Englishes as local repertoire(s)
	nationally-defined native Englishes	global English as a plural system (lingua franca)
	language as homogeneous	language as hybrid
	native and non-native speakers	speakers of varying degrees of proficiency
	nativeness as target	local norms of relevance
	language and discourse as static	language and discourse as dynamic
	language as context-bound	language as context-transforming
	correctness	negotiation of meaning
	mastery of grammar rules	metalinguistic awareness
	focus on rules and conventions	focus on strategies
	L1 as problem (interference)	L1 as resource
cultural norms	›target‹ cultures and communities	cultural diversity, hybridity and heterogeneity
expertise	established universal knowledge	context-specific local knowledge
	uni-directional knowledge flow	multi-directional knowledge-flows
	academic scholarship	reflective practice
	information/knowledge transmission	inquiry orientation / collaborative knowledge transformation
curriculum	prescription of innovation and change, top down-transmission	bottom-up processes equally supporting continuity and development
pedagogy	methods-dominated	postmethod practices
	skills-based, skills-focused	project-based, skills-in-context
materials	authenticity	relevance
	centrally generated and distributed	locally generated

Table 3.2: Shifts in professional discourse on language teacher education and pedagogical practice

method altogether and proposes a postmethod pedagogy as a necessary redefinition of foreign language teaching and teacher education. By searching »an alternative to method rather than an alternative method« (Kumaravadivelu 2012, 16), a postmethod pedagogy tries to respect **individual, situational and local circumstances of foreign language learning** and the demands this puts on teachers and their education. In agreement with the notions of reflective practice and independent professionalism, a postmethod pedagogy requires a large amount of **teacher autonomy** and **teacher agency** as explained by Bach (2015, n. p.). The ensuing freedom of choice corresponds with a greater responsibility concerning

Language teaching
and technological
development

the necessary processes of decision-making and, thus poses additional challenges to English language teachers.

Technological pedagogical content knowledge: While the social dynamics of globalisation probably have the most profound impact on the language teaching profession and individual teaching practices, they interfere with at least two more aspects that need to be mentioned here: technological advancement (cf. chapter 12 in this volume) and inclusive education (cf. chapter 2 in this volume). Both aspects put tremendous challenges on teachers of English as a foreign language and their educators, but also contribute to the vitality of the profession. As mentioned above, teachers have to be open-minded towards technological developments and understand the **affordances and limitations of both existing and newly developing technologies**, i.e, how these influence the teaching and learning of English as a foreign language. Koehler and Mishra (2009, 66) assume that a well-developed technological pedagogical content knowledge is

> [...] the basis of effective teaching with technology, requiring an understanding of the representation of concepts using technologies; pedagogical techniques that use technologies in constructive ways to teach content; knowledge of what makes concepts difficult or easy to learn and how technology can help redress some of the problems that students face; knowledge of students' prior knowledge and theories of epistemology; and knowledge of how technologies can be used to build on existing knowledge to develop new epistemologies or strengthen old ones.

An important aspect of the language teaching profession is that many technologies cannot only be used for the acquisition or retrieval of subject-specific content knowledge or as a tool for learning, but also for facilitating communication with real speakers. Learners of English have the opportunity to feed their contributions into existing discourses, which might contribute to their motivation for learning the foreign language. At the same time, Internet-based structures of communication and language use follow different rules compared to the traditional speaking or writing (cf. Elsner/Viebrock 2013). To deal with this and turn it into a valuable learning experience is another challenge for the teacher.

Inclusive education: Another recent socio-political development which has an enormous impact on classroom interaction and on the teaching profession is the turn to inclusive education. While inclusion ultimately describes a comprehensive, all-embracing way of teaching, in which **diversity** and **heterogeneity** are the norm, in the meantime a more realistic goal consists in developing immediate accommodations for learners with learning differences (cf. Kormos/Smith 2012, 105). It becomes apparent that again the teachers' mind-sets are crucial to the success of inclusive education. In particular, when it comes to putting inclusive education into practice and communicating its merits, »there is some responsibility on teachers to choose to use more empowering discourses that reflect inclusive approaches to education« (ibid., 15). As a conclusion, an **awareness and appreciation of learning differences** needs to be developed in language teacher education in order to be able to cope with inclusive settings in the foreign language classroom and beyond.

3.5 | Conclusion

The purpose of this chapter was to discuss the characteristics of a professional English language teacher and good teaching practice in the English language classroom. By taking the teachers' experiential knowledge acquired prior to and during their formal education as a starting point, the peculiarities of the teachers' mind-sets and how these influence their professional development have been described. A review of the existing research has shown that among the necessary characteristics of good teaching, ›reflective practice‹ and ›independent professionalism‹ are the most important ones since they take the dispositions of the individual teacher as a starting point and explain how experiential knowledge and theoretical academic knowledge are integrated and utilised in a repetitive circular course of action and reflection. Professional competence is the result of a successful completion of these processes. The reflective practice model also lies at the core of foreign language teacher education, which combines phases of academic training and practical experience and reflection. As a final point, this chapter looked at the most salient challenges of the teaching profession: the effects of globalisation, the growth of technology and the implementation of inclusive education. Through their profession, foreign language teachers have to assume the role of agents of change in many respects and meet the challenges with a great amount of flexibility and expertise, which in turn contributes to the vitality of the profession. Wright's (2013, n. p.) statement sums up nicely what this chapter set out to explain:

Being a teacher is more than simply having an occupation, a job. Teaching is a way of life defined by learning and by relationship; it is always a »work in progress«, a potentially lifelong endeavour in which we continually reinvent ourselves as we learn more about what it is we are doing and who we—teachers and learners—are. Not only are we helping others learn, but we are also learning about how to do that, which means learning about learning itself. We develop knowledge, expertise and awareness about learning; we become teachers.

Further Reading
Bach, Gerhard (⁵2013): »Alltagswissen und Unterrichtspraxis: der Weg zum *reflective practitioner*«. In: Bach, Gerhard/Timm, Johannes-Peter (eds.): *Englischunterricht. Grundlagen und Methoden einer handlungsorientierten Unterrichtspraxis* [1989]. Tübingen/Basel, 304–320.
Helmke, Andreas (⁶2015): *Unterrichtsqualität und Lehrerprofessionalität. Diagnose, Evaluation und Verbesserung des Unterrichts* [2009]. Seelze.
Kumaravadivelu, Balasubramanian (2012): *Language Teacher Education for a Global Society. A Modular Model for Knowing, Analyzing, Recognizing, Doing, and Seeing.* New York/London.
Richards, Jack C. (2010): »Competence and Performance in Language Teaching«. In: *RELC Journal* 41/2, 101–122.

Britta Viebrock

4 Language Learners — From Learning Styles to Identity

From a global perspective, education is the key to democratic participation and personal welfare. Therefore, providing as many people with as much education as possible is a fundamentally democratic endeavour. From a historical point of view, it is thus very consistent that the humanist approaches to public schooling for an increasing number of people in the 17th and 18th century drew on the idea of instructivist teaching to large numbers of students, crowded into large classrooms. In the 20th century, various reform pedagogical movements and an increase in pedagogical research raised awareness that learning is a fundamentally individual and even idiosyncratic process. Therefore, uniform instruction to large groups was increasingly seen as problematic. The idea of learner orientation was born.

About a century later, it cannot fully be claimed that this learner orientation has actually become a reality. Nevertheless, there is a lot of evidence that suggests that learner orientation improves the quality of EFL classrooms. In fact, there are various approaches that look at the language learner from different perspectives, thus highlighting a multitude of aspects that together constitute learner orientation in a complex way. The following chapter will first set the stage for learner orientation by putting it into the context of individualisation. It will then consider it from a psycholinguistic point of view, highlighting learners' individuality of processing language. Afterwards, it will discuss learner orientation from a socio-cultural perspective, exploring what it means to understand language acquisition as a process embedded in cultural contexts. Finally, the chapter will present implications of these different approaches to learner orientation for the EFL classroom (cf. also chapter 11 in this volume).

> Learner orientation in FLT means making language teaching adaptive to the learners by taking into account their individual psychological dispositions (e. g. their learning styles) as well as their individual constructions of identity (e. g. their cultural and linguistic positionings) in order to foster learner autonomy with respect to its functional (i. e. manage their own language learning) and critical (i. e. take up a reflected stance to school as an institution) aspect.

Definition

4.1 | EFL in the 21st century between learning and education

Change: ›The only constant is change‹. Arguably, this saying attributed to Heraclitus has never been more appropriate in its 2500 years of existence than in the early 21st century. Social change is fuelled by migration and alternative constructions of social identity. **Globalisation** and **digitalisation** have speeded up technological change dramatically and altered the work place fundamentally. Technological change in turn has altered the patterns of the use of foreign languages in that there is an ever increasing number of devices (e.g. electronic translators) that support everyday communication across languages.

Impacts on FLT: What has all this to do with foreign language teaching and learning? A preliminary answer could be that it impacts on the goal of the EFL classroom. Where there might have been a time when competence in the target language (i.e. English), perhaps complemented by a smattering of intercultural skills, was the goal, this is not satisfying anymore. Today, English is the most important global *lingua franca*. Who dares to say that this will still be true when today's students are graduating or when they are at the peak of their career? Will it probably be Chinese by then? Or Spanish? We do not know. This is exactly the point.

Learner autonomy: Target language competence is the goal that teachers will probably devote most of their time in the EFL classroom to. But it is only learner autonomy which gives their students the opportunity of extending their language competence in the best possible way for the course of their future life and career. On the one hand, this means that learners become autonomous in terms of organising their own **lifelong language learning** (cf. Benson 2011). On the other hand, it means that they become autonomous in terms of understanding the **biographical and political relevance of language and language learning** (cf. Fairclough 1999). Both elements, functional autonomy to be able to participate and reflexive autonomy to be able to become critical and emancipated, are two sides of the same coin. The question, this chapter is going to address then, is: How do learners become autonomous in these two respects?

Language learning: The first path to autonomy is looking at TEFL as language *learning*. Learners have long been considered trivial machines imitating interlocutors and making transfer mistakes that need to be erased by drill exercises. Selinker's seminal paper (1972) has taken seriously that learners are by no means trivial machines but intelligent processors of input constructing and testing language hypotheses. For the first time, learners became a relevant object in foreign language research in their own right. This coincided with the communicative turn, shifting attention from form to message and content.

Following from an ever increasing conceptualisation of **language acquisition as a constructive process**, learners were re-conceptualised as acting rationally or even strategically and therefore in need of an extended amount of **reflexivity**. Parallel to this, learners were no longer reduced to solely cognitive creatures but also considered having emotional needs. This led to looking at the **emotional aspects** of language acquisition, taking into account aspects of anxiety, motivation or self-efficacy. Summing up this strand of research, language learning is considered a constructive and strategic activity of processing input, negotiating meaning and producing output to bring about a complex cognitive and emotional deep structure.

Language education: The second path to autonomy is looking at TEFL as language *education*: Historically, there have always been educators such as Wilhelm von Humboldt, who foregrounded the educational potential of foreign languages. While Humboldt still had a somehow cognitive approach to what constitutes the educational potential of foreign languages, he arguably paved the way for taking the learners into account in a holistic way. This led to reform pedagogical approaches to language learning that stressed the **educational potential of foreign languages** rather than functional language competence (e. g. the Steiner movement that introduced foreign language learning at elementary level in the early 20th century already). It was the cultural turn (i. e. the notion that cultural context strongly influences human actions), though, and the emergence of understanding language acquisition as intertwined with learners' identity constructions that led to viewing learners as human beings with complex biographical and cultural roots and resources that strongly influence their language acquisition. This chapter will first elaborate the two perspectives in terms of their central concepts and their conceptualisation of the foreign language learner and second provide examples of teaching strategies and classroom activities putting these conceptualisations into practice.

4.2 | Language learners from a psycholinguistic point of view: learners as non-trivial machines processing language

Learner features: From a cognitive point of view, language acquisition is a process that is relatively similar across individuals, which runs through comparable states in a similar order and which is influenced by individual features of learners in a systematic way (cf. Wolff 2010a, 293). It is considered a mental activity of receiving and processing input, negotiating meaning in interactions with interlocutors and generating output that aims at reaching the speaker's communicative goals. The underlying mental activity is seen as a **constructive process** of generating linguistic hypotheses and learners are seen as testing these in interaction. From this point of view, learner orientation means optimising the language acquisition process by taking into account different **learner-specific variables** that influence this process.

There are various ways of organising and relating these different features. In his concise overview, Wolff (2010a, 294 ff.) compares different attempts of defining relevant categories and comes to the conclusion that researchers have agreed on most of the categories« and that there is very little that is still contested. It does not make sense to present all the different taxonomies here, because they partly overlap or give different names to similar concepts. Therefore, it might suffice to identify the relevant areas. According to the literature, learners are significantly different with respect to different domains.

> **Dimensions of learner differences**
> - **age**
> - **affective state**, i. e. their emotions in the course of acquiring a foreign language, influenced by features such as anxiety or uncertainty tolerance
> - **aptitude**
> - **attitudes** towards (learning) foreign languages
> - **beliefs** about language acquisition and favourable conditions of the language classroom
> - **motivation** to learn foreign languages
> - **strategic repertoire**
> - **cognitive style**, such as a rather analytic or holistic way of approaching problems

An introductory text does not allow going through all the features in turn, hence one of the particular features will be dealt with in more detail. This will demonstrate (1) that each of the features is complex in itself and can be conceptualised in different ways, (2) that these features are not fixed but can be influenced by individual ways of teaching and (3) that looking at the different features allows for drawing very practical consequences with respect to managing a specific classroom. Because of its importance, the topic chosen is the concept of motivation.

Motivation: Dörnyei, one of the most prolific experts on motivation in the foreign language classroom, begins one of his books by saying that »strictly speaking, *there is no such thing as ›motivation‹*« (2001, 1; italics in the original). Of course, the point he wants to make is not that the phenomenon known as motivation does not exist. He rather wants to stress that it is very complex and needs to be approached from various angles to get a grip on what it means or even take it into account in the classroom. He goes on defining it as an »aspect of the human mind [...] related to what one *wants/desires* [...], in contrast to characteristics related to what one rationally *thinks* [...] or *feels*« (ibid., 2; italics in the original).

Early research into motivation: Having established this, the question is where do these desires come from? According to self-determination-theory (cf. Deci/Ryan 1985), they can originate from internal driving forces such as a positive attitude towards foreign language learning or foreign languages or they can be instilled externally by positive rewards or threatened punishment. With respect to foreign language learning the specification of this by Gardner and Lambert (1972) is a very useful tool to show how motivation can vary across individuals based on their individual **attitudes**. In their model, an integrative orientation is given if learners have a positive attitude towards the foreign language and the assumed community of speakers of this language, which they want to interact with. In contrast to this, an instrumental orientation means that a learner wants to acquire a language because of non-linguistic goals, such as success in the labour market.

Motivation and the self: Moving into the 1990s and 2000s the concept of motivation has become increasingly complex. It may suffice here to introduce one other important aspect, the concept of **self-efficacy** (cf. Bandura 1997). It describes the effect that even if an individual may have an instrumental orientation towards the foreign language, this may not lead to high motivation if the individual considers him/herself not capable of mastering the language. The important point about this concept is that self-efficacy and actual performance in the classroom have a reciprocal relation, i.e. they are two sides of the same coin. On the one hand, high self-efficacy leads to high **persistence** and high **intensity** of a learner's activities, which in turn is likely to have a positive influence on the learner's **performance**—a self-enforcing cycle. On the other hand, low performance and failure reduce a learner's self-efficacy, which in turn lowers persistence and intensity of activities—a vicious circle.

Anxiety: An aspect of this specific to the foreign language classroom is the notion of anxiety. It is considered a major factor influencing to what extent a person is able to process input or to engage in interaction, which in turn helps to clarify the learner's linguistic hypotheses. Again, it can be said that anxiety and comparable phenomena such as uncertainty tolerance are acquired in early stages of a person's biography: students bring this disposition to the classroom. Nevertheless, anxieties are not fixed. They have been learned and they can be transformed. Therefore, your classroom needs to be a place which not only reacts to students' dispositions but tries to influence them positively. This aspect will be taken up in the final section of this chapter.

Multiple intelligences: This closer look at motivation has already demonstrated that viewing learners' individuality as a programmed set of fixed features is very questionable. Therefore, there are models that look at learners' individuality in a more flexible way. One such approach is the model of multiple intelligences (Gardner 1993). It assumes that human intelligence does not only consist of cognitive capacities, but that other areas such as aesthetics or movement are of equal importance, i.e. that humans possess multiple intelligences with individual strengths and weaknesses. It is certainly questionable whether individuals could be put into a box according to their particular mode of intelligence. This would create the same problems as assuming that a lack of aptitude is the end of the story of learning a language for an individual with this assumed deficit. The point rather is that the model of multiple intelligences shows to what extent EFL classrooms have a **cognitive bias**, particularly if following the prevalent form-orientation of textbooks.

Learning styles: Another way of dealing with individuality without putting learners into individual boxes (perhaps at the price of using collective boxes, though) was developed in the 1990s as part of a broader movement to take the cultural embeddedness of learners' individuality into account. Oxford and Anderson (1995) summed up the existing literature and identified the following eight learning styles:

Learning styles	Description
global vs. analytic	the disposition to start with the whole picture rather than looking at details first, going along with a verbal orientation and liking of linguistic form rather than a visual/spatial orientation and liking of communication
field dependent vs. field independent	»the degree of ability to separate insignificant background details from truly significant details« (205), going along with the disposition to understand a situation through logic analysis rather than through interpersonal communication
feeling vs. thinking	the disposition to base one's decision-making on social and emotional factors rather than on logic and analysis
impulsive vs. reflective	the disposition to communicate spontaneously and fast with a high acceptance of inaccuracy rather than to communicate slowly, deliberately and with great accuracy
intuitive-random vs. concrete-sequential	the disposition to »build a mental model of the second-language information« (207), going along with creativity, the application of compensation strategies and high acceptance of topical deviation, as opposed to analysing and combining linguistic information, going along with task- and teacher-orientation and avoidance of compensation strategies and topical deviation
closure-oriented vs. open	the disposition to do tasks on time and to avoid »ambiguity, uncertainty or fuzziness« (ibid.) as opposed to operating on flexible time-management and possessing »high tolerance for ambiguity« (ibid.)
extroverted vs. introverted	the disposition to »gain their energy and focus from events and people outside of themselves« (208) leading to a liking of co-operative interactional activities, as opposed to be »stimulated by their own inner world of ideas and feelings« (ibid.) and disliking continuous work in great groups
visual vs. auditory vs. hands-on	the disposition to prefer visual stimulation leads to anxiety in the face of merely oral input, whereas the disposition to prefer auditory information does not cause this problem; the disposition to prefer hands-on experience leads to an increased need of physical action and the manipulation of »tangible objects, collages and other media« (209)

Table 4.1:
Learning styles according to Oxford/
Anderson (1995)

Learning styles and culture: Oxford and Anderson's point was not to open just another taxonomy, but rather that the combination of learning styles to sets is culture-specific. This means that certain learning styles may be preferred on the basis of one's cultural background. If, for example, a person grows up within a small nuclear family with a strongly individualist and emancipatory orientation, s/he may find it difficult to adjust to a teacher centred instructivist classroom. If a teacher does not share the students' background, s/he may find it difficult to understand the students' difficulties in adjusting. S/he may therefore attribute learning difficulties to a student's lack of aptitude or intellectual capacity rather than to a difference in learning style. Therefore, a teacher's awareness of the potential differences in learning styles and their cultural roots is required to correctly identify learning difficulties that could be reduced by responding to the learners' different styles. If this is not done, the »foreign language classroom becomes a place of inequity, where some students receive what they need and others do not« (Oxford/Anderson 1995, 201).

This **culture specificity** opens up a point of view, from which »cross-cultural style conflicts« (ibid., 210) become visible. A relevant study by Wallace and Oxford (1992) in North America showed that the teachers were significantly more oriented towards introversion and thinking, whereas their ESL students seemed to be much more oriented towards extroversion and feeling. The study also shows that these differences negatively influenced grades, most intensely when it comes to writing. The authors conclude from their data that the style incongruities originate from cultural differences and recommend more awareness and sensitivity in this area.

Stereotype threat: One possible criticism of this approach is that the seeming complexity of describing individual dispositions in eight different categories is significantly reduced by the authors themselves. By constantly establishing connections and interdependencies between categories they create an overarching dichotomy between analytical-reflexive-uncertainty tolerant learners as opposed to global-impulsive-uncertainty intolerant learners (cf. Bauer 2015, 23). This simplifies the complexity they created in the first place and may lead to put learners into boxes too readily and inappropriately.

Another possible criticism concerns the application of this list in the classroom. Their suggestion is to use questionnaire-like style inventories to establish students' styles and teachers' styles as well. Could there be anything wrong with this? The authors say no, because: »A questionnaire is by nature non-threatening« (Oxford/Anderson 1995, 210). There are researchers, however, who would be rather unhappy with this (cf. Steele/Aronson 1995). They draw on the finding that students' **performances** in the classroom are influenced if features of their **identity**, such as gender or ethnicity, are made salient. This phenomenon is called ›stereotype threat‹ and was first discovered in the context of post-segregational college education in the United States. There, African-American students in an ethnically diverse setting performed significantly worse in tests that were introduced as achievement tests as compared to tests that were introduced as research tests, for example in order to measure the co-ordination of hand and eye. Also, the effect was found when students were asked to name the relevant feature, such as ethnicity or gender, in the header of the test, as opposed to if they were not.

How stereotype threat works: The explanation of this phenomenon is that people tend to accept the stereotypes attributed to the social group they are identified with, i. e. the stereotype that minority students are less competent or that women can't do maths. When the stereotype is made salient in a classroom situation, students implicitly or even explicitly spend cognitive and emotional capacity on dealing with the **social expec-tations** that the stereotype evokes. This can mean that students' **stress levels** rise because they are anxious not to conform to the stereotype by performing badly; which sadly enough is what happens in this situation. And this is exactly what could happen if style inventories are used in the classroom, because these inventories—even more so if their presumed cultural background is mentioned—may well be threatening by empha-sising cultural stereotypes.

Othering: The discussion of different concepts has shown the com-plexity of the problem. The concept of learner styles even tries to account for cultural effects. Besides the stereotype threat problem, however, it only works under the assumption that certain orientations are stable. Combining this assumption with the cultural attribution underlying the concept may enhance stereotype-threat. It may even lead to attributing individual differences to an assumed cultural and therefore collective background. And this in turn positions a student in a **minority position**, a phenomenon social scientists call ›othering‹. Where, with good inten-tions, a teacher wants to acknowledge a student's individuality, s/he ac-tually excludes him or her by stressing that the difference is cultural and not just individual. In order to take this into account, the following sec-tion will look at approaches that view learner orientation from a so-cio-cultural angle.

4.3 | Language learners from a socio-cultural point of view: learners as human beings and meaning makers

Cultural and bio-graphical resources and limitations

Whereas psycholinguistic approaches argue that learners can be charac-terised with respect to features they possess and that are stable across situations, socio-cultural approaches refute this assumption. They argue that language acquisition is a culturally and biographically embedded process and learners are acting on the basis of their cultural and bio-graphical resources and limitations. They also argue that foreign language classrooms are situated in institutions and thus objected to institutional as well as personal **power relations**. Because of this, language acquisi-tion can hardly be described solely by sets of cognitive and affective var-iables, which leads Krumm (2011, 79) to »distrust typologies of language learners« (translation AB).

Context-sensitivity: An example of this is that students may use and value the languages they speak totally differently in different contexts: multilinguals may consider and use their heritage languages as **cultural capital** at home and in their community, whereas they feel forced to hide them at school where they may be considered a sign of social and cogni-tive deficits. That is why Krumm (2011) argues that learner orientation has been proposed for decades but has never been achieved, neither in research, nor in the classroom. What would have to be done, to make EFL classrooms learner-oriented in a sense that multilingualism is looked at very carefully and seen as a resource where this is appropriate.

Socio-cultural approaches: First of all, one needs to understand what exactly is meant by the idea that language acquisition is a situated and socio-cultural phenomenon. This can be done by looking at what Norton, one of the pioneers of identity and foreign language learning, observed time and again with minority students of ESL (English as a second language) (cf. Norton 2013). Although they spoke more than one language and showed high metalinguistic awareness, these students would not **participate** in the ESL classroom and thus underperform as compared to their majority peers. Why?

Exclusion of multilingualism: From a psycholinguistic point of view, the students would be looked at as motivationally deficient. So, the first step was to establish their motivation for foreign languages. As opposed to what researchers expected, it was high. In the interviews conducted with the students it showed that the students felt **excluded** from the classroom because they were constantly addressed as problematic as their multilingualism would cause problems in ESL and they were excluded by being addressed as representing a minority and thus different and not belonging. This led the students to **withdraw** from classroom activities although their motivation for foreign languages and for cultural learning was high.

Investment: This is why Norton introduced the concept of investment. It describes the degree to which a person mentally and physically **engages** in a foreign language classroom or—more broadly speaking—in language learning activities. The punch line of this concept is that it acknowledges that a person's investment and his/her motivation can be quite different. That raises the question what a student's investment originates from. This can be understood by looking at Darvin and Norton's (2015) model of identity and investment in the foreign language classroom. They argue that investment is constituted at the intersection of **identity**, **capital** and **ideology**.

Identity: Identity denotes »how a person understands his or her relationship to the world, how that relationship is constructed across time and space, and how the person understands possibilities for the future« (Norton 2013, 45). The term ›understand‹ does not mean that a person is necessarily aware of all this. One might as well say how a person *enacts* his or her **relationship to the world**. This means how a person positions him- or herself and how that person is positioned with respect to his or her languages and cultural identity but also with respect to gender, age or political or religious beliefs.

Capital: The concept of capital refers to sociological theory, here Bourdieu's (1986) theory of habitus. It describes that in a given society, each member of this society possesses valuable commodities that help everyone reach their goals. Whereas **economic** capital is easily understood as money or other equivalent assets, such as real estate or shares in a company, two other types of capital are of equal importance but easily overseen. **Social** capital refers to the set of relationships a person has. Even in a seemingly meritocratic society, these relationships strongly influence whose support someone can draw on and what access a person gets to the labour market. Finally, and this is where foreign languages come into play, there is **cultural** capital. It refers to the languages a person speaks or the soft skills s/he possesses.

Ideology: The important point to note is that cultural capital is defined by ideology. In other words: the value of a person's linguistic assets depends on the value a language is given by society and its reigning ideologies, i.e. the ideas that most of its members share. In many Western countries, the reigning ideology is as follows: multilingualism is considered an asset, if it concerns high-**prestige** languages such as English or Spanish, but considered a threat and a problem if it concerns minority languages such as Arabic languages or Turkish. Informed by a still predominantly monolingual habitus (cf. Gogolin 2008), this is mirrored in the educational system, which favours monolingual instruction in the majority language or in high-prestige former colonial languages, whereas it sidelines low-prestige minority languages.

Inclusion of multilingualism: This may create a rather schizophrenic situation: A multilingual student may perceive his/her heritage language as an acknowledged asset and thus cultural capital in his own community. This leads to himself/herself feeling a strong sense of belonging and cause investment into this language. The same student may be given the impression that his/her heritage language and culture are a burden in school, and the monolingual practice rejects and gradually alienates him/her from the foreign language classroom, leading to disinvestment into and underachievement in English. This frequently observed pattern requires change on the side of the teacher by **acknowledging** students' multilingualism, **valuing** their heritage languages and thus **welcoming** these in the foreign language classroom (cf. chapter 3 in this volume). This will lead to increased investment and subsequently participation.

A developmental perspective: Looking at a second very powerful model of students' identities, a *sine qua non* becomes visible—a condition that applies to both minority and majority students, because beyond their mono- or multilingualism they are all **children** or later on **adolescents**. There may be the case that cultural and linguistic identity is acknowledged, that motivation for foreign languages is there and that a student still does not engage in the FL classroom. Why may this be the case? It may be, because the student unconsciously prioritises other issues than those dealt with in class over what the teacher has on offer. This is particularly true when students enter adolescence.

Developmental tasks: This phenomenon has given rise to the concept of developmental tasks. It was first introduced in the 1950s by Havighurst and conceptualised as follows:

A developmental task is a task which arises at or about a certain period in the life of the individual, successful achievement of which leads to his happiness and to success with later tasks, while failure leads to unhappiness in the individual, disapproval by the society, and difficulty with later tasks. (Havighurst 1953, 2)

The tasks originate from the interaction of the individual with society. In terms of the investment model, one could say that they reflect the individual's need to position him- or herself relative to reigning ideologies, such as ideologies about gender, about culture(s) and language(s), about sexual orientations, about careers, to name just a few. Over the last decades, research has focussed on the developmental tasks of early adolescence and a list of these issues has been compiled. Havighurst's initial list has been criticised for a strong white-protestant-middle class-bias. Therefore, in the German context, the list has been reworked and empirically tested. The psychologists Dreher and Dreher (1985) have empirically established a very influential list, which has been updated by the educational researchers Hericks and Spörlein (2001). The following developmental tasks can be considered accepted state of the art:

Developmental task	Description
peer	establishing new and deepened relationships to peers of both sexes
role	establishing a gender identity and relating to social expectations of male and female behaviour
body	accepting one's own body and its physical transformations
independence	gradually becoming independent of one's parents
partner/family	developing ideas about future partners and potential family structures
desire	starting close and increasingly sexual relationships with a boy- or girlfriend
job	developing job aspirations and understanding the competences one needs to achieve one's goals
future	developing a perspective of one's own future, targeting goals and planning their achievement
values	creating a set of values by dealing with moral, political, religious or other ideologies
self	developing a self-concept

Table 4.2: Developmental tasks according to Hericks/Spörlein (2001)

How do developmental tasks relate to teaching foreign languages? There are two options to you as future teachers. If you consider them, they may be your **allies**: introducing content, such as coming-of-age-fiction, that offers students the opportunity to deal with their developmental tasks in the foreign language classroom, you can cash in on the motivation and investment this creates. If, however, you ignore them, they may become your **rivals**: if you do not take them into consideration, students will pursue their own activities in the foreign language classroom and the teacher will have to compete for the students' investment. Unfortunately for the teacher and fortunately for the students' personal growth, the teacher will lose this competition.

Goal autonomy: One may conclude that both the investment model and the concept of developmental tasks foster goal autonomy and show two aspects of it: The first aspect concerns the students' identity. It means that by acknowledging their linguistic and cultural identity and by inclusively reflecting on heterogeneity and hybridity in the classroom, students become aware of what languages mean to them. Bringing in the idea of capital and connecting this to developmental tasks such as finding a personal vocational perspective leads students to become goal autonomous in that they **connect foreign languages to their personal aspirations**.

Critical autonomy: The second aspect, i. e. the socio-political dimension as foregrounded by Fairclough's (1999) concept of ›critical language awareness‹ is particularly fostered by the element of ideology as part of the investment model. If students reflect on the linguistic and cultural ideologies of their classroom and if they compare this to their everyday experience, they see how the majority society conceptualises them. They understand how they are influenced by stereotypes or **implicit rules** of access to institutions such as higher education. In this respect, students (and teachers) become critically autonomous. This in itself is a fruitful way of dealing with students' developmental tasks. The perk of this is that teachers' professional development can be described in terms of developmental tasks as well, and that acknowledging students' developmental task is a powerful source of successful professional development (cf. Hericks et al. 2018). The final part of this chapter will deal with how the principles explained above can be put into practice.

4.4 | Implications for the EFL classroom

Of course, there is no way of dealing with all the principles and there is no way of giving you simple tools to take with you to the classroom tomorrow. Some of the following illustrations and explanations will provide some general ideas. Starting from the assumption that learning a foreign language is a very individual, even idiosyncratic endeavour, it becomes clear that the individual's needs as well as their (and the teacher's) social embeddedness need to be taken into consideration. The following conclusions could give directions as to how to achieve this (cf. also chapter 11 in this volume). Psycholinguistic aspects will be looked at first:

Enhancing motivation

Motivation theory provides very useful suggestions and mentions all sorts of consequences, which Dörnyei (2001) has put together in a very hands-on manner. The key point is: do not simply react to students' motivation, but **shape it**. Three examples may suffice in order to illustrate how to do this:

- Try to positively transform students' motivational orientation. This can be done by influencing their attitude, for example by inviting **positive role models,** such as senior students or adults who used their foreign languages in an inspiring way or by having gained instrumental benefits from their FL mastery such as a job.
- Try to increase students' self-efficacy. This can be done by very carefully adjusting and preparing tasks, providing **scaffolding** and making the **goals** as **transparent** as possible. Also, negotiate FL goals with your students to make sure that they accept the classroom goals.
- The ultimate prerequisite for motivation is that the students see the

relevance of any classroom activity. This can be achieved by explaining how which classroom activity contributes to which goal. It can also be achieved by taking into account students' interests. It sounds as if the developmental task model could come in handy here (cf. table 4.2).

Emotionality: Whereas motivation is linked to the students' emotionality, which should be taken into account in general, it is worth highlighting **anxiety** as a particular factor. In order to minimise this, students need to be dealt with in a very individual way. This is beyond the scope of this chapter. There are three measures, however, that reduce anxiety in a systematic way. First of all, it requires a classroom that **welcomes mistakes** and that encourages students to test their linguistic hypotheses by participating in classroom communication. Second, it requires **message-orientation** before form-orientation in order to provide the opportunities for communication and in order to direct students' attention away from accuracy and towards communicative goals. And it requires a differentiation between phases of learning and phases of assessment in order to help them switch on and off their accuracy monitor depending on whether it is required or not. Third, it requires **mastery goals** (i.e. success is defined as making progress towards a defined and shared competence goal), rather than performance goals (i.e. success is defined as performing better than others).

Eliminate stereotype threat: Anxiety can also be influenced positively by eliminating elements that cause stereotype threat. This can only be done by identifying the relevant features of your students, such as a minority status and by being very careful about how to address this. The line between positive acknowledgement and negative othering is very thin. The rule of thumb is to **address students as individuals** and not as members of an assumed cultural group. It makes a lot of sense to ask each student how they spent their weekend or celebrated a festivity and let them decide how much they conceptualise this as a result of their cultural background. It is rather detrimental, though, to address students as members of a minority group in the first place and make them an expert for this cultural group. Their expertise for this group comes at the price of not belonging to the majority of the classroom. A price you should not make them pay.

Create relevance: The all-important aspect of relevance can best be addressed by allowing for the students to work on their **developmental tasks**. On the one hand, this can be done by facilitating extended social learning in co-operative settings. This gives students the opportunity to develop their peer-relations and to put to the test their values like solidarity or justice. On the other hand, this can be enabled by dealing with topics that directly address selected developmental tasks. This could mean dealing with literature, particularly with adolescent fiction, in a learner-oriented mode (cf. chapter 10 in this volume). Coming-of-age-novels or other fiction that explicitly addresses issues like gender roles, intimate relationships or child-parent-relationships, offer opportunities to discuss these issues in the safe space of communicating about fictional characters.

Create ownership: Dealing with literature in this open way also sets the principle of **participatory teaching**. Asking students directly or following their ideas in discussions (bottom-up adaptivity) is even better than choosing content on the premise of expected interests (top-down adaptivity). Therefore, learner orientation means asking for the students' participation in determining the content of the EFL classroom and thus creating a sense of ownership.

Plurilingualism: The movement towards plurilingualism in the foreign language classroom has also come up with many suggestions that make EFL classrooms relevant to students. On the one hand, there are methods that highlight individual multilingualism, such as **multilingual picture books**. Reading them acknowledges multilingualism in an inclusive way. Making them creates opportunities for using target and heritage languages in a productive way and providing creative opportunities of raising language awareness. The same is true for using **linguistic landscaping** in the classroom, in the school and in the community. It creates an authentic product orientation and again provides opportunities to acquire critical language awareness.

Openness

Uncertainty and sense construction: This is the moment to raise the question, why—although accepting the need and wanting to do it—teaching often does not offer the required openness, why opportunities of individual sense construction are closed when they occur. There are two important reasons: One has to do with a teacher's tolerance towards **uncertainty**. Individual sense construction is necessarily unplannable and to a certain extent subversive. It perturbs the teacher's plan. This is by no means a phenomenon exclusive to the EFL classroom. Gruschka (2013), who has done extended classroom research in various subjects, almost always observed the following pattern. Whenever individual **sense construction** led to students uttering creative thoughts that showed lateral thinking but led away from the lesson's immediate goal, these contributions were not taken up but postponed and forgotten, sidelined or openly dismissed. This may well be a sign of the ubiquity of assessment. Research on teachers introducing co-operative learning (e. g. Bonnet/Hericks 2014) shows that innovation raises uncertainty and in turn creates anxiety on the teacher's side. Whenever teachers leave the planned route, they ask themselves: Will I reach the required goals? How do my colleagues feel about this? Will I cover all the necessary content the curriculum tells me to teach? Are my grades valid?

Assessment and Co-operation: One way of dealing with this is consulting the state curricula and probably being surprised that they are not the place of endless lists of mandatory content (cf. chapter 2 in this volume). With respect to some aspects, even the opposite is true. The state curriculum of Hamburg is a case in point. It extensively asks for **co-operative, participatory grading** and **self-assessment** of the students. Another is to realise that the persistent teacher-centredness is something that cannot be overcome individually. It strongly calls for **teacher co-operation** to pave ways for the learner to be at the forefront. As far as assessment is concerned, co-operatively developing criteria-referenced-assessment is called for (cf. chapter 14 in this volume). When developing the grids, teachers discuss and negotiate goals and expectations and thus reduce uncertainty. As far as the assessment of products that students are familiar with—such as presentations—is concerned, the students can join in developing the grids. This empowers students and enhances transparency.

Reflexivity: This is also, where the classroom becomes reflexive of its own institutional framework and where students can become **critical of the educational machinery** that permanently acts in a catch 22 between creating and selecting a qualified labour force and fostering students' critical thinking and emancipation. If a classroom can be said to have brought this about, and if students are at some point able to discuss this in the target language, teacher and students deserve to be congratulated.

4.5 | Conclusion

Teacher-centred and instructivist teaching made an important contribution to overcoming education being a privilege to the rich and powerful. At the turn of the 19th to the 20th century, though, it became apparent that this way of teaching and learning needed reform. Although student-centred teaching and learning have by no means become an educational reality, they are considered an ideal to aspire to. In this chapter, learner orientation is approached from two different perspectives. From a psycholinguistic point of view, learner orientation means taking into account learner specific features, such as aptitude or motivation and adapt one's teaching to these. Also, this approach highlights the importance of cultural aspects that may overtly or covertly influence individual learning and performance. A socio-cultural point of view explains how individuals are influenced by societal or institutional norms. Also, attention is drawn to the fact that while the individual's biography is a strong influence to reckon with, there are models—such as the idea of developmental tasks— which allow teachers to see patterns, which at first glance seemed to be idiosyncrasies. The principles, highlighted by the different approaches, can be put into practice by applying motivational strategies, taking seriously students' developmental tasks (e. g. by dealing with coming-of-age-fiction), reducing anxiety by putting accuracy in its place, welcoming minority languages and identities and by giving students ownership (e. g. by way of co-operative- or self-assessment).

Further reading

Bauer, Viktoria (2015): *Englischlernen—Sinnkonstruktion—Identität*. Opladen/Berlin/Toronto.

Dörnyei, Zoltan (2001): *Motivational Strategies in the Language Classroom*. Cambridge.

Fairclough, Norman (1999): »Global Capitalism and Critical Awareness of Language«. In: *Language Awareness* 8/2, 71–83.

Norton, Bonny (²2013): *Identity and Language Learning. Extending the Conversation* [2000]. Bristol/Buffalo/Toronto.

Trautmann, Matthias (2014): *Fremde Sprachen und Fremdsprachenlernen aus Schülersicht*. Opladen/Berlin/Toronto.

Andreas Bonnet

5 English Language Learning—
An SLA-based Approach

This chapter introduces basic concepts of a Second Language Acquisition-based approach to English language teaching. It briefly discusses why it is necessary for every (future) foreign language teacher to be familiar with at least some key results of second language acquisition research. Throughout the chapter, the key notion of **interlanguage** and its development will be the focus of description, analysis and explanation of the psycholinguistic background of language learning. From that perspective, important suggestions for the teaching of English as a foreign language will be derived. Only if a teacher understands the basic psycholinguistic background of what happens in the mind of a learner when learning another language s/he will be able to make appropriate pedagogical and methodological choices to support each individual learner in his/her EFL classroom.

5.1 | Why every foreign language teacher needs
to know about second language acquisition

More than 30 years ago, Allwright (1984, 3) asked the question »Why don't learners learn what teachers teach?«. Pienemann (1989) went even further and asked »Is language teachable?«. Both questions clearly reveal a possible gap between foreign language teaching and its prospective outcomes. One example that can be found in the literature (cf. e. g. Wanders 2006; Keßler 2009) and is well experienced by every English teacher almost every day in her/his EFL classroom is the phenomenon of ›3rd-person singular s‹. Every learner can easily recite the rule of when this structure has to be produced, however, in spontaneous language production many of these learners do not apply it.

»Why don't learners learn what teachers teach?«

Complexity of language teaching: Both questions as well as the example show a common problem in traditional language instruction. Teachers often believe that the EFL classroom mainly serves as a platform for teaching language. Though this is obviously true, it is only one aspect of a far more complex story. When perceiving the EFL classroom only as a place for teaching, one does not take into account that any classroom accommodates both teachers and learners. From a more learner-centred perspective, it needs to be considered that learners need to process what is being taught to them (cf. Keßler/Plesser 2011, 135). This language processing is an active procedure that learners have to engage in and which can take place implicitly as well as consciously.

Language as psychological phenomenon: Here, psycholinguistics in general and second language acquisition (SLA) in particular play a major role for the EFL classroom. Psycholinguistics examines language as a »psychological phenomenon« (Garman 1990, XIII). Since the 1990s, psychologists and linguists have worked on theories that explain language development (cf. Lightbown/Spada 2006, 38). Psycholinguistic approaches to language acquisition consider language learning as a gradual development within the mind of the learner. Individual learners need to build up their own (psycholinguistic) knowledge-system and language awareness. In addition, they have to be **developmentally ready** (cf. Mansouri/Duffy 2005) in order to notice and process linguistic structures of the target language.

Psycholinguistic constraints

Psycholinguistics deals with either first language acquisition (i. e. the mother tongue) or second language acquisition (i. e. any language learned after the acquisition of the mother tongue). This discipline also studies possible differences between first and second language acquisition. Second language acquisition as a sub-discipline of psycholinguistics examines the psycholinguistic constraints involved in learning a second language. SLA research focuses on **learner-immanent processes** as a gradual development of second or foreign language learning. It does, however, not distinguish between acquisition and learning in natural or instructed settings but looks at the gradual development of processing skills in either environment:

Norman Segalowitz (2003) and others have suggested that learners have to pay attention at first to any aspect of the language that they are trying to understand or produce. ›Paying attention‹ in this context is accepted to mean using cognitive resources to process information. However, there is a limit to how much information a learner can pay attention to. Thus, learners at the earliest stages will use most of their resources to understand the main words in a message. In that situation, they may not notice the grammatical morphemes attached to some of the words, especially those that do not substantially affect meaning. Gradually, through experience and practice, information that was new becomes easier to process, and learners become able to access it quickly and even automatically. This frees them to pay attention to other aspects of the language that, in turn, gradually become automatic. (Lightbown/Spada 2006, 39)

Instructed language learning as a developmental process indeed follows a trajectory similar to the one found in natural acquisition. For a long time, however, many teachers have understood language teaching as a way to only externally steering the learning process. As could be seen with the example of the ›3rd-person singular s‹, things are not that simple in the EFL classroom. This is one of the reasons why foreign language teaching needs to consider a psycholinguistic basis.

Interlanguage development: Foreign language teachers who know about the psycholinguistic basis of SLA and language learning will have a better understanding of this developmental path. Thus, they will not only be in a position to better classify their **learners' output and errors** (cf. Keßler/Plesser 2011, 136) but could even »tweak their syllabi according to their learners' states of interlanguage development« (ibid., 150). Instruction that incorporates the basic psycholinguistic features of language acquisition can be beneficial for more successful language learning in the classroom. In other words, a SLA-based approach to the EFL classroom may contribute to a far more learner-centred foreign language teaching.

Focusing on internal factors of language learning does not imply that external factors do not play a role, either. This chapter, however, does not deal with the external factors of instructed language acquisition. These factors will be addressed in chapters 6–8 and 11–13 of this volume. The following sections will give a short explanation of the general idea of second language acquisition with a special focus on what happens in the mind of the learner when learning another language.

5.2 | The theoretical basis of second language learning

5.2.1 | Explaining second language learning

Lightbown/Spada (2006) dedicate a full chapter of their book to explaining second language learning. They point out that second language learners have already acquired a first language (i. e. mother tongue) and are therefore in a way more experienced language learners as compared to first language learners. So according to Lightbown/Spada (2006, 30 ff.), both **learner characteristics** (e. g. the degree of metalinguistic awareness) as well as **learning conditions** (e. g. informal to formal settings) influence second language learning.

Second language learning—as well as first language learning—can be based on various theories. When explaining second language learning one has to consider the contexts for learning another language. Although some authors distinguish not only between first and second language learning but also investigate third language learning (cf. e. g. Cenoz/Jessner 2000; Aronin/Hufeisen 2009), a distinction between second and third language learning will not be made in this chapter. Second language learning is understood as the acquisition of any other language than the mother tongue, no matter if it is learned as second, third or other language.

Several theories have tried to explain second language learning. The following section can only very briefly introduce the main theoretical approaches. For a deeper insight and a wider scope, please refer to Lightbown/Spada (2006), VanPatten/Williams (2015), Larsen-Freeman (2000) and Gass/Mackey (2012).

Major approaches in SLA

Behaviourism: In the past, Behaviourism played an important role. Derived from a psychological approach in the 1940s and 1950s, people thought that language learning was a habit formation and that second language learners just had to memorise and imitate patterns from the input. The underlying idea of Behaviourism was that imitating language input and reproducing structures and lexical items for which the learners had received a positive feedback from their interlocutors (i. e. **positive reinforcement**) was beneficial for the acquisition of the target language. Thus, Behaviourists considered imitation and practice, guided by positive reinforcement to be the driving forces for language acquisition. A prominent approach based on Behaviourism is the audiolingual method (cf. Larsen-Freeman 2000, 35 ff.).

Innatist perspective: Another theoretical approach discusses the »innatist perspective« (Lightbown/Spada 2006, 35). The underlying theory is **Chomsky's Universal Grammar (UG)**. Though UG mainly is considered a theory of first language acquisition, some researchers apply it to also explain second language learning because Universal Grammar can account for the so-called logical problem, i. e. the »mismatch between the input that children are exposed to and their ultimate attainment« (White 2007, 37). The logical problem obviously occurs both in first as well as in second language learning. Researchers who use this approach to explain second language learning are mainly focused on the learners' competence (cf. Lightbown/Spada 2006, 36; White 2015).

Monitor model: In 1982, Krashen developed his monitor model in order to explain second language learning. His model comprises five hypotheses: ›acquisition-learning hypothesis‹, ›monitor hypothesis‹, ›natural order hypothesis‹, ›input hypothesis‹ and ›affective filter hypothesis‹ (cf. Krashen 1982b).

Monitor Model

Krashen's monitor model in a nutshell (cf. Lightbown/Spada 2006, 36–38)
1. **Acquisition-learning hypothesis:** Acquisition refers to the unconscious process of picking up of the target language in natural settings; learning takes place in the language classroom as a conscious process of form and rule application.
2. **Monitor hypothesis:** Each learner has a ›monitor‹ in his/her mind that checks utterances by comparing them to the language system already acquired by the learner. The use of the monitor is constrained by time, i. e. in spontaneous oral language production it is weaker than in written language where the speaker has more time to apply his/her monitor to edit his/her language output.
3. **Natural order hypothesis:** This hypothesis is based on findings that language acquisition follows predictable sequences. It accounts both for first as well as second language acquisition.
4. **Input hypothesis:** Input is a necessary prerequisite for acquisition. Comprehensible input which follows the concept of »i plus 1« is considered to be most beneficial for acquisition/learning. In this formula »i« stands for what the learner has already acquired and »plus 1« symbolizes language features that are slightly above what the learner already knows in the target language.
5. **Affective filter hypothesis:** The affective filter is a metaphor for a blockade that might prevent the learner from acquiring or applying structures from (comprehensible) input. Anxiety increases the learner's affective filter.

Krashen's model has been challenged for a number of reasons, mainly because his hypotheses are not falsifiable and thus neither testable nor verifiable (cf. Gass/Mackey 2015). Yet, his work has been very influential and sparked a lot of research.

Output hypothesis: In answer to Krashen's ›input hypothesis‹, Swain (1985; 2005) developed her ›output hypothesis‹ which basically claims that second language learners need »**sufficient opportunities for language use** [... because] language production forces learners to move from comprehension (semantic use of language) to syntactic use of language« (Gass/Mackey 2007, 179, emphasis added).

Interaction hypothesis: As neither the ›input hypothesis‹ nor the ›output hypothesis‹ can fully account for second language learning, Long (1996) developed the ›interaction hypothesis‹. This hypothesis »attempts to account for learning through the learner's **exposure** to language, **production** of language, and **feedback** on that production« (Gass/Mackey 2015, 181, emphasis added).

Interactional modification: By making input comprehensible (i. e. according to Krashen's ›input hypothesis‹ by using less complex grammatical structures, shorter sentences, clearly articulated oral speech) language acquisition can be promoted. In addition to the ›input hypothesis‹, input can also be made more comprehensible through interactional modification, e. g. through negotiation of meaning and the feedback the learner receives from her/his interlocutors.

Definition

According to Lightbown/Spada (2006, 43), the general idea of the ›interaction hypothesis‹ is as follows: »(1) Interactional modification makes input comprehensible. (2) Comprehensible input promotes acquisition. Therefore (3) Interactional modification promotes acquisition.« Modified interaction as promoted by the ›interaction hypothesis‹ comprises amongst other features comprehension checks, clarification requests and self-repetitions.

Input processing: VanPatten (2015, 113) elaborated the idea that »acquisition is [...] a byproduct of comprehension« and coined the term ›input processing‹. Important features of input processing according to VanPatten (ibid., 114) are form-meaning connections (e. g. ›-ed‹ for past tense, ›-ing‹ for something in progress), processing (i. e. the mapping of form and function to create meaning), parsing (i. e. the assigning of syntactic structures to input) and effortful comprehension (i. e. the development of the ability to understand).

Processability theory: Taking the concept of processing as his yardstick, Pienemann (1998; 2011) developed a theory of second language development called ›processability theory‹ (PT). This theory is designed to explain second language learning as a staged development where learners acquire incremental processing strategies. A complete overview of PT's psycholinguistic approach to language processing and development is provided in chapter 5.2.3.

In this respect, PT's approach might sound similar to Krashen's »i plus 1«, however, a major difference is that PT is underpinned by extensive research on second language learners with different first languages learning various second languages (cf. Pienemann 1998; 2005; Pienemann/ Keßler 2011; 2012). PT describes and explains the development of learner language (i. e. interlanguage; see chapter 5.2.2 for details) as an »acquisition sequence from simple to complex forms [...] which, in turn, puts constraints on teaching« (Grimm et al. 2015, 49). Teaching can only support second language learning if the learner's state of interlanguage development has reached the stage where the learner can comprehend and produce the very structure. In other words, learners need to be developmentally ready to be able to process the language structure and, by doing so, converting input into intake.

5.2.2 | Interlanguage

According to Long (2003), learners are on their way from the **initial state of the target language** to its target-like use. Interlanguage contains features from the first language of the learner as well as features from the target language.

Definition | Interlanguage is a term coined by Selinker in 1972. »It describes the state of language that has not yet been fully developed by a learner. Interlanguage refers to the individual mental grammar of each language learner of a second (or foreign) language who has not yet fully acquired the target language but only approximated to it. Interlanguage contains features of the target language but also ›innovations‹ by the learner that are neither target-like nor totally in line with the learner's first language« (Keßler/Plesser 2011, 42). Though it is the individual mental grammar representation of a learner, it is yet rule-governed and thus predictable.

Interlanguage development | In contrast to interlanguage development in the first language, however, there is no guarantee that second language learners will actually reach a target-like command of the second language (cf. Selinker 1972; Cherrington 2000; Long 2003).

IL [Interlanguage] posits that learners are involved in a continual process of hypothesis formulation and testing. As new elements of L2 are acquired, language is tested and assessed. L2 items are also constructed through analogy with items and rules already known. This may be carried out subconsciously, along with the processing of feedback and how this may or may not change the IL as the learner moves along the continuum. The changes may bring the IL closer to the desired L2 form, but not necessarily. (Cherrington 2000, 307 cited in Grimm et al. 2015, 94)

Predictable path: Long (2003) states that the concept of interlanguage draws from the thought that psychological structures within the learner's mind constrain the development of the target language. This development from the initial state to target-like use is far from being random but follows a predictable path (cf. Pienemann 1998; 2005; Long 2003). According to Pienemann (2005, 48) »it is defined in an *a priori* manner by the learner's current level of processing«.

Illustration 5.1 (Lightbown/Spada 2006, 16) shows the mental representation of interlanguage structures in the mind of the learner and also clearly points out that any correction of non-target-like interlanguage structures is in vain if the learner is not yet developmentally ready to process the target-like structure. As the little boy in the cartoon is not yet developmentally ready for the mother's correction, he misinterprets this correction as a semantic one rather than a morphological correction (cf. Keßler/Plesser 2011).

Mental representation

Illustration 5.1:
Interlanguage
(taken from
Lightbown/Spada
2006, 16)

Overgeneralisation: Moreover, illustration 5.1 demonstrates that interlanguage structures are **rule-governed**. The little boy in the picture has already acquired the concept of the simple past (›-ed‹). This concept is now overgeneralised by the learner to any situation that is set in the past. Overgeneralisations are a typical feature of interlanguage and its development. In the EVENING study (cf. Engel/Groot-Wilken/Thürmann 2009; Börner/Engel/Groot-Wilken 2013) plenty of spontaneous speech samples were collected from learners of English in German primary schools. Here, interlanguage structures such as »The dog is grabing« (Keßler/Lenzing 2008) were found. This particular learner mixed the L1 German verb for digging (›graben‹) with the L2 English progressive verb form (›-ing‹) and created the word ›grabing‹ by using the ›-ing‹ as a verb marker in her interlanguage.

> **Overgeneralisation** refers to the phenomenon that language learners who have acquired a certain grammar rule ›overuse‹ it by applying it to all contexts even when there are exceptions from that rule. One example is the overgeneralisation of the past-ed-morpheme also for irregular verbs (cf. illustration 5.1).

Definition

Interlanguage is a crucial feature of any language acquisition, be it first or second language acquisition, be it acquisition in natural or instructed settings. In the following section interlanguage development for English as a second or foreign language will be explained.

5.2.3 | Interlanguage development through the second language learning process

Interlanguage development is rule-governed: Interlanguage and its development through stages are an essential part of the psycholinguistic basis of second language learning. It has been shown above that interlanguage development is rule-governed and predictable. Research into developmental sequences has

a long research history, and the question of the existence of universal sequences in SLA is currently regarded as being ›one of the central issues in understanding phenomena of second language acquisition‹ (Hulstijn 2015, 1). Although discussed heatedly, developmental sequences are regarded as an established finding in current SLA textbooks (see e. g. VanPatten/Williams 2015; Ortega 2009). (Lenzing 2016, x)

Processability theory: As mentioned previously, the most prominent theory that explains second language processing is Pienemann's processability theory (cf. Pienemann 1998; 2005; 2011). PT is a psycholinguistic theory of SLA »designed to explain the phenomenon of staged development in SLA« (Pienemann 2011, 3). It explores what goes on in the mind of a second language learner during the acquisition process. In chapter 5.2.1 above the logical problem (i. e. why are learners able to produce an infinite number of sentences in the target language despite a limited amount of input?) was introduced. Although PT in its original version from 1998 was designed to address the so-called developmental problem (i. e. why do second language learners follow the same developmental trajectory?) PT was developed further (cf. e. g. Pienemann 2005) to also account for the logical problem. Yet, to keep things simpler and digestible the following section is limited to the explanation of the developmental problem.

Stages of acquisition: Regardless of the learner's first language s/he will go through the stages of acquisition spelled out in PT for the respective target language:

Table 5.1 provides a short overview of the developmental stages found for English as a foreign or second language. Stage 1 consists of single words or formulaic speech chunks which at that stage, are not yet analysed by the learner. The main syntactic feature of stage 2 is the SVO-pattern (subject, verb, object) which the learner can use for statements, questions and negations. At this stage both target-like as well as non-target-like structures can be produced. Stage 3 develops the SVO-pattern from stage 2 further and extends it to the fronting of either an adverb (e. g. ›today‹), an auxiliary (e. g. ›can‹ or ›do‹) or a wh-question marker (e. g. ›where‹ or ›what‹). At stage 4 the learner acquires how to invert sentence structures in order to ask questions. Here, s/he can either produce questions starting

Stage	Structures	Examples
6	Cancel Aux-2nd	I wonder what he wants.
5	Neg/Aux-2nd-? Aux-2nd -?	Why **didn't** you tell me? Why **can't** she come? Why **did** she eat that? What **will** you do?
	3sg-s -	Peter likes bananas.
4	Copula S (x) Wh-copula S (x) V-Particle	**Is she** at home? **Where** is she? Turn it **off**!
3	Do-SV(O)-? Aux SV(O)-? Wh-SV(O)-? Adverb-First Poss (Pronoun) Object (Pronoun)	**Do** he live here? **Can** I go home? **Where** she went? **What** you want? **Today** he stay here. I show you **my** garden. This is **your** pencil. Mary called him.
2	S neg V(O) SVO SVO-Question -ed -ing Plural –s (Noun) Poss –s (Noun)	Me **no** live here. / I don't live here. I am John. / Me John. You live here**?** John play**ed**. Jane go**ing**. I like cat**s**. Pat**'s** cat is fat.
1	Words Formulae	Hello, dog, green How are you? Where is X? What's your name?

Table 5.1: Stages of acquisition in L2 English as spelled out in processability theory

with the copula (i. e. the verb ›to be‹ as the only verb in the sentence) or questions that start with a Wh-question word in front of the copula (e. g. ›Why is psycholinguistics important?‹). The main feature of stage 5 is that the learner acquires to put the auxiliary (i. e. ›do‹, ›have‹, ›can‹) in the second position of the question (e. g. ›What do you want to know?‹). Additionally, only at stage 5 the learner acquires the ›3rd-persons s‹-morpheme; this explains why so many learners in the EFL classroom struggle with this structure so long. At stage 6, the learner acquires indirect questions.

Psycholinguistic basis: These stages of acquisition for L2 English form the psycholinguistic basis of L2 English development and outline the acquisition of procedural skills in »the sequence they become available for the learner« (Pienemann 1998, 3). This sequence cannot be altered through instruction. Does this, however, imply that instructed second language acquisition would be fruitless? This question can be answered by a clear ›no‹. Although every L2 English learner has to go through this sequence, PT does not make any claims in terms of how fast a learner might go through this sequence. As will be explained below, teaching that considers the current state of the learners' interlanguage development may be beneficial for the acquisition process.

Furthermore, PT distinguishes between the developmental features introduced above and learner variation (cf. Pienemann 1998; Liebner/Pienemann 2011). Despite the fact that all learners have to go through the

Psycholinguistic Constraints

sequence of the developmental stages and **no stage can be skipped** it is commonplace that not all learners actually do exactly the same or are even at the same stage of development within the same language classroom. Learner variation as outlined in PT is also constrained by the architecture of the human mind (cf. Pienemann 1998). Learner variation can well be altered by instruction.

Interlanguage variation

Examples: If a learner is on stage 3 and has not yet reached stage 5 and, therefore, is not yet able to spontaneously produce a question such as ›Where is he going?‹ (= aux-2nd question) s/he has the following three options that are psycholinguistically constrained: omitting a feature, violating a rule, avoiding the problem. An asterisk put in front of a sentence (e. g. in (1) and (2)) indicates a non-target-like utterance. Though these utterances are non-target-like they are, however, valid interlanguage examples found in speech samples produced by learners of L2 English.

(1)   *Where he going?   (**omission**)
(2)   *Where he is going?   (**violation**)
(3)   He is going where?   (**avoidance**)

In order to develop a standard-oriented interlanguage variation the learner ought to ›choose‹ option (2) because this option contains all morpho-syntactic features of the question and is also semantically closest to the targeted question. Omitting features as in (1) would be the worst choice because that could lead to a simplified interlanguage and lead to stabilisation before having reached a target-like command of the language. The avoidance strategy (3) is not really harmful but does not promote second language learning. This might sound strange at first sight as (3) is the only target-like option of our three examples. However, this SVO-structure is a structure of stage 2 (cf. table 5.1) and therefore does not increase the processing skills of the learner.

At stage 2, examples of more standard-oriented or more simplified learner variation can also be found:

(4)   He is Tarzan.
(5)   *He Tarzan.

Although both sentences follow the SVO-pattern of stage 2, example (5) is problematic for the learner's future interlanguage development. Due to the fact »that for every L2 grammatical structure learners make choices and **bad choices will accumulate** as the learner moves on« (Liebner/Pienemann 2011, 73) learners might get stuck easily if they do not develop an interlanguage variation as close as possible to a standard-oriented version. If, as in example (5), the learner does not acquire the grammatical function of the copula, s/he will not be able to process and produce copula questions (e. g. ›Is he Tarzan?‹ or ›Where is he?‹) as acquired at stage 4.

These examples show that psycholinguistic approaches to SLA (e. g. PT) distinguish between **developmental errors** (cf. examples 1 and 2 above) and **variational errors** (cf. example 5 above). This has important repercussions for the foreign language classroom.

> Developmental Errors occur when a learner is not yet developmentally ready to process and therefore produce a certain structure. A learner who has acquired stage 3 of the processability hierarchy cannot produce ›3rd-person singular s‹ yet. In syntax s/he cannot produce questions with the auxiliary in second position. Both structures are acquired only at stage 5. So, a question like ›*What you want?‹ is a valid stage 3-question and an example for a developmental error.
>
> Variational Errors occur when a learner is developmentally ready for the processing and production of a structure but makes a mistake. A learner who has acquired stage 2 of the processability hierarchy can produce utterances such as ›He is Tarzan‹. If the learner, however, leaves out the copula and says: ›*He Tarzan‹, s/he makes a variational error by choosing a simplified variety of the more standard-oriented version of this statement.

Definition

Variational errors ought to be addressed and corrected in instruction in order to prevent the learner from acquiring a simplified variety of the target language at an early stage of the acquisition process. Developmental errors need not be corrected for the individual learner as s/he is not yet ready to notice or understand this correction due to limited processing capacities at that stage. However, some corrective feedback might also be beneficial, especially in heterogeneous classrooms where some learners might already have acquired the higher stages.

Corrective feedback

5.3 | Interlanguage and the foreign language classroom

Instruction: The role of instruction has always been one of the main concerns in SLA (cf. Baten/Keßler 2018). According to Spada/Lightbown (2013), there are basically three questions that have been examined by SLA research in order to determine whether grammar instruction is effective:

1. How **effective** is grammar teaching in terms of L2 proficiency levels?
2. Compared to natural exposure, can grammar teaching change the **rate of acquisition**?
3. Can grammar teaching alter the **route of acquisition**?

All three questions are of importance both for researchers as well as for teachers because the answers to these questions have a direct impact for the language learner. As could be seen above, psycholinguistic research can promote more successful language learning in instructed settings if teachers are aware of its findings and calibrate their language classrooms accordingly. In this section, emphasis will be laid at question 3 because this question is highly related with the psycholinguistic basis of language learning and teaching.

As early as 1984, Pienemann claimed that »an L2-structure can only be learned by instruction if the learner's interlanguage is close to the point when the structure is acquired in the natural setting« (Pienemann 1984, 198). This was the beginning of what is known today as ›teachability hypothesis‹ (TH). TH has been incorporated into PT in 1998 and has been an integral part of this theory.

Definition

> Teachability hypothesis: »Developed since 1984 and incorporated into processability theory by Pienemann in 1998 it states that no stage can be skipped or altered by instruction. The teachability hypothesis implies that foreign language teaching is most successful when its curriculum follows the stages of the processing hierarchy« (Keßler/Plesser 2011, 247).

Developmental and variational features: In line with the staged development as predicted in PT (cf. chapter 5.2.3 and table 5.1) TH distinguishes between **developmental** and **variational features** in the foreign language classroom. The TH has been tested by many studies (for an overview cf. Keßler/Liebner/Mansouri 2011).

There has been some concern in the field about the claims made by TH. Lightbown (1998, 2000) criticised that more empirical evidence was needed, especially from learners with non-Germanic L1s. In addition, she warned that a too close adoption of the concept of developmental readiness might lead back to teaching structures in isolation (cf. Lightbown 1998, 188). This point was also addressed by Long/Robinson (1998) as well as Ortega (2009).

Some of the concerns have been addressed by other researchers (cf. e. g. Keßler/Liebner 2011; Keßler/Liebner/Mansouri 2011; Baten/Keßler 2018). As Baten/Keßler (2018) summarise: »[...] the main merit of the teachability hypothesis is that it provides teachers and students with realistic knowledge of what to expect as a result of classroom instruction.«

The question remains, however, if grammar ought to be taught explicitly in the foreign language classroom. This chapter started with a look at the ›3rd-person singular s‹-problem. As has been explained, psycholinguistic research provides a yardstick for understanding *what* can be taught *when*. Therefore, it depends on the conceptualisation of grammar. Keßler/Plesser (2011) point out that different representations of grammar imply different approaches to its teaching. They make a case for the incorporation of learner grammars (i. e. interlanguage grammars) as the mental representation of what learners have already acquired and, therefore, are ready to learn next.

Route vs. rate of acquisition

It has been shown that the **route of acquisition** cannot be altered by instruction. The **rate of acquisition**, however, can be influenced by the teacher. Language teaching that is geared towards the developmental readiness of the learners in the classroom is far more likely to support individual learners in their acquisition process. Needless to say, that this again leads to a whole range of questions concerning grammar teaching

e. g. how language teachers can easily and reliably diagnose the current state of their learners' state of interlanguage development.

Diagnosis: The issue of **diagnosing learner progress** has been tackled from various angles (cf. Keßler/Plesser 2011). There are competing approaches to diagnosing learner progress in the language classroom. On the one hand, there are proficiency-based measures such as the *Common European Framework of Reference* (CEFR) (cf. chapter 2 in this volume). On the other hand, there are acquisition-based diagnostic tools such as approaches to linguistic profiling (e. g. Rapid Profile; cf. Keßler 2006; Pienemann/Keßler 2012). Acquisition-based diagnostic tools are based on a theory and are criterion-referenced. This means that they do not compare learners within a certain reference norm but look at individual learners and their interlanguage state. Therefore, they provide a valid analysis of what a learner can as well as cannot do at a certain point in time during her/his acquisition process. This helps the teacher to validly decide what this very learner can learn best and what s/he would not yet be developmentally ready to learn.

Rapid Profile: One diagnostic approach based on psycholinguistic theory is **linguistic profiling**. This approach was first introduced by Crystal et al. (1976). Linguistic profiling has been applied for many languages, very often in a pencil-and-paper procedure. Rapid Profile is a computer-assisted short-hand version of linguistic profiling based on PT. It is a »useful diagnostic tool« (Grimm et al. 2015, 93) which has been developed and calibrated over a long period (e. g. Keßler 2006; Pienemann/Keßler 2012). Rapid Profile is a criterion-referenced procedure utilising the morpho-syntactic structures spelled out in PT for L2 English. The software utilises the developmental features for L2 English and the teacher can key in the structures produced by the learner during the diagnosis. With its inbuilt knowledge-system Rapid Profile then calculates the stage acquired by the learner. By doing so, the procedure diagnoses both what a learner can and cannot do at a given point in the EFL classroom.

To start the diagnosis, a speech sample is collected from a learner working on **communicative tasks** (cf. Pienemann 1998; Keßler/Plesser 2011). The speech sample contains linguistic structures that can be measured against the developmental hierarchy of PT. Illustration 5.2 shows an example of what such speech samples look like. In an online-screening, the software compares the structures against the developmental hierarchy and calculates the acquired stage within a 10 to 15-minute speech sample (Keßler 2006; Pienemann/Keßler 2012).

As the diagnosis is based on a psycholinguistic theory, it provides a quick valid and reliable picture of which grammatical structures a learner can acquire next in the EFL classroom. Because the diagnosis actually also elicitates what a learner cannot produce yet due to the constraints within the processability hierarchy it also informs the teacher of why certain structures cannot yet be produced by the learner in spontaneous speech production, namely those structures beyond the current stage acquired by this learner. Keßler (2008) introduced the **diagnostic task cycle** showing how the underlying communicative tasks can be used for the diagnosis of the individual learner's progress as well as for practicing new

Illustration 5.2:
Communicative
tasks and exam-
ples of speech
samples
(taken from
Keßler/Liebner
2011, 143)

C02: there she write on the computer
C05: she writes on the computer
C07: then she's work at her computer

C01: next she (em) goes by bus
to work
C04: then.. she's going to drive
with the bus
C10: she go by bus to the town

structures in the foreign language classroom. Based on the diagnosis as point of departure for TBLL (task-based language learning) in a pre-task activity, a language learning task can be administered. Here the teacher can set the scene (e. g. vocabulary) for tasks for instructed second language learning. In the tasks for instructed second language learning the learners can apply their linguistic knowledge according to their current state of interlanguage development. For example, in a ›Spot the differences‹-task they can ask questions at any stage (1–6) in order to find out what is different in a partner's picture.

5.4 | Input—output—interaction revisited

Negotiation of meaning: Input, output and interaction play a major role in language acquisition both in natural as well as instructed settings. One crucial feature of the ›interaction hypothesis‹ is what Long (1996) introduced as ›negotiation of meaning‹, i. e. »that both interlocutors need to express, comprehend and adjust utterances in order to offer and receive comprehensible input« (Grimm et al. 2015, 55).

Task-based language learning (TBLL): One promising way of providing learners with opportunities for negotiating meaning is the task-based approach (cf. chapter 11 in this volume). Though there are many definitions of what a task is and how it functions in the foreign language classroom there is common understanding that a task contains some kind of a gap (e. g. information gap, opinion gap) and needs to be open in outcome. Though TBLL primarily focuses on problem-solving by negotiation of meaning, form also plays an important role. This is how modern foreign language pedagogy (practice) and findings from SLA research (theory) come together and to life in the classroom. Tasks that are tuned according to the developmental readiness of the learners provide a good opportunity for learners to actually notice gaps between the input they receive and the output they produce. This may lead to a growing **language awareness** as well as to noticing, both important aspects of language learning.

Definition

> Language awareness: According to the Association for Language Awareness (ALA) language awareness is the »explicit knowledge about language, and conscious perception and sensitivity in language learning, language teaching and language use«.
> Noticing refers to the moment when an L2 learner registers a particular linguistic form, e. g. the plural-s in English as a second or foreign language, in the input s/he receives. In order to make input become intake, the learner has to notice gaps or differences between the input and her/his current interlanguage.

Spot the difference

Example

One example for a task in the EFL classroom is the so-called bike-task which has been described in detail in Keßler (2008). It is a ›Spot the difference‹-task and has been designed to provide meaningful language use in the classroom:

Two learners receive pictures of bikes which are similar but not the same. By comparing the pictures orally (each learner can only see his/her picture), this task offers opportunities for communicative language use according to each learner's individual developmental stage. Learners have to ask questions about their partner's picture in order to find out a certain number of differences between the two pictures. By doing so, learners communicatively focus on question formation. As could be seen in table 5.1, questions are one decisive feature of syntactic structures within the PT-hierarchy. Each learner can ask questions according to his/her current state of interlanguage development.

During this phase, this task provides authentic opportunities for communicative language production as well as for language awareness. Learners need to negotiate meaning in order to find out the differences between their pictures. Teachers can choose if they want to combine two learners who are currently at the same developmental stage and can thus practise their accuracy and fluency. Alternatively, teachers can match learners whose interlanguage states are one stage apart. Then, one learner can serve as a peer-scaffold for the other one.

In a post-task activity, either the same pairs or the whole class can discuss the merits of biking and spark a discussion on what they like or do not like to use their bikes for. Again, this activity provides opportunities for authentic language production through interaction according to each learner's individual state of interlanguage development.

5.5 | Conclusion: a role for psycholinguistics in the EFL classroom

Psycholinguistics provides a good measure for teachers to understand how language learning works in the minds of their learners. By knowing about the basic concepts of psycholinguistics, SLA research and their findings teachers can better support their learners on their individual ways on the developmental trajectory. The ›teachability hypothesis‹ contributes to a classroom application of psycholinguistics that helps both teachers and learners to acquire the target language more efficiently.

Role of errors
reconsidered

From a psycholinguistic perspective, the role of **errors in the EFL classroom** ought to be reconsidered. The distinction between developmental and variational errors helps teachers to select those errors that ought to be corrected in order to support a more standard-oriented interlanguage of the learners. Errors, however, that are developmental need not be addressed for the learner who makes them, as this very learner will not be able to notice the correction in order to make the correct form part of his/her intake. Yet, corrective feedback might be useful here, too, as there will be learners in the same classroom whose interlanguage is at a more advanced developmental stage and who might use this corrective feedback for a better integration of this structure into their own interlanguage.

A psycholinguistics-based approach to the foreign language classroom automatically contributes to supporting each learner individually according to his/her stage of development and is therefore a good means to teach in **heterogeneous** or even **inclusive classrooms** (cf. Keßler 2005). Lessons and teaching units that have a diagnostic basis do not only increase the chances of the learners to learn the target language more efficiently and smoothly but also contribute largely to a more **learner-centred approach** to communicative foreign language teaching and learning.

This chapter started by asking two important questions: ›Is language teachable?‹ and ›Why don't learners learn what teachers teach?‹. It has explained that language is teachable, however, that not everything can be taught at any time because learners need to be developmentally ready to actually learn (i. e. notice and intake) what they are taught. In a way, this is already the answer to our second question. If learners are not developmentally ready they cannot learn what they are taught (remember the example of ›3rd-person singular s‹). This is why Allwright's question from 1984 was rephrased to »Why don't teachers teach what learners can learn?« (Keßler et al. 2011, 149).

Further reading

Keßler, Jörg-U./Plesser, Anja (2011): *Teaching Grammar*. Paderborn.
Lightbown, Patsy/Spada Nina (³2006): *How Languages are Learned* [1993]. Oxford.
Ortega, Lourdes (2009): *Understanding Second Language Acquisition*. London.
Pienemann, Manfred/Keßler, Jörg-U. (eds.) (2011): *Studying Processability Theory*. Amsterdam.
VanPatten, Bill/Williams, Jessica (eds.) (²2015): *Theories in Second Language Acquisition* [2007]. New York.

Jörg-U. Keßler

6 Receptive Competences—Reading, Listening, Viewing

Traditionally, reading and listening have been considered to cover the range of receptive skills which learners in the English language classroom need to develop. Since the 1990s with the growing importance of images and audiovisual texts in our daily lives and the increased integration of audiovisual material in English classes, viewing and so-called audiovisual comprehension (*Hör-Seh-Verstehen*) have been incorporated as receptive skills. Additionally, the emphasis on images and the analysis of visual information in a number of subjects in the humanities have had a significant influence on foreign language teaching methodology in terms of content, materials and skills. Learners are expected to demonstrate competence in their interaction with texts transmitted via a variety of media. In other words, they should learn:

- to understand written and spoken texts: factual texts, literature, emails, blogs, public announcements, podcasts, radio programmes
- to decode still and moving images: photos, diagrams, documentaries
- to connect text or speech and images: in comics, newspaper articles, advertisements, digital texts, films, presentations, conversations

In this way, meaning(s) embedded and intertwined within the content can be interpreted and the information and knowledge gained can be used to further think, speak and/or write about related topics. Learners should also be able to recognise the role and impact various media and genres have on their audience. It therefore goes without saying that the information technology focus of the world in which today's learners interact, coupled with the shift from a simple development of reading or listening comprehension skills into what can be considered expansive **multiliteracy training** (cf. Hallet 2011, 110 f.; Küster 2014), has placed new demands on foreign language teaching and learning.

In this chapter, the various receptive competences (based on a number of codes, symbols and modes of communication) which learners are expected to develop in the English language classroom will be examined both as an integrated system of competences as well as in terms of how they differ from each other. In this context, a broad understanding of the concept of texts (and the word ›text‹ itself) is adopted as constituting not only a written form, but also oral, visual and hybrid forms.

6.1 | Reading, listening and viewing as interactive processes

Actively engaged recipients: At first sight, and as a narrow semantic view of the term ›receptive competences‹ might suggest, reading, listening and viewing tend to be associated with passive consumerism. In the case of viewing in particular, which could conjure up the image of the so-called ›couch potato‹, taking in whatever the mass media dishes out, it might be a challenge to move beyond this notion of passiveness. However, as readers, listeners and viewers, we are actually actively engaged during the receptive process.

The interaction model has therefore been established as a means of defining this aforementioned process (cf. Hudson 2007, 32 ff.). It states that reading is a continuous process of constructing meaning from and based on the input we receive. The same applies to the process of listening and viewing. The understanding of the **construction of meaning** as inherent within the receptive process is essential when it comes to developing the range of literacies which facilitate foreign language learning in the classroom.

Definition

> Starting from a broad notion of ›text‹, text comprehension can be defined as the uptake and processing of information emanating from spoken, written or even visual forms of language. This requires physiological as well as psychological effort; a process which starts off with the recognition of sounds, words and sentences or images and ultimately leads to comprehension.

Bottom-up processing: Among the processes which support the construction of meaning during reading, listening or viewing is that of bottom-up processing. As represented in illustration 6.1, the construction of meaning is, on the one hand, **data-driven**. This process starts with decoding words (from word-building and derivations to making connections within the text) and moves to chunks and sentences (at which point larger **units of meaning** can be deciphered). During listening, this is accompanied by the recognition of sounds and phonemes, the characteristics of spoken language and the prosodic (intonation, speed, volume) or non-verbal aspects of language (facial expressions, gestures). In multimedia texts, we also construct meaning on the basis of pictures, symbols or other forms of visual signs like colours or camera perspectives.

Bottom-up processing tasks in class use the written, audio or visual text as their starting point. Based on the text, learners are encouraged to extract **general**, **specific** or **detailed information**. Bottom-up processing supports learners in decoding information by utilising strategies involving cues within the text itself like deciphering the meaning of an unknown word from the context or from its use within a chunk. Learners are also encouraged to use linguistic aspects found within a text, like connectors (*firstly*, *secondly*, etc.) or adverbs of time (*yesterday*, *later*, etc.) which

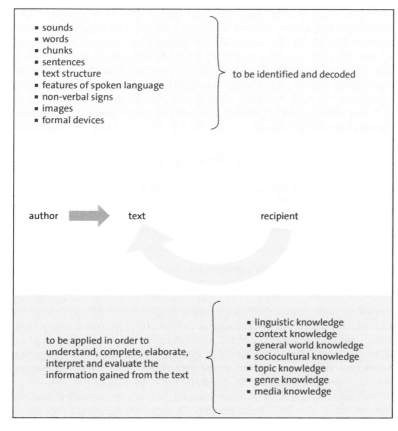

- sounds
- words
- chunks
- sentences
- text structure
- features of spoken language
- non-verbal signs
- images
- formal devices

to be identified and decoded

author → text   recipient

to be applied in order to understand, complete, elaborate, interpret and evaluate the information gained from the text

- linguistic knowledge
- context knowledge
- general world knowledge
- sociocultural knowledge
- topic knowledge
- genre knowledge
- media knowledge

Illustration 6.1:
Text reception as an interactive process
(cf. Hedge 2000, 188 f.)

might indicate the sequence of events, to draw meaning from the text. In the case of visual texts like movies, camera angles or editing techniques are among the specific features of audiovisual communication which can be used as the basis for understanding.

Top-down processing: On the other hand—as the illustration also shows—, there is more to the process of understanding when it comes to reading a text, listening to the radio or watching a movie. Each input is also influenced by **inference** and **hypothesis building**, that is, by interpretations arrived at or conclusions drawn as a result of predictions made about the development of the text (cf. example on page 92). This so-called top-down processing takes place on the basis of cognitive patterns by means of which the recipient is able to draw on personal experience, context related frames of reference and different types of knowledge (context knowledge, general world knowledge, genre knowledge, etc.). The information gathered from within a text is therefore processed (cf. Hedge 2000, 189) and specific importance is ascribed to it on the basis of **knowledge-driven/concept-driven construction of meaning**.

When it comes to listening comprehension, we use, for example, our knowledge about the social context and about the typical flow of a conversation to be able to understand the information communicated. Our experience helps us to identify a speaker's mood, intentions and the situation within which the conversation is taking place—based, for example, on indicators like facial expression, gestures, intonation, speed and volume. When viewing a film, we use our previous knowledge about the topic or the typical plot structure of a particular genre (for example, fairy tales, crime stories, romantic comedies, westerns or horror films) to be able to predict upcoming events or incorporate new information into our current knowledge base.

Example **Try to solve this riddle**

A man and his son are driving in a car one day, when they get into a fatal accident. The man is killed instantly. The boy remains alive, but is severely injured. He is rushed to the hospital for emergency surgery. The surgeon enters the emergency room, looks at the boy and exclaims: »I can't operate on this boy! He is my son!«

How is this possible?
Explanation: This familiar riddle makes the different ways in which reading can be processed quite evident. Readers generally come up with completely different solutions to the riddle since the text gives no specific information about who exactly the surgeon might be. In addition to this, the English language does not provide any clues about gender in this profession. Using bottom-up processing alone does not help much in this situation. However, should we use our general world knowledge, personal experience or common cultural understandings, then we could assume that ›the surgeon‹ might be, for example, the stepfather of the injured boy or the second father in a homosexual parental constellation. But the mother could also have been implied. In this way, top-down processing offers different options for ascribing meaning. Some readers, however, do not solve the riddle, because they cannot imagine any of these solutions—including a woman as a surgeon—as a possible option. This means that our assumptions can awaken awareness in the process of comprehension, just as much as they can inhibit this process.

Development of mental models: New perspectives on reading in the area of cognitive psychology emphasise the production of complex mental models during reception (cf. Hallet 2008). A similar process occurs while listening to a text and while viewing a film: the recipient very often fills gaps and adds information which has not been made explicit by using the support of visual representations. In this context, cognitive **schemata** (such as knowledge about school as an institution or about family structures) and so-called **scripts**, that is, mental structures about conventional daily situations and associated forms of behaviour (for example, in a restaurant, at a concert or at the doctor's office) play a significant role. Owing, however, to their specific cultural orientation, schemata and scripts can also negatively influence comprehension. This can occur if personal interpretations are practically forced upon the text without adequate consideration of its cultural and/or historical context (cf. Hermes 2017a, 228).

> Mental models refer to a range of complex cognitive structures in which information from the text is combined with the recipient's culturally framed schemes and scripts to build patterns. These are then brought together to form a coherent mental concept which facilitates comprehension (cf. Hallet 2008, 149).

Definition

Top-down processing tasks support learners in recalling and using previous knowledge in order for them to be able to use this knowledge in the process of understanding a text. In this way, for example by means of **action- and production-oriented tasks**, such as the scenic interpretation of the relationships among characters in a play or writing the continuation of a story, can encourage an examination of personal experiences as they relate to the content of a text. Such creative tasks also support learners in hypothesis building and filling gaps, as they do not have to come up with unknown content (for more on working with literary texts and films, cf. chapter 10 in this volume).

Visualising tasks are just as stimulating for understanding texts since they activate important aspects of this process of developing models while reading or listening. This is due to the fact that they help learners to reorganise the information via a different medium, for example, to show via symbols (circles, arrows) how people, places or events in a text are related. Such tasks include the creation of a topographical sketch or even of abstract forms of representation, so called graphic organisers (diagrams, grids or mind maps), based on the content of a text (cf. Hallet 2008, 155).

The herringbone technique

Example

With the help of a graphic illustration in the form of a fishbone, learners can be guided through the procedure for answering the key wh-questions (who?, what?, when?, where?, why?) related to a narrative (novel, radio play, film, etc.). In this way, the plot structure can be presented in a clear and simple manner. This can then be used in a post-phase as the basis for writing a content summary, for recounting the story orally or for a plenary discussion on the text. Additionally, this can be used as a means of assessing the learners' comprehension.

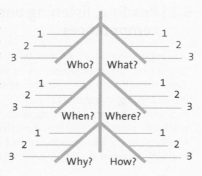

The role of feelings in text reception: Alongside the skills of being able to interpret the language and structure of a text and ascribe meaning to it, the feelings and subjective reactions of the recipient are also important in understanding a text. Emotions connect the content presented in a text with one's own reality. Feelings capture attention, influence perception and also help in recollecting what was read, heard or seen (cf. Donnerstag/Bosenius 2000, 153). In this way, they play an important role in the development of relevant hypotheses and in testing them during the receptive process. This means that the emotional dimension of text reception in the classroom has to be taken into consideration and supported.

Key points

The active process of understanding a text
- We do not simply extract meaning from a text, but we actively assign meaning to individual text elements.
- We think while reading, listening and viewing, anticipate further information, review what we have already gathered, make hypotheses and confirm or reject them during the reception process.
- We fill in gaps of information which have not been explicitly delivered, for example on the basis of our world knowledge.
- We activate different levels of understanding and emotions in connection with the context, the topic and the genre of the text.
- We enter into a dialogue with the text by asking questions, for example about possible interpretations and/or about the context.
- We make judgments about what we have read, heard and seen and develop the need to communicate these judgments.
- In participatory reception situations like conversations, we react to what we hear, comment on it and even make enquiries.

6.2 | Reading, listening and viewing as complex competences

Reading competence: As has been seen, when we receive information from a text, different processes of comprehension take place simultaneously. Hurrelmann (2003) therefore sees the following factors as constitutive of reading competence:
- cognitive factors (decoding skills, the application of schemes)
- affective factors (emotional participation)
- reflection on what has been read
- ability to generate follow-up communication

This demonstrates that reading is more than just a skill; it is an extensive competence with different sub-competences. Successful readers distinguish themselves by mastering not only **lower-order skills** (decoding single words), but also **higher-order skills** (overarching text comprehension) (cf. Hudson 2007, 83):

- They can decipher the meaning of unknown words.
- They use pre-, while- and post-reading strategies and adapt these to their reading goals.
- They plan, direct and monitor their reading process.
- They are able to examine and critically reflect on what they have read.

> Competence, according to Weinert (2001b, 27 f.), should not be simply reduced to skills, but it points to different types of knowledge (declarative knowledge) as well as skills and strategies (procedural knowledge). Additionally, personality-related aspects, such as attitudes, motivation and emotions, form part of each competence.

Definition

Listening comprehension, too, not only relies on the perception of sounds (cf. Blell 2017). Competent listeners are also able to capture, process and interpret different types of listening texts and contexts, that is, audible language input (including intonation, prosody and rhythm) as well as tonal and musical impulses (for example, sounds, songs, film music). They can picture different conversational situations (job interviews, arguments) and recognise the emotional undertones of an utterance (for example, irony). Beyond that, they possess the ability to concentrate on what they are listening to and to monitor their own listening comprehension process. Additionally, they can cope with what they have not understood, critically reflect on their own understanding of the text and accept different possible meanings.

Visual competence: In a similar manner, visual competence (or visual literacy) is not equivalent to simply possessing a visual sense, that is, perceiving visual stimuli (cf. Hecke 2017). The visual sense, as it functions to perceive the environment, is a genetic predisposition which develops as a skill throughout the process of maturation. Visual competence, based on the ability to perceive (in sensory terms) and identify visual stimuli, however, involves critical and cultural components. Reception requires the construction of meaning on the basis of the formal characteristics of a picture (such as its colour, design or composition) and the context in which it is presented. When it comes to interpretation, the impact and message inherent in the picture has to be considered carefully. Competent viewers are aware of various types of pictures or images (photographs, picture series, diagrams, sculptures) and the effect these may have on them. They have also developed an awareness that pictures do not have an illustrative nature in and of themselves, but rather that they are subjective interpretations and cultural products (cf. Hecke/Surkamp 2015).

Combined text comprehension: A further aspect of complexity related to receptive processes comes as a result of the fact that learners have to meet a number of simultaneous demands made by **multimodal texts**. Should the receptive signals be channelled via different senses or come from different sign systems, for example, reading and visual comprehension, that is, written text and pictures, as is the case in graphic novels (cf. Ludwig/Pointer 2013), or listening and viewing comprehension, that is, oral text and images, as is the case with films (cf. Henseler et al. 2011), then these different signals must not only be simultaneously captured and processed bottom-up and top-down, but they also have to be connected to each other. For example, sound design (such as film music) and the content inherent in pictures in audiovisual texts can complement or mutually reinforce each other (as in the case of romantic background music during a love scene). A divergence can also result between image and sound (for example, images of war accompanied by a peace song), the so-called picture-sound dichotomy, which might provide a new, perhaps surprising meaning on a higher level of understanding.

Reception of hypertexts: An integrated process of comprehension is also associated with **digital texts** (cf. Möller/Netz 2009). Non-linear digital texts can be classified as individual, interlinked units of information which make various navigation pathways and an endless array of options available, so that recipients can construct their own texts (cf. Schmidt 2010). The interaction between text and recipient is particularly high since on the one hand, the recipient has to decide which path to follow within the network of hypertexts. On the other hand, the recipient himself/herself is compelled to construct a coherent text from a variety of specifically selected connections. In addition to this, along with elements of language mainly in written form, hypertexts also incorporate pictures, diagrams, sound files or embedded films which give quick access to different items of information, but which can also make orientation difficult for the recipient (cf. Murray/McPherson 2006). At any rate, the recipient is particularly challenged by the multimodal coding of information, also in terms of managing his/her own direction of focus.

6.3 | Challenges of receptive processes in foreign language contexts

Reasons for a deficit in receptive competences: Competent foreign language learners use top-down as well as bottom-up processes while reading, listening and viewing. In contrast, less successful learners often concentrate mainly on bottom-up strategies. This presents the risk of them stopping at the level of word meaning, often attempting to understand single units and, in this way, read mainly without an awareness of the meaning of groups of words (chunks).

A holistic receptive process can also be impeded if barely any connection is made between the information in a text and one's own reality. Further reasons which account for receptive competences not being well developed would be a lack of motivation and/or adequate receptive strategies, the failure to monitor one's own comprehension as well as insufficient opportunities for practice.

Errors in dealing with texts in the classroom: The development of foreign language learners into good readers, listeners and viewers is one of the main goals of foreign language teaching. Working with texts in the classroom, however, often stands in the way of the development of for-

eign language receptive competences. In the case of reading and as contradictory as it might seem, it has been noted that even though the goal
is to promote reading comprehension, there is hardly any free time for
learners to read at school, to select what interests them or to experience
reading texts which are not filled with difficult language and/or content
(cf. Ivey/Fischer 2006). Also, in terms of actually working with texts, a
number of poor choices are sometimes made:

- Texts are preceded by a lot of ›relief‹ exercises like listing or discussing   Poor choices
  most of the words belonging to the word field of the topic addressed in
  a text: this works against decoding skills and promotes word-for-word
  comprehension, which should rather be avoided.
- Unknown texts are read aloud: this prevents the silent uptake of information.
- Texts are listened to and read at the same time: this can lead to colli-
  sions between the channels via which information is processed on a
  sensory level.
- Reading strategies are not practised: this prevents learners from dealing with texts in an autonomous manner.
- Details on the text are often checked or working with texts is dominated by language exercises: this works against reading motivation
  and individual text interpretation.

Motivation and competence development: The close connection between
motivational aspects and the development of receptive competences is
not to be underestimated. The development of receptive competences
among learners who are motivated to read or listen to foreign language
texts or watch foreign language films on a regular basis outside the classroom tends to increase as a result of this constant training. On the contrary, learners who do not have any positive receptive experience are not
able to break the vicious circle: they have no interest in reading or listening to texts or even watching foreign language films because they have
difficulty with reception; they therefore do not make the effort and are, as
a result, unable to practise their receptive competences. For reading and
listening, this means that the identification and interpretation of lexical
chunks and grammatical structures (cf. chapter 8 in this volume) are not
automatic and that learners allow themselves to be easily distracted if
they do not understand something or tend to look up every single word
and lose their flow. Consequently, learners develop neither the ability to
cope with frustration nor strategies to compensate for what they do not
understand.

Difficulties during listening comprehension can also result from the fact
that, generally speaking, foreign language learners themselves do not determine the pace at which reception takes place while listening. Furthermore, spoken language differs in many respects from written language
(incomplete utterances, contracted forms, colloquial language, restructur-
ing, slurring between word boundaries, etc.). Similarly, texts with unfamiliar topics can pose a serious challenge to learners since they have so
many prerequisites and do not allow them to make connections to their
prior knowledge. Authentic listening texts with several speakers, unfamil-

iar accents, sociolects or dialects as well as distracting background noises can also produce difficulties while listening. This does not mean, however, that such texts should not have a place in the English language classroom; on the contrary, because of their close connection to daily life, reception of this type should actually be practised on a regular basis.

Challenges of films: When it comes to film, listening comprehension is coupled with viewing or—in the case of sub-titles or intermittent texts—even reading. Foreign language learners are thus faced with a huge challenge. The simultaneous interpretation of language and further auditory as well as visual information is not so easy for them to manage. Additionally, reception necessitates multimodal knowledge and skills for dealing with texts, such as knowledge about film specific techniques, which goes beyond pure language comprehension. Furthermore, as in the case of simple listening texts, fast-paced dialogues in films with multiple interchanging speakers and a variety of accents as well as an intricate storyline and complex character constellations can make comprehension difficult. The combination of image and sound can, on the other hand, also facilitate comprehension if learners are able to compensate for gaps in language by using visual signals like the facial expressions and body language of the speakers. Moreover, the capacity for retention is greater if image and sound work together.

6.4 | Implications for teaching reading, listening and viewing

6.4.1 | Practising on different levels

The challenge of teaching and learning these very complex receptive competences is based mainly on the fact that various sub-competences have to be practised on different levels (cf. Lütge 2012e). First, there is the issue of the actual execution of reading, listening and viewing as an activity. Second, learners have to develop an awareness of the best use of available strategies and techniques (cf. Helbig 1998). Third, in the end, learners have to learn to constantly review their own success in terms of reception. They also have to be further motivated to read, listen and view texts in the foreign language (cf. Henseler/Surkamp 2007).

Components of a curriculum for reading: Using the example of **reading competence**, this section illustrates which aspects a curriculum for the foreign language classroom should incorporate (cf. Rosebrock/Nix 2006; Henseler/Surkamp 2009):

1. **Interest in reading:** As reading motivation serves as an important prerequisite for the development of reading as a competence, a foreign language class should attempt to establish an age-appropriate reading culture and develop a love for reading in the foreign language. This also includes pupils' confidence in their own language competences. Learners acquire this confidence with practice and early success, for example through the use of picture books in lower foreign language

classes. In order to establish long-term reading motivation, pupils should be encouraged **to read extensively** using interesting texts, for example, with choices from children's and young adult literature (cf. Henseler/Surkamp 2007).

Examples

Methods to support extensive reading

- Setting up a **class library** or mobile book treasure chest with a wide range of authentic texts (non-fiction, popular fiction, magazines, comics, etc.).
- Regular **story time sessions** (also with excerpts to promote interest in reading whole books).
- Arranging free, ritualised reading time in class (**leisure time reading**).
- **Conversations** about individual reading experiences in the form of book conferences, reading syndicates (small group discussions about different books), battles of the book (pupils ask and answer questions, in battle style, about books they have read) or book clubs (groups of 4 to 6 pupils read a book chapter by chapter and have regular discussions about their views and ideas about the book).
- **Book presentations** in the form of a book slam, a book review or book report, or in the form of a book poster.
- Genre conversion **reading events** (pupils read stories or excerpts from a selected book in the style of a different genre, for example, reading a fairy tale in the tone and style of a horror story with background sounds and expressive intonation).
- **Reading week** or bring-a-book-to-school day (can also be organised as a cross-curricular event).

2. **Reading skills:** For many pupils, the so-called lower-level skills are not yet an automatic process. These skills refer, for example, to techniques for visually capturing text elements, supported by a high level of concentration and good memory. Practice in this area should include the following aspects: the range of words captured at a glance, close reading, reading words faster and recognising sentences as whole units. The following exercises, among others, are useful to support the development of these skills (cf. Haß 2016, 144):
   - sight-word practice exercises to encourage word recognition at a glance: pupils identify words displayed for an instant via electronic media or in the form of flash cards
   - exercises to practise focal width: pupils focus on a fixed point and try to identify the words on the right and on the left side at the same time
   - segmenting exercises: pupils dissect sentences into units of meaning

3. **Reading fluency:** Pupils whose fluency is not that advanced at the word and sentence level struggle through a text. Particularly weak

readers therefore have to improve their technical reading skills to achieve a higher level of comprehension. Through **paired reading**, an oral reading routine in fixed reading tandems, reading fluency can be increased and reading comprehension skills can be developed by means of a discussion about what was read (cf. Grieser-Kindel et al. 2016, 152 ff.).

4. **Reading strategies:** Good information processing is based, in the first instance, on the use of reading strategies. To promote effective reading processes, successful exercises like reciprocal reading, for example, combine strategy instruction and strategy implementation with reciprocal teaching and learning (cf. ibid., 217 ff.; cf. example below). Learners are supported by competent peers while reading in order to manage their own reading process as they become familiar with strategies for working autonomously with texts to understand, analyse and interpret them.

One strategy before beginning the receptive process, for example, is to formulate one's own questions about the text based on the title and topic in order to be clear about what one's expectations are (cf. top-down processing). Another strategy, this time to support the actual process of reception, is to prepare notes. In this way, higher-level skills can be practised which help learners reach a level of understanding that goes beyond the sentence level.

5. **Reflective skills:** In order to be able to manage the reading process, pupils need to reflect on the path their learning follows and on their learning progress. A number of methods can be helpful here: using a reading goals chart, learners set themselves goals for the reading process (cf. Gaile et al. 2007) or they observe themselves while reading with the help of an observation form, a reading journal or a reading portfolio (cf. Bertschi-Kaufmann 2007, 104 f.; Henseler/Surkamp 2009, 12 ff.).

Example
Reciprocal Reading group work—from Grade 7 onwards (cf. Grieser-Kindel et al. 2016, 222)

The content of a text (for example, the chapter of a book) is examined systematically, paragraph by paragraph, in groups of four by:
- reading the text together
- working together to clarify open questions
- formulating the content of the text using their own words
- speculating about what follows in the text

The text is divided into paragraphs. The first paragraph is read silently by all the members of the group. Then, each group member receives a role card. Each role card is printed on different coloured paper. For each new paragraph, the roles are rotated clockwise among the members of the group.

1. Questioning

Read the passage aloud to the members of your group.
Ask questions about unclear parts, puzzling information or anything that could be misunderstood.

2. Summarising

Briefly summarise the content of the passage which has just been read aloud. Try to use your own words.

3. Clarifying

Ask the members of your group to explain what certain words/chunks mean or how they are pronounced correctly.

4. Predicting

Make predictions. Imagine how the story could continue. What do you think will happen next?

The roles in your group change as you pass your card one person to the right and read the next paragraph. Repeat the process using your new roles. This continues until the entire text is read.

6.4.2 | Process-oriented text reception

In order to respond to the complexity of reading, listening and viewing as processes and to take learners through the various stages of text comprehension, a process-oriented approach to the development of receptive competences has established itself within the field of foreign language teaching methodology. In this approach, working with texts has been divided into the three phases of pre-, while- and post-reading/listening/viewing tasks. The tasks in this three-step structure serve to facilitate interaction between learner and text and also support oral and written language production (for productive language competences, cf. chapter 7 in this volume).

Pre-reading/-listening/-viewing activities pave the way for the receptive process. They also help prepare learners topic-wise and emotionally to work with the text, to incorporate their own experience, to activate their prior knowledge, to generate expectations about the text, to familiarise themselves with the word field and make possible contextual knowledge readily available. In other words, they establish context, activate knowledge and schemata and prepare learners for the main receptive event. For example, we can support comprehension by asking the pupils to make predictions about what they might read, hear or see.

While-reading/-listening/-viewing activities provide structure and support for text reception. These activities should guarantee text comprehension, focus learners' attention and occasionally redirect them (for example, through observational tasks) to active reception as well as to come into dialogue with the text. Active reading and watching films, for example, can be supported by encouraging learners to reflect on the impressions they have gathered and to articulate their personal reactions. Different forms of creative interaction with the text can also support specific subjective comprehension processes during this phase and promote the creation of meaning (for example, through testing hypotheses already built in the pre-phase).

Post-reading/-listening/-viewing activities help learners to evaluate the reception process, take a deeper look at the text and engage in further language or topic-specific work with the newly acquired information. It is considered a meaningful approach to first give pupils the opportunity to express their personal reactions to the text. Further activities should then, in keeping with the process nature of text comprehension, link to tasks in the pre- and while-phases. Learners should therefore be able to refer back to their personal impressions and observations and build on new insights which they will have obtained during the receptive process.

Dos and Don'ts: Even if the three-phase sketch of the process of text comprehension should support learners and offer teachers a helpful instrument for planning classes, its use should be given careful consideration. Too much of a mechanical application makes the classroom event too predictable and brings about boredom rather than raising awareness and practising strategies for working effectively with texts. Additionally, there should not be so much preparatory work that learners are not allowed to activate their own previous knowledge or work more independently on further aspects of knowledge (for example, contextual aspects), which are needed in order to interpret the text. Moreover, it should be ensured that the individual phases are approached with as much variety as possible and that the different activities also offer variety in terms of social form, that is, individual-, pair-, small group and whole group work (for further ideas on working with literary texts, cf. Surkamp/Nünning 2016, 78 ff.; for ideas on working with films, cf. Henseler et al. 2011, 97 ff.).

6.4.3 | Different genres, goals, purposes and strategies related to reception

The interdependence of genre, receptive goals and applied strategies: The choice of methods selected by a teacher to support the development of receptive competences depends predominantly on the genre of the text and the specific reading, listening or viewing goals pursued. The genre and receptive goals can in fact complement each other. In this way, we set the goal for reading a recipe on gathering detailed information, while we allow ourselves to be captivated by the emotional aspects of a film and therefore aim to have our learners follow the main plot in the foreign language without necessarily having to understand all the details. Being aware of one's own receptive goal prior to the actual reception of a text is an important sub-competence, since this will determine the choice of reading, listening or viewing strategies and techniques. This also applies particularly to reception when dealing with hypertexts, as the variety of information sources via the different sensory channels requires the recipient to be able to carefully select relevant texts (cf. Schmidt 2010, 31).

Phase	Pre-reading/-listening/-viewing	While-reading/-listening/-viewing	Post-reading/-listening/-viewing
Objectives	preparing for comprehension: • introducing the topic • making emotional connections • incorporating personal experience • activating prior knowledge • becoming familiar with the word field • making contextual information available • generating expectations or hypotheses about the text	structuring and supporting comprehension: • recognising and organising content elements • reflecting on and linking preparatory activities to the content • focussing attention on the topic • actively engaging with the topic • testing hypotheses	evaluating comprehension and communicating meaning: • (inter-)linking and advancing the newly acquired content • making cross-references between preparatory and supporting activities as a basis for creating new texts • critically reflecting on developments within the text • coming to conclusions about significance of the outcomes of the text
Possible activities	• speculating about the text on the basis of the title, book cover or film poster • looking at a picture representing a listening scene and describing the possible communication situation • revising word fields and chunks related to the particular topic • researching background information on the topic presented in a text • organising screen shots of a film in a meaningful sequence • watching a film scene without sound and speculating about the topic/issue at hand and the dialogue	• visualising the logical structure of a text with the help of graphic organisers • taking notes on the most important arguments or events • annotating a text with personal reactions or previously generated ideas • observational tasks on the development of a character • identifying a route on a map while listening to instructions • watching the scene of a film previously viewed without sound to test hypotheses generated about the topic/issue and the dialogue	• creating a title for a text (e. g. a poem or a newspaper article that has been read without the title) • annotating each paragraph of a non-fictional text with a key word or expression • discussing specifically identified aspects of or meanings ascribed to a text, e. g. in a debate • writing a review • acting out a scene • writing additional texts, e. g. thought bubbles in a graphic narrative or another episode in a story to fill a time-gap within the plot • converting a text or a part of a text into another medium (e. g. drawing a picture based on a listening text or writing a film script to a short story)

Table 6.1:
A three-step structure for process-oriented text reception

Everyday genres and goals: As already alluded to, the main goal of the foreign language classroom is to prepare learners to communicate in a variety of everyday situations. Therefore, in selecting texts to support reading, listening and viewing competences, it is those genres which learners are most likely to encounter in their daily life, which should be considered. Similarly, receptive goals should be formulated in accordance with everyday listening, reading and viewing events. Therefore, instead of only exposing learners to pedagogically tailored school book texts, everyday texts like brochures, articles, schedules, poems, maps, diagrams, radio interviews, loudspeaker announcements, TV news, documentaries, vlogs or theatre performances should also be part of the foreign language classroom experience. The prerequisite here, however, is that texts should be appropriate for the class level in terms of language and topic, so that the learners can make connections to their reality during top-down and bottom-up processing activities. Then, instead of always letting them draw details from or respond to mechanical comprehension questions in a text, learners should be engaged in receptive activities which relate as closely as possible to or actually reflect everyday situations. This could include, for example, silent reading and listening and viewing for pleasure—within the classroom as well.

Purposes for reading and listening: In real life, we read and listen for various reasons. The reasons determine how much and what exactly we need to or want to understand in the text. In this context, Hedge (2000, 195) states that we read

- to get information
- to respond to curiosity about a topic
- to follow instructions to perform a task
- for pleasure
- to keep in touch with friends
- to know what is happening in the world
- to find out when and where things are taking place

Listening
situations In a similar manner, listening in real life is dependent on different listening situations in which we may find ourselves (Müller-Hartmann/Schocker-v. Ditfurth 2004, 76):

- listening to public announcements: information, instructions, warnings, etc.
- listening to media: radio, TV, recordings, cinema
- listening as a member of a live audience: theatre, public meetings, public lectures, entertainment, etc.
- overhearing conversations

To this list, we can add so-called participatory listening; the kind of listening we do during conversations, debates or telephone calls (cf. ibid., 72), where as listeners we can contribute with our (even non-verbal) reactions to maintaining communication and also have to switch quickly to the role of the speaker. This shows that reading, listening and viewing can all aim at different receptive goals which can be achieved using different receptive strategies and techniques as table 6.2 illustrates.

Goal: reading/ listening/ viewing ...	Description	Strategy	Example	Techniques
... for gist	▪ obtaining an overall impression or capturing the main idea ▪ serves to provide general orientation on the content ▪ recipient formulates hypothesis about the content	▪ skimming or listening or viewing without paying attention to details	reading a newspaper article to be able to identify generally what it is about and if it is of personal interest (What is this article about generally? Would I like to read it in more detail?)	While reading, for example, I take note of the headline, glance at illustrations or pictures, read short summaries in italics or sub-headings and look out for highlighted words.
... for specific information	▪ glossing over or filtering out details to pick up a specific bit or bits of information ▪ serves to provide selected information or key pieces of information which can be quickly identified (for example, names, dates, locations) ▪ recipient sorts through information and excludes whatever does not fall in line with the nature or form of the information being searched for	▪ scanning or listening or viewing for specific types of information	listening to an announcement at the train station to be able to select the departure time and platform of a particular train (Which train number or description and destination do I need to listen for? Which time and platform number are mentioned immediately following this latter information?)	While listening, for example, I tune into names, locations, times and numbers.
... for detailed understanding	▪ paying careful attention to minor details of information ▪ serves to provide detailed information via careful examination ▪ recipient examines all the details provided to obtain an intimate view of the information	▪ close reading/ listening/viewing	researching online for information about a festival in a specific country to be able to share these details (Which variety of details can I gather in which series of hyperlinked texts? Which additional details for further reference can I examine closely to complement the information I have gathered so far?)	While reading and exploring hyperlinked information, I read for details and can, for example, create a text document with referenced information including highlighted relevant details.

Goal: reading/ listening/ viewing ...	Description	Strategy	Example	Techniques
... to follow lines of arguments	■ engaging intensely with content ■ serves to develop a sense of logical (though not necessarily linear) and analytical thinking ■ recipient examines the relevant aspects of a text which help to form a cohesive understanding of the information	■ intensive reading/listening/ viewing	reading academic texts to be able to get a clear understanding of the development of ideas	While reading, I take notes as I go through the lines of thought, for example, about my conclusions. I also keep a record of my subjective evaluations and assessments of what I have read.
... for implications	■ detecting a speaker's mood, underlying intentions and the atmosphere of the context ■ serves to provide implicit information by looking beyond what is read, heard or seen ■ recipient examines all the intricacies of the interaction presented	■ reading/listening/viewing while paying attention to non-verbal and paralinguistic signs	viewing a talk show interview to be able to determine the participants' attitude and disposition towards a particular issue	While listening and viewing, for example, I pay attention to the participants' tone, body language, reactions as well as their responses to each other's utterances.
... for critical engagement	■ interacting with content in such a way that subjective and often manipulative intentions are identified and put into a broader historical and/or cultural perspective ■ serves to develop critical media literacy by encouraging further investigation using multiple sources of information, for example ■ recipient takes a critical view of contextual factors and attempts to view content from an objective standpoint	■ contextually sensitive reading/listening/ viewing	watching a documentary about a historical event to be able to critically assess its impact (Does the documentary present various perspectives on the issue? Who was interviewed under which circumstances?)	While viewing and listening, for example, I observe and consider the impact of the visual effects and images selected. I reflect on my own attitude toward and previous knowledge on the event. I try to match this up against current events in the context and compare this with my own subjective views.
... for general understanding/ for fun	■ exploring content for pleasure	■ extensive reading/listening/ viewing	reading novels and magazines; listening to music and watching films of personal interest	While reading/listening/viewing, I allow myself to be motivated by the leisurely experience the texts offer.

Table 6.2: Goals and strategies of text reception (cf. Hedge 2000, 195)

6.5 | Questions of assessment

Challenges: It is not only teaching receptive competences, but also assessing the performance of learners in the areas of reading, listening and viewing comprehension which poses challenges (cf. chapter 14 in this volume). These challenges are linked to the process nature and complexity of text comprehension. As a result, both product-oriented and process-oriented tasks should be included in assessing pupils' performance. For example, when working with films, writing a summary of the film (**product-orientation**) should be complemented by keeping a film response journal (**process-orientation**) in which the learners can engage on an individual level with the audiovisual text to give them the chance to record their spontaneous impressions, feelings, thoughts and opinions (cf. Henseler et al. 2011, 106 f.). Additionally, it is important to consider the learners' skills in bottom-up as well as top-down processing activities, that is, not only to assess the decoding of language, auditory or pictoral elements in a text, but also the interaction with and evaluation of what was read, heard and seen.

Task format: However, it is important to note that task formats which require lengthy answers reveal more about the pupils' skills in text production and allow receptive skills to be only marginally assessed. As a result, it should be ensured, particularly among younger learners, that when working with texts, activities should be included which simply evaluate language comprehension and therefore demand little or no language production (speaking or writing) in the foreign language. Thaler (2012, 163) differentiates between **closed**, **half-open** and **open formats**, whereby closed formats do not require learners to produce any formulated output and half-open tasks only require single-word responses. Some examples of such tasks types are (cf. ibid., 164; Haß 2016, 132, 148):

- multiple choice or true/false tasks
- tasks which require a solution performed by a mere mechanical operation, for example, making changes or corrections in a picture
- total physical response tasks, like ›listen and draw‹, ›listen and act‹, ›listen and point‹
- matching tasks (matching people with utterances or connecting parts of a text with headings)
- organising a chain of events into the right order
- ticking off on a list what was seen and heard following the viewing of a film
- choosing the right text summary from among a larger selection
- filling in a gap text
- using information gathered to fill in a grid

Task types

Closed and half-open tasks focus particularly on learners' lower level skills. Once the learners' interaction with the text content has to be assessed, then they have to also actively produce language. In this context, story reproduction (accompanied by some task support in the form of a story structure guide, for example), presents itself as a reasonable assessment tool for learners who do not yet have advanced production skills. Other possible activities include questions on the text (related to content) as well as beyond the text, discussions on a statement made in a text or the comparison of content from the text with previously formed opinions as well as creative tasks like transforming texts into new forms or scenic representations.

6.6 | Conclusion

The difficult question regarding appropriate tasks to assess performance levels as far as receptive competences are concerned is again an indication that—as stated throughout this chapter—competences in the foreign language classroom should not be addressed in an isolated, but rather an integrated manner. Learners can only become competent in the foreign language if they can draw simultaneously on receptive and productive competences in communication situations. Just a simple dialogue shows, for example, that »listeners play a very important and active role in keeping conversations going, by showing interest and sympathy, and by causing speakers to modify or repeat things« (White 1998, 6). Furthermore, and according to Schwerdtfeger (1989, 24 f.), visual competence is not only important for language comprehension, but also for training individual speaking skills and speakers' willingness to communicate.

Text competence   The educational standards (*Bildungsstandards*) in Germany (cf. chapter 2 in this volume) also articulate the need for developing an **overarching text competence**—oral, written and audiovisual—in advanced foreign language classes which goes beyond a purely functional communicative competence. This can also mean, for example, supporting text production competences through text reception: knowledge about different genres facilitates writing one's own texts. Conversely, text reception competences can also be developed via productive processes, if creative writing tasks contribute to making narrative and lyrical models clear to learners.

Ultimately, it is not only receptive and productive competences that contribute to developing an overarching foreign language discourse skill set (*fremdsprachliche Diskursfähigkeit*). Beyond this, there is need for an **intertextual** and **intermedial competence** which enables learners to recognise the manner in which texts and utterances are intertwined in various discourses (e. g., religious discourse, gender discourse, etc.), to determine the place of a single text in a specific discourse framework and to link or position their own utterances in a reflective manner within this constellation (cf. Hallet 2002).

Further Reading
Grabe, William/Stoller, Fredricka L. ([2]2011): *Teaching and Researching Reading* [2002]. Harlow.

Henseler, Roswitha/Möller, Stefan/Surkamp, Carola (2011): *Filme im Englischunterricht. Grundlagen, Methoden, Genres*. Seelze.

Henseler, Roswitha/Surkamp, Carola (eds.) (2009): Special Issue »Lesekompetenz«. *Der Fremdsprachliche Unterricht Englisch* 100/101.

Hudson, Thom (2007): *Teaching Second Language Reading*. Oxford.

Kieweg, Werner (ed.) (2003): Special Issue »Hörverstehen«. *Der fremdsprachliche Unterricht Englisch* 64/65.

Lynch, Tony (2009): *Teaching Second Language Listening*. Oxford.

Carola Surkamp / Tanyasha Yearwood

7 Productive Competences—Speaking, Writing, Mediating

Traditionally, the content of English language teaching was conceptualised in four skills: listening and reading (receptive skills), speaking and writing (productive skills). More recently, the categorisation of language knowledge and performance has changed: Now the use of our own language, e. g. when mediating, is also taken into consideration and the scope of our lessons is extended by teaching a combination of reading, viewing and listening (audiovisual skills, cf. chapter 6 in this volume). Therefore, some researchers now speak about five or even six skills (listening, reading, speaking, writing plus mediation and audiovisual skills). Furthermore, our learners' abilities have been conceptualised as a **complex communicative competence**, which includes more than just knowledge and practical skills but also, for example, strategies, attitudes, emotions and motivation.

This chapter provides an overview over speaking, writing and mediation. First, the processes underlying these competences are outlined before moving on to issues relating directly to teaching and assessment of the productive competences.

7.1 | Speaking: the nature of spoken discourse and how to teach it

The development of oral communicative competence has taken centre stage in most English language classes and being able to speak fluently is a major goal of many students of English. In fluent conversations, speakers seem to perform almost effortlessly. This performance can only be achieved by diverse and interrelated cognitive processes:

Talking is one of our dearest occupations. We spend hours a day conversing, telling stories, teaching, quarrelling [...] and, of course, speaking to ourselves. Speaking is moreover one of our most complex cognitive, linguistic, and motor skill. (Levelt 1989, XIII)

As speaking is highly complex, being able to speak fluently and accurately does not follow naturally from grammar, vocabulary and pronunciation instruction. In order to become a fluent speaker of a foreign language, plenty of practice, meaningful repetition and some level of automatisation are crucial.

7.1.1 | Understanding speaking

Speaking is a competence that demands knowledge of language and discourse, a sound mastery of the sub-skills of speaking and also a good command of **communication strategies**.

Knowledge base of speaking: Successful speakers of English draw on a wide knowledge base of the nature of spoken discourse they might not necessarily be aware of. Not only do they know a lot about the language in terms of grammar, vocabulary (cf. chapter 8 in this volume), pronunciation, discourse and genre, but they have also gained **intercultural awareness** (cf. chapter 9 in this volume) and valuable insights into the **sociocultural knowledge** base of local and international English-speaking cultures.

Apart from knowledge about discourse, sociocultural knowledge is an important prerequisite for successful and respectful communication between people from diverse cultural backgrounds, as language and non-verbal behaviour are closely linked to the culture and the society it is used in. Sociocultural rules for certain speech events can differ from one social and/or cultural group to another. Shaking hands when meeting a person from a cultural group with strict rules on bodily contact and proximity could, for instance, be taken as an offence. Therefore, L2 users need to be aware of their own culturally formed communicative behaviour and that of others (cf. Baker 2012).

Knowledge about the nature of spoken discourse is also necessary for successful speaking. The term **discourse** signifies either the use of language in a specific context or the use of language in units that exceed the length of a sentence. Here, discourse is concerned with how sentences and larger units are connected to form **coherent** and **cohesive** speech.

Definition

> **Coherence** and **cohesion** are the two qualities of a text that create a sense of unity and purpose.
> Coherence refers to the structure and unity of a text as far as meaning is concerned. In a coherent conversation, a question by a speaker is followed by an answer to that question by the next speaker. Cohesion refers to the use of linguistic devices to join sentences and paragraphs together, like conjunctions, reference words, substitutions and lexical devices such as collocations and lexical groups.

Beyond formulating individual sentences, speakers need to connect individual utterances to form a meaningful text. They also need to know how to take turns in a conversation or discussion with the help of **discourse markers**.

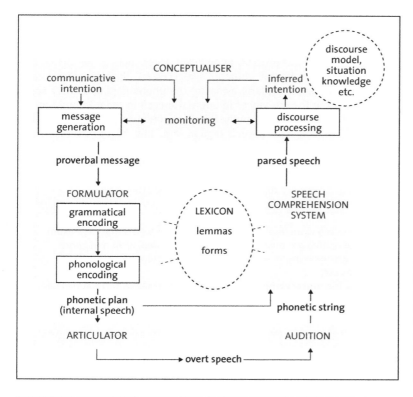

Illustration 7.1:
Blueprint of speech
production. Boxes
represent process-
ing components;
circles represent
knowledge stores
(adapted from
Levelt 1989, 9)

Discourse markers are words and phrases used as ›signposts‹ in speak-ing as well as in writing. Discourse markers can initiate turns and signal links to something previously said, like *well* in the following extract from a conversation.
James: *Oh, let's just say, I am not crazy about traditional British food.*
Pete: <u>Well</u>, *but just think about ...*

Definition

The speaking process: Being able to produce fluent speech is the main goal of most foreign language learners. But what does speaking fluently involve? In spoken interaction, we react to the person we are talking to (our interlocutor). In response, we produce two or three words per sec-ond in a linear fashion, where one utterance follows the other. **Fluent speakers** often plan what they are about to say while they are still artic-ulating their previous idea. This spontaneous and overlapping decoding and processing of information in real time is highly demanding. Levelt (1989, 8 ff.) divides the underlying processes of speech production into three interrelated components: conceptualisation, formulation and artic-ulation.

Once a message has been processed in the **speech comprehension system**, the speaker interprets the parsed speech and conceives of what to say as a response in the **conceptualiser**. According to Levelt (1989), a preverbal message is generated. In the **formulator**, this preverbal message is formed into a phonetic plan by grammatical and phonological encoding. During this process, knowledge stores such as the mental lexicon (cf. chapter 8 in this volume) are accessed. Speakers of a foreign language may be particularly aware of the phonetic plan as they sometimes sound out the utterances in internal speech in order to monitor and warm up for speaking out loudly. Finally, overt speech is articulated (**articulator**) by using our speech organs, e. g. lips, teeth, alveolar ridge, hard and soft palate and glottis. All the while, overt speech is **self-monitored**. Here, speakers strive to notice self-generated failures with respect to meaning or well-formedness. Consequently, failures can be self-repaired, e. g. by simply repeating or rephrasing utterances.

Definition

> A lemma is a word or phrase as it is entered in a dictionary. For example, the lemma *go* consists of *go* with *goes*, *going*, *went* and *gone*.
> Forms are meaningful units of speech like sentences, phrases, morphemes etc.
> Parsing is a process whereby the syntactic and semantic relations between linguistic elements are analysed in order to derive the meaning of an utterance.

Communication strategies: Speakers of a foreign language frequently encounter communication problems due to the demands of the cognitive process and/or a lack of language resources. What can learners do when they have problems expressing themselves? They might draw back on conversation strategies to convey their message, win time for processing or, simply, keep the conversation going. Common communication strategies for foreign language learners are:

- **Paraphrasing:** Speakers express what they want to say by using different words. Instead of saying *She is generous with her time.* Somebody might say *She is willing to give away her time freely.*
- **Code switching:** Speakers use more than one language within a single conversational turn or interaction, e. g. *All the Bratwürstel were eaten.*
- **Use of all-purpose words:** Speakers use words like *thing*, *stuff*, *make*, *do*.
- **Word-coinage:** Speakers turn a word of another language into an English-sounding word. Somebody not being able to retrieve the word ›map‹ might try to use *Karte* instead, saying, *Can I have a look at your Karte?*
- **Non-verbal/paralinguistic communication:** Speakers might use gestures and facial expressions to get their meaning across.
- **Asking for help and clarification:** Speakers ask directly for clarification and help.
- **Avoidance:** When faced with too great a challenge to express a certain idea, speakers simplify their intended message to a less complex statement.

7.1.2 | Spoken discourse: linguistic features, genres and pronunciation

Knowledge about **linguistic features** of spoken language, **genres** of speaking and **pronunciation** are highly relevant for teaching and learning how to speak accurately, fluently and with an appropriate level of complexity. A comparison of written and spoken English highlights significant linguistic features of spoken language. Speakers and listeners share the same time and context, which allows them to negotiate and construct meaning, e. g. by asking for clarification, confirmation or rephrasing. In contrast to writing, we usually have very limited time to plan what we are about to say. In addition to that, we simultaneously listen to and observe our partner's reaction. Moreover, spoken language is ephemeral.

Even though there are great differences between written and spoken discourse, new communication technology has created a mix of the two modes. Communication in social media, such as instant messaging or networking sites, is mostly written, but shows distinct features of oral communication.

Purposes of speaking: There are two main purposes of speaking: interactional and transactional. **Interactional speaking** centres on engaging in direct social interaction with a strong focus on building a relationship as we do in small talk, joke telling and conversations. In contrast to that, **transactional speaking** is mainly about conveying and receiving information, e. g. in a speech or when ordering in a restaurant.

When we interact, meaning is not simply transferred from one person to the next, but it is negotiated. In this process, called negotiation of meaning, speakers try to reach a clear understanding of each other. It has been proposed that negotiation of meaning is at the heart of language development. Thus, teachers in a communicative classroom seek to elicit this process by introducing jigsaw activities, communicative crosswords, opinion gap activities or more elaborate tasks.

Definition

Spoken language	Written language
dialogic/interactional/transactional	monologic/non-interactional
co-constructed by more than one speaker	constructed over time by individual writers/readers
shared knowledge of context	assumed knowledge of context
unplanned and negotiated	planned and redrafted
impermanent (produced in ›real time‹)	permanent (produced for ›long term‹)
close to action in time and space (context-embedded)	distant from action in time and space (context removed)
uses more informal language	uses more formal language
performance effects (e. g. hesitations, repeats, false starts, incompletion, syntactic blends)	no performance effects

Table 7.1:
Spoken vs. written language

Transactional encounters often follow a script and a high amount of formulaic language is used to keep the exchange going (cf. Brown/Yule 1983). For instance, when checking into a hotel the receptionist usually welcomes the guest, who would give their name and booking details in order to receive a key for the hotel room. In return, the receptionist would provide some information on how to get to the room, before wishing a pleasant stay.

Genre: A great part of our everyday communication is shaped by genres like small talk and conversational storytelling. Learning not just useful chunks of language in isolation, but also gaining insights into the pragmatic function of a genre, helps learners to successfully engage with their partners in communication (cf. Freitag-Hild 2014). At the opening of a conversation, small talk, for instance, often serves to gain common ground by talking about the weather or weekend activities before moving on to more serious topics.

Definition

> The term genre classifies different types of spoken or written discourse. A genre is characterised by typical features and characteristics such as content, language, purpose and discourse conventions. In this sense, small talk, presentations, stories, e-mails and letters can be characterised as genres. Those features and characteristics are culturally specific and subject to continuous negotiation and change.

Interactive speaking: Particularly interactive speaking, where two or more speakers engage in conversation, is often seen as the most difficult of all the skills (cf. example for interpretation). Here, speakers negotiate and co-construct meaning and manage taking turns in conversation. Almost simultaneously they need to conceptualise, formulate, articulate and monitor their own speech production (cf. the illustration of cognitive process in chapter 7.1)

Example   **Mastering small talk**

The following extract is taken from a small talk at a party. It contains typical features of spoken English and gives us a sense of what is involved in the mastery of seemingly easy small talk.

A	*Hi.*
B	*Oh hi, how are you?*
A	*Good, good, fine.*
B	*So you have just arrived from Tel Aviv.*
A	*Yes, Tel Aviv.*
B	*All right (nods). ... Are you here on vacation?*
A	*No, no holiday.*
B	*Ah, I see. You are here for work?*
A	*No, family. My friend ... er ... partner is from New York.*

B	*Oh, that's nice. So, you must know the place already.*
A	*No, not really.*
B	*Ah, so …*
A	*Well. Actually, we live in Tel Aviv all the time … since 2010.*
B	*Really, so there is a lot to discover. What are you interested in?*
…	
B	*It was a pleasure talking to you.*
A	*Yeah, bye.*
B	*Bye.*

In this short exchange, the speakers co-operate in negotiating meaning. Partner B, who is highly proficient, helps partner A, who is a basic user of English, to manage the genre of casual conversation. In order to be successful speakers, they need to

- understand the pragmatic function of small talk, here establishing a friendly relationship with a stranger in interactional speaking;
- use fixed expressions and routines commonly used as discourse markers in small talk at their proposal (e. g. *all right, I see, really, well, it was a pleasure talking to you*);
- be able to manage the flow of conversation;
- be able to understand and produce formal or casual speech depending on the situation and the partners in communication;
- be fluent in making small talk on topics that are culturally acceptable/appropriate to make each other feel comfortable in the conversation (e. g. what do to in New York);
- use back-channelling which signals interest in the oral interaction verbally (e. g. *ah, that's right.*) or non-verbally (e. g. nodding of head);
- have a good command of opening and closing strategies.

Pronunciation: To get meaning across, speakers require knowledge about the phonological system of English on two levels: the **segmental level** (micro-level) that is concerned with individual vowels and consonants and their combinations, and the **suprasegmental level** (macro-level) that goes beyond the individual word and deals with stress, rhythm and intonation. In our mental lexicon, form and meaning of a word are usually connected to its pronunciation and need not be reconstructed every time we speak, whereas stress and intonation depend on the message a speaker wants to convey. Surprisingly, these suprasegmental features are particularly important with regard to the intelligibility of a speaker's message (cf. Setter/Jenkins 2005, 9). **Intelligibility** is the degree to which a speaker's utterance can be understood by a listener. Consequently, teaching learners stress, rhythm and intonation directly impacts on communicative success. Therefore, pronunciation practice should be incorporated from the very start of language learning with a focus on segmental as well as suprasegmental features.

It is a well-known phenomenon that we tend to perceive every new language through the lens of the languages we have learned in the past. The pronunciation of these languages and, in particular, our mother tongue (L1) interfere with the way we speak English. As the pronunciation of any language is closely linked to our identity, some learners may not strive to annihilate all traces of their mother tongue from English. Thus, intelligibility should be the primary goal of pronunciation instruction in most contexts.

Native-like accent versus intelligibility: In former times, pronunciation that fell short of a native-like accent was considered defective and an obstacle to intelligibility. The goal of a native-like accent has since been heavily questioned and is thought to be largely unattainable (cf. Han/Selinker 2005, 457). Researchers like Jenkins (2000) have pointed out that mutual intelligibility is a far more realistic and desirable target, as English is increasingly used as a Lingua Franca (ELF). It has been shown that when focussing on intelligibility, explicit instruction can have a significant impact on the quality of language (cf. Thomson/Derwing 2015).

Definition	English as a lingua franca (ELF) refers to the use of English as a shared language of communication across linguacultural boundaries among people who speak different first languages.

Non-native speakers of English: Statistics suggest that, nowadays, about a quarter of the world population is fluent in English and three in four speakers of English are non-native speakers (cf. Crystal 2003). Gradually, researchers have accumulated data and knowledge about ELF as a potential basis for informed educational decisions on how to foster international intelligibility (e. g. VOICE 2013). But whether a non-regional, common core form of English should serve as a basis for language learning curricula is up for debate (cf. Schneider 2011, 215 ff.).

The quality of learners' speech: Knowledge of language and discourse, active command of communication strategies and mastery of the skill of speaking under the pressures of cognitive processes as shown in Levelt's model of speech production (cf. illustration 7.1) form the basis of speaking. Cognitive and affective demands have a high impact on the quality of spoken language. Time constraints and the demand to process and produce language simultaneously may lead learners to the limits of what they can achieve in real-time communication. Thus, in a challenging situation, speakers may not be able to produce a correct grammatical structure even though they know the underlying rule.

As speakers mainly focus on meaning in oral interaction, they might sacrifice accuracy to get their message across. Under such constraints, spontaneity and creativity in using the foreign language can enable a foreign language speaker to produce a maximum of meaning with a minimum of language knowledge.

Key features of learners' speech: The quality of a learner's speech is determined by its fluency, accuracy and complexity.

Levels of proficiency: Of course, foreign language learners achieve different levels of oral proficiency in the target language due to various individual factors of second language acquisition (e. g. motivation, language

	Definition	Focus
Fluency	speech where message is communicated coherently with few pauses and hesitations, causing minimal comprehension difficulties	meaning
Accuracy	speech where the message is communicated using correct grammar, lexis and pronunciation	form
Complexity	speech where the message is communicated precisely and appropriately to the context and the partners in communication, using more advanced grammatical forms and differentiated lexis	meaning and form

Table 7.2:
Key features of
learners' speech

learning aptitude and age) and due to differences in the instructional environment (e. g. number of teaching hours, exposure to target language and quality of learning opportunities).

Common European Framework of Reference: The *Common European Framework of Reference* (CEFR) issued descriptions of proficiency in the form of can-do-statements (cf. chapter 2 in this volume). The CEFR provides a basis for the design of modern language syllabuses, examinations, textbooks etc. across Europe. »It describes [...] what learners have to do in order to use a language for communication and what knowledge and skills they have to develop so as to be able to act effectively« (Council of Europe 2001). Table 7.3 contains characteristics of social conversation on the levels of the CEFR.

7.1.3 | Approaches to teaching and learning speaking

From awareness-raising to appropriation to autonomous speaking: Knowing about processes of oral language production, the nature of spoken discourse and about the quality of learners' speech forms the basis for teaching speaking in the foreign language classroom. From a methodological perspective, speaking skills can be developed by moving from awareness-raising activities to appropriation before encouraging students to communicate autonomously, flanked by continuous training of pronunciation.

Three different perspectives: From a **behaviourist perspective**, mastery of speaking can be attained by habit formation through repetition and reinforcement. From the perspective of **sociocultural theory**, learning is socially mediated (cf. chapter 5 in this volume). This implies that language learners continuously improve their speaking skills by interacting with a peer or teacher (interlocutor) in a scaffolded environment. From a **cognitivist perspective**, learners are equipped with a capacity for information processing. Therefore, learning a complex competence such as speaking is viewed as a learning process that moves from noticing to controlled processing to automatic processing. Theorists, coming from these perspectives, try to explain how humans acquire a language within diverse social and instructional settings. An all-encompassing theory of language learning is still a long way off, though (cf. Lightbown/Spada 2013, 120 f.).

Proficient user	C2	Can converse comfortably and appropriately, unhampered by any linguistic limitations in conducting a full social and personal life.
	C1	Can use language flexibly and effectively for social purposes, including emotional, allusive and joking usage.
Independent user	B2	Can engage in extended conversion on most general topics in a clearly participatory fashion, even in a noisy environment. Can sustain relationships with native speakers without unintentionally amusing or irritating them or requiring them to behave other than they would with a native speaker. Can convey degrees of emotion and highlight the personal significance of events and experiences.
	B1	Can enter unprepared into conversations on familiar topics. Can follow clearly articulated speech directed at him/her in everyday conversation though will sometimes have to ask for repetition of particular words and phrases. Can maintain a conversation or discussion but may sometimes be difficult to follow when trying to say exactly what he/she would like to. Can express and respond to feelings such as surprise, happiness, sadness, interest and indifference.
Basic user	A2	Can establish social contact: greetings and farewells; introductions; giving thanks. Can generally understand clear, standard speech on familiar matters directed at him/her, provided he/she can ask for repetition or reformulation from time to time. Can participate in short conversations in routine contexts on topics of interest. Can express how he/she feels in simple terms, and express thanks.
		Can handle very short social exchanges but is rarely able to understand enough to keep conversation going of his/her own accord, though he/she can be made to understand if the speaker will take the trouble. Can use simple everyday polite forms of greeting and address. Can make and respond to invitations, suggestions and apologies. Can say what he/she likes and dislikes.
	A1	Can make an introduction and use basic greeting and leave-taking expressions. Can ask how people are and react to news. Can understand everyday expressions aimed at the satisfaction of simple needs of a concrete type, delivered directly to him/her in clear, slow and repeated speech by a sympathetic speaker.

Table 7.3: Characteristics of conversation in the Common European Framework of Reference (CEFR)

> Scaffolding has become a much-used term in English language teach-
> ing. Originally, Bruner (1978) defines scaffolding metaphorically as
> »the steps taken to reduce the degrees of freedom in carrying out
> some tasks so that the child can concentrate on the difficult skill she is
> in the process of acquiring« (quoted in Gibbons 2015, 16). In this defi-
> nition, scaffolded learning is a process whereby learners take on more
> and more control of their language production in a framework of repe-
> tition and variation of complex linguistic actions provided by teachers.
> Gibbons (2015, 13 ff.) views scaffolding as »situated help« in what Vy-
> gotsky (1978) terms the zone of proximal development. Here scaf-
> folded situations are created by helping learners to achieve beyond
> their current language proficiency by asking questions or providing
> prompts.

Definition

Thornbury (2005a, 38 f.) points out that each of these theories is based on
a different concept of mind, but, nevertheless, they all incorporate similar
stages of learning how to speak:

1. First, learners need to become **aware of new linguistic and cultural
   aspects** of spoken language.
2. Then, the new knowledge needs to be **appropriated** by integrating it
   into already existing systems with speakers gaining more and more
   control over their mental processes and their knowledge.
3. And finally, each theory acknowledges that the new forms become
   available to the speakers by some form of automatisation, making
   them more and more **autonomous.**

Speaking activities for different stages (cf. Thornbury 2005a)

Example

1. **Awareness-raising activities:** Listening to scripted, semi-scripted or
   authentic recordings while focussing on features of spoken language,
   e. g. organisation, sociocultural aspects, topic, performance effects,
   communication strategies, speech acts, discourse markers, features of
   spoken grammar and vocabulary, stress and intonation.
2. **Appropriation activities:** Practice with less and less control by teachers and peers, e. g. starting with chants, writing as preparation for
   speaking, reading aloud, flow-diagram conversations and dialogues
   with assisted performance and scaffolding.
3. **Fostering automaticity and autonomy:** Tasks with minimal assistance from the teacher under real operating conditions, e. g. academic
   presentations, drama, role-plays and simulations, discussions and debates and outside of class speaking.

On their path to fully **autonomous speakers** of a foreign language, learners move through stages of becoming aware of relevant new input to ap-
propriating new language and, finally, to building up routines and automatising language use. At this last stage, speakers have more cognitive

room for higher level processes like spontaneously adjusting to a new communicational situation.

Pushed output: Researchers, like Swain (1985), stress that being pushed to use the language is imperative for learning how to perform in a foreign language (comprehensible output-hypothesis). Therefore, designing tasks that elicit the use of English should be at the centre of our language classrooms. Using group work or pair work, starting out with easy language and carefully choosing topics and tasks that stimulate interest as well as providing a friendly, non-threatening learning environment stimulate a high level of participation in speaking activities, like jigsaw tasks, ranking activities, problem-solving activities or role-plays (for concrete examples cf. Klippel 2012; Ur 2015). Ideally, learners are given the opportunity to repeat tasks to maximise effects of automatisation.

Teaching pronunciation: Not all students might want to acquire native-speaker-like proficiency, still their English should be intelligible. To avoid fossilisation of erroneous articulation, there should be a focus on pronunciation in the early years of language learning. Most important features to teach are:

- **consonants:** students might mispronounce consonants as in */ba-nilla/ milkshake
- **consonant clusters:** students might miss out consonants in a cluster and replace them with vowels, */sipot/ for spot
- **vowel length:** students might mix up long and short vowels, e. g. tins vs. teens, this /thees/ these
- **word stress:** students might stress the wrong syllable as in *Event instead of eVENT, *baby-SIT instead of BABy-sit
- **tonic words that bear the principal stress in the sentence:** students might not focus on the most important word as in A: *»Was it expensive?«, B: »It was quite exPENsive!«

A basic cycle of pronunciation teaching moves from modelling and focused language perception to choral repetition on to individual repetition of segmental and suprasegmental features. It is particularly beneficial, though, to start with awareness-raising activities and explicit explanations of how to articulate sounds and patterns to imitation and free production.

Definition

> Fossilisation is a phenomenon whereby inaccurate linguistic items become permanent in a learner's interlanguage (cf. chapter 5 in this volume). A foreign accent can be interpreted a result of fossilisation. Experts suggest that fossilisation occurs in case of insufficient attention to accuracy in teaching. Therefore, learners need exposure to form-focussed as well as meaning-focussed activities.

Teaching speaking to young learners: In the primary classroom, children develop their speaking skills in a playful way, often using songs, games and role-play on top of varied practice with a strong element of repetition. In order to give them the opportunity to experiment with language, young learners of English need input that focuses on verbs and structure words, not just on nouns (cf. Groot-Wilken et al. 2007, 32). A strong focus on pronunciation is important, as errors in pronunciation are prone to fossilisation. Legutke et al. (2014, 53 f.) list the following principles for developing speaking skills in the primary classroom:

- Find a balance between listening and speaking.
- Use English as a means of communication in the classroom.
- Present new language using gesture, mime and action.
- Encourage learners to interact spontaneously and give them support to get their message across.

Empirical data on the outcome of English language teaching in primary school are provided by the EVENING- and the BIG-study (cf. Engel et al. 2009; BIG-Kreis 2015).

7.1.4 | Assessing speaking

For test designers and test administrators, testing speaking is a challenge of its own due to the varied nature of the competence itself and issues of test quality criteria (cf. chapter 14 in this volume). Now, standardised oral tests have become established on all levels of teaching and learning English in German secondary schools. Particularly high-stakes tests like university entrance exams must be valid, objective and reliable. Therefore, testers need to have a clear idea of the construct that is tested. Standardised test formats and task types as well as testing scales for speaking and observation sheets serve as a basis for good testing practice.

Formats of speaking examinations: Speaking examinations are notoriously difficult to design and organise. Formats vary from non-interactive tasks, where test takers respond to verbal, visual or written prompts to one-on-one interactive tasks to discussions and role-plays with multiple partners. Oral test types include:

- **Live or recorded presentations:** Here, test takers prepare and present a short talk on pre-selected topics. If recordings are made, they can then be graded independently by different raters.
- **Role-plays:** Candidates are asked to take on a role well known to them, like being a customer in a restaurant. The other role is either played by another student or the tester. Students could, for example, discuss preparations for a birthday party.
- **Interactive tasks and discussions:** As the candidates are not asked to take on roles based on additional information, the stimulus should include material that is already known and appealing to the test takers.

Some genres of speaking hardly ever get tested. Interactive conversation is by far the most prominent genre of speaking, but it is also the most elusive: In social conversation information is co-constructed and shared just as much as relationships and social identities are formed. Performative, emotional and creative aspects of language use like jokes, storytelling and word-play are the vital ingredients of this kind of interaction. None of these skills get focused on in most current tests of spoken English. Thus, the construct of spoken English has not yet been fully taken into account (cf. Hughes 2011, 84).

Marking and assessment criteria

IELTS speaking test: »IELTS (International English Language Testing System) is the world's most popular English language test« (British Council 2017, emphasis PK). As part of this extensive test, speaking is assessed for 11 to 14 minutes in a face-to-face interview. Candidates are assessed on their use of spoken English to answer short questions, to speak at length on a familiar topic and also to interact with the examiner. The following criteria are used in the IELTS speaking-test (cf. UCLES 2015, 18):

- **Fluency and coherence:** This criterion refers to the ability to talk with normal levels of continuity, rate and effort and to link ideas and language together to form coherent, connected speech. The key indicators of fluency are speech rate and speech continuity. The key indicators of coherence are logical sequencing of sentences, clear marking of stages in a discussion, narration or argument and the use of cohesive devices (e. g. connectors, pronouns and conjunctions) within and between sentences.
- **Lexical resource:** This criterion refers to the range of vocabulary the candidate can use and the precision with which meanings and attitudes can be expressed. The key indicators are the variety of words used, the adequacy and appropriacy of the words used and the ability to circumlocute (get around a vocabulary gap by using other words) with or without noticeable hesitation.
- **Grammatical range and accuracy:** This criterion refers to the range as well as the accurate and appropriate use of the candidate's grammatical resource. The key indicators of grammatical range are the length and complexity of the spoken sentences, the appropriate use of subordinate clauses and the range of sentence structures, especially to move elements around for information focus. The key indicators of grammatical accuracy are the number of grammatical errors in a given amount of speech and the communicative effect of error.
- **Pronunciation:** This criterion refers to the ability to produce comprehensible speech to fulfil the speaking test requirements. The key indicators will be the amount of strain caused to the listener, the amount of the speech which is unintelligible and the noticeability of L1 influence.

7.2 | Writing: the process of writing and how to teach it

There are many uses to which writing is put in the real world. We use writing in order to transcend time and space when we record something for later or send a message to another person at the other end of the world. We also write to store information either electronically or on paper and we use it to clarify our ideas. To language learners writing is also important as a mnemonic technique, e. g. when revising vocabulary.

7.2.1 | Understanding writing

Recently, researchers have often focused on the spoken word rather than on the written. But written language cannot just be seen as spoken language fixed in a text that can be read. In comparison to speaking, written English tends to be more uniform. In writing, we are much more conscious of the formal aspects of language and, often, we have more time to consider the quality of our texts.

Text types: Writing has very distinct text types, for example, a narrative text, a letter of application, a dictionary entry or a letter to the editor of a newspaper. Visual information can be included to produce discontinuous texts, e. g. tables, graphs and diagrams and computer mediated communication have created new genres of written texts.

Writing and technology: A major part of our daily writing activities is carried out in computer networked environments. New genres such as e-mail, social media posts and texts have emerged and expanded the traditional boundaries of the English language classroom. In blogs, for example, regular journal entries are published including text, audio and/or video for means of self-expression and creativity. Consequently, L2 learners need to develop multiliteracies (cf. chapter 12 in this volume) beyond mere writing of texts to be able to comprehend and create combinations of word, image and video to form multimodal texts.

Now, English language learners can use and develop their newly acquired writing skills for online communication across the globe. Online corpora and dictionaries can be accessed to facilitate writing. Word processors make it easy for L2 learners to draft, re-draft and edit texts either on their own or in collaborative learning arrangements. Teachers and peers can provide context-specific feedback using a track changes function via e-mail (cf. Levy 2009).

Developing writing skills not only involves **linguistic development** (accuracy, complexity, fluency, cohesion and coherence), but also **knowledge** about genre and text production processes, **metalinguistic knowledge** (planning, monitoring and evaluating) and **use of strategies**, writing goals and motivation (cf. Polio 2017, 261). In developing as writers, learners also focus on different goals in different phases. Whereas beginners in writing might concentrate on increasing the complexity of their syntactical constructions, more advanced writers might work on aspects of style and register.

7.2.2 | Approaches to teaching and learning writing

Table 7.4:
Overview of main
approaches to
writing

Process-based approaches	Genre/text-based approaches
Focus on the process of writing mainly from a cognitive point of view	Focus on the product of writing by examining e. g. the formal surface elements and discourse structure of sample texts
How do writers create good texts?	What makes a good text?

In teaching writing, two major approaches can be identified, each of them focussing on different aspects: **a process-approach** and a **genre-approach**. Moreover, reader-based and creative writing approaches now play a role in classroom instruction.

Process-based approach: ›How do writers create a good text?‹ is the underlying question of a process-based writing approach. This approach focuses not so much on the product, but on the process of writing. In this process, writers gradually create a text by means of discovery and thinking. Here, writing is seen as a dynamic, non-linear and recursive process in which meaning is generated and knowledge is transformed into texts. This process takes place in phases that were described by Flower and Hayes (1981). The main sub-processes of the cognitive engagement of producing a written text are:

1. setting goals
2. generating ideas
3. organising information
4. selecting appropriate language
5. making a draft
6. reading and reviewing
7. revising and editing

During this complex process, writers might start by planning, drafting and revising and then go back again to re-planning and drafting before they move on to checking spelling in their final draft. With growing experience and skill, writers start to compose in different ways than novices. Overall, skilled writers achieve more positive effects by using planning and revising strategies.

Following a process-approach to writing, teachers would set **pre-writing tasks** to generate ideas about the content but also the structure of a piece of writing. They would encourage brainstorming and subsequent structuring activities. Often teachers require their students to produce several drafts based on teacher and peer feedback while asking their learners to postpone surface corrections until the final editing. Finally, a lot of teachers would display finished work (cf. Hyland 2009, 24).

Genre-/text-based approaches: Genre- or text-based approaches focus on the question ›What makes a good text?‹ as well as taking into account their own communicative intentions. Hence, analysing and imitating the style and content of sample texts and their sociolinguistic context is at the heart of genre-/text-based approaches.

In genre-based pedagogy, developing an understanding of the social context within which texts are situated is the proper entry point of instruction. A focus then on the linguistic and rhetorical features of a text should only come after a social context has been established (cf. Myskow/Gordon 2010, 284).

Genre-/text-based teaching of writing regularly follows a step-by-step procedure:

1. helping students to identify their writing needs
2. building awareness of discourse organisation
3. helping students to develop crafting skills
4. enabling students to apply criteria of an effective text

Working with standardised texts: Genre-/text-based writing approaches are particularly effective when working with highly standardised texts, such as postcards, letters, different newspaper genres, essays or academic papers. Learners with less command of the target language and reading experience often find this approach highly effective, as it provides concrete orientation and, above all, chunks of language to use in their own writing (cf. Hallet 2016). According to Hyland (2009, 17 f.), additional advantages to genre-based writing instruction are:

- Genre-based writing instruction tends to be highly explicit, as the end-product is the primary focus.
- A focus on genre offers a framework for concentrating on language, textual organisation and communicative contexts alike.
- Genre-based approaches help identify the student's immediate needs for writing a specific text. Ideally, learners can choose language and textual organisation from a variety of model texts.
- Genre-based instruction can have an empowering effect on the learners.

Creative writing: Communicative language teaching has put great emphasis on utilitarian aspects of language use. In creative writing, students rather produce texts that have an aesthetic value. Stories, poems, letters, blogs, travelogues, dialogues, jokes and a huge number of other genres are created. Drawing on close observation, imagination, personal memories but also the experience of reading creative texts, English learners engage with the foreign language in a playful way. In creative writing, the knowledge of a particular genre serves as a necessary starting point for the student's own playful and imaginative engagement with the English language and its literary forms. Here, the restrictions of the genre often foster rather than impede the writer's imagination.

What benefits could creative writing bring to the ELT classroom? Ideally, L2 learners become sensitised to rhyme, rhythm, stress and intonation of the foreign language and by attempting to express personally relevant meanings, the language used becomes all the more memorable. Learners might also feel empowered by realising what they can achieve with the English they have already learned (for teaching ideas see Spiro 2004; Wright/Hill 2009; Sara/Elis 2017).

Empirically validated writing strategies: Research into L1 writing suggests several writing strategies that can be transferred to L2 writing context. Based on a meta-study of research publications, Graham and Perin (2007, 11) recommend a list of scientifically validated writing strategies for L1 writing, in particular, self-regulated writing strategies. Some of the following strategies are genre-specific and others rather general (cf. Graham/Harris 2009, 39 ff.):

Writing strategies

- **TREE** (topic sentence—reasons—examine each reason—ending) is a planning strategy for argumentative texts. First, writers would formulate a topic sentence, then give at least three reasons to support the topic sentence. Next, they would explain their reasons and, lastly, they would formulate a statement to summarise the topic sentence.
- **Vocabulary** is a strategy for writing narrative texts. Here, learners are asked to brainstorm actions for telling a story and to describe words and phrases to use it in. In the next step, they formulate full sentences and paragraphs based on the chosen vocabulary.
- **CDO** (compare—diagnose—operate) is a revising strategy for all text genres, where each sentence is evaluated and modified according to criteria.

Strategy use: Most L2 writing strategies are similar to strategies used in the L1, but the transfer from L1 to L2 writing strategies is influenced by the learners' language proficiency as well as cultural and contextual factors (cf. Manchón et al. 2007). In writing, students need to engage proactively in a range of strategies to generate ideas, monitor and evaluate their progress and revise their texts. On top of that, they also need to actively regulate their motivation and use social-behavioural strategies, especially for feedback-handling but also for peer learning (cf. Zimmermann 2011). A first empirical study indicated that self-regulated learning strategies have significant predictive effects on EFL writing proficiency (cf. Teng/Zhang 2016).

Effects of feedback: Intervention studies that investigate the effects of instruction or the effects of different kinds of feedback and assessment are still thin on the ground. Polio (2017, 269) sees a particular need for well-designed longitudinal experimental studies in order to ascertain the most effective source of students' development in writing in a foreign language. Overall, there is no approach that would inevitably produce good writers. Apart from well-managed cognitive processes, general experience in writing as well as a sense of self and audience form the basis of writing competence. Therefore, teachers should carefully monitor the writing needs of their students and combine a variety of approaches throughout the L2 writing development accordingly.

7.2.3 | Feedback and the assessment of writing

A growing body of research is investigating the effect of corrective feedback on L2 writing. Recent studies indicate that provision of error correction is effective (cf. Bitchener/Storch 2016). As a basis for future studies and pedagogical decision-making, Ellis (2009) identified various options to provide and to process corrective feedback in the ELT classroom. According to him, teachers' strategies for providing feedback are:

- **direct strategies:** indicating and/or locating the error
- **meta-linguistic feedback:** use of error codes (e. g. V = vocabulary, G = grammar, T = tense) or brief grammatical descriptions
- **scope of focus:** unfocused feedback (extensive) on all errors or focussed feedback (intensive) on pre-selected types of errors
- **electronic feedback:** indication of error and hyperlink to concordance with examples of correct usage

Feedback strategies

Peer-feedback refers to »the use of learners as sources of information and interactants for each other in such a way that learners assume roles and responsibilities normally taken on by a formally trained teacher, tutor or editor in commenting on and critiquing each other's drafts in both written and oral formats in the process of writing« (Liu/Hansen 2002, 1). Peer-feedback is increasingly used in ELT classrooms, not least because its use has been supported by a number of theories of second language acquisition and writing, like process writing theory, collaborative learning and sociocultural theory. Researchers have intensively invested in the following question: How effective is peer-feedback compared with teacher and self-feedback? Hard evidence on the causes of improvements in writing skills is not yet available, but most recent studies on immediate impacts of different forms of feedback on text revision and the quality of writing indicate that teacher feedback and peer-feedback can serve different purposes in students' text production: peer-feedback can offer the opportunity to discuss topics and contents whereas teacher feedback provides information on how to improve linguistic form and style of a text. Therefore, multiple sources of feedback should be used in lessons on writing (cf. Yu/Lee 2016). Curiously, one study suggests that students who give feedback benefit more than students who receive feedback (cf. Berggren 2015).

Students' use of feedback: Students may be required to use the feedback for a revision of their texts and for future orchestration of their writing strategies. Students could, for example, apply an additional proofreading technique like scanning individual words rather than proofreading entire sentences. Not surprisingly, no ›best way‹ to give feedback to students' writing was found. This is probably due to the complex nature of teaching contexts and individual learner differences. Different learners at different stages of their foreign language development need different kinds of feedback to their written texts. Therefore, it is important for teachers to have a repertoire of techniques to choose from.

Writing tests: Like in any other area of language testing, writing tests can serve the purpose of diagnosis, testing proficiency or measuring achievement. Writing tests can range from mere assessment of the language that is used, e. g. in sentence-completion tasks, to tasks that correspond closely to real-world writing tasks, e. g. writing a letter to the editor. Writing can be assessed in one-off in-class tests or over a course of time in the format of a portfolio.

Example **Portfolio assessment**

A writing portfolio is a collection of written texts for different purposes over a period of time. Portfolios allow the learners to display a range of writing performances in different genres. They reflect the learning situation and demonstrate what the writer has achieved over time. Students have the opportunity to select the writing pieces to be included. Therefore, they have a high level of control and the chance to reflect and self-assess. Evaluation is delayed and provides the means to measure development over time. One of the most prominent benefits of portfolio assessment is that it comprises a variety of writing samples. Also, including multiple drafts of essays gives the teacher insights into how the L2-writers master different sub-skills of writing, like drafting or revising (cf. Cushing-Weigle 2002, 202 ff.).

Criteria for test usability: When devising a test, language teachers need to consider the use it is put to. Bachman and Palmer (1996, 17 f.) defined six criteria for test usability: **reliability, construct validity, authenticity, interactiveness, impact** and **practicality**. As Cushing-Weigle (2002, 175) notes, in-class tests devised by teachers are mainly interested in questions like »How can I tell whether my students have met the writing goals of the class? How will the results of this test help my students improve their writing? How can I design writing prompts that my students are interested in?« In order to maximise the positive effect of writing assessment, Cushing-Weigle (ibid.) suggests the following principles:

- Evaluate not just in-class but out-of-class writing.
- Evaluate more than one writing sample.
- Build authenticity and interactiveness into timed writing tasks.
- Use scoring instruments that are specific to the assignment and to the instructional focus of the class and that provide useful feedback to the students.

7.3 | Foreign language mediation: new skills for English language teaching

Over the past years, mediation tasks have become a core component in English language courses. This could be due to their relevance for everyday multilingual communication, where English is used as a **lingua franca**. On top of that, mediating between two languages also helps to extend the variety of interaction in the communicative classroom. Moreover, the general value of own-language activities for the language learning process has been recognized (cf. Kerr 2014).

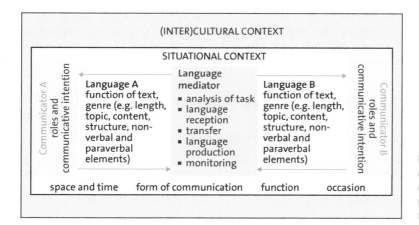

Illustration 7.2:
Model of language
mediation
(adapted from
Kolb 2016, 137)

7.3.1 | Defining foreign language mediation

In the Common European Framework of Reference, mediation is defined as a process where »the language user is not concerned to express his/her own meaning, but simply to act as an intermediary between interlocutors who are unable to understand each other directly—normally (but not exclusively) speakers of a different language« (Council of Europe 2001, 87 f.). Whereas translation is often viewed as a close reproduction of the original text, mediation focuses on communicating the most relevant information for a particular audience (cf. E. Kolb 2016, 12 f.). Further research has shown that mediators also transform the information and the language of a source text to a target text, depending on the communicative purpose set by the task and the context (cf. Stathopoulou 2015, 32).

Different strategies: Transformation takes place as mediators apply **information strategies** (e. g. making explicit connections between ideas) or **language strategies** (e. g. paraphrasing key words from the original text). When mediating the content of a holiday brochure to a much younger sibling, for example, the mediator might leave out information that would be too difficult to understand (information strategy) and paraphrase vocabulary that could be unknown to the younger sibling (language strategy). Kolb (2016, 179 f.) has shown that successful mediation requires activating linguistic, cultural, pragmatic, strategic, social interactive and discourse competences. Because of this complexity, she argues, mediation could be seen as a fifth competence and not just as another format of activities within the framework of task-based teaching.

As shown in illustration 7.2, a mediation between two or more speakers is framed by a specific (inter)cultural and situational context. In this context, the language mediator transfers a text from language A to language B taking into account the communicators' roles as well as their perceived communicative intentions. In this complex task, the mediator needs to analyse the task, decode the information provided, transfer the relevant information to the other communicator bearing potential (inter-) cultural gaps in understanding. Additionally, the mediator has to monitor language perception and production (cf. the model of language production by Levelt in illustration 7.1).

7.3.2 | Developing foreign language mediation skills

Example **Instructions and shortened text for mediation**

A German class is about to go on a high-school exchange to New York. Before they are about to leave, the exchange coordinator in New York informs the German class that extensive security measures are in place at the school in New York.

The US teacher and his students would like to know about security issues and measures at German high-schools. You have found the following interview in a German newspaper. Write an e-mail with the most important information for your counterparts.

Kameras lösen keine Probleme
Der CDU-Politiker Altmaier plädiert für Videokameras in Schulen. Der Sozialforscher Nils Zurawski sieht die Gefahren und meint: Dicke Schlösser schrecken genauso gut ab.

ZEIT online: Herr Zurawski, der CDU-Politiker Altmaier spricht sich auf Twitter für die Video-Überwachung unter anderem in Schulen aus. ...
Nils Zurawski: Sinnvoll ist die Videoüberwachung, wenn kein Schüler und kein Lehrer mehr auf dem Gelände ist [...]

Source: Parvin Sadigh, »Kameras lösen keine Probleme«, in: http://www.zeit.de/gesellschaft/schule/2011–11/schule-kamera-zurawski, 09.11.2011 (last access: 26.03.2012)
(adapted from: Sächsisches Staatsministerium für Kultus 2012, 3 f.)

Complex processes: The mediation task above was set to prepare students for the German A-levels. Typically, the task involves complex receptive and productive processes. Furthermore, the learners need to be aware of intercultural aspects, in this case, legal and cultural differences on the use of firearms and resulting dangers for public life. This example serves well to show the significance of **intercultural communicative competence** (cf. chapter 9 in this volume) for successful mediation.

Task formats for teaching mediation: From a teacher's perspective, mediation demands a high amount of teachers' content knowledge and pedagogical skill. Because of the multitude of demands while mediating, it is still difficult to establish a fixed progression for teaching. Therefore, Kolb (2016, 182 ff.) suggests offering a variety of tasks and formats, like role-plays, in order to fully develop this competence. In teaching and training mediation, teachers can break down the process of mediation into individual steps:

1. understanding context and task
2. setting goals for text reception
3. listening, reading and/or viewing
4. evaluating and selecting
5. creating and editing of new text

In class, they would provide help and practice in pre- and post-mediation activities, e. g. paraphrasing and vocabulary activation activities (pre-mediation) and comparing learners' versions to sample texts or evaluating the difficulties during the process (post-mediation) (cf. Kolb 2009).

7.4 | Conclusion

In class, most English learners strive to improve their productive language competences. Particularly in primary and lower secondary school, a strong focus has been put on speaking and to a lesser extent on writing. The mediation between two languages has become a frequent activity in English language classrooms. One must not forget, though, that productive competences can only develop on the basis of sound receptive competences: good readers, for example, often make good writers. Therefore, the teaching of competences should follow an integrated approach that balances all competences.

This chapter has set out to demonstrate that in order to design a useful methodology for teaching these competences, a deeper understanding of the complex underlying types of knowledge, processes, skills and genres is required. Speaking, writing and mediating fluently and accurately require concentration, effort and regular practice. The more often students need to communicate in writing and speaking, the more likely they are to improve. Clear tasks on interesting topics or questions guided by stimulating materials and a relaxed supportive atmosphere contribute to the students' willingness to communicate in speaking and writing. The repetition of tasks and activities also impacts highly on the development of productive competences.

However, it is also instrumental to positive learning outcomes in the English classroom that teachers experiment with different types of activities, topics and teaching objectives. As a consequence, every teacher needs to develop a principled approach to the teaching of the productive competences on the basis of their students' needs. But teachers also need to reflect on classroom dynamics, foreign language use and, ultimately, learning outcome. Finally, a high level of teachers' classroom management skills paves the way for adapting to the learners' needs by offering challenging activities and tasks that focus on language production.

Further reading

Goh, Christine/Burns, Anne (eds.) (2012): *Teaching Speaking. A Holistic Approach*. Cambridge.

Hallet, Wolfgang (2016): *Genres im fremdsprachlichen und bilingualen Unterricht. Formen und Muster der sprachlichen Interaktion*. Seelze.

Hyland, Ken ([2]2009): *Teaching and Researching Writing* [2002]. Harlow.

Kolb, Elisabeth (2016): *Sprachmittlung. Studien zur Modellierung einer komplexen Kompetenz*. Münster.

Thornbury, Scott (2005): *How to Teach Speaking*. Harlow.

Petra Kirchhoff

8 Focus on Form—The Lexico-Grammar Approach

Traditionally, there has been a clear-cut distinction between vocabulary and grammar in foreign language teaching. The prevailing attitude has been that **vocabulary** is about learning words, whereas **grammar** is about learning rules and generalisable patterns based on sentences. Vocabulary consists of a specific set of lexical items while the main function of grammar is to put words together in a rule-governed manner to construct new phrases and sentences. On the one hand, therefore, we talk about grammar lessons, pedagogic grammars and grammar tests. On the other hand, there are vocabulary lists, dictionaries and vocabulary tests.

However, this sharp distinction is misleading in many ways since there is a much greater closeness between both domains than is often perceived. In the following sections, the strong links between vocabulary and grammar will be outlined and the implications for the EFL classroom will be discussed.

8.1 | Lexico-grammar

Interaction between grammar and lexis: In English, as in any other language, there is a great deal of interaction between grammar and lexis. The main reasons for this are that every word has its own grammar (cf. Thornbury 2002, 122; Lewis 2008, 142) and words have specific grammatical relationships with others. Hence, each word contains a substantial amount of grammatical information and has its own grammatical profile, including, for instance, categories such as word class, tense or person. The adjective *good*, for example, has the comparative forms *better* and *best*. In addition to this, it is also often used in combination with other words: *fairly good, good-natured, good-humoured, to be no good, good to see you, be a good boy, good luck, have a good time* and so on.

Recurring patterns: When we look at the examples with *good*, it is obvious that we also find specific recurring syntactic patterns such as

- »to be + good + at + noun« (e. g. *to be good at maths/sports*),
- »to be + good + V-ing« (e. g. *to be good at skiing, keeping appointments, making friends*),

- »in + a + good + noun« (e. g. *in a good mood/state/way/condition*, etc.).

Proficient speakers use a vast array of such language patterns (cf. Willis 2003, 40) and it is obvious that language learners must recognise and gradually become familiar with these patterns as well.

Hence, it has become clear that »every word in a language is involved in a complex and unique network of patterns and relationships« (Swan 2005, 35). In particular, we may distinguish between **lexical patterns** (i. e. collocations) and **grammatical patterns** (i. e. colligations) words can be associated with. Both concepts refer to the likelihood with which lexical items can co-occur with other lexical items or with specific grammatical categories, respectively.

Collocations refer to the habitual co-occurrence of words, i. e. the ways words are combined to form multi-word units (cf. McCarthy et al. 2010, 28), such as *to have breakfast, a quick glance, to set a record, a good cause, to waste money, odd numbers* or *null and void*. It is obvious that words are attracted to some words more than to others. We talk about *fast food*, but not **quick food*. On the other hand, you can have a *quick lunch*, but not a **fast lunch*; people may *still their hunger* and *quench their thirst*, but not the other way round. These words are closely linked in the mind (cf. chapter 8.1.2) so that a word ›triggers‹ its associated collocates (cf. Willis 2003, 48).

Colligations (from Latin »tie together«), on the other hand, work on a syntactic level and refer to how words form specific grammatical patterns with other words. Words colligate, i. e. are tied together, with certain grammatical patterns.

Example | **Colligation patterns**

verb + -ing (*I started watching*)
verb + infinitive (*I began to watch*)
verb of perception + adjective (*it sounds great, it looks good*)
a + noun + of + noun (*a flock of seagulls, a school of fish, a group of people*)

Lexical items: These common language patterns demonstrate how »difficult it becomes to uphold the traditional split between vocabulary and grammar« (Cameron 2001, 72). It also shows that the term ›vocabulary‹, which typically only refers to single words, is not sufficient as a concept. Instead, it is more advisable to talk about ›lexis‹ and ›lexical items‹. The concept of ›lexis‹ is more comprehensive than ›vocabulary‹ since it does not only include single words (e. g. *bad*), but also habitual combinations of words (e. g. collocations such as *bad cold, bad dream, bad luck, bad mistake, bad press, bad blood*) and fixed or semi-fixed combinations of words or ›lexical chunks‹ (cf. chapter 8.1.2) that we seem to store and recall as single meaningful units (e. g. *to go from bad to worse, to have a bad time, things are in a bad way, that's bad for your health, in good times and bad*, etc.).

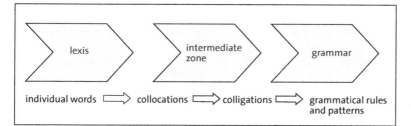

Lexico-grammatical approach: The relationship between grammar and lexis must rather be seen as a continuum (cf. e.g. Swan 2005, 38 f.) or spectrum (cf. Lewis 2008, 37). On one side of the continuum we find individual lexical items which are semantically strong (e.g. *Caution! Stop! Thanks a lot!*). On the other side of the continuum we find patterns which are purely grammatical (e.g. the use of the present continuous to indicate ongoing action: *She's working day and night to finish the deadline*). However, in between these extremes there is a large middle ground where the distinction between grammar and lexis can sometimes be rather unclear. For example, some lexical items such as prepositions, determiners or auxiliary words are almost ›meaningless‹ since they fulfil a purely grammatical function. The auxiliary verb *do* as in *Do you know where Peter is?* or *I don't know* simply helps to construct questions or negatives, but has no lexical meaning as such in these sentences. Prepositions can have a clear temporal meaning (*after, before, on*) or spatial meaning (*under, above, in*), but are still often seen as part of grammar. Like other function words—such as determiners (*a, the, that*) or pronouns (*she, her, herself*)—prepositions have little or no referential meaning per se, but simply serve a grammatical purpose (cf. Swan 2005, 35). It might also be argued that collocations and colligations represent an intermediate zone between vocabulary and grammar (cf. Scrivener 2011, 187).

Thus, rather than regarding grammar and lexis as two different entities, which need to be treated in an isolated way in the classroom, it makes much more sense to adopt a lexico-grammatical approach for the classroom (cf. Müller-Hartmann/Schocker-v. Ditfurth 2011, 210). If we accept this perspective, this also means that vocabulary and grammar should not be learned and taught separately, but in combination. While it is important that learners can draw on a broad grammatical outline, it is at least equally important that they become familiar with the specific patterning of individual words and how they combine with other words.

8.1.1 | Focusing on chunks of language

Lexical chunks: Much of what we say or write consists of multi-word expressions. Some estimates have claimed that the amount of formulaic language in ordinary English usages ranges up to 80 per cent (cf. Swan 2005, 38). For instance, a single lexical item such as ›time‹ can be found

Type	Form	Examples
Collocation	e.g. adj. + noun	*light winds, torrential rain, thick fog, heavy rain*
Compound	e.g. noun + noun	*fingerprint, lawsuit, textbook, living-room, distance learning*
Prepositional phrase	e.g. preposition + noun phrase	*in a few days, in three years, in a fortnight, in a week*
Phrasal verb	verb + particle	*to get by, get away with sth., get across, get around, get into sth., get on with sb., get off, get over sth.*
Binominals	noun + and + noun; adj. + and + adj.; verb + and + verb	*fish and chips, salt and pepper, sick and tired, rant and rave*
Trinominals	noun + noun + and + noun; adj. + adj. + and + adj.	*lock, stock and barrel; left, right and centre; signed, sealed, delivered*
Simile	as + adj. + as	*as dry as a bone, as hard as nails, as free as a bird*
Idiom	whole clause or sentence	*to get on like a house on fire, to kill two birds with one stone, to sell like hot cake, Elvis has left the building.*
Proverb	full sentence	*Every dog has its day. A rolling stone gathers no moss. A stitch in time saves nine.*

Table 8.1:
Types of lexical
chunks

in hundreds of so-called ›lexical chunks‹, for example *a long time, all the time, any time soon, in time, idle time, time limit, to ask the time, all time high/low, to have a good time, a stitch in time saves nine, from time to time, once upon a time.*

Definition

> **Lexical chunks** may be defined as prefabricated strings of words that are frequently used in spoken or written interactions and that are typically stored as ready-made units in our memory (cf. Lindstromberg/ Boers 2008, 8).

Lexical chunks can occur in very different shapes (cf. McCarthy et al. 2010, 51 ff.; Hutz 2014) and can vary considerably in terms of fixedness. While some of these ›chunks‹ form relatively loose or semi-fixed combinations (e. g. collocations), others appear to be almost ›frozen‹ (e. g. idioms and proverbs).

Advantages of lexical chunks: Knowing and using lexical chunks is very beneficial in the context of second language learning. In particular, the following benefits can be mentioned:

- **Successful interactions**: Lexical chunks help learners to communicate successfully because they serve many relevant interactive functions. For example, many social formulae consist of lexical chunks (e. g.

Have a good time! See you later. Pleased to meet you.). Some expressions may help to soften a message (e. g. ›hedging expressions‹ such as *if you know what I mean* or *as far as I'm concerned*); alternatively they may serve as discourse markers or text connectors (e. g. *by the way, as a matter of fact* or *the point is*).

- **Idiomatic use of language:** Using frequent chunks makes learners sound natural and idiomatic. For example, there are numerous phrases which include *'ll* (e. g. *I'll give you a call. I'll drop by. I'll be back in a minute. I'll get back to you. We'll see. It'll be alright. That'll do.*). Lewis (2008, 97) claims that such highly institutionalised phrases and sentences often seem much more natural and idiomatic and help learners to avoid unnatural ›EFL-speak‹ which is often found in textbooks.
- **Fluency:** Multi-word items are learned, stored and retrieved as one lexical unit which also makes language processing and recall faster and eventually leads to greater fluency (cf. McCarthy et al. 2010, 54). Breaking down fixed phrases into their constituent parts or composing such phrases anew each time only slows down the process of language comprehension and production.
- **Accuracy:** Lexical chunks help learners to create ›islands of accuracy‹ since learners do not have to worry about formal correctness.
- **Flexibility:** Chunks provide learners with lexical alternatives and stylistic choice. For instance, instead of using the common intensifier *very* expressions such as *bitterly cold* and *pitch dark* can be used (cf. McCarthy/Dell 2005, 6).

Thus, having a stock of ready-made chunks at one's disposal should be an essential part of the learning process. However, there are also numerous problems associated with the learning of fixed phrases (cf. McCarthy et al. 2010, 34 f.). Since English is a highly idiomatic language, even language learners with a high degree of proficiency have problems with fixed expressions. Here are some of the most common problem areas:

Problem area	Comment	Examples
Meaning	The metaphorical meaning may not be transparent for learners.	The meaning of idiomatic expressions such as *to be out on a limb, once in a blue moon, to be snowed under* or *at your fingertips* may be opaque for learners.
Cross-linguistic influence	Learners may feel inclined to transfer idiomatic expressions from their mother tongue to English.	*A drop in the ocean* (in German *ein Tropfen auf dem heißen Stein*), *to beat someone black and blue* (*jemanden grün und blau schlagen*)
Frequency	Learners often find it difficult to know whether a chunk is frequently used or not.	A phrase like *it's raining cats and dogs* tends to be overused by learners while some other common expressions *it never rains but it pours* or *rain or shine* are often rather underused.

Table 8.2:
Lexical chunks:
common problem
areas

Problem area	Comment	Examples
Fixedness	Some lexical chunks tend to be rather loose combinations of words while others tend to be fixed.	*Sick and cold* appear to be a rather loose combination, whereas *sick and tired* is a fixed combination.
Collocations	It can be difficult for learners to predict the collocations of specific words, in particular with regard to words which are close in meaning.	*Make and do* collocate with different nouns: e. g. *do homework, do damage* vs. *make coffee, make breakfast*.
Register	Some lexical chunks may only occur in informal speech, others may sound formal or even archaic.	Phrases like *to kick the bucket* or *to be pushing up the daisies* are associated with informal speech.

Table 8.2
(continued):
Lexical chunks:
common problem
areas

Thus, lexical chunks are very complex and a lot of information needs to be stored and recalled by learners if they want to use these words correctly. A great amount of information about lexical items has to be stored in the mind, including information about the meaning, the form (e. g. pronunciation and spelling) and its use (cf. chapter 8.2.1).

8.1.2 | The mental lexicon

When we communicate with other people, we can recognise and produce words in fractions of seconds. This is only possible because we have the ability to store and retrieve words very efficiently in a word archive, which is commonly referred to as the ›mental lexicon‹.

Definition

The mental lexicon is the human word store, i. e. that part of our long-term memory where the words are linked systematically in terms of conceptual, semantic and phonological similarity.

Semantic network: Slips-of-the-tongue such as *all men are created evil* (instead of *equal*) provide us with indirect evidence in this respect since they result from the wrong selection of a lexical item (cf. Hutz 2017). In other cases, we may simply choose an item which is semantically related (e. g. *Saturday* instead of *Sunday* or *apple* instead of *peach*). Slips-of-the-tongue show that words, concepts and sounds must be interconnected in semantic, lexical and phonological networks and that we sometimes fail to activate the correct link, for instance because of the phonological similarity between the words *evil* and *equal* or the semantic similarity between different days of the week. Several words seem to be triggered simultaneously through a process of »interactive activation« (Aitchison 1994, 206 f.) and we sometimes fail to suppress a word which is not appropriate in a particular context. Thus, words are not stored randomly, but seem to be organised systematically in our minds. It is probably best to imagine the mental lexicon to be organised like a »word-web« or a »semantic network« (Aitchison 1994, 82 ff.) which consists of words and their semantic relations with other words.

Types of association: Schmitt (2000, 39 f.) makes a distinction between three types of association or types of storage: clang association, paradigmatic association and syntagmatic association.

- **Clang associations** include words that are stored closely together purely as a result of their phonological similarity, e. g. words like *evil* and *equal* or *compensation* and *consolation*.
- In **paradigmatic associations** words are grouped in the same word classes. This would include semantic relations such as synonymy (e. g. *get* and *receive*), antonymy (e. g. *high* and *low*, *rich* and *poor*) or hyponymy, i. e. a hierarchical arrangement between superordinate and subordinate words (e. g. *flower* and *daffodil/daisy/rose*).
- Finally, words can also be connected through **syntagmatic associations**, i. e. by linking words from different word classes syntactically, for example in the case of collocations and lexical chunks (e. g. *to wear a hat*, *bright colours*).

The following word-web shows some potential syntagmatic and paradigmatic associations for the word *car* (see illustration).

Such a word-web or semantic network must be very flexible and dynamic since it needs to be constantly revised. When new vocabulary is acquired, the entire network has to be modified and updated: New lexical entries must be added and linked to already existing items while some existing connections might just be strengthened through increased use (cf. Ellis 2005).

Storing and retrieving words are interrelated processes: The better words are organised in the learners' mental lexicon, the easier it will be to access and retrieve them. As far as comprehension is concerned, learners need to find a match between the input and the stored sounds and spellings as quickly as possible. As far as the productive use of vocabulary is concerned, learners have to activate not only appropriate words, but also additional information concerning the words' form and use. Fast retrieval and the productive use of vocabulary, therefore, also depend greatly on the systematic presentation and practice of vocabulary, which is the topic of the following chapters.

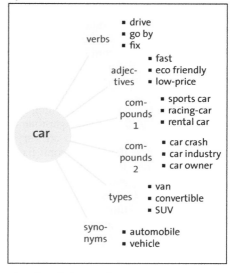

Illustration 8.2:
Example of a
word-web: ›car‹

8.2 | Building lexical knowledge

One of the key competences of a teacher should be to help learners establish connections between lexical items and gradually build up semantic networks in the mind. Thus, there are important implications for selecting, presenting and practicing vocabulary in the classroom (cf. chapter 8.3) and for integrating words into the mental lexicon.

8.2.1 | Knowing words and lexical items

Teachers often ask the question *Do you know all the words in the text?* Likewise, learners often either say *I know this word* or *I don't know this word*. But what exactly does it mean ›to know a word‹? Obviously, the meaning of the word is crucial, but knowing a word also involves two other main dimensions, namely form and use (cf. Nation 2001, 27). This is demonstrated in the following table based on the verb *to lose*.

Form and meaning: The process of acquiring new vocabulary is very complex. Initially, learners need to go through a labelling process, i. e. they have to establish links between form and meaning and discover the basic meaning of lexical items. Then they need to find out about semantic restrictions and more specific meanings. Eventually, they need to ascertain how the lexical item is used, for example, which other words it can be combined with.

Receptive and productive learning: All three dimensions of ›knowing‹ a word involve receptive aspects (i. e. recognising the meaning and form) and productive aspects (i. e. being able to say or write a word with its correct meaning and form in an appropriate context). Hence, we need to make a distinction between receptive and productive learning. Both in L1 and in L2 learning a speaker's receptive repertoire of vocabulary tends to be much larger than the productive one. This is often due to the fact that some words are very rare or restricted in use. Thus, it is not very likely that they become part of a speaker's productive competence (cf. Channell 1999, 85) since there are not enough opportunities to use the lexical item actively.

For productive use, learners also need to know more distinctive features of the form (cf. Nation 2001, 28), for example how a word is pronounced, stressed or spelled. Receptive learning, on the other hand, re-

Dimension	Types of ›knowledge‹ involved	Examples
Meaning	e.g. knowing the core meaning and additional meanings	*lose* (= the opposite of *win*)
Form	e.g. knowing about pronunciation, spelling, word stress, morphology, colligations	e.g. *lost, losing, loses*
Use	e.g. collocations, register, semantic range, context, constraints of use	e.g. *losing one's mind, lose control, lose weight, lost in translation*

Table 8.3: Knowing about a word

quires less amount of knowledge. Even if we have never come across a word, we can make educated guesses about the potential meaning based on the co-text, the word-class and the surrounding words. In other words, we can rely on our linguistic knowledge, the contextual knowledge and our world knowledge (**top-down processing**; cf. chapter 6 in this volume). For example, even though learners may not know the meaning of the word *acclaim* in the sentence *Nelson Mandela gained international acclaim for his activism*, it is still quite possible for them to figure out the meaning based on their knowledge of Mandela's merits as well as the surrounding words (*to gain, international*).

With regard to the active use of words, there are numerous problems for learners, however. In particular, the following areas may cause problems:

Dimension	Difficulty	Comment	Examples
Meaning	false friends	Semantic interference between L1 and L2 words may occur as a result of a phonological similarity perceived by learners.	*actual*/aktuell, *fatal*/fatal, *become*/bekommen
	synonyms	True synonyms hardly exist in a language—learners have to find out about the subtle differences between near-synonyms.	*to get* vs. *to receive* or *to obtain*; *to buy* vs. *to purchase*
	antonyms	Antonyms may vary according to the surrounding words.	*light wind* vs. *strong wind*, but: *light colour* vs. *dark colour*
Form	spelling	In English there is a great discrepancy between spelling and pronunciation, i. e. the same sound is often reflected in different spellings.	The phoneme /i:/ can be spelled in various ways: e. g. *bee*, *be*, *receive*, *meat*, *police*, *key*, *quay*, P*ho*enix
	word stress	Word stress patterns can be very complex—even the meaning can change depending on word stress.	*object* vs. *to object*, *to desert* vs. *desert*
Use	collocation	Knowing how words combine with other words is a very complex issue.	*to watch TV*, but not *to see TV*
	degree of formality	It is important to know which words are associated with a very formal or rather informal register.	*to begin* or *to start* vs. *to commence*

Table 8.4:
Lexical challenges
for language
learners

When new words are introduced, both receptive and productive skills must be given adequate attention. But teachers need to be aware of the fact that more time and repeated effort is needed to learn new vocabulary for productive use (cf. Nation 2001, 32). Just providing an explanation of the meaning of the word and then expecting the learners to actively use the words instantly in a correct manner is usually insufficient. Quite often, receptive knowledge might be the first step towards active usage, but due to the complex nature of lexical items a great amount of practice might be needed before learners can appropriately apply the rules concerning the meaning, the form and the use of lexical items.

8.2.2 | The lexical approach

It is a common observation in language acquisition that words come first. When children produce their first utterances in their first language, they normally do not speak well-formed grammatical sentences. At first, they typically focus on single content words which convey a maximum of meaning (e. g. *ball*, *give*) and largely ignore function words (e. g. determiners and prepositions). Even when they produce longer utterances during the two-word stage or multi-word stage, they usually focus on content words (mainly nouns and verbs) and pre-fabricated chunks which are still relatively ungrammaticised (e. g. *daddy go*). Only at later stages the process of ›word grammaring‹ sets in and gradually more and more grammatical structures are discovered and used.

In a similar way, most foreign language learners initially focus on lexical items to get meaning across, too, i. e. they move in a »lexical-to-grammatical direction« (Thornbury 2005b, 17) as well. The idea that lexis is the basis of language production and the key to meaningful communication is also one of the main assumptions of the ›lexical approach‹ by Michael Lewis. According to this approach, vocabulary should be placed at the centre of teaching methodology.

Grammaticalised lexis: Lewis also challenges the traditional dichotomy between grammar and vocabulary. He states that »language consists of grammaticalised lexis, not lexicalized grammar« (Lewis 2008, 89). Main emphasis should be given to the teaching and learning of lexical chunks which are made up of lexico-grammatical patterns. Thus, the lexical approach emphasises the teaching of multi-word items or so-called ›institutionalised expressions‹ such as *just a moment, please, that's all very well, but ...* or *sorry to interrupt, but, ...* (cf. Lewis 2008, 94). Such institutionalised phrases are often acquired in a context in which incidental learning takes place, for example, when watching a film or reading a novel. However, it may also be helpful to make learners aware of the chunks in a text (cf. Lewis 1997, 55), to make them search for patterns and regularities and possibly to let them discover similarities and differences between English ›chunks‹ and ›chunks‹ in their L1. The following activities aim at raising some consciousness concerning the use of collocations.

Example   **Teaching collocations**

In the following activity the learners are asked to match adjectives denoting the concept of ›speed‹ with specific nouns. The idea is that learners learn to distinguish between adjectives that can be collocated with numerous other nouns and those which are much more restricted in use.

a) **Which of the following adjectives and nouns may form a ›lexical chunk‹? Which items do not really match? In case of doubt, you can put a question-mark.**

	computer	breakfast	train	response	action	decision
fast						
quick						
rapid						
speedy						
swift						
hasty						

Collocations with ›make‹ and ›do‹ are potentially difficult for German learners since both verbs may correspond to the German *machen*. Therefore, this activity attempts to raise awareness for cross-linguistic differences.

b) **Make ten collocations from the following words using either ›MAKE‹ or ›DO‹**

homework	damage	a mistake	a meal	your duty
some noise	a mistake	some coffee	harm	someone a favour

Learners may research collocations for specific adjectives, nouns or verbs in order to make them aware of the wide semantic range of individual words.

c) **Finding collocations**
What can you ›tell‹? Find at least ten collocations, e. g. *tell a joke*, …
What can be ›heavy‹? Find at least ten collocations, e. g. *heavy traffic*, …
Write down at least ten lexical chunks which contain the word ›end‹, e. g. *in the end*, …

8.3 | Selecting, presenting and practising lexical items

The teaching and learning of vocabulary is associated with several important processes: Specific lexical items need to be selected, introduced and explained. Learners need to understand their meaning and integrate the items into their mental lexicon by linking the words with as many lexical fields as possible.

8.3.1 | Selecting lexical items

Since the English vocabulary contains approximately between 500,000 and 1,000,0000 words, it is obvious that it is virtually impossible to learn all the words. Even native speakers have an active command of only a tiny fraction of the entire English vocabulary. It is often estimated that between 500 and 700 words can be introduced per school year. Since not all the words are equally important for everyday communication, this means that words need to be carefully selected based on specific criteria. The most crucial criteria for word selection are frequency, semantic range, relevance and learnability.

Frequency: It is obvious that it is useful to select those lexical items which are frequently used. Linguistic corpora can provide very good surveys of words which are used frequently. The following survey is based on the Oxford English Corpus which contains nearly 2.5 billion lemmas, which were collected mainly from pages on the Internet (https://en.ox forddictionaries.com/explore/what-can-corpus-tell-us-about-language; a lemma is the base form of a word, e. g. *plays, played* and *playing* are all examples of the lemma *play*):

Vocabulary size (no. of lemmas)	% of content in OEC	Example lemmas
10	25 %	*the, of, and, to, that, have*
100	50 %	*from, because, go, me, our, well, way*
1,000	75 %	*girl, win, decide, huge, difficult, series*
7,000	90 %	*tackle, peak, crude, purely, dude, modest*
50,000	95 %	*saboteur, autocracy, calyx, conformist*
>1,000,000	99 %	*laggardly, endobenthic, pomological*

Table 8.5:
Frequency of
lexical items

The main conclusion which can be drawn from this table is that relatively few words account for a huge part of the entire communication on the Internet. In other words, a great deal can be expressed with a limited number of words. If just 7,000 words are sufficient to cover 90 % of all the text, this may suggest that it is not necessary to learn more than this. However, the remaining 10 % of the words are often crucial to understand the main message since they tend to be content words (cf. Gardner 2013, 45). Although English is known for its extremely rich vocabulary, many words are extremely rare and occur only in very special contexts. Quite often, they are of Latin or Greek origin and are rather part of the passive vocabulary, even among native speakers.

When we take a closer look at only the Top 30 words, nearly all of them are so-called **function words**, for example determiners, prepositions, conjunctions and pronouns. They have significant grammatical functions, but very little meaning can be expressed by them.

Table 8.6:
Most frequently
used words in
English (Top 30)

1	2	3	4	5	6	7	8	9	10	11	12	13	14	15
the	be	to	of	and	a	in	that	have	I	it	for	not	on	with
16	17	18	19	20	21	22	23	24	25	26	27	28	29	30
he	as	you	do	at	this	but	his	by	from	they	we	say	her	she

Semantic range: The second criterion, semantic range, is indirectly related to frequency as well, since it refers to the potential meanings a word may have and the potential contexts it might be used in. There are words with a very broad semantic range (e. g. *bad, make, get, take*), i. e. words that can be used in many different contexts (*a bad guy, a bad experience, a bad day*, etc.) while other words with a similar meaning are much more restricted (e. g. *wicked, vicious, vile*) and others are probably in between (e. g. *evil*). Since the meanings are restricted and the number of possible collocations is limited, their frequency is also reduced.

Relevance is a criterion that is much harder to define since it involves making predictions about the learners' future needs. Lexical fields that are usually included in textbooks as part of everyday vocabulary which learners are likely to come across, include domains like traffic, pets, sports or directions. However, some lexical fields such as tools or kitchenware are hardly ever included in textbooks although they might be considered part of everyday vocabulary as well. In this case the prediction seems to be that learners are not very likely to come across these terms.

Learnability refers to the difficulties caused by various aspects concerning the meaning, form and use of individual lexical items (cf. chapter 8.2.1). This criterion is often based on assumptions concerning the proximity between two languages. However, what might be difficult for one learner, may not present any difficulty for another learner. In fact, predicting learning difficulties is a very complex matter.

8.3.2 | Presenting lexical items

It is usually helpful to group lexical items for teaching purposes so that learners can connect the words more easily. When teaching a set of lexical items, it might be useful to teach
- lexical items associated with a specific location, phenomenon or event (e. g. words related to ›money‹ or ›traffic‹)
- lexical items that share the same grammatical and lexical function (e. g. adjectives to describe feelings or verbs of perception like *look, sound, hear*)
- lexical items that can be used in a specific communicative event (e. g. giving directions or agreeing/disagreeing).

If the meaning of individual words needs to be explained, teachers may rely on a variety of presentation techniques to ensure that words are understood (cf. Hutz/Kolb 2010). We can distinguish between verbal and non-verbal techniques.

There are also techniques which more or less directly or indirectly involve the learner's L1 or another language the learner is familiar with (e. g. by demonstrating the similarity between cognates, e. g. *brother* and *Bruder*). A direct translation might be the fastest way to convey the meaning—however, it may also be the least effective one in terms of recall since learners are not cognitively involved enough.

Probably the most common way of learning vocabulary is through

Presentation technique	Example
Non-verbal techniques	
realia	bringing real objects into the classroom, e. g. vegetables or fruits
drawings and pictures	drawing a house with different rooms and furniture or using pictures as visual support
gestures	making gestures to explain the meaning of words, e. g. *swimming*
facial expressions	demonstrating moods like *frightened, disappointed* or *shocked*
pointing	pointing to objects, e. g. *chalk, blackboard, sponge*
acting out	demonstrating the meaning of words by miming or acting it out in class, e. g. *jumping, bouncing, chasing*
Verbal techniques	
synonyms	using words which are close in meaning (e. g. *deceptive* is similar to *misleading*)
antonyms	using words which have the opposite meaning (e. g. *a heavy suitcase—a light suitcase*)
hypernyms	using a superordinate term (e. g. *a pineapple is a tropical fruit*)
definition	A round-robin letter is a letter which is sent to a number of people at the end of the year in which the writer describes the year's events for himself/herself and/or his/her family.
explaining/ paraphrasing	You use a *corkscrew* to open wine bottles.
word-formation	The noun *strength* comes from the adjective *strong*.

Table 8.7: Presentation techniques for lexis

wordlists. Typically, the individual words are listed in a chronological order as they appear in the textbook units. However, this way of learning new lexical items has numerous disadvantages. Above all, the words included in such more or less random lists appear not to be connected with each other, i. e. there is only little information about potential collocations or multi-word items the word is associated with. All of this makes long-term storage in the mental lexicon and eventually recall more difficult for learners.

Integrating words into the mental lexicon: Words need to be embedded in the mental lexicon, i. e. they need to be put properly into storage by creating links to already existing lexical items. This can be achieved, for instance, by topic-based **word networks** (e. g. ›school‹, ›means of transport‹), which allow for the integration of **syntagmatic associations** (collocations, idiomatic expressions) and **paradigmatic associations** (synonyms, antonyms, hyponyms; cf. Klippel 1995; Kielhöfer 1994). Such semantic networks resemble the structures of the mental lexicon and facilitate lexical retrieval by grouping and connecting numerous lexical items. The main objective is to store words in the long-term memory, not in the short-term memory. Thus, it is a good idea to follow the following principles:

Principle	Explanation	Implications for teaching
connecting words	It is essential that words are not presented and learned in isolation, but that learners can make as many connections to other words as possible.	presenting words in topic-based networks, semantic fields, lexical patterns and colligations; demonstrating lexical relations between items (e. g. synonyms, antonyms, subordinate/super-ordinate terms)
processing words in a multi-sensory approach	The more channels and senses are involved in processing lexical input, the more easily the information can be stored and retrieved.	providing visual support (e. g. through pictures), auditory support (e. g. rhymes) or kinaesthetic support (i. e. linking the lexical items with physical motion)
contextualising words	Learners need to explore how the new lexical items are used in specific contexts.	using authentic texts; using index cards with sentences that show how the lexical item is used
repeating words	Words need to be repeated at certain intervals.	revising vocabulary in certain intervals in transfer activities (e. g. role plays)

Table 8.8: Integrating words into the mental lexicon

8.3.3 | Practising lexical items

After learners have encountered a new lexical item, they need to have opportunities for practice concerning its meaning, form and use.

Meaning-related practice: The following activities are typically used to focus on the meaning of lexical items and to integrate them into semantic networks:
- matching pictures to lexical items
- categorising items
- odd one out (*Which word is different from the others? E.g. carpenter, painter, boss, mechanic*)
- memory game
- taboo game (explaining a word on a card without using it—other learners have to guess it)

Form-related practice: These activities may be used to practise certain aspects related to pronunciation, spelling or grammatical aspects:
- pronunciation drills (e. g. varied speed, volume, mood)
- filling in grids or crosswords to practise spelling
- reconstruction exercises (e. g. jumbled letters)
- filling in gaps to practise word grammar (e. g. tenses)

Use-related practice:
- matching lexical items to other words, e. g. collocations, antonyms, synonyms
- writing a story based on a number of key words (e. g. *Tell a funny story based on the following words: teacher—forget—maths—lesson*)

- information gap activities (e. g. finding differences between two similar pictures)

The following activity includes all three dimensions. Learners are asked to categorise the lexical items of a specific word-field semantically (meaning) as well as according to their word-class (form) and eventually use them in a context (use).

40 Words about Money

dollar, waste, coin, legal, receipt, pocket money, cash, time is money, bank, foreign, not for all the money in the world, shop, spend, pay, charge, sell, save, illegal, withdraw, savings bank, it's worth the money, borrow, invoice, payment, money doesn't grow on trees, finance, the money is rolling in, short of cash, bill, pound, euro, out of money, huge amount of money, money box, transfer, money is power, hard-earned, to be in need of money, money can't buy it, good value for money

Underline all the verbs that you can find in green, nouns in blue, adjectives in yellow and longer phrases in red.
Decide where to put the words and phrases and fill in the columns (see following table).
Which words go together? Try to find some common collocations.
Circle 5 words and write a short story which includes these words.

Currencies (nouns)	What you can do with money (verbs)	What money can be like (adjectives)	Types of money (nouns)	Phrases about money	Things associated with money (nouns)
dollar ...	spend ...	illegal ...	pocket money ...	It's worth the money ...	money box ...

8.4 | Building grammatical knowledge

Grammar teaching has been a controversial topic throughout the history of foreign language teaching. The role of grammar has been debated for a long time, in particular with regard to the following questions:
- Should grammar be taught explicitly or implicitly?
- If so, how much grammar teaching should there be?
- What are the most effective ways of teaching grammar?

8.4.1 | Interventionist and non-interventionist grammar instruction

Non-interventionist instruction: Concerning the first question two main approaches can be distinguished: an interventionist and a non-interventionist position (cf. Summer 2011, 57 ff.; Timmis 2017). In the latter case, the idea is that grammar is acquired subconsciously and mainly through exposure to comprehensible input. Learners form hypotheses about specific rules and patterns in the foreign language, this is similar to the way a first language is acquired. In terms of methodology, this is an approach which is reflected in the strong version of **Communicative Language Teaching** or in immersion programmes.

Interventionist instruction: However, in the history of foreign language teaching, an interventionist position towards grammar, i. e. an explicit focus on discrete grammatical items (e. g. tenses, relative clauses or adverbs, etc.) has been much more dominant. The degree to which interventions have been used differs considerably. In some cases, the interventions were very direct and explicit, in other cases more indirect and implicit. Two of these approaches (›Presentation—Practice—Production‹ and ›Focus on Form‹) will be briefly characterised in this chapter.

Proactive and reactive grammar teaching: On a more practical level, another general distinction can be drawn between proactive and reactive grammar teaching (cf. Doughty/Williams 1998). Proactive grammar teaching involves the planned instruction of specific grammatical phenomena, for instance, through course books, materials or grammar exercises. In contrast, reactive grammar teaching refers to rather unplanned instances of grammar teaching, for example when teachers see the need to deal with specific grammatical items during or after a communicative activity. This may just involve a short explanation or in some cases simply correcting the learner's utterance.

The two general positions towards grammar instruction can be illustrated as follows:

Interventionist grammar instruction	Non-interventionist grammar instruction
conscious ›learning‹ of grammatical rules	›acquiring‹ rules subconsciously through exposure to input and communication
planned materials and activities to introduce and practise language items (proactive approach)	incidental instruction in the context of communicative activities (reactive approach)
deductive approach based on providing explicit rules which aims at general orientation	inductive approach based on examples which promotes explorative learning
linear progression	non-linear progression
drills and exercises to practise new forms	tasks which involve a focus on form
focus on discrete grammatical forms	focus on meaning and communication
focus on accuracy	focus on fluency
explicit error correction	implicit error correction
strong use of metalinguistic terminology	focus on using structures; no need to acquire special terminology

Table 8.9: Interventionist and non-interventionist grammar instruction

Two approaches: Methodologically, this opposition can be illustrated by two well-known approaches. A good example of an interventionist grammar instruction is the so-called **PPP (Presentation—Practice—Production)** approach while the **Focus on Form (FonF)** approach represents a rather reactive and non-interventionist approach to grammar instruction. A PPP approach is typically characterised by the following pattern:

Stage	Explanation	Examples
P Presentation	Learners are exposed to a new language item (e. g. the simple past). The new item is explained and the rules are presented.	A text or dialogue is presented which contains numerous examples of the simple past, for instance.
P Practice	Learners are provided with opportunities to practise the selected grammatical items in controlled ways.	Drills or gap-filling exercises, where learners are asked to fill in the correct simple past forms.
P Production	Learners use the form more or less freely in communicative activities.	Learners are supposed to talk or write about an event where they are required to use the simple past (e. g. their last holidays).

Table 8.10:
PPP approach

The PPP approach has been criticised for various reasons, in particular because of the great emphasis it has placed on the teaching of isolated grammatical phenomena. The forms are typically introduced by means of non-authentic texts which were specifically written to showcase as many examples of the new form as possible. The gap-filling exercises were often out of context and devoid of meaning. In addition to this, the expected transfer did not automatically take place when learners had to use the structures in free production.

Focus on form (FonF): The concept was suggested by Long (1991). A FonF approach draws the students' attention to linguistic structures as they arise incidentally in lessons which are mainly based on meaning and communication. He makes a distinction between a focus on form and a focus on forms (plural), i. e. the teaching of discrete grammatical items without a specific focus on meaning. Long assumes that language development takes place, above all, implicitly and therefore, interventionist approaches like PPP which are based on a linguistic syllabus are not very helpful, in general. Van den Branden (2006b, 5) also states that learners do not learn »isolated items in L2 one at a time, in an additive, linear fashion, but rather as parts of complex mappings of form-function relationships«.

In a similar way, Ellis (2005) distinguishes between a focus on form which can be either incidental or planned. **Planned FonF** tasks are meaning-centred (e. g. a task which involves learners predicting the future), but also include a pre-determined focus on a linguistic element (e. g. will-future) whereas **incidental FonF** rather follows a ›learning-by-opportunity‹-approach. With regard to planned FonF tasks, Müller-Hartmann/Schocker-v. Ditfurth (2011, 215) point out that learners often focus strongly on meaning and may circumvent the structures in question.

Overall, however, most researchers seem to agree that a focus on form is beneficial and necessary so that learners can develop their interlanguage and avoid the risk of »freezing« their linguistic system (Thornbury 2005b, 31). Cameron (2001, 108) points out that »the grammar of a foreign language is ›foreign‹, and grammar development requires skilled planning of tasks and lessons, and explicit teaching«.

8.4.2 | The development of grammar instruction

In the past, the pendulum has swung back and forth between periods which were characterised by either an »instruction plus« or an »instruction minus« attitude (Thornbury 2005b, 31). When looking at the development of grammar instruction, three main phases can be distinguished where grammar played a role in different approaches.

Grammar as the basic foundation of language production: Initially, grammar was often viewed as the most central aspect of language production. This resulted in a strong focus on teaching grammatical forms and accuracy. The **grammar-translation method**, for instance, was based on classical language teaching, i. e. the explicit teaching of prescriptive grammar rules as in Latin or Greek (cf. chapter 1 in this volume). After grammatical rules had been stated explicitly and deductively, texts were translated into and out of the target language.

Later on, **the audiolingual/audiovisual method** focused on grammatical accuracy as well, even though grammar was taught rather implicitly. A particular grammatical phenomenon was selected and then practised in numerous **pattern drills**. The idea underlying this method, which was largely based on the theory of behaviourism, was that grammar and speech production needed to be automatised through imitation and repetition.

These methods, however, were often criticised for numerous reasons, in particular because of their strong focus on grammar and formal accuracy. In addition to the monotony and lack of creativity, learners were often unable to transfer their explicit or implicit grammar knowledge to other situations (cf. Keßler/Plesser 2011, 31).

Grammar as an inhibition to language production: As a result of the numerous problems associated with the methods mentioned above, it was not surprising that there was a strong counter-reaction. Due to the communicative paradigm shift in the mid-1970s, grammar tended to be seen as a factor which often inhibited rather than promoted language production. Instead, emphasis was placed on meaning and the ability to communicate, not on producing language forms correctly. ›**Meaning before form**‹ and ›**fluency before accuracy**‹ became well-known principles. Thus, in the most radical version of the communicative approach, grammar teaching almost became a taboo. However, it soon became clear that some attention needed to be drawn to accuracy as well so that learners would not ›fossilise‹ in their development.

Grammar as a tool to create language awareness: In the 1990s, a revival and renewal of approaches to teaching grammar (›**Focus on Form**‹) began since cognitive processes were considered to be crucial for promoting learners' linguistic development. The role of the teacher is to help learners notice specific grammatical features and to engage them in a creative construction process (cf. Müller-Hartmann/Schocker-v. Ditfurth 2011, 212). However, **noticing** is an active process in which learners become aware of specific patterns as well as links between form and meaning and compare a new form or rule with already known patterns. The process of noticing enables the learners to revise and modify their internal grammar. This process can be further reinforced through activities which help the learners to restructure their grammatical knowledge, for instance by means of controlled practice. Ideally, grammatical patterns are eventually ›proceduralised‹ (cf. Batstone 1994, 42 ff.) through automatised and repeated use in free production.

8.4.3 | Sequencing grammatical activities

It is reasonable to sequence grammatical activities in such a way that new forms can easily be noticed, (re-)structured and proceduralised by learners (cf. Batstone 1994). Several sequences have been suggested which follow these three phases, e. g. the sequence »Discovery—Consolidation—Use« (Gerngross et al. 2006) or the sequence »Non-communicative learning—Communicative language practice—Authentic communication« (Littlewood 2007).

What these sequences have in common is that they gradually move from focus on form to focus on meaning and from consciousness-raising via controlled practice towards free use of language. The sequence suggested here is similar (»**Raising awareness—Guided production—Creative production**«), but adds a potential fourth stage (»**Exploring language**«).

Raising language awareness: Initially, learners need to discover and notice new grammatical patterns. During this phase of explorative learning they need to focus on the new structures of language, how they are formed and what their functions are (cf. Gnutzmann 1995). This active process of noticing or »recognition« (Willis 2003, 8) can be supported with data which illustrate the targeted feature. The main idea is that learners are encouraged to form hypotheses about new patterns.

Example | **Language awareness**

Awareness for conditional sentences may be raised with the help of the following activity:

Look at the following three sentences:
If I had set the alarm-clock, I wouldn't have missed the plane.
If I had more money, I could buy a new air ticket.
If I ask my Dad, maybe I can borrow some money from him.

Questions: How do the three sentences differ in form? Which sentences are realistic, which ones are hypothetical? Which sentences are related to the past, the present and the future?

Meaningful practice: It should not be assumed, of course, that a consciousness-raising activity is likely to result in immediate acquisition. The new patterns need to be practised by the learners, which may happen in different ways. The most basic forms include pattern drills and gap-filling exercises, since it is useful to give learners the opportunity to form their own sentences according to a set pattern. However, the objective is to practise the language items, above all, in a meaningful context—perhaps involving some unpredictability.

Chain-story

Example

This activity aims to practise conditional sentences in a rather controlled way by creating a story in the classroom together.
The teacher begins a story, then the pupils create their own story spontaneously sentence by sentence. Each student adds a new sentence.

If I had a million dollars, I would travel around the world.
If I travelled around the world, I would meet lots of people.
If I met lots of people, I ...

Creative production: In order to proceduralise the knowledge it is essential that learners get the opportunity to use the structures in free production tasks as well (cf. Gerngross et al. 2006; Hutz 2006). This could involve activities such as creative role-plays, debates or problem-solving tasks. Since this stage is strongly meaning-based, it may happen, of course, that learners make little or no use of the new pattern. For example, in the activity below, specific tenses (here: present perfect and going-to-future) might be practised, but learners may also see the need to use other tenses as well.

Faces

Example

Photos of faces are shown which require the use of specific tenses (e. g. present perfect).
What do you think has happened here? What do you think is going to happen next?

He has just dropped a hammer on his foot. I think he is going to see a doctor very soon.

Or: He has just found out that his favourite football team lost the cup final ... I think he is going to ...

She has just lost her front teeth and is looking at the mirror for the first time. I think she is going to eat a lot of soup in the next few weeks.

Or: She has just seen a huge spider. I think she is going to ...

Exploring language: Corpus-based studies can help to engage advanced learners in meaningful activities that involve them in learning more about language items (cf. Reppen 2010, 5; Hutz 2016). Linguistic corpora, which are available online, such as the Corpus of Contemporary American English (COCA) can provide excellent samples of actual language use which can be explored in the classroom. Hence, learners can become ›linguistic detectives‹ or researchers who analyse specific grammatical phenomena in authentic speech by searching the online corpora.

Example **Research Tasks**

Do you say ›fewer people‹ or ›less people‹ in English?
Can ›yet‹ and ›already‹ be used with simple past?
Can ›always‹ be used with verbs in the progressive form
(e. g. *she is always smiling*)?

8.5 | Implications for the communicative English classroom

In the past, grammar and lexis were usually seen as two different entities which were taught separately. The final chapter aims to show how both domains can be combined in the framework of a communicative classroom. First of all, some basic principles will be summarised and finally some communicative activities will be presented.

8.5.1 | General principles of a lexico-grammatical approach

Teaching grammar and lexis together: There are numerous reasons why teaching lexis and grammar should not be artificially separated. Words have an internal grammar, hence knowing a word also implies knowing about its form, e. g. how the past of a verb is formed. On the other hand, a functional view of grammar implies that grammar is also ›meaningful‹. For instance, the continuous form can be used to indicate the speaker's meaning. Grammar can thus also be conceptualised »as patterns of language through which meaning is created and shared« (de Oliveira/Schleppegrell 2015, 11). In particular, lexis and grammar should be viewed as a continuum since lexical and grammatical patterns are stored together in the mental lexicon. Thus, it makes no sense to teach isolated words or to teach grammar only for its own sake.

Working from lexis to grammar: Communication is, above all, meaning-centred. Initially, learners often focus on lexical items to convey messages. Therefore, it is usually reasonable to focus first and foremost on lexemes to help learners to express meaning. However, formal correctness is crucial to convey precise and accurate meaning as well, for example when a learner wishes to express time differences or notions of space and time. Therefore, when introducing new vocabulary, it is essential to deal with some formal aspects as well (e. g. spelling, pronunciation, stress and grammatical patterns that a word is associated with). In particular, attention should be directed to those grammatical features of a language that are different from the first language or that cannot be easily noticed (cf. Cameron 2001, 110). In other words, the principle ›form follows function‹ should be maintained in a lexico-grammatical approach, but form should not be neglected.

Creating language awareness through noticing: Learners need to notice how specific lexical items or grammatical features are used so that they are able to revise and modify their interlanguage. They need to integrate new words into their mental lexicon and make new connections between words. They also need to revise their hypotheses about grammatical patterns and rules. After all, the learner has to do the learning—merely presenting vocabulary or grammatical rules does not necessarily lead to learning. Instead, learners need to be cognitively engaged as much as possible. They should be encouraged to make intelligent guesswork. When learners ask for the meaning of a specific word, a teacher might simply reply with the question »Well, what do YOU think it means?« Quite often, the learners are capable of figuring out the meaning from the context or their prior knowledge. Likewise, instead of explaining grammatical items it is usually helpful to let students discover grammatical patterns by themselves. Even though such an **inductive** and **explorative approach** may appear to be more time-consuming at first, the main advantage is that the rule becomes the learners' rule and not the teacher's or the textbook's rule. Eventually, following this principle also facilitates retrieval since words and structures are much better integrated in the mental lexicon and the learners' internal grammar.

Integrating focus on form into task-based language learning: Although **task-based language learning** (cf. chapter 11 in this volume) is primarily meaning-centred, a focus on form is usually considered to be an essential part of TBLL since it appears to be crucial for the learners' language development. However, there are two main challenges. The first challenge is: How can teachers make sure that learners also pay attention to formal accuracy when they are, above all, interested in conveying meaning? In general, language support and implicit feedback can be provided at all points of a task sequence while the focus on meaning is maintained, for example when learners are looking for a word or if they misuse a pattern (cf. Müller-Hartmann/Schocker-v. Ditfurth 2011, 222). More complex forms (e. g. tenses, passive voice), however, may have to be dealt with in an extra session.

The second challenge is: When should focus on form be provided, for example during the pre-task phase or the post-task phase? Several researchers, Van Gorp/Bogaert (2006, 103) and Müller-Hartmann/Schocker-v. Ditfurth (2011, 223), for instance, agree that a focus on form can be integrated into almost any of the phases of the task framework. In particular, the post-task phase seems to offer an appropriate opportunity, for example when learners are supposed to present their final product—in this case, a focus on lexical items and grammatical patterns may be an important step during the editing stage. The pre-task phase which serves to activate the learners' pre-knowledge is perhaps less ideal for a focus on form, at least with regard to grammar. However, it might be helpful to activate the learners' pre-knowledge also by introducing some key lexical items in a meaningful context.

8.5.2 | Communicative Activities

The following activities try to combine a focus on meaning and a focus on form. In each case some potential lexico-grammatical aspects are mentioned which could be practised. The activities are intended to engage learners in free language production. It is often helpful to include the focus on form after the introductory phase in order to take advantage of the full potential during the communicative activity itself. In addition to this, a second focus on form might be useful after the task has been accomplished, for example after the presentation in order to ›polish‹ the learners' output.

Example **A class trip to London**

In this consensus-finding task or WebQuest students have to organise a 5-day class trip to London. They only have a small budget of 200 € per person. They have to discuss and select the attractions they want to visit, find some appropriate accommodation and calculate the costs for travelling in London and for entrance fees. Each group has to present its findings—afterwards the entire class decides on the best arrangement for the class.

Focus on form:
Lexis: attractions, directions, means of transport, agreeing/disagreeing
Grammar: will-future, modals like *may, might, could, should, must*

Example **Brick by brick**

In this information gap activity learners are asked to construct an object (e. g. a building, a plane or perhaps just a ›piece of art‹) with a set of small bricks. The object must not be shown to their partner. Their partner has the same set of bricks and has to reconstruct the same object just based on the description provided by the partner who built the object. Thus, the learners are forced to negotiate the exact position of the individual bricks. Afterwards, the objects can be compared and, if necessary, re-arranged. A final exhibition of all the objects may also be part of the activity.

Lexis: shapes, colours
Grammar: prepositions (e. g. *under, next to, on top of*), modals (e. g. *have to, should*)

Emojis

In pairs or small groups learners choose four or five different smileys and develop a story just based on the faces. A particular context may be provided by the teacher to indicate a special focus on form (e. g. simple past: »Once upon a time there was a ...«). Then the group has to decide on a specific sequence in which the faces occur. Afterwards the story is presented to the entire class.

Focus on form:
Lexis: adjectives to describe emotions and verbs related to senses (e. g. *to look angry, to feel happy, to feel sad, to look confused*)
Grammar: tenses (e. g. simple past)

8.6 | Conclusion

Words in discourse are held together by grammar, which in turn largely depends on sets of words or phrases that are frequently used with them. Thus, grammar and vocabulary are intrinsically linked. The main idea of a lexico-grammar approach in language teaching is that vocabulary and grammar are not taught separately, but in combination. The knowledge of lexical items is essential for communication and may serve as a stepping stone for learning grammar. However, within the framework of a focus on form approach grammar also has a place in the classroom, but it needs to be integrated into tasks and activities which are meaningful for learners. Authentic texts and interactions offer numerous opportunities for grammar and vocabulary learning—learners and teachers simply need to explore these linguistic patterns.

Further reading

Aitchison, Jean ([2]1994): *Words in the Mind. An Introduction to the Mental Lexicon* [1987]. Cambridge, MA.

Lewis, Michael (2008): *The Lexical Approach. The State of ELT and a Way Forward*. Andover, Hampshire.

McCarthy, Michael/O'Keeffe, Anne/Walsh, Steven (2010): *Vocabulary Matrix. Understanding, Learning, Teaching*. Andover, Hampshire.

Thornbury, Scott (2005b): *Uncovering Grammar*. Oxford.

Willis, Dave (2003): *Rules, Patterns and Words. Grammar and Lexis in ELT*. Cambridge.

Matthias Hutz

9 Teaching Culture — Intercultural Competence, Transcultural Learning, Global Education

The idea that teaching a foreign language always includes teaching another culture has guided foreign language education since Kramsch's (1993) *Context and Culture in Language Teaching*. Because language is used in a cultural context and this context is reflected in the language and how it is used to communicate, foreign language learning needs to make this cultural context available to language learners: If we assume that EFL learners in a German secondary school have learned words and phrases to talk about their school day, they may be equipped with the linguistic means to share their daily school experiences (teachers, subjects, activities, tests, etc.) with pupils from an English speaking country. However, it may already be difficult for them to understand and translate words like ›school assembly‹ (UK), to understand the significance of school uniforms or grasp the role that sports play in US high school communities. These examples may illustrate that it is not only necessary to focus on language as a linguistic system, but that we also need to help our learners understand the **cultural contexts** which are reflected in the language and which are necessary to understand if they want to communicate successfully in a foreign language.

Over the last decades, a number of different concepts, approaches and methodologies have been developed which provide suggestions about what exactly culture pedagogy should focus on and how ›culture‹ can be taught in foreign language education. This chapter introduces readers to basic concepts, theories, models and methods for teaching culture in the foreign language classroom. It sets out to define ›culture‹ and provide a brief outline of how the teaching of culture in English Language Teaching (ELT) has changed over the last decades. In addition, the chapter will present **educational objectives**, **basic assumptions** and concepts of **relevant approaches** such as Cultural Studies in ELT, intercultural learning, transcultural learning, global education and multilingualism, thus providing insights into the pedagogical and methodological repertoire that foreign language education can rely on for teaching ›culture‹. Three teaching examples at the end will serve to illustrate some of the pedagogical principles and propose ideas for putting educational objectives for cultural

Culture pedagogy

learning processes into practice. The **teaching proposals** will focus on three relevant aspects: (1) representing and exploring culture, (2) understanding culture and reading literary texts, (3) participating in cultural discourses.

9.1 | What is culture? Definitions and concepts

The idea that a foreign language cannot be taught without the culture(s) in which this language is used to communicate has generally been accepted in foreign language education. However, the ideas about ›what‹ exactly should be taught when teaching culture and the ideas about ›why‹ and ›how‹ it should be done, have changed over the last decades. These changes can be seen as a reflection of the academic discourse in the field of **Cultural Studies** about how culture can be described, explained and understood as well as a reflection of the role that teaching and learning about culture(s) is assigned in society. It is necessary, first of all, to reflect what ›culture‹ is or how it can be defined and explained before taking a closer look at approaches and concepts of how it can be taught.

Culture as a controversial term: The term ›culture‹ is a controversial term which has had many different meanings. One of the past controversies is connected to the idea of culture as something that can be classified as valuable to a greater or lesser extent: In colonial times, for example, the cultural achievements of ›civilisation‹ were contrasted with more ›primitive‹ or ›uncivilised‹ ways of life in order to justify colonial oppression (cf. Sommer 2003, 7). Another distinction that is or was often made is one between ›**high‹ culture**, for example the arts, literature or architecture, and ›**low‹ culture**, which usually refers, for example to popular culture, mass media etc. Modern approaches within Cultural Studies as a discipline avoid such evaluations of culture and aim at describing, explaining and understanding culture and processes of cultural change instead.

Culture as a set of shared meanings: While there are still many different concepts and definitions of ›culture‹, it has generally been agreed upon that, as Hall (1997, 1) suggests, »culture is about ›shared meanings‹«:

> To say that two people belong to the same culture is to say that they interpret the world in roughly the same ways and can express themselves, their thoughts and feelings about the world, in ways which will be understood by each other. Thus culture depends on its participants interpreting meaningfully what is happening around them, and ›making sense‹ of the world in broadly similar ways. (ibid., 2)

The idea of culture as a set of shared meanings among the members of a cultural group, however, does not mean that culture could be seen as a homogeneous, stable or fixed entity. Instead, it needs to be conceived of as heterogeneous and always in a flux. As Hall points out, »in any culture, there is always a diversity of meanings about any topic, and more than one way of interpreting or representing it« (ibid., 2). Any representation

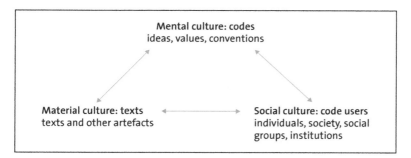

Illustration 9.1:
Three dimensions
of culture
(according to
Posner 2003, 47 ff.)

of culture in the classroom therefore needs to make sure that this **diversity of meanings** is also made accessible to learners so that they can understand **cultures as complex, heterogeneous entities**.

Three dimensions of culture: Cultural Semiotics distinguishes three dimensions of culture: a **material**, a **mental** and a **social dimension** (cf. Posner 2003).

- Material culture refers to texts (literature, theatre, film, etc.) and other artefacts (art, architecture, clothing, products of everyday life).
- Mental culture includes collective ideas, norms and values, perceptions of self and other, worldviews or ideologies.
- Social culture consists of society, social institutions (educational, administrative, political, judicial) and cultural agents (individuals, collective groups, etc.).

Of course, these dimensions do not exist separately, but are linked and interact with each other constantly: Children's books, for example, are part of the material dimension of culture, but also reflect cultural norms and values (mental dimension) and there are also rituals like reading a bedtime story to young children which fulfil different social functions within the family and society (social dimension). If we look at how children's books have developed over time, it is easy to see how changes in cultural norms and values have also led to a change in the way children's stories are told (e. g. with or without moralizing undertones) and, possibly, even in the way the bedtime story ritual is performed.

Representing culture in the classroom: The three-dimensional model of culture is not only relevant for Cultural Studies, but also for the EFL teacher who chooses or designs materials and makes decisions about how culture can be represented in the classroom: Teaching culture, in fact, means exploring the ›shared set of meanings‹, the values, norms and ways of thinking of the participants of a cultural group, as well as the social and institutional forms in which they live. However, the opportunities to observe the social dimension in the EFL classroom directly are limited and the mental dimension can only be observed and interpreted indirectly with the help of cultural manifestations or phenomena (cf. Hallet 2007, 38 f.). While it is, of course, desirable to provide opportunities for learners to experience the social dimension of culture directly through **school exchanges** or **telecollaboration**, the FL classroom is still to a large extent dependent on the **representation of culture through artefacts** like texts, visuals, music or realia (street signs, clothing, decorations, etc.).

›Culture as text‹ vs. ›culture as discursive practice‹: Another concept or idea that is relevant for the representation of culture in the FL classroom originates in Cultural Anthropology: The metaphor of ›culture as text‹ suggests that cultures can be read and interpreted like complex texts and that every cultural text is linked to many other cultural texts (cf. Bachmann-Medick 2004). In Cultural Studies, however, the metaphor of ›culture as text‹ has also been criticised, because it neglects the **›cultural agents‹**, who exchange, share and negotiate cultural meanings. This leads to an understanding of ›culture as discursive practice‹, which assumes that culture is a dialogic and discursive process in which cultural meanings are negotiated among the participants of a culture (cf. Küster 2005).

Modelling cultural discourses: Hallet (2002) therefore suggests that cultures can be conceived of as a vast ensemble of texts and cultural discourses, as a **›textual and discursive space‹**, which can be made accessible to learners in the FL classroom by modelling cultural discourses: If every cultural text is linked to other cultural texts which together make up a particular cultural discourse (›**intertextuality**‹), then reading this cultural text allows learners to access or interpret the cultural discourses that constitute the respective culture. This idea, of course, relies on the assumption that any cultural text can only be read or understood within the **cultural context(s)** to which it belongs and that it is necessary to provide opportunities for learners to read a text within the relevant cultural contexts. The idea of representing cultures by modelling cultural discourses therefore implies that teachers (or course book editors) have to select a combination of texts and materials which can open up the complexity and diversity of cultures and cultural meanings to their learners.

According to Decke-Cornill (1994) and Hallet (2002), **intertextuality** and **multiperspectivity** should be guiding principles and criteria for the selection and combination of texts: The complexity of cultures and the polyphony of cultural discourses can only be represented by a multitude of texts which open up a **diversity of voices** within a culture. In addition, text arrangements also need to take into account that real-life discourses are **multimodal**, i. e. they draw on various genres and media.

Key points

> **Principles for modelling cultural discourses (cf. Hallet 2007, 39 ff.)**
> - relevance of topics and issues: selected texts need to be relevant for a particular cultural context
> - openness of text combinations: learners should be encouraged to research and find additional texts
> - multitextuality and multiperspectivity: text combinations should represent diverse voices of cultural discourses
> - intertextuality: texts need to be perceived as linked but not redundant
> - multimediality and multimodality: cultural discourses should be represented through a variety of texts, media and modes
> - relevance of literary texts and films: learners can access the com-

> plexity of cultural discourses through literary texts because they represent a diversity of meanings and voices, and because they take up ideas, modify them or create new meanings with the help of literary devices (cf. Surkamp/Nünning 2016, 41 f.)

Participating in cultural and global discourses: The ability to participate in cultural discourses can be seen as a central educational goal of foreign language learning because it enables pupils to take part in social processes and to shape their own real-life worlds (cf. Hallet 2011, 54 ff.). Learners can develop this ability by dealing with or reacting to the texts they encounter in the foreign language classroom. If we imagine that the texts introduced into the classroom belong to real-life discourses, then the production of the learners' own (oral or written) texts as a reaction to the original one can be seen as their participation in the discourses of the respective culture. If the texts are also shared with others outside the classroom, the pupils can even be viewed as ›cultural agents‹ who take part in shaping processes of cultural negotiation.

In that respect, foreign language learning has also benefited from the introduction of new media technologies. The term ›web 2.0‹ refers to different tools and applications like blogs, chats, wikis, online communities, etc. which invite Internet users to share their texts, pictures or videos with others outside the classroom and to collaborate with them, for example in the production of written or multimedia texts. These technologies help to **connect learners** with people all over the world, thus providing **new opportunities for interaction** with real audiences and for taking over new roles (cf. chapter 12 in this volume).

9.2 | Intercultural approaches: concepts, models and dimensions

The role of teaching culture in foreign language education has, just as other educational activities or processes, always been influenced by social norms and values as well as by different ideas about what knowledge, skills and attitudes learners need to acquire in order to be able to satisfy their individual needs, meet the requirements of the job market or take up social, economic and ecological challenges in a globalised world. In our world today, which is characterised by mobility and migration, digitalisation and globalisation, the ability to communicate and interact with people across languages and cultures has become a key competence. This idea is also reflected in the German educational standards and curricula as well as European educational documents like the CEFR (*Common European Framework of Reference for Modern Languages*), which put a special focus on the development of ›**intercultural communicative competence**‹ **(ICC)** in foreign language education (cf. chapter 2 in this volume).

Development of intercultural approaches: While in the 1970s (and before), the teaching of **Landeskunde** (area studies) was often reduced to the acquisition of knowledge about so-called ›target cultures‹, their history, political institutions and society, the idea of intercultural learning was developed in foreign language education in the 1980s and 1990s. As Delanoy and Volkmann (2006) state in their book *Cultural Studies in the EFL Classroom*, intercultural learning has challenged the notion that culture was something fixed and objective. In addition, the role of the learners has become a more active one as »they were invited to become personally involved in the exploration of English-speaking cultures as self-reflective co-constructors of cultural meanings« (ibid., 13). The idea that cultures must be understood as complex, dynamic and always in a flux and the notion of **learners as ›intercultural agents‹** (Hallet 2002) must not be misunderstood in the way that knowledge about culture has become obsolete, but that the role of attitudes and skills has finally been acknowledged, which had not been in the focus of teaching *Landeskunde*.

Intercultural communicative competence: ICC as an educational aim and concept for English language teaching has mostly been influenced by Byram (1997). The term refers to the ability to communicate and interact with people who speak a different language and come from a different cultural background. The shift from ›communicative competence‹ to ›intercultural communicative competence‹ as the educational goal of foreign language learning and from the role model of the ›native speaker‹ to the ›**intercultural speaker**‹ implies a special focus on the sociocultural context in which people communicate and on their cultural identities: It can be assumed that both the context and cultural identities influence the way people in a particular situation interact with and perceive each other. Byram, therefore, argues that foreign language learners need to acquire a set of knowledge, skills and attitudes in order to become ›intercultural speakers‹.

Definition	An intercultural speaker is somebody who has acquired the necessary knowledge, skills and attitudes which allow him or her to manage intercultural encounters or solve intercultural conflicts. He or she has also acquired what may be called ›**critical cultural awareness‹**, which means that he/she is generally aware of how an intercultural situation and the way participants communicate may be influenced by their cultural identities and backgrounds (cf. Byram 1997).

The model of ›intercultural communication‹, which is used by Byram to define the required knowledge, skills and attitudes of an ›intercultural speaker‹, includes five dimensions (Byram 1997, 49 ff., cf. table 9.1):

1. **Attitudes**: curiosity and openness, readiness to suspend disbelief about other cultures and belief about one's own
2. **Knowledge** of social groups and their products and practices in one's own and in one's interlocutor's country, and of the general processes of societal and individual interaction

3. **Skills of interpreting and relating**: ability to interpret a document or event from another culture, to explain it and relate it to documents from one's own

4. **Skills of discovery and interaction**: ability to acquire new knowledge of a culture and cultural practices and the ability to operate knowledge, attitudes and skills under the constraints of real-time communication and interaction

5. **Critical cultural awareness/political education**: ability to evaluate critically and on the basis of explicit criteria perspectives, practices and products in one's own and other cultures and countries

Byram's model was intended to help language teachers plan and assess intercultural learning processes in classroom settings and it has therefore also been used as a basis for defining different competences of ICC in the CEFR, in the *Bildungsstandards* and in the design of teaching materials and tasks (cf. Tesch et al. 2008). Recent research shows, however, that ICC continues to be an elusive concept which is difficult to assess or evaluate (cf. Hu/Byram 2009) because attitudes like ›respect for others‹ or the ability to reflect critically about one's own views cannot be categorised or measured easily. In addition, intercultural learning continues to be a **lifelong learning process** and the question what FL learners can be expected to be able to do at different levels of proficiency still needs more investigation.

Didaktik des Fremdverstehens: Intercultural learning has also been the focus of approaches in German ELT research that were developed by the research group *Didaktik des Fremdverstehens* since the 1990s (cf. Bredella/Christ 1995; 2007). These intercultural approaches aim at developing learners' ability to understand people who speak a different language and have a different cultural background. They rely on the basic assumptions that (1) there is a (cultural) gap which needs to be bridged and (2) in order to enable intercultural understanding, it is necessary to enter into a dialogue between ›self‹ and ›other‹.

Dialogue between self and other: The notion of ›dialogue between self and other‹ includes the idea that the ›self‹ needs to turn to other positions in order to learn from them and that previous assumptions, ideas or attitudes about the ›other‹ are changed in the process. This view implies that it is necessary to ›**decentre**‹, i. e. to **become aware of and reflect one's**

	Skills interpret and relate (savoir comprendre)	
Knowledge of self and other; of interaction: individual and societal (savoirs)	Education political education critical cultural awareness (savoir s'engager)	Attitudes relativising self valuing other (savoir être)
	Skills discover and/or interact (savoir apprendre/faire)	

Table 9.1:
Factors in
intercultural
communication
(Byram 1997)

own views and perspectives, in order to **overcome ethnocentric judgments**. Instead of reducing the ›other‹ to one's own interpretations, *Fremdverstehen* aims at giving the ›other‹ a voice and at reconstructing his or her views and ways of seeing or interpreting the world.

Self and other as subjective, relational and dynamic categories: While the concept of *Fremdverstehen* relies on the categories of self and other, at the same time, they need to be reflected critically: If self and other are understood as ontological, fixed categories where ›one's own culture‹ is contrasted with ›the other culture‹, they may lead to exclusion and stigmatisation of the ›other‹ (cf. Bredella/Delanoy 1999, 14). It is therefore important to understand self and other as subjective, relational and dynamic categories which are defined differently for each individual and are subject to change: What may be considered as ›other‹ by an individual at some point, can become familiar and may even be integrated into one's own identity; and whatever view or position is considered part of one's identity or self may suddenly, through experience or reflection, seem strange or unfamiliar to us so that we decide to distance ourselves from this part of our identity or ›self‹.

Changing perspectives and negotiating meaning: *Fremdverstehen* aims at **critical self-distancing (›decentring‹)**, at understanding the other's views and perspectives and at a ›negotiation of meaning‹ which evolves from this dialogue between self and other. The ability to decentre, to change and take over another perspective in order to see the world with different eyes is therefore central to this idea of intercultural understanding. However, it is also important to understand that *Fremdverstehen* does not end with a reconstruction of the other's perspective, but includes the idea of dialogue, of an interplay in which different views or perspectives are negotiated so that pre-existing views are critically reflected and, possibly, changed. This does not imply that learners need to agree with the other's views or perspectives, but that they at least arrive at a more reflected understanding of their own views and perceptions as well as those of the other.

9.3 | Transcultural perspectives in culture pedagogy

Transculturality and hybridity: Due to the fact that our world and our societies today are largely influenced by migration, cultural change and the global exchange of information as well as goods, terms like ›interculturality‹ and ›multiculturality‹ have been found to be unsuitable to come to terms with the growing heterogeneity and entanglements of cultures. ›Transculturality‹, like ›**transnationality**‹ or ›hybridity‹, are concepts that have therefore been used in Cultural Studies to describe **cultural complexity**, the **dynamics of cultural change** as well as the internal differentiation within and the **interconnectedness of cultures** (cf. Antor 2006; Risager 2006). According to Welsch's (1999) conceptualisation of the term, modern cultures can all be described as ›transcultural‹ and ›hybrid‹ because they share certain characteristics: inner differentiation and complexity; external networking and entanglements of cultures; hybridisation, i. e. a mix(ing) of different cultural elements (like, for example, in the mix of Western and Indian music styles in Bhangra music).

> Transculturality refers to a number of characteristics that are shared by modern cultures: inner differentiation, polyphony, cultural complexity, hybridity, external networking and entanglements with other cultures. Cultures and identities can be described as ›transcultural‹ if traditional categories of, i. e. national, cultural, religious communities, are deliberately questioned, broken up or transgressed.

Definition

Transcultural identities: In addition, we also have to assume that the multiplicity and diversity of lifestyles in a society leads to **multiple identifications** of individuals: The term ›transcultural identity‹ refers to the idea that individuals can identify with multiple cultural or collective groups that cut through traditional cultural boundaries.

Ae Fond Kiss

Example

The example of a young woman in the film *Ae Fond Kiss* (Loach 2004) illustrates how individuals develop hybrid cultural identities. The character Tahara Khan describes herself as a »dazzling mixture«, when she states »I am a Glaswegian, Pakistani, teenager, woman of Muslim descent who supports Glasgow Rangers in a Catholic school«, thus challenging notions of what it means to be ›Glaswegian‹, ›Pakistani‹, ›Muslim‹, ›Woman‹ and ›Catholic‹. The concept of ›transculturality‹, as used in Cultural Studies, therefore implies an understanding of culture as hybrid, polyphonous and entangled with other cultures and draws attention to the choices of identification that individuals have when constructing their identities.

The FL classroom as ›third space‹: Hallet (2002) has elaborated ›transculturality‹ as a concept for structuring and designing the language classroom: With reference to the postcolonial concept of ›third space‹ (Bhabha 1994), he suggests that the foreign language classroom itself can be viewed as a ›third space‹, as a **›hybrid space‹** for cultural encounters in which learners are confronted with and acquire previously unknown cultural meanings, in which they negotiate or reinterpret these new cultural meanings. The **›interplay of texts and cultures‹** (cf. Hallet 2002) is initiated by feeding texts from different cultural spheres (e. g. L1 cultures, L2 cultures, transcultural or global discourse communities) into the FL classroom, which are then processed and negotiated by the learners. Foreign language learners thus become ›**intercultural agents‹** themselves who exchange cultural meanings, values and perspectives and thus participate in the processes of **cultural negotiation** and even cultural change. Intertextual arrangements are seen as necessary for a negotiation of diverse cultural meanings and for broadening the learners' repertoire of cultural orientation and identification.

Transcultural approaches in ELT: Transculturality is also seen as a useful concept by other researchers who emphasise that, in foreign language education, too, cultures need to be understood as complex, hybrid and always in a flux. While some argue that the intercultural approach needs to be replaced by a transcultural approach (cf. Eckerth/Wendt 2003; Fäcke 2006), others argue against a transcultural approach (cf. Bredella 2012), because it assumes that there are no cultural differences and because it disregards the recognition of the ›other‹ and a dialogue in which the notion of ›self‹ can be challenged.

Dialogue between inter- and transculturality: Delanoy (2006) is in favour of a dialogue between intercultural and transcultural approaches. In his view, intercultural learning and its focus on a dialogue between self and other has always included the idea of a continuous negotiation of meaning, which also leads to the transformation of existing views and the development of new, hybrid positions. Delanoy, therefore, views intercultural approaches as compatible with a transcultural agenda as long as they are aware of internal cultural differences and hybridity and as long as they view cultures as dynamic, heterogeneous, hybrid entities. Regardless of these controversies, what transcultural approaches have in common is the basic assumption that contemporary culture pedagogy needs a focus on issues like cultural **diversity**, internal differentiation, **hybridity** and transcultural identities: The selection of input, goals and activities for the FL classroom should draw the learners' attention to the complexity and hybridity of cultures and identities. In this respect, multi- and transcultural literary texts offer a high potential, because they portray characters' conflicting loyalties and their hybrid identities (cf. Delanoy 2006; Schumann 2008; Freitag-Hild 2010).

Principles for inter- and transcultural learning

There are several pedagogic and methodological principles which can help with the selection of materials and the design of tasks or even learning arrangements.

1. **Multiperspectivity:** In order to sensitise foreign language learners to the diversity and hybridity of cultures as well as people's complex cultural identities, teachers need to make sure that multiple perspectives and diverse voices are represented and ›heard‹ in the classroom. This requires the integration of literary texts and intertextual arrangements that assemble a multiplicity of perspectives (cf. Hallet 2002) and that draw attention to cultural hybridity and transcultural phenomena, thus pointing to the fact that ›culture‹ is always heterogeneous and in a flux.

2. **Dialogue:** Inter- and transcultural learning also includes the idea of entering a dialogue between the learners and a literary text, a literary character or different cultural views. It is important for the learners to recognise views and cultural perspectives that are different from their own and to negotiate these different positions. The task design therefore needs to make such dialogue possible (cf. table 9.2 on page 171; Surkamp/Nünning 2014, chapter II.2).

3. **Reflection:** Inter- and transcultural learning aims at developing the

learners' ability to reflect critically about their own perspective and to break up ethnocentric views or essentialist concepts of culture and identity. They are encouraged to distance themselves from their own perspective.

Global education: A new, transcultural and even interdisciplinary approach to teaching culture is »global education«, an approach to education which—according to Cates (2000, 241)—»aims to promote students' knowledge and awareness of world peoples, countries, cultures and issues«. Its basic idea is enabling young people to become **responsible global citizens** and actively take part in shaping a better, shared future in the world. Global education takes up the ideas and principles of approaches like peace studies, environmental education, intercultural learning or human rights education. It involves integrating a global perspective in the language classroom through a **focus on international themes and global issues** (cf. Lütge 2015a).

While culture pedagogy in EFL sets out from a focus on English speaking countries and cultures, global education rather starts from topics of global relevance and from English as ›lingua franca‹ which is used to communicate with people all over the world. The activities in the classroom should provide opportunities for learners to build up **knowledge** about various countries, cultures and global issues, to develop their **skills** of intercultural communication, to develop **attitudes** like global awareness, respect for diversity and empathy and to become aware of their social responsibility as world citizens. This includes becoming aware of how lives, lifestyles and economies throughout the world are interconnected and dependent on each other: Both in the foreign language classroom and in CLIL settings, learners can be encouraged to do some research about the T-Shirts or sports shoes they are wearing or to find out about where the food they buy in the supermarket comes from. Thus, the English classroom can also contribute to raising the learners' awareness of how their own lifestyles or decisions to buy certain products may be connected to mechanisms of the global economy, to the working conditions of textile workers in Asia or to a changing planet, to name but a few examples.

Multilingualism and the multilingual subject: Further developments in culture pedagogy highlight the close connection between language and culture teaching, which has been an issue for foreign language education since Kramsch's (1993) *Context and Culture in Language Teaching* and is also relevant in Risager's (2006) concept of ›languaculture‹. In her book *The Multilingual Subject*, Kramsch (2009) also calls for a more dedicated recognition of language learners' **multilingual subjectivities** by taking into account the different languages (and their different identities) that learners bring to the classroom. She argues for developing language learners' ›**symbolic competence**‹ which refers to the ability to use different symbolic systems (i. e. languages and their semiotic resources) in order to share, exchange and reflect on people's experiences: Being a multilingual subject, in Kramsch's (ibid., 201) words, means

[...] having the choice of belonging to different communities of sign users, resonating to events differently when expressed through different semiotic systems, positioning oneself differently in different languages, and ultimately having the words to reflect upon this experience and to cast it into an appropriate symbolic form [...].

9.4 | Teaching literature and culture

The potential of literature for intercultural learning: One of the research areas within culture pedagogy is concerned with the question how literary texts can be used to promote intercultural understanding and intercultural competence (cf. Bredella 2002; Burwitz-Melzer 2003; as well as chapter 11 in this volume). There are different reasons why literary texts are considered valuable in that respect:

1. Readers as spectators, participants and critics: First of all, literary texts invite readers **to engage with the text** (cf. Bredella/Burwitz-Melzer 2004): as a ›spectator‹ who observes what is happening in the fictional world, as a ›participant‹ who uses his/her imagination to ›take part‹ in the events of the story, who learns to see the world with the characters' eyes but also evaluates their behaviour, and as a ›critic‹ who reflects on how the text affects him/herself and on the views that are presented. Thus, literary texts can provide insights into different cultural realities and real-life worlds, they invite readers to **change perspectives** and they can also challenge the learners' views and prompt a **critical reflection** or **negotiation of self and other**.

2. Literary texts as part of cultural discourses: Secondly, literary texts are no mimetic reflection of reality, but use literary devices (e. g. point of view, plot, characters) to present a particular view of reality: they may draw attention to individual voices and experiences, exaggerate or distort social developments, question dominant ideas in society or present utopian or even dystopian visions of what life could be like (cf. Surkamp/Nünning 2014, chapter III.1). Literary texts, in that sense, take part in the cultural discourses of a society and can therefore also provide access to the cultural discourses to which they belong (cf. Hallet 2002; 2007).

3. Multi- and transcultural literature: Thirdly, transcultural approaches highlight literature's potential of drawing attention to the diversity and complexity of cultures and cultural identities: Internal differences, conflicting ideas and multiple, hybrid identities are especially portrayed in postcolonial literature or multi- and transcultural literary texts. Dealing with culture and cultural hybridity as well as cultural identities can raise the learners' **awareness** of the complexity and diversity of cultures and identities (cf. Schumann 2008; Freitag-Hild 2010).

Empathetic and cultural reading: When teaching literature to promote intercultural understanding and transcultural learning, there are different ways of reading literary texts that can be used to support different cultural learning processes (cf. Schumann 2008): Empathetic reading refers to methods that help learners to take over the perspective of various characters, to reconstruct their views and understand their situation and behaviour from the inside. Cultural reading aims at reading a literary text as part of a cultural discourse. This includes **contextualisation**: in order to understand how a literary text responds to or comments on cultural discourses, it is necessary to read further fictional and non-fictional texts to be able to reconstruct the particular voice of that literary text. These different ways of reading literature are also represented in the task typology for teaching literary texts as presented by Freitag-Hild (cf. 2010, 120 f.).

Task type	Task function (aims)	Task formats and examples
1. warming up / tuning in	developing curiosity and readiness to deal with cultural ›otherness‹	▪ pre-reading tasks: building hypotheses and expectations about characters, topics, etc.
2. self-reflection	creating awareness and critical reflection of self	▪ sharing reader reactions: reading log, discussing and reflecting reactions to characters, events, etc.
3. interpretation and change of perspectives	understanding perspectives: interpretation, change of perspectives, coordination	▪ while-reading tasks: character profiles, run-on diaries ▪ assignments and tasks with a focus on characters and their relationships ▪ creative tasks: scenic interpretation, rewriting texts
4. analysis and reflection	understanding and reflecting effects of literary devices	▪ literary analysis of characters, content, literary devices ▪ reflection about reader reactions
5. negotiation and participation	negotiation of meaning, dialogue	▪ class discussions about reader reactions and interpretations ▪ class discussions about cultural views, experiences, perspectives ▪ writing a review
6. contextualisation	contextualising and cultural reading: understanding a text within its cultural context(s)	▪ researching background information, cultural knowledge ▪ intertextual comparison of different texts ▪ relating a text to one's own lifeworld
7. reflection	self-reflection, awareness of requirements for intercultural learning and understanding	▪ reflecting self and other ▪ reflecting one's own intercultural learning process

Table 9.2:
Task types for promoting intercultural competence through literature

9.5 | Teaching culture in and beyond the classroom: three teaching examples

The following examples serve to illustrate how these theoretical considerations about why and how we need to teach culture in foreign language education can be put into practice.

Putting theory in practice

1. Representing and exploring culture: a learning circle about South Africa: The first example refers to a learning circle about »Exploring South Africa: The rainbow nation« and provides some ideas for representing culture in the classroom. It was designed for a class of 10th graders in the year 2010 when South Africa was hosting the Fifa World Cup. The fact that the eyes of the world were focused on South Africa, but the pupils' knowledge about the ›rainbow nation‹ was rather limited, was the reason for the class to take a closer look at this country, to find out more about its past and present, its society, culture and political issues—and about the question what hosting the World Cup meant for South Africa and its people.

Modelling cultural discourses: The teaching unit started by working with two short films about teenagers in Cape Town: *Teens in South Africa* (Download: http://www.planet-schule.de). They provided insight into the everyday lives of the two teenagers and their families, whose lives were also linked to social, cultural and historical issues of the country (Apartheid, sports, living in a township, education, AIDS). The fact that the films were linked to several relevant discourses of the country's past and present made it possible for the teacher to look for additional texts (e. g. pictures, photos, postcards, articles, cartoons, film trailer, map, statistics, etc.) that would open up these cultural discourses to the learners. The topics that were touched upon in the film and taken up again for the learning circle included Apartheid, the film *Invictus* (as an example of how a nation can be united through sports, cf. also Alter 2016), education, facts and figures and a reading corner about Nelson Mandela. These five topics were chosen as stations for the learning circle and learners had to work through three of them in small groups.

In addition to modelling cultural discourses of South Africa's past and present, the learning circle engaged learners with texts and materials by providing authentic, **complex target tasks** (cf. chapter 6 in this volume): While working their way through different assignments for the selected materials, learners had to use their knowledge and skills, for example to design a poster about how apartheid violated human rights or prepare a one-minute-speech about why the class should go to see the film *Invictus* in the cinema. After the learning circle, the students were encouraged to work on a magazine which would open up relevant aspects about South Africa's past and present to other people in and outside their school. Every group of students was responsible for a double page on a topic of their choice (e. g. Fifa World Cup, Apartheid, Kwaito Music, etc.). Thus, it was also possible for the learners to research topics and relevant texts independently and to present to others what they thought was relevant to know about the host of the 2010 Fifa World Cup.

2. Understanding culture and entering a dialogue with literary texts: The second example refers to teaching a young adult novel: **Sherman**

Alexie's *The Absolutely True Diary of a Part-Time Indian* (cf. also Eisenmann 2016). It is the story of fourteen-year-old Arnold Spirit (Junior), a member of the Spokane tribe living on a reservation in the north-west of the USA. His life at the ›rez‹ (reservation) is characterized by poverty, violence and alcoholism, but he can also rely on his loving parents and grandmother for support. However, due to brain damage, he is a fragile character who is continually beaten up by the other children at his Native American school. His only friend is violent Rowdy, who protects him. When one day, Junior realizes that he is still taught with the same old books his mother had had at school, he becomes angry and throws the book at his teacher. It is the turning point of the story where Junior has to decide whether he wants to stay at his old school without any hope or perspective for the future or transfer schools to Reardan, which is attended mostly by wealthy white children. At the new school, he is an outcast again because he is the only Indian, but he also makes new friends and we follow his first year at the new school with a number of ups and downs.

Teaching potential: The novel is a good choice for 14–15-year-olds for a number of reasons: First of all, it is told by a 14-year-old himself whose voice is that of a youngster speaking to other young people and the way he tells the story is quite humorous. In addition, the story focuses on topics like first love, friendship and striving to be accepted, which can help teenagers to identify with Junior, although he is not a typical hero. What makes the novel interesting for intercultural learning is that the narrative perspective (Junior as I-narrator) invites readers to take over Junior's perspective and therefore also helps to understand what life is like for him or how he feels about some of the (tragic) events that happen throughout the story. The novel can provide learners with an inside view of one young (fictional) Native American who lives on a reservation but takes up the challenge of attending an all-white school nearby. From a transcultural point of view, it is also interesting to look at Arnold's complex (trans-)cultural identity which he develops throughout the story: »I realized that, sure, I was a Spokane Indian. I belonged to that tribe. But I also belonged to the tribe of American immigrants. And to the tribe of basketball players. And to the tribe of bookworms« (Alexie 2009, 198).

Empathetic and cultural reading: The teaching unit should include a focus on both empathetic and cultural reading as suggested in inter- and transcultural approaches: empathetic reading can be encouraged by focusing on Junior, his identity and self-image and/or his experiences throughout the novel. It is advisable to invite learners to work on a number of tasks and activities supporting the interpretation and change of perspectives (cf. table 9.2 on page 171): collecting important information about Junior, an interpretation of his cartoons, writing a characterisation or role biography, retelling an event at school to his grandmother, acting out a role interview, as well as an analysis of Junior's development throughout the novel. At the same time, it is also necessary to provide opportunities for learners to read about reservations and to inform themselves about their past and present. Thus, learners can compare Junior's story to other information they find about reservations and relate the different texts to each other. Tasks for contextualisation (cf. table 9.2) are relevant to make learners aware of the fact that this particular novel is not a mirror of real life, but presents a unique voice (e. g. both funny and tragic) within the cultural discourses about reservations and Native Americans: Junior's story needs to be understood as a fictional account of life on a reservation; it is not a reliable source of information, but can be seen as one out of many possible voices which enables readers to see the world through this particular character's eyes.

3. Participating in cultural discourses: »Raise your voice—change climate change«: The final example is a project on climate change in grade 11. The students in the class were especially talented in the natural sciences so that the teaching unit matched their interests. Before the project started, the students had already studied various materials on the topic (articles, statistics, documentaries, etc.). The project itself was based on an idea which had been pursued by YouTube and CNN in the weeks leading up to the Climate Change Conference in Copenhagen in 2009. YouTube and CNN had started a campaign with the name »Raise your voice—change climate change« which was aimed at individuals who also wanted to have a say in the climate change debate and who wanted to ›raise their voice‹ for politicians and world leaders to hear. They invited people to upload their videos with a message on climate change, and the online community could vote for the best video. The winners were invited to join in a TV debate with global leaders during the Copenhagen Conference.

Unfortunately, when the project started in December, the Conference had already ended so that the audience for the pupils' videos was a lot more limited than it could have been. Nevertheless, the project task for the pupils was to raise their voice, too, and in groups produce a video, poster, cartoon or presentation with their message on climate change. The final products were then presented to the classmates in a gallery walk so that every pupil had the chance to raise his/her voice in front of an authentic audience and to discuss their personal viewpoint with a small group. Each group of learners had prepared a statement that they wanted to make—about climate change, about an individual's responsibility, about ways for reducing one's carbon footprint, about the state of the earth. By researching and selecting relevant information, by choosing an adequate format for communicating their message and by voicing their ideas during their presentations, learners were given the opportunity to participate in the global discourses and exchange their views with their classmates. Using Internet tools, telecollaboration or projects like the one by YouTube and CNN, of course, even extends the ways of communication as it includes a global audience of world citizens (cf. also chapter 13 in this volume).

9.6 | Conclusion

The intention of this chapter was to introduce readers to the basic questions of culture pedagogy: What is culture and how can we teach it? As the brief survey of different approaches for the teaching of culture has shown, culture pedagogy has witnessed some profound changes over the last decades and has been influenced to a great extent by developments in Cultural Studies. We have seen that cultures can be defined as ›shared sets of meaning‹, but that we also need to include the material and social dimension. The notion of culture as a vast textual and discursive space which can be made accessible to learners can be a useful idea for the representation of cultures in the classroom. Byram's model of ICC and the concept of *Fremdverstehen* can be used as a basis for planning learning processes because they draw attention to the different skills, attitudes and knowledge that are required for successful intercultural encounters. In addition, literary texts can be valuable for cultural learning processes because they provide opportunities to change perspectives, to reflect about one's own and other people's views and because they can prompt an exchange and negotiation of meaning.

Further reading

Delanoy, Werner/Volkmann, Laurenz (eds.) (2006): *Cultural Studies in the EFL Classroom*. Heidelberg.
Hallet, Wolfgang/Nünning, Ansgar (eds.) (2007): *Neue Ansätze und Konzepte der Literatur- und Kulturdidaktik*. Trier.
Risager, Karen (2007): *Language and Culture Pedagogy. From a National to a Transnational Paradigm*. Clevedon.

Britta Freitag-Hild

10 Literature and Film—Approaching Fictional Texts and Media

»Literature is back, but wearing different clothes«, as Maley (1989, 59) pointed out some years ago. In recent years, the **role of texts** in the teaching of literature in ELT has developed a number of new facets and dimensions that have completely changed in comparison to earlier decades. The didactics of literature has explored many questions such as **how and why** texts—both literary and audio-visual formats—should be introduced to the English language classroom and which **goals** might be followed at different levels. The advent of new media or transcultural and global issues, the inclusion of younger or generally neglected learner groups, broader definitions of what constitutes literature and, consequently, broader concepts of classroom methodology in ELT are mirroring current trends in literary and cultural studies and in foreign language pedagogy. This chapter provides an introduction to basic concepts and competences of teaching literature and refers to questions of text selection and different literary genres. Different approaches and methods of teaching literature and film as well as perspectives and challenges for the literature classroom will be discussed.

10.1 | Literature matters: a rationale for teaching literature and film

The question why we teach literature at all, particularly in the context of foreign language education, has raised a lot of interest among literary scholars and teacher educators in the relatively new research field of *literature didactics* which first emerged at universities in the German-speaking countries in the 1970s. Influences from neighbouring disciplines such as literary studies and pedagogy as well as the general impact connected to developments in education policy and curriculum design must also be taken into account.

Why literature?

Long tradition: The teaching of literature in modern language lessons has played a prominent role ever since the 19th century and has undergone considerable changes over the decades. Originally, learning objectives as well as teaching practice were both modelled on ancient languages and focussed strongly on the translation of significant works of

English and French literary history (cf. also chapter 1 in this volume). The goal was to convey cultural achievements of the so-called target cultures with a strong educational, rather than specifically linguistic focus in literature lessons, which were often taught in German (cf. Surkamp 2012, 488). Back in 1943, Leavis (34 f.) characterised literature study as a »supremely civilising pursuit«, in fact, his view was that it »trains, in a way no other discipline can, intelligence and sensibility together, cultivating sensitiveness and precision of response and a delicate integrity of intelligence«. Such a view has now been discarded as a purely academic if not downright elitist opinion. Similarly, the establishment of an allegedly elite literary ›canon‹ was seriously challenged and led to a gradual opening for new texts—and films.

Two major currents

The twentieth century witnessed the development of two major currents in literary studies, i.e. the New Criticism in the first half of the century and Reader Response Theory in the 1970s and 1980s. The **New Criticism** can briefly be summarised as a text-centred current with a focus on ›objective literary studies‹ and structuralist methods of interpretation and the formal elements of literary texts. As a contrast, the influence of the **Reader Response Theory** focussed on the reading process as a creative act involving the reader and his or her exchange with the literary text which was more received as a process of negotiation and not so much as a kind of decoding of the ›hidden meaning‹ of a text. Both currents have influenced the teaching of literature and led to a number of coexistent classroom approaches mirroring also diverse paradigm shifts in literary and cultural studies. New notions of culture and text developed that fundamentally changed the role of the reader, in other words the learner in the foreign language classroom in an attempt to educate »the whole person« (cf. Gilroy/Parkinson 1997, 215).

Experiencing literary texts: Literary texts and films can help learners to experience multiple perspectives provided through the narrative structure or the character constellation. The limitedness of one's own world views, the ability to possibly even empathise with others and to change perspectives are important facets of the literary experience—not only with regard to inter- and transcultural learning. In addition, experiencing a sense of ambiguity of literary language is an important issue, ideally leading to some degree of **tolerance of ambiguity**, a prerequisite both for indulging in literature as well as for analytical approaches. In fact, the experience of literary texts and films is not restricted to issues of personal response and motivation but serves an important function concerning the distinction of fictional and non-fictional texts. Developing an **awareness for the differences between fictional and non-fictional texts** is eminently important. Reading a newspaper article about, for example, migration, offers a very different kind of reading experience than reading a short story or novel on the same topic.

Reasons for the teaching of literature sometimes refer to the long tradition of literature but frequently also stress a number of different dimensions hinting at its potential for the foreign language classroom.

Motivational-affective dimension: One aspect of experiencing literature is the possibility of **entering a ›new world‹** via texts and films. Immersing oneself in this new world conjured up by an author or filmmaker can be an exercise that appeals to the learner's emotions and also focuses on the ›literariness‹ of literary texts taking into account descriptions of people, places and settings (cf. Paran/Robinson 2016, 19). Although sometimes discarded as being a rather ›escapist‹ reason, according to many authors, the genuine feel of literary texts acts as a powerful motivator and touches on themes to which learners can bring a **personal response**. Ideally, texts arouse the learners' interests, involve them emotionally and can even encourage their individual feedback. To be sure, not every literary text may be equally interesting for every learner and in some cases there might even be downright rejection. However, literary texts (as opposed to non-fictional texts like newspaper articles) quite generally have the potential to evoke a personal response, i. e. positive, negative or ambivalent reactions that can lead to interaction in the EFL classroom and prepare for communicative and creative tasks.

Aesthetic and formal dimension: The experience of literary texts and films offers encounters with formal, for example genre-specific features that constitute the language of literature. Analytical approaches dominated the teaching of literature for a long time but should not be regarded as obsolete in the context of learner-oriented approaches. A focus on formal aspects of literary language and aesthetic enjoyment are often interdependent. Literary language is sometimes regarded as challenging, it may be intense, memorable, even sometimes question syntactic norms. Aesthetic enjoyment can partly be derived from innovative variations of literary genre conventions. Formal aspects of literary texts play an important role both in analytical and creative approaches of teaching literature.

Dimension of language learning and competence development: Among the reasons for teaching literary texts in the EFL classroom, competence and skills development, namely reading skills are also frequently mentioned. Literature can also be employed for oral and written work and encourage learners to become more creative and adventurous. Connected with this line of argumentation, it is commonly assumed that learners may thus begin to appreciate the richness and variety of the language they are trying to master. It seems important to stress that the teaching of literature and allegedly more practical and ›sober‹ aspects of language learning need not be seen as an antagonism.

The cultural dimension of language learning: Cultural approaches have had an influence on the teaching of literature—or in fact sometimes referred to as *literatures* in the plural form, addressing different ethnic backgrounds and literary traditions. As important authentic cultural products, films as audiovisual texts have strongly influenced the role and perception of literature in the classroom (see 10.2 below). Both print text and its mediatised forms such as film are regarded as sources for cultural learning. A perspective on literary texts and films as a medium in which culture materialises has fundamentally changed text selection as well as teaching goals and methods (cf. Delanoy 2015).

In fact, literary texts and films can be used for a multitude of reasons, not all of which can or must necessarily be fulfilled in every single literature lesson. Summarising the above one may largely categorise the following different dimensions concerning the teaching of literature and film:

Motivational-affective dimension	Dimension of language learning and competence development	Aesthetic and formal dimension	Cultural dimension
Literature and film …			
involve learners personally and can be motivating	provide extensive and authentic language input from the target culture	are aesthetically satisfying or challenging and therefore often memorable	allow for the change and coordination of (different) perspectives
allow for emotional and individual reactions	help develop reading competences and film literacy, oral and written skills	enable learners to experience aesthetic learning	can provide specific insights into stories narrating about other people or cultures
provide *protective spaces* for learners' imagination and personal response	can help develop critical abilities concerning text reception and production	enable learners to encounter the formal characteristics of different text genres	can connect literary and inter- and transcultural learning
provide the potential for creative follow-up activities	can support the development of general text and media competences	help learners to experience the connection of formal analysis and aesthetic enjoyment	may sensitise for the representation of cultural topics in literary texts

Table 10.1:
Dimensions
concerning the
teaching of literature and film

Depending on the goals of the respective lesson, different dimensions of working with literary texts may be accentuated. It is important to note that there is no functional mapping, i. e. that a certain text does not automatically address a certain dimension only.

10.2 | Literature and film—concepts and competences

The role of literary texts and films on ELT is sometimes regarded as ambivalent. **The *Common European Framework of Reference for Languages*** (cf. Council of Europe 2001) has been reproached for neglecting or marginalising literary and aesthetic learning. **The German educational standards** and the examination requirements issued by the Standing Conference of Ministers of Education and Cultural Affairs of the German Länder (cf. KMK 2004) have partly been criticised for focussing too strongly on testable output in the areas of communicative, intercultural and methodological competences. Usually, these refer to competences like understanding and reproducing content, analysing and re-organising texts, evaluating and producing texts. However, the aspect of individual cultivation (for the German word *Bildung*) is sometimes felt to be lacking in the reception of language policies and curricula. Multiple educational purposes of literature and film or the pleasure of reading texts and watching films exceed more functional aspects of literary learning by far. Recent publications refer to the significance of literary texts and films on **competence development**, thus integrating different dimensions of foreign language learning and literary learning with a view to *functional, aesthetic* and *communicative goals* (cf. Hallet 2015; Surkamp 2012; Grimm et al. 2015, 176; Kimes-Link 2013).

Development of communicative competences: In fact, literary texts are also ideally suited for developing the competences required in the foreign language classroom. Here, communicative competences are at the centre of foreign language teaching. Fostering these competences with literary texts and films can address aspects of *spoken and written interaction, interpretation* and *identity formation*. As with non-fictional texts foreign language reading competences play an important role. These refer to questions of automatising the recognition of words and sentence structures, of expanding the vocabulary and acquiring strategies for extensive reading. With regard to literary texts, the development of hypotheses about the literary text, of relating back to one's own experiences and reflecting about the reading process is particularly important. Literary competences, sometimes also referred to as literary literacy, can be based on some of the following and partly interrelated aspects (cf. Grimm et al. 2015; Burwitz-Melzer 2007; Diehr/Surkamp 2015; Lütge 2012c):

- **motivation, orientation and emotional involvement with literature**: involvement with the text, pleasure of reading, recognition of the relevance of literature for life
- **subjective response and creative production**: individual reactions, personal perspectives
- **cognitive understanding and co-creation of meaning**: gap filling, forming hypotheses, forming of mental models
- **linguistic-discursive competence**: in interaction with literary reading, follow-up activities, negotiation of meaning
- **cognitive-aesthetic understanding and methodological competences**: contextual readings, textual impact and functions, media literacy, narrative, performative and poetic competence
- **reflection and critical judgement** of cultural dimensions of literature, (inter)cultural and critical reflections

Inter- and transcultural learning with literature and film: Literary texts and films are **authentic cultural products** and can provide insights into foreign cultures and contexts. This is based on the assumption that fictional characters and settings can help develop an understanding for other norms, values and world views. Encountering alternative worlds, changing and coordinating perspectives, developing empathy and sensitivity—these concepts are most commonly referred to as central cornerstones of inter- and transcultural learning with fictional texts (cf. Bredella/Burwitz-Melzer 2004; Eisenmann 2015; Volkmann 2015; Surkamp/

Nünning 2016). However, a word of warning should be addressed with a view to a naive perception of ›understanding otherness‹ via literature and film. Literary texts do not automatically—let alone simplistically—lead to cultural learning. They can, however, support reflection processes about the literary and medial presentation of cultural contexts. Foreign language literature lessons should therefore not be restricted to thematic aspects of cultural learning but should themselves be subject to media-critical or aesthetic analyses. The following three stages have been suggested in order to account for cultural learning with literature and film (cf. Lütge 2017):

Stages of cultural learning

1. Culture-sensitive perception: Working on a culture-sensitive perception is an important goal of inter- and transcultural teaching. Among other things, the dramatisation of cultural and global topics in literature and in films should take into account the ›constructedness‹ of all literary representation and the depiction of otherness in text and film. Possible tasks may include questions like:

- What roles do specific nations/ethnicities play in the context of the text?
- How are members of different ethnic groups depicted?
- How are intercultural encounters dramatised?

2. Evaluating cultural images and global views: Coming to terms with and evaluating the representations put forward in literary texts with regard to the depiction of cultural topics requires careful analyses which take into account literary devices and the focalisation of attention in different narrative stances. Starting-points for discussions may include questions like:

- How does an author construct perceptions of cultural or global issues?
- Which characters are depicted positively/negatively? Can they be ascribed to specific cultural or ethnic groups?
- Are there stereotypical views about cultural topics? What problems or topics are displayed most prominently? Are they connected with specific cultural backgrounds?
- Which solutions for global problems are offered? Are they culture-specific?

3. Developing a cultural and global awareness: Understanding ideological undercurrents and developing an awareness for cultural subtleties is an important goal that may be focussed on in the literature classroom. Questions may include examples like:

- Are there clichéd views and conventions about the narrative?
- Does the text (or film) follow a specific ideology or a certain culture-specific bias?

10.3 | Literary genres and text selection

Beyond the canon: Planning teaching units requires a careful selection of texts and films and their relevant organisation within a sequence of lessons. Debates about the usefulness of a literary canon in the EFL classroom have had a long history (cf. Surkamp 2013). Certain shifts away from an emphasis of more traditional texts towards more recent and contemporary texts—and films—mirror changing discourses in literary studies and in the TEFL discourse. In some federal states there are fixed texts for the school-leaving certificates (*Abitur*), which impacts on publishing houses and their production of teaching materials.

Criteria for text selection: While there is no recipe for text selection, which must always account for the specific requirements of the individual group of learners, there is some general agreement as to the following aspects (cf. Grimm et al. 2015; Surkamp/Nünning 2014; Heinz/Hesse 2012). Texts and films should be:

- manageable in length and difficulty
- interesting, engaging, motivating and appealing to pupils
- authentic and ideally also representative, for example with regard to the depiction of cultural phenomena
- adequate in terms of the topic and age group

However, any selection of criteria may hardly serve as a simple checklist because different dimensions may interact and have to be evaluated with close reference to the specific goals of a teaching unit. Thus, it may be adequate to work with a short, but highly demanding text (e. g. a poem), which has a special importance for the specific learner group, that ideally suits the teaching unit and may just be in line with the goals of the teacher. Authenticity and representativeness may also be criteria that are quite hard to match. Not only is it extremely difficult to define what makes texts both authentic and representative but it is also highly questionable whether these alleged norms are fixed or whether they rather mirror an attitude of common sense in teaching practice. As hardly any single literary text or film may qualify as fully authentic and representative (according to whose standards?) such a criterion may rather be considered as an approximation towards general principles of text selection. There are other criteria in addition. The text/film:

- can easily be structured into a number of different sections
- provides various options for follow-up communication
- offers multiple perspectives that can be made use of in formal and aesthetic analyses and creative text productions

One may concede that there is a certain split between teachers who wish to *teach* literature and literary skills and teachers whose aim it is to *use* literature in the foreign language classroom primarily for language development purposes. Accordingly, as Paran (2010, 143) points out, *teaching* literature and *using* literature are not necessarily the same. Ideally, different dimensions of teaching literature (e. g. language learning and competence development *and* the aesthetic and formal dimension as mentioned above) are taken into consideration simultaneously. While all fictional texts as well as films offer an abundance of options also for foreign language classrooms, the major challenges concerning text selection, classroom methodology and the question of evaluation are all more or less dependent on the decision of the teacher to define the goals of a literature lesson. It is a decision that cannot be separated from questions of **content**. A Shakespeare drama such as *Macbeth* requires different decisions than a short animation film such as *The Present*. In addition, the respective **genre** with its special characteristics has an impact on questions of text selection and methods.

Narrative texts—novels and especially short stories, but also picture books—are most commonly used in the foreign language classroom. For younger learners an early encounter with literature can be motivating and foster extensive reading, while more advanced learners might focus on cognitive and aesthetic approaches. Telling stories—and listening to them—mirrors a basic anthropological need. Narrative texts can be analysed and discussed with a view to the *event structure* as well as the *discourse structure* (cf. Paran/Robinson 2016, 61). In more detail, the following different aspects of narration in literary texts can be distinguished (based on Surkamp/Nünning 2014, 39):

Aspects of narration

- **story-level of characters (what?):** plot (content, topic, structure), characters (techniques of characterisation, character constellation), setting (presentation of space, depiction of setting)
- **discourse-level of narration (how?):** communicative situation (Who speaks?), presentation of the narrative stance (Who perceives? Who feels?)
- **extra-textual level:** context of origin, historical background, biographical information

It is vital not to restrict oneself to an analytical approach. These aspects are supposed to provide starting-points for a more detailed and integrative approach that does not necessarily and exclusively focus on the above-mentioned ›wh‹-questions in brackets. Instead, the exploitation of the narrative stance or the depiction of the setting for creative purposes may be emphasised so as to focus the learners' attention to the fact that a certain novel or short story has been meticulously designed and deliberately composed into the form that we encounter as readers.

Poetry is not always adequately represented in foreign language teaching in spite of its great potential in terms of brevity and memorability. The specific features of poetry can be made fruitful for creative and student-oriented approaches to literature, also for creative writing purposes, for gap-filling exercises or more complex forms of text production (cf. Heinz/Hesse 2014; Lütge 2012d; Paran/Robinson 2016).

The connection of form and content should not be marginalised and—depending on the age group, be part of teaching (about) poetry. The following aspects are particularly important (for more details see Surkamp/Nünning 2014, 34):

Aspects of poetry

- **content:** topic and content structure, atmosphere
- **structure:** composition, metre, rhythm, rhyme

- **rhetorical devices:** on a phonological, morphological, syntactic, semantic or pragmatic level
- **historical background:** context of origin, historical background, biographical information

Poetry often displays emotions, provides insights into an individual's interior thoughts or mirrors a certain moment in time—almost like through a looking glass—and sometimes seemingly distorted from a specific perspective. In order to come to terms with these (and other) features of poetry some of the above-mentioned aspects may be addressed in tasks specifically integrating formal and creative approaches. Alliterations and other repetitive structures serve a function, for example create a certain mood and possibly even stick in the learners' mind, which allow for a playful or more serious response, thus enabling readers to see the connection between form and function.

Dramatic texts: Considering the nature of drama it is important that its special features are taken into account, especially the lack of a narrative stance as a contrast to narrative fiction. Dramatic texts offer experiences that go beyond the printed text. Performative approaches have become very popular in the foreign language classroom, not only in terms of acting out but also through reflecting and discussing performances or film versions. A wide selection of short plays is available for young and intermediate learners (cf. Ahrens et al. 2008; Lütge 2015b; Paran/Robinson 2016). The following aspects are particularly important for classroom discussion and can be made fruitful also for creative and action-oriented activities (for more details see Surkamp/Nünning 2014, 37; Surkamp 2015):

- **characteristics of dramatic texts:** verbal and non-verbal codes, relation between text and performance

Aspects of dramatic texts

- **plot and composition:** structure, scenes and acts, open and closed forms
- **characters:** *dramatis personae,* character constellations
- **dialogues:** dialogues and monologues and their functions in a play, structure of speech
- **presentation of space and time:** setting, techniques of presentation of time and space

Dramatic texts are based on the development of action through dialogues and introduce their characters in a different way than narrative texts do. Learners should develop an awareness for these differences. Discussing the passing of time as represented in a dramatic text (and in contrast to a narrative text) or the depiction of character traits require careful observation and an understanding for the subtleties of this literary genre.

Films have become very popular in the EFL classroom. For many learners, they are even more accessible than print texts. Film is an important part of popular culture and can be used in the classroom for various aspects of competence development in the foreign language, for developing **film literacy** and also in order to promote an understanding of literature and culture. Audiovisual aspects of language teaching (*Hör-Seh-Verste-*

hen; cf. chapter 6 in this volume) are integrated into the curricula of most federal states and have been discussed in detail in many publications, also with a view to activities and methods (cf. Henseler et al. 2011; Lütge 2012a; Thaler 2014; Viebrock 2016). The following aspects of approaching films should be considered so as to ensure the multitude of dimensions of the medium film (cf. Surkamp/Nünning 2014; Lütge 2012a; Viebrock 2016):

Aspects of films
- **literary aspects:** character constellations, symbolism, plot structure, presentation of space and time
- **dramatic aspects:** casting, dialogues, non-verbal communication, props
- **cineastic aspects:** editing, montage, composition of pictures and cuts, colours, sounds and lighting

In order not to use films exclusively for communicative follow-ups or as simple ›quarries‹ for discussions about the film's topic or context an awareness for these different dimensions and various different devices of the medium should be systematically developed. The appreciation of a literary work of art can also be additionally supported through literary adaptations and comparisons of different film versions of the same literary text (cf. Lütge 2012c).

10.4 | Teaching literature and film—approaches and methods

Approaches to teaching literature, questions of text selection and classroom methodology have always been influenced by underlying concepts from literary studies and foreign language pedagogy. The formal analysis of texts and films—usually following a teacher-centred pattern—was partly informed by the school of the **New Criticism**. Here, the sequence of summary of content was followed by the formal analysis of stylistic devices and often rounded off by a comment on ›the message‹ of the text, thus implicitly aiming at an alleged author's ›intention‹, which only needs to be carefully dug out and laid bare for meticulous academic inspection.

Today's didactics of literature is influenced by the **Reader Response Theory**, which builds on the learners' cognitive and emotional processes of sense-making. Methodologically, this led to activities that not only focus on the text but more on the reception process of a text or film. The learners' individual response gained ground so that individual reactions and subjective readings came into play. In spite of diverse theoretical pendulum swings and their reverberations in didactic materials there is some interaction between different and in fact complementary approaches to teaching literature that ideally interact with each other (cf. Grimm et al. 2015, 189):
- subjective response and reflection
- creative transformation and performance
- aesthetic and cultural analysis and interpretation

Phase	Pre-reading/ pre-viewing	While-reading/ while-viewing	Post-reading/ post-viewing
Purpose	▪ activation of schemata and prior knowledge ▪ facilitation of language input	▪ enhancement of involvement ▪ support of text-reader-interaction and more intense reflection	▪ reflection on the reading/viewing experience ▪ creative or analytical follow-up work
Activities	▪ brainstorming on the topic/title/ book cover/film poster ▪ predicting plot or central conflict	▪ step-by-step reading or viewing ▪ reading/watching for gist ▪ reading/watching for details	▪ filling imaginative gaps (creative writing) ▪ transforming or amending a text/ film

Table 10.2: Examples of pre-, while- and post-reading/ viewing activities

Recently, the foreign language classroom has seen the rise of student- and action-oriented as well as holistic approaches. The focus on the learner with attention to affective and human factors has led to an interest in more personal approaches. Thus, ideas from communicative language teaching and humanistic schools of language teaching that put the learner more in focus seem to converge with recent developments in Reader Response Theory (cf. Gilroy/Parkinson 1996).

In line with this development a certain task sequence has emerged, a **three-phase model of pre-, while-** and **post-activities**, which in itself does not automatically guarantee high quality lessons. This tripartite division, however, has the potential to support the learners' processes of constructing meaning with regard to the content, the textual or aesthetic structure, the (literary or filmic) language or cultural implications. The goal is interaction between the learner and the text, both in written or oral language production and an enhanced sense of reflection about the ambiguities of a literary text or film, and thus about a basic characteristic of literature, for example questions of perspectivity and interpretation. With a view to the challenge of mastering a literary or filmic experience in a foreign language this sequence of processing a text is particularly relevant in order to overcome linguistic or cultural obstacles and to reduce the complexity of the reading or viewing process (cf. Surkamp 2012; Surkamp/Nünning 2014).

A word of warning should be addressed here concerning the schematic application of the three-phase-structure, which, if over-exerted, may tend to appear ›prescriptive‹ and thus possibly be rather detrimental than conducive to goals of the literature classroom. This sequence of processing a text may, however, be regarded as a kind of methodological scaffolding rather than a universal remedy or recipe, based on the very same heavily-used ingredients.

Much more intricate and specialised types of methods and activities—depending on the age level and the literary genre—open up a wide scenario of tasks that foster motivation and help build up competences. The most often cited are usually categorised as **production-oriented** or **ac-**

tion-oriented activities, both of which can of course be integrated into the pre-/while-/post-sequence of working with a text (cf. Surkamp 2012).

Examples **Production-oriented activities**

Production-oriented activities aim at generating new texts, at rewriting, creatively expanding or alienating the original. Examples include:
- personal response in a reading or viewing diary or log, email or blog
- transformation of a film scene into a poem, a poem into a newspaper article, a film clip into a vlog
- poster, a character profile of a protagonist, digital collage
- book or film reviews edited digitally in teams and published online
- alternative endings and various forms of rewriting from different perspectives or in different genres

Action-oriented activities

Action-oriented activities aim at acting out or transposing a text into a different medium. Examples include:
- reconstructions of a text or film script from jumbled fragments
- scenic re-enactments of a film scene or a dialogue, freeze frames and spatial arrangements of certain scenes or conflicts
- fake interviews with the film director or author
- transformations into a different type of medium, for example text into film, an image, a pantomime, music or radio play

In this context, **creativity and performativity** are important keywords for the teaching of literature, sometimes overlapping with concepts of action-oriented or student-oriented approaches to literature. Generally, creative approaches tend to focus on individual recreations and try to open room for less desk-based or teacher-centred activities. However, sometimes used as a buzzword, creativity can materialise very differently in foreign language literature lessons, for example regarding oral or written response, out-of-classroom scenarios, joint teaching formats with arts or music teachers, innovative and original forms of response and recreation in groups or individually (cf. Hesse 2016). Considering the goals for an individual lesson, teachers should be aware that creative approaches are not *per se* ›better‹ (or ›worse‹) than analytical approaches but that ideally the two complement each other. It is indispensable, therefore, to always closely connect one's decision for the activities with the goals of the respective literature lesson:
- What are the main goals for the literature lesson I am planning?
- What competences are to be fostered in this literature lesson?
- How can those be best achieved? What methods/tasks can be helpful in order to reach that goal?
- Are my planned activities/methods really in line with the overall goal?

Or:

- Have I chosen creative tasks that seem original and interesting but that may not be fruitful for the text I have in mind? (E.g. brainstorming or prediction activities about a book or film title everyone knows anyway.)
- Am I constantly following a (maybe even predictable) sequence of some three to five pre-, while- and post-reading or viewing activities?

Performance-based approaches such as role-play, simulations, the creation of audio plays, improvised dialogues etc. regard the role of the learner as a constitutive part of the literary reception process. Here, learners are asked to actively take up another person's perspective, to imaginatively swap places with a literary character or protagonist of a film and thus interact with the text or film more deeply and—hopefully—with more motivation. Innovative performance-based activities can foster the reader's sense of engagement and his or her willingness to interact with the text in the foreign language.

It is important to be aware of the enormous range of performance-based approaches and not to restrict oneself to the demanding task of staging a scene with foreign language learners. Examples for slowly progressing formats of performativity in the context of literature and film can be remodelled on the following ideas for using a dramatic text (Shakespeare's *Hamlet*) and its literary adaptations as a starting point (cf. Lütge 2007):

Activities with drama   Example

- **active silences:** group presentation of a monologue, decisions about the number and length of pauses
- **nonverbal text responses:** pantomime and nonverbal presentations of a monologue
- **verbal improvisations:** changes in intonation, volume, pitch and other forms of verbal presentation
- **group encounters with the text:** group presentations or joint recitations of monologues

Resulting from the shift away from cognitive and teacher-centred approaches to more innovative formats of teaching literature there is a rising dimension of complexity and involvement required on the part of the learner and the teacher. ›Doing‹ literature as a synonym for increasingly demanding literature projects refers to the more active role of the learner (cf. Grimm et al. 2015, 187).

Aesthetic aspects: However, the **aesthetic and cultural analysis, interpretation and evaluation** of fiction must not be neglected. Context and culture shape the conditions in which literature materialises. In order to teach literature one needs to be aware of the fictional character of literary and filmic works. Thus, asking questions like »what can be learned from this text/film about India?« would be reductionist and possibly lead to stereotypical or single-minded perspectives. Fiction is not an imitation of reality and should not be misinterpreted as a mirror of reality. Thus, both essentialist as well as mimetic approaches should be avoided. Quite generally, different texts and films about the same topic or cultural background might be combined so as to provide a context for encountering a specific target culture. Alternatively, it is the *depiction* of cultural phenomena themselves that should be scrutinised, for example:

- How are camera angles, lighting or music employed to create a certain atmosphere in a film about India (e. g. *Slumdog Millionaire*)?
- How can the narrative stance, the choice of figurative language and the composition of flashbacks evoke an impression of India in the corresponding novel?

Formal aspects: Questions concerning the form as well as the content of literary works need to be taken into account. While it may well be recommendable to start off teaching a Shakespearean sonnet by inviting the learners' personal response, the question how **form shapes meaning** requires careful analysis, too. Literary or filmic devices and their functions including a reflection on the connection of form and content are indispensable. Depending on the framework of the chosen genre aspects like voice, style and structure play an important role. The narrative stance and its different realisations need to be systematically approached, also concerning production-oriented activities: without a basic understanding of how a narrator's presence or absence shapes meaning no creative transposition into a different genre would be possible.

Overcoming the dichotomy of analytical versus creative approaches is an important goal for any conceptualisation of literature didactics. Both perspectives are significant and may indeed be merged in activities stressing both formal aspects of a text or film and their creative transformations, for example in tasks that allow for personal responses to certain formal devices. Rather than just using (or abusing) literature and film for communicative follow-up activities, i. e. as a kind of quarry for topics and plots, the potential of literature in its ambivalence, complexity and multiperspectivity should be systematically developed (for detailed accounts see Surkamp/Nünning 2014; Delanoy et al. 2015; Lütge 2015b).

10.5 | Perspectives for the literature classroom

Whereas some recent criticism regarding the neglect of aesthetic learning in various educational curricula has been voiced, the field of literature didactics has developed various new trends and topics introducing innovative projects for teaching and research. Among the most visible developments **literature for all levels** can be identified as a consequence of student-centred approaches and a generally renewed interest in the reader. Literary texts and films should in fact be employed from the very beginning starting with **picture books**, **short poems**, **nursery rhymes** and songs but also **short animation films**. Storytelling and the playful repetition of rhyme and rhythmic patterns, of nonsense songs and elementary children's literature should be systematically integrated into beginners' foreign language classrooms.

Basic and intermediate levels of literary learning often refer to visual elements, on the interplay between words and pictures, watching and listening, for example in storytelling events in a classroom. Suspense, adventure, imaginative gaps and surprising twists are important elements of literary encounters for younger learners and they are constitutive for what is essential in reading for pleasure or extensive reading (cf. Krashen 2004). Visually supported materials (texts and films) can be used for different levels and age groups.

Picture books

Example

Barack Obama: *Of Thee I Sing* (2010)
Drew Daywalt: *The Day the Crayons Quit* (2013)
Neil Gaiman: *The Day I Swapped my Dad for Two Goldfish* (2004)

Short animation films

The Present (2014. Dir. Jacob Frey, 4:18 minutes)
John und Karen (2007. Dir. Matthew Walker, 3:56 minutes)
Father and Daughter (2000. Dir. Michaël Dudok de Wit, 9:22 minutes)

The potential of multimodal literature addressing different modes of understanding is gaining ground in recent literature didactics (e. g. Mark Haddon's novel *The Curious Incident of the Dog in the Night-time*, 2003 or Sherman Alexie's *The Absolutely True Diary of a Part-Time Indian*, 2007). Graphic novels (in some cases in word/image combinations like Shaun Tan's *The Lost Thing*, in some cases completely without language like Shaun Tan's *The Arrival*) can be used as starting-points for developing students' visual and critical literacy and for introducing skills that are also important for film literacy. An understanding for the aesthetics of composing a film as a sequence of pictures can be prepared by an analysis of the different panels of a graphic novel, which may be judged as a ›missing‹ and very welcome ›link‹ between literature and film.

With the goal of supporting literary learning in the foreign language classroom, one may concede that pictures can provide a narrative scaffold to help the reader follow the story and to provide a meaning-anchor effect that supports inexperienced L1 readers. The potential of multimodal texts for foreign language learning can be seen in the contribution to the narrative in multiple forms (e. g. pictures, words, design, the peritext of picture books), which may either overlap, complement, amplify or contradict each other. Multimodal literature can thus provide rich opportunities for negotiation of understanding and meaning (cf. Bland 2015; Bland/Lütge 2013). According to Bland (2015), the following aspects play an important role in this context:

- Pictures can be used as a shortcut to deep reading.
- Access to cultural context can be provided through pictures.
- Amplification through simplification can serve as an important principle for visual literacy.

Global topics: Newer thematic developments in literature and film integrate topics of a more global scope. Concepts like global issues in ELT are mirrored in materials, often in the context of inter- and transcultural learning (cf. chapter 9 in this volume). **Global Education** strives to promote the awareness of social values, ethics and the environment. Similarly, **Global Citizenship Education** is focusing on goals that emphasise cultural and political issues. Increasingly transcultural approaches to ELT with an interest of overcoming the binary model of ›us‹ and ›them‹ lay more emphasis on the commonalities between people from different cultural, ethnic or religious backgrounds (cf. Byram 2008; Lütge 2015a).

While the ultimate goal of a ›global citizen‹ may not always realistically be in the centre of the foreign language literature classroom, it is important to note that these concepts have partly been mirrored in texts and films now available for teaching, for example (cf. Lütge 2015a):

- **films** such as *An Inconvenient Truth* by Davis Guggenheim
- **short stories** such as *FREE? Stories Celebrating Human Rights* (2009), an anthology of fourteen short narratives
- **picture books** with a global focus such as *We Are All Born Free. The Universal Declaration Of Human Rights in Pictures* by Amnesty International (2008)

Children's and young adult literature (CYAL) has been another prospering field over the past 10 years. This increase of popularity has been fruitful for the EFL classroom and has contributed massively to a widening of the literary canon. The advantages of these—sometimes—shorter literary works include more straightforward plotlines, simpler forms and often less complexity in their character constellations, which can help young readers to identify with protagonists of their age groups (cf. Bland/Lütge 2013; Bland 2015; Hesse 2016; O'Sullivan/Rösler 2013). Often CYAL takes up the experience of ›secondary worlds‹ (e. g. historical fiction, religious, mythical figures, supernatural powers).

Debates about the teaching of literature in a foreign language are also led with regard to the legitimacy of using **graded or simplified readers**, i. e. adaptations of original texts to be applied for extensive reading and with a view to their most recent transformation into digital formats. Graded readers can be helpful in order to introduce younger learners to literature and to allow for reading experiences at a very early stage. In some cases, extreme simplifications of classics are felt to be counter-productive, though, for example when the literary language is ripped off all its challenges—and charms (cf. Hermes 2017b for a detailed discussion).

The interplay of texts, their intermedial connections and various media adaptations, sometimes simplifications, provides a rich web of literary and filmic encounters for EFL teaching. In the case of Neil Gaiman's prize-winning **young adult novel** *Coraline* (2002), the charming **graphic novel** illustrated by Craig Russell with the same title (2008) allows for film-analytical tasks (e. g. camera angles) or pre-viewing activities for the **film version** (animation film by Henry Selick, 2009). Reading images in literature and film in various forms, for example using picture books, graphic or multimodal novels or films as literary adaptations and feature films plays an important part in establishing literary and film literacy (*Text- und Medienkompetenz*) (for more details see Henseler et al. 2011; Lütge 2012a). Comparing different realisations of *Coraline* can make it very obvious for learners that the same story can be told, shown, narrated or mediated very differently. An awareness for the intricacies of the narrative stance, for necessary omissions, specific visual elements, music and sound can be fostered systematically considering the following questions:

- How is atmosphere created in the novel and in the film? What literary or filmic devices contribute to this impression? How would other choices have changed the impressions of the reader or viewer?
- How is the narrative stance depicted in the literary text? And how does narration work in the film?
- What are the differences between different versions or formats of the same text (novel, graphic novel, film, different film versions)?

Multiple texts and media are assumed to generate communication and to attract learners with their rich input. However, critical literacy as part of media-sensitive approaches to teaching literature in the foreign language must also take into account questions concerning the dispersal of the learners' attention. Digital tools can also support collaboration in and beyond the literature classroom but more research into this field is still lacking. Modern classroom technology and media-based innovations do not necessarily pose a threat to creativity or individual enjoyment. Educational apps might even facilitate the following methodological aspects: reflection, modification, communication, multiplication, creation and collaboration. Interactive digital narratives can allow for individual response and creative approaches (cf. Merse/Schmidt 2012; Cope/Kalantzis 2013; Grimm/Hammer 2015).

Digital Apps   Example

These digital apps can be used in the context of literary learning:
popplet: visualises (changes in) character constellations, plot lines, timelines, etc.
flipsnack: creates flip books and/or book brochures
little bird tales: creates stories with pictures and sound
glogster: creates an interactive book poster with text boxes, pictures, audio and video files and links

Testing and evaluation: Another challenge often mentioned in the context of teaching literature refers to aspects of testing and evaluation (cf. chapter 14 in this volume). Depending on the overall goals of individual lessons or teaching units, teachers are confronted with a number of questions:

- What is the role of testing and evaluation in my foreign language literature classroom?
- Does testing refer to language and reading skills or literary aspects of the fictional text?

- Does testing refer to knowledge about content and form or rather to the individual appreciation of literature and its personal response?
- What tasks are adequate?
- How can individual response be judged?

Current models on literary competences integrate aesthetic aspects as well as questions of language development and evaluation. Various suggestions for task-based foreign language learning scenarios try to overcome alleged contradictions of the foreign language literature classroom (cf. Hallet et al. 2015).

10.6 | Conclusion

As has been pointed out above, *using* literature and *teaching* literature may not always be the same thing, thus implying different approaches to texts and films, questions of text selection and classroom methodology. Referring to another dichotomy mentioned in this chapter, for example analytical and creative approaches, it is important to consider that integrating different dimensions of teaching literature and film is helpful in overcoming apparent contradictions. Similarly, content and competence-orientation should ideally complement each other; the goals for a lesson or a teaching unit will necessarily define the road to be taken as a starting-point into the complex world of literature. Literature lessons in the foreign language classroom are not supposed to be static units following simplified recipe-like routines. Teachers are faced with various challenges considering questions of text selection, methodological flexibility, evaluation and competence development, as well as foreign language development and literary learning.

Literature in the digital age will pose even more challenges (cf. Hammond 2016) but may open up new doors into imaginative worlds. Interactivity instead of passive reception is very interesting from an educational perspective in this context and might offer some chances for the future—and especially for the literature classroom. Whether Alan Maley (1989, 59) is right in pointing out that »literature is back, but wearing different clothes« may be a completely new chapter in the (digital) future of teaching literature.

Further reading

Delanoy, Werner/Eisenmann, Maria/Matz, Frauke (eds.) (2015): *Learning with Literature in the EFL Classroom*. Frankfurt a. M. et al.

Hallet, Wolfgang/Surkamp, Carola/Krämer, Ulrich (eds.) (2015): *Literaturkompetenzen Englisch. Modellierung, Curriculum, Unterrichtsbeispiele*. Seelze-Velber.

Lütge, Christiane (2012a): *Mit Filmen Englisch unterrichten*. Berlin.

Paran, Amos/Robinson, Pauline (2016): *Literature*. Oxford.

Surkamp, Carola/Nünning, Ansgar (⁴2016): *Englische Literatur unterrichten. Grundlagen und Methoden* [2006]. Seelze-Velber.

Viebrock, Britta (ed.) (2016): *Feature Films in English Language Teaching*. Tübingen.

Christiane Lütge

11 Principles and Methods—Focus on Learners, Content and Tasks

The question of how languages are taught and learned most effectively has been controversially discussed throughout the history of foreign language teaching. To answer this question, a variety of language teaching methods have been promoted over the years (cf. chapter 1 in this volume). The choice of method influences the activities learners will be expected to perform in the classroom, the roles teachers and learners are assigned, the content they are expected to work with and the material that is being used (cf. Harmer 2015, 62; Richard/Rogers 2014, 29).

What is a method? The term ›method‹ is used in a variety of contexts in foreign language teaching. Methods can be used to describe comprehensive concepts of language teaching such as the audiolingual or the grammar-translation methods (cf. chapter 1 in this volume). They are based on specific theories of how languages are learned and can be understood as links »between the actions of a teacher in the classroom and the thoughts that underlie the actions« (Larsen-Freeman/Anderson 2011, 1). It is also common to use the term ›approach‹ for these underlying theoretical principles of language learning (cf. Richards/Rogers 2014, 3). *Questions of terminology*

In contrast, the term ›method‹ as it is commonly used by teachers also describes specific classroom **activities** and **techniques** (cf. e. g. Grieser-Kindel et al. 2016). With these techniques, approaches to language learning and teaching are put into practice and certain principles are realised: for example, the activity ›think-pair-share‹, in which students first think individually about a problem and then share results with their classmates, might be an activity that learners do in a classroom that subscribes to **task-based language learning** (cf. section 11.4) and helps to implement the principle of **learner-orientation.**

While some methods and approaches come with a fixed set of procedures (for example, the audiolingual method that relied heavily on repetition and pattern-drill), others are characterised by a wide variety of activities and procedures and are therefore more difficult to be labelled as methods. Another reason why the concept of ›method‹ is rather fuzzy is that their implementation will vary from teacher to teacher and classroom to classroom. Teachers will interpret methods depending on their own experiences as students, their beliefs and their teaching style (cf. Larsen-Freeman/Anderson 2011, xiii f.). The same is true for learners who also have considerable influence on the success of methods and will bring their experiences, needs, interests and motivation to the classroom.

The idea that there is one right method that can live up to the complexity of every classroom situation seems no longer appropriate. Instead of methods, some researchers talk of **principles** or **macrostrategies** that should guide teachers' behaviour in the classroom (cf. Ellis 2014; Larsen-Freeman/Anderson 2011; Kumaravadivelu 2006b). These principles can help teachers to reflect on their teaching and raise their awareness of the ideas underlying their teaching (cf. chapter 3 in this volume).

This chapter will first show how the **communicative turn** has laid the foundation for current methodology with the idea that a language is learned through using it. It will then present principles and approaches for teaching and learning foreign languages that are currently being discussed, grouped into three categories—focus on learners, focus on content and focus on tasks (cf. Klippel 2016, 317 for a similar structure of principles: *Schüler-, Sach- und Handlungsorientierung*).

11.1 | The communicative turn and its implications

The emergence of **communicative language teaching (CLT)** in the early 1980s is commonly referred to as a paradigm shift in foreign language teaching (cf. Richards/Rogers 2014, 151). The core question of the discourse at that time was how a foreign language is learned and what consequences the knowledge of this learning process has for language teaching.

Definition	Communicative language teaching is an approach to language teaching that highlights real-life interaction as the goal of language learning.

Learning the language by using it: Does learning refer to the knowledge of the system of a language such as lexis and grammar or is it rather about the ability to use the language and develop language skills? Today, most language teaching approaches follow the idea that a foreign language is best learned by using it actively. Towards the end of the 19th century, movements such as the reform movement had rejected the idea that language skills develop through explicitly teaching the structures of the language alone, as it was typical of the traditional **grammar-translation method** (cf. chapter 1 in this volume). Contexts of using English as a foreign language had changed because people in Europe increasingly needed to use English for communicative purposes while travelling or as immigrants to the United States. This shows that one good reason for centring language teaching on actively using the foreign language in the classroom is that learners need to be prepared for using the language in specific communicative contexts.

The audiolingual approach, which was very popular in Europe and the USA between the 1950s and the late 1970s, also follows the principle of learning the language by using it. The core idea of **audiolingualism** derives from **behaviourism** and defines language learning as the oral mastery of the elements and building blocks of the language (cf. Richards/Rogers 2014, 55). Although active language use in the classroom is widely acknowledged as a central element of foreign language teaching today, audiolingual methods are no longer popular in Europe because they limit communication in the classroom to a set of drill sentences without sufficiently enabling learners to communicate in real-life contexts. One of the main criticisms of audiolingual methods was that although they claimed to promote communicative competence, they were based on the use of one specific language structure at a time, which does not reflect how languages are used in real communication, when meaning can be expressed in a variety of ways (cf. Morrow 1977, 12).

The communicative turn of the 1980s was, on the one hand, rooted in a critical response to these pre-communicative structuralist approaches to foreign language teaching and, on the other hand, in findings of second language acquisition researchers during the 1970s. A distinguishing feature of communicative language teaching was therefore to use learning activities in the classroom which represent communication as it actually occurs outside of the classroom. Proponents of the communicative turn saw real-world communicative competence as a main goal of language learning and criticised audiolingual methods for their lack of including the social dimension of interaction between speakers into the classroom (cf. Widdowson 1972; Morrow 1977).

Communicative activity: Talk about your weekend Example

In a 5-minute activity, the students talk about their weekend to one of their classmates. This activity is based on their real-life contexts and has a social dimension of sharing own experiences with peers.

In the plenary, the teacher can ask for feedback from the pair activity. In that way the foreign language classroom becomes a space of social interaction.

Language acquisition research and language learning: The idea of the communicative turn that authentic communication supports language learning, was not only brought up by foreign language teaching practitioners, but it was also shared by second language acquisition researchers. One influential theory in second language acquisition research is the **input hypothesis** (cf. Krashen 1981; Krashen 1982b). Krashen, a linguist, argues with this hypothesis that the only thing that matters for language learning is that learners get authentic spoken or written language input. Furthermore, he puts forward that a language is subconsciously acquired and conscious learning has therefore no influence on developing language competences (cf. Krashen 1982a, 97).

Output and interaction: Although many experts in the field have shared Krashen's theories, research on classroom teaching has shown that learners' output and interaction matter as well, particularly where accuracy is concerned. The Canadian second language acquisition research group led by Swain, which researched French immersion programmes in Canada, claimed that comprehensive input alone was not sufficient for acquiring communicative language competence (cf. Swain 1985). During their extensive research studies in bilingual classrooms they found that learners' language output and **corrective feedback** on the output is also crucial for language learning (cf. Swain 2000, 201). This means that learners need to have the opportunity to experiment with language in order to test their subconscious hypotheses about how the language system works. Learners get feedback through ›trial and error‹ with their output and become aware of mistakes, which gives them the opportunity to revise their hypotheses and improve their language competences. These research findings show that language learning occurs when learners have both comprehensible input and the opportunity to produce and experiment with language. The implication for the classroom is that language teaching must include activities which encourage the learners to interact with others in the foreign language in meaningful communication. Face-to-face interaction in the classroom is therefore a key element to support foreign language learning (cf. Long 1996).

Claims how to teach a foreign language: Communicative language teaching has never been a distinctive language learning theory but as has been shown, it stands for an essential turn in our understanding of how languages are learned (cf. Richards/Rogers 2014, 161). Research in second language acquisition and classroom-based research have informed the main claims of the communicative approach. Today, the language learning claims which have evolved from the communicative turn are broadly accepted as the foundations for contemporary language teaching and learning. Two basic claims have to be highlighted which are central to the following parts of this chapter.

- The first claim is that teaching should be oriented around **authentic situations of language use**. This implies a shift from learning about language forms to looking at what learners can *do* with language while communicating with others (cf. Littlewood 1981, 2). Classroom teaching should therefore not be organised around grammar forms to be learned but rather around functional contexts of using the language so that learners can develop competences of using the language in authentic real-world contexts (cf. chapter 8 in this volume).
- The second claim for language teaching is to create **opportunities for learners to interact with others** by using the foreign language. When learners see themselves as active participants of a group they want to share meaningful content with, they are more likely to participate in communication which leads to language competence (cf. Breen/Candlin 1980, 90). This way, learners will be prepared for using the foreign language to negotiate meaning in diverse contexts.

The two claims are seen as a basis for methods which follow a communicative approach to foreign language teaching. It is not possible and maybe not even helpful to list each of these methods and concepts here. Instead, the main principles and approaches which have evolved from these two claims are described.

11.2 | Focus on learners

Learners as individuals: One major idea that the communicative turn has brought about is the shift from the teacher to the learners as the central point of reference for foreign language teaching (cf. also chapter 4 in this volume). As the learners are the ones who have to engage in communication, their needs and interests are what matters and their learning process should be central to all efforts. Research on **individual differences in language learning** (cf. e.g. Dörnyei 2005; Riemer 1997) and on learners' perspectives on their language learning experiences have shown that this language learning process is a very individual one—something that teachers experience on a daily basis. Learners differ in regards to their prior experiences, languages they know, interests, social background, motivation, cognitive abilities, strategies, learning styles etc. A significant number of students report that they are under- or overchallenged as early as in primary school (cf. Haenni Hoti 2007). Studies have shown that students' competences across school types vary considerably at secondary school level (cf. DESI 2008). Depending on their interests and prior experiences, students' motivation and commitment in certain topics differ significantly; while some students might be interested in computer games and music, others need English to watch specific arts and craft tutorials on YouTube. It currently appears as though **diversity** in classrooms is increasing due to growing immigration or educational reforms (such as efforts on **inclusion** or the *Gemeinschaftsschule*, a comprehensive school that tries to overcome the traditional streaming of students in different types of secondary schools). Nevertheless, **heterogeneity** of learners has always been a constant factor in the language classroom.

Language teaching principles which take this heterogeneity of learners into account emphasise **learner-centredness**, which means using learners' interests and needs as well as their abilities and skills as the starting point for teaching (cf. Schocker 2016). These principles also require a certain view of learners that goes beyond their role as passive students, but rather sees students as whole people with diverse identities which they bring to the classroom (cf. van Lier 2007, 62).

1. Differentiation and individualisation: Starting from the assumption that students learn a language in different ways—that is they begin from different starting points, can make use of different types of support and progress at their own pace—a one-size-fits-all approach to language teaching would not make sense. In contrast, differentiated and individualised learning provides strategies to cope with heterogeneous groups of learners, which are also discussed in the context of efforts to make the English language classroom a more inclusive one (cf. Börner/Lohmann 2015). Differentiated and individualised learning can mean giving students choices regarding tasks, topics, social forms, materials, methods or learning strategies. On the level of tasks, many current course books offer material on **different competence levels**. This form of differentiation can either be of quantitative or qualitative nature:

Major principles that focus on learners

- **Quantitative differentiation** is achieved through a reduction or expansion of activities and material.

- **Qualitative differentiation** tries to make the same tasks more accessible for weaker students through, for example, less complex sentences, a smaller range of vocabulary and more task support.

Definition

> The term differentiation describes the use of strategies and techniques to teach groups of learners with different abilities, interest and learning needs.

While in the beginning teachers might have to assign certain task levels to students, learners can gradually take over the selection of their respective level (cf. Haß 2006, 252). Differentiation and individualisation further implies the following:

- **Choice of content:** If personally relevant content is one basis for students' engagement with tasks (cf. chapter 11.4), this content cannot be the same for everyone, but will vary according to students' interests. Thus, learners should be able to participate in the selection of topics, for example for a presentation, a blog, a book report, etc.
- **Individualised settings**, in which learners are given a choice of activities, partners and materials (like *Wochenplan*—weekly plans with learning activities, or *Stationenlernen*—rotation learning), enable them to progress at their own pace and choose their preferred ways of learning. For teachers, these settings can provide opportunities to support individual students.
- **Reflective and introspective activities** such as learner diaries and portfolios in which students collect samples of their work and reflect on their learning process, add relevance to the learners' perspectives. They can help learners to show their individual learning paths, reflect on the progress of their work and also provide possibilities for alternative assessment (cf. chapter 14 in this volume).

2. Learner autonomy: If learners are given an active role in the learning process, they are more involved in decision-making regarding the learning process. Learner autonomy is a buzz word that is often used in this context.

Definition

> Learner autonomy focuses on the ability to plan, monitor and evaluate one's learning process and is seen as a prerequisite for self-directed learning (cf. Holec 1981).

One way to give students responsibility for and control over their own learning is to support their use of **learning strategies**. Research with successful language learners (cf. Oxford 1990) has identified a large number of learning strategies such as:

- guessing meaning of unknown words from context
- using visual support for learning vocabulary
- focusing on key information in a text

Although the value of strategy training is not evident (cf. Little 2013), students will probably benefit from reflecting on their strategy use and from trying out new strategies to broaden their repertoire. In the classroom, they could, for example, talk about successful strategies to remember vocabulary or try out different reading strategies when dealing with a difficult text (cf. chapter 6 in this volume).

Learner autonomy should not be reduced to a mere strategy training and the individual occupation of students with pre-set material. A comprehensive understanding of the concept includes an emancipatory dimension (cf. Schmenk 2008; 2016). In the context of learner-centred principles, learner autonomy means giving students responsibility for their own learning. This does not imply leaving them alone, especially because language learning takes place through interaction and the support of the teacher and their peers plays a major role for the students' learning process (cf. Dam 1994, 505; Little 1994, 435). In a learning environment that encourages **collaboration** and **reflection**, learner autonomy can be promoted by, for example, letting students choose the title of a novel they want to read or decide between different tasks, and by encouraging individual mini-research projects on a topic learners are interested in.

3. Holistic learning: A focus on learners that takes learners' whole selves into account has to consider not only cognitive, but also **sensory, emotional and affective aspects** of language learning. Although concepts such as different learner types (cf., for example, Skehan 1986), learner styles (cf. e. g. Cohen 2010) and multiple intelligences (cf. Gardner 1983) overlap and have been controversially discussed, they have drawn our attention to the fact that learners vary according to their preferred mode of learning. Activities in the classroom should therefore appeal to different senses, for example by including pictures, physical activity, video and audio material. Learners should be encouraged to become aware of their own preferences and to try out new strategies (cf. Riemer 2013).

Language learning is not only a cognitive endeavour, emotions also play a crucial role in the learning process. Students' attitudes towards language learning in general and the target language, as well as their motivation and fear, significantly influence their success. Early research studies claimed that learners' motivation depended on their interest in and openness towards the target culture and their beliefs in the usefulness of the language for their future lives (cf. Dörnyei/Ryan 2015, 72 ff.). In contrast to this, Dörnyei's concept of the ideal L2 self emphasises the role of the learner's **identity**. The motivation to learn a foreign language is closely linked to the goals that are personally relevant for each learner and the ability to imagine oneself as a competent user of the language, that is to develop a positive self-conception (future self). Motivation is therefore not significantly shaped by a learner's interest in the target culture. Students are more likely to be motivated if the foreign language allows them to express their own identity and allows for interesting encounters.

While motivation can positively influence foreign language learning, negative emotions like foreign language classroom anxiety (cf. Horwitz

2010) can hinder the learning success. Language anxiety is mainly attributed to communication apprehension, fear of negative evaluation and test anxiety. A positive classroom atmosphere and encouraging feedback techniques can help students to overcome these fears.

Language
awareness and
translanguaging

4. Multilingualism: Another principle that has to be taken into account when considering heterogeneous groups of learners is working with linguistic diversity. For quite some time, a **monolingual habitus** (cf. Gogolin 2008) had been prevalent in foreign language teaching. This means that the mainstream school language and other previously acquired languages were excluded from the (foreign language) classroom. Teachers feared that the transfer of structures from the L1 would lead to mistakes, that there would be too little exposure to the target language and that learners would make too little efforts to use the target language (cf. Hall/ Cook 2012). This approach does not take into account that first and second language learning processes differ: when learning a second language, learners have already acquired concepts and categories in their first language and use these as a point of reference (cf. Butzkamm 2013, 473). Instead of seeing the learning of each language as a separate process, research has highlighted the interconnectedness of all language learning. Already acquired languages influence the learning of another language, affecting for example identity development and the development of **language awareness** (the ability to reflect on the function and form of language). Concepts such as **translanguaging** (the ability of multilingual speakers to make use of their different languages in a communicative situation, for example reading a text in one language and discussing it in another; cf. Garcia/Wei 2014) aim at exploiting multilingual speakers' full potential of language competences.

A strategic use of the language of schooling can include psychological support (for example establishing a positive relationship and ensuring understanding), opening up possibilities for participation (for example allowing students to give their ideas in German or their native language) and offering opportunities for metalinguistic learning such as comparison between languages or mediation (for varied examples cf. Butzkamm/ Cladwell 2009).

To enable students to draw on their full linguistic potential, **migrant languages** that the students speak should also have a place in the foreign language classroom. They could be used for **cross-linguistic comparisons** or to support understanding in small groups and foster **cultural learning** (cf. Hu 2003; Jakisch 2014; also cf. chapter 9 in this volume).

5. Competence orientation: An additional dimension of a focus on learners is the shift in curriculum design from the input the teacher provides to the competences learners should develop (cf. chapter 2 in this volume). In line with communicative approaches, this principle takes into consideration what learners can do with the language and focuses on language in use, rather than targeting at a native speaker-like competence. Competence orientation has now become the basis for both the nation-wide educational standards and the curricula of the different federal states, following the disappointing results of German students in large-scale studies like PISA and DESI. The principle is based on Wein-

ert's (2001b) concept of competence that includes knowledge, skills, strategies, actions, attitudes, experience, motivation and social abilities and that enables people to solve problems in specific situations. This means that competences are complex and comprise a variety of dimensions; they are not just individual skills such as being able to answer questions about a text.

Competence models in the area of foreign language teaching that are also based on the **Common European Framework of Reference** try to display foreign language competences in a matrix with different levels. What is problematic about this approach is that while it is possible to display the traditional four skills in a model with different levels, this is much more difficult for additional, but equally important dimensions of foreign language competence (for example, cultural and aesthetic aspects or attitudes; cf. Bonnet/Breidbach 2013). As a result, the sum of the parts (the individual skills like listening and speaking) very often does not mirror the complexity of the whole (foreign language competence). Competences are not developed by training individual skills but in complex communicative situations that ask for problem-solving activities in interaction with others (cf. Hallet 2011). If this is the case, competence-orientation can contribute to a learner-centred perspective on teaching and allows teachers to focus on what students are able to do with language.

11.3 | Focus on content

Content matters: Authentic language use in the foreign language classroom requires a focus on content. Meaningful content with personal relevance to the learners is the starting point for any communicative interaction when authentic language use is concerned. Why should learners make an effort to express themselves in a foreign language if there is nothing relevant to talk about? This refers to the primacy of content over form, which has been a core message of the communicative approach. A popular German supporter of this focus on content in foreign language teaching was Piepho, who started publishing about it in the late 1970s. He criticised that English lessons in German classrooms would not focus on meaningful content and therefore learners would just learn formal aspects for tests instead of using the language to develop communicative competence (cf. Piepho 1979, 9). Although today school curricula in Germany generally follow the idea of a content-oriented approach, the question is how meaningful content actually is integrated in language teaching.

Teaching literature and culture: The teaching of authentic literature in the foreign language classroom involves a focus on content and has been part of foreign language learning from the beginning of modern language teaching. In current EFL classrooms, young adult and children's literature provides relevant content for students (cf. chapter 10 in this volume). In a similar way, culture as content has always been an important dimension of foreign language teaching. Intercultural communicative compe-

Meaningful content

tence as a major goal again involves addressing relevant content, for example if students compare their favourite music or places they like to go (cf. chapter 9 in this volume).

Content and language integrated learning (CLIL): More specific content-based approaches have become internationally known under terms such as content-based instruction (CBI), bilingual instruction, sheltered instruction or English as an additional language (EAL or Structured English Immersion). All of these concepts can be grouped under the umbrella term ›Content-based language teaching‹ (CBLT).

<table>
<tr>
<td>Definition</td>
<td>Content and Language Integrated Learning (CLIL) denotes an approach to learning content through a foreign language and teaching content and language at the same time. As a rule, CLIL is used to describe all types of teaching that use any second language (foreign language, regional languages, minority languages etc.) to teach up to 50 % of certain content subjects (e. g. history or biology) at school.</td>
</tr>
</table>

In Germany, the term ›Content and Language Integrated Learning‹ (CLIL) and, more often the term *Bilingualer Sachfachunterricht*, are used when a content subject is taught in the foreign language. CLIL in this context means that a school subject is taught in English as a foreign language and both the subject and foreign language skills are in the focus of learning. This of course raises several questions: How much focus should be on the subject matter and how much focus on supporting the development of the foreign language skills? Can the content of the school subject be sufficiently learned when the learners are not proficient in the foreign language? Should the teaching material of the subject be translated from German into English or is it better to use authentic material from English-speaking countries? Most of these questions have been discussed since CLIL became part of school curricula (cf. chapter 2 in this volume). This discussion resulted in principles of CLIL methodology that give orientation of how to integrate CLIL in the classroom.

CLIL goals and principles: Contemporary approaches of CLIL follow the principle of putting a focus on teaching the content subject and supporting the foreign language at the same time (cf. Wolff 2010b, 299). The organisational forms of CLIL can vary from bilingual streams in schools (*bilingualer Zug*) when several subjects are taught in the foreign language through all grades, to teaching one content subject in the foreign language for one or more school years. Even weaker forms such as teaching one module of a particular subject in the foreign language can be considered as CLIL education.

A common practice with teaching materials is to simply translate German textbooks of the subject into English. Proponents of CLIL however argue that translating content into the foreign language is not sufficient because language is always closely connected to **cultural contexts**. The teaching material thus has to represent the cultural contexts of the target language. More recent CLIL approaches therefore see bilingual education as cultural teaching and they try to integrate **authentic teaching material** from the target countries instead of translating German textbooks (cf. Sudhoff, 2010). For history lessons, this CLIL approach could for example mean including texts and sources from English-speaking countries, which represent perspectives from these contexts on historical events.

CLIL in history: World War II Example

Teaching World War II in history with a CLIL approach opens up new opportunities of using authentic texts from American or British sources. This enables learners to get to know the events of WW II from different authentic perspectives. Historical and cultural learning is extended towards a global and intercultural perspective.

Scaffolding: Learners in CLIL classes are faced with complex learning processes through the combination of learning contents of the subject and doing so in the foreign language with authentic texts. In this **complex learning environment**, learners need support to understand authentic texts, for example, through teaching aids being used in the classroom. Therefore another important principle of CLIL is scaffolding (cf. Thürmann 2010).

> The term scaffolding refers to forms of language support, learners are offered during the learning process. Texts often need to be adapted to the language level of the learners and additional visuals or demonstrations support the comprehension of the content. Another important principle is the use of the first language as a support of the learning process. Although the classroom language should primarily be the foreign language, the first language of the learners can be used to support the comprehension of complex contents. The goal is, however, to reduce the use of the learners' first language step by step while the learners make progress in using the foreign language in the CLIL class.

Definition

CLIL and focus on language teaching: What sets CLIL apart from other language teaching approaches is the assumption that academic subject matter and new language features can be taught by the teacher and learned by the students at the same time. Although this expectation might have its rationale in **SLA theory** and in foreign language research, the question is in how far this expectation can be met in the classroom. As Lightbown (2014, 65) points out, language learning in content-based classes can only be successful if classroom teaching also includes an explicit **focus on form**. Through her analysis of research findings on content-based foreign language classrooms, she comes to the conclusion that there is not enough focus on teaching the foreign language and that subject learning and foreign language competence can suffer from this. But how can teachers focus on language teaching in the CLIL classroom and support subject learning at the same time? One way is to introduce **speech acts**, which are typical of discourse in the subject. Learners need to learn how to express themselves in the context of the specific subject field. Learning terminology of the subject, as it was practised in former CLIL approaches, is not sufficient because terminology alone does not help learners to (inter)act in the language.

11.4 | Task-based language learning

Based on the two major claims that a foreign language is best learned through communication in authentic situations and in interaction about meaningful content, relevant principles and approaches which help to realise both learner- and content-orientation have been spelled out. An established approach which brings these principles together is task-based language learning.

Action-orientation: Task-based language learning takes up the principle of action-orientation which emphasises the use of the target language as an instrument of action, for example to get in touch with people, to communicate ideas, wishes, thoughts, etc. Action-orientation is seen as both the method and the goal of the language learning process (cf. Bach/Timm 2013b, 8): Language is learned through the accomplishment of communicative tasks and actions and by preparing students for communicative situations that they have to deal with. Authentic communicative situations are created by performing tasks in which students use the language for personally **meaningful purposes**, for example presenting their dream house as in the sample task below. Since tasks take the learners' interests, needs and competences as a starting point, task-based language learning realises the principle of learner-orientation. It is also in line with a focus on significant content, because language use becomes meaningful for students if they have the opportunity to talk about topics that are personally relevant to them. In tasks, language is used as a means to pursue a communicative goal. TBLL usually follows the structure of a TBLL framework that takes into account the importance of activating prior knowledge (pre-task), sequencing activities (sub-tasks) that prepare students for the target task and evaluating the outcome. An explicit language focus may be integrated.

Definition	According to Van den Branden (2006, 4), a task »is an activity in which a person engages in order to attain an objective, and which necessitates the use of language.« In contrast to exercises (for example, gap-filling activities), tasks provide communicative and meaningful situations and generally focus on meaning rather than on form.

Task-based language learning is promoted by the *Common European Framework of Reference* (CEFR), emphasising the fact that language competence enables people to participate in society (cf. Council of Europe 2001). A distinction is made between **task-based language teaching** (TBLT) and **task-supported language teaching** (TSLT) depending on the degree to which language learning is centred on tasks. In task-based language teaching, the whole curriculum is grounded on tasks, whereas in task-supported language teaching tasks are one element among others in an otherwise topic- or form-focused syllabus (cf. Ellis 2003, 27). TBLT contexts are not very common in Europe. English teachers in Germany usually work in a TSLT context in which the course book plays a very important role.

Features of TSLT: In extensive classroom studies, Müller-Hartmann and Schocker-v. Ditfurth (2011; 2013) have identified several features of tasks that support language learning:

1. Involvement: Students will only be motivated to get involved in a task if it enables them to communicate about content that is personally relevant to them. This implies letting students participate in the selection of topics and giving them tasks that can be completed with a wide range of content, for example ›friends‹, ›songs and idols‹, ›future plans‹, ›holidays‹, ›eating habits‹, etc. (cf. Müller-Hartmann et al. 2013). Tasks do not prescribe specific linguistic forms that the learners are required to use but give them choices according to their level and preferences. Learners can activate their resources and use whatever linguistic means they have at their disposal to get their meaning across. In the task example on dream houses, students can use the given language chunks, but are free to include details and descriptions that go beyond the model text. The task can be completed on a very basic level giving only limited information about the dream house, but the description of the house and the interaction with the partner can also be very elaborated. Involvement is also supported if »tasks are clear about why learners do what they do with language« (Müller-Hartmann/Schocker-v. Ditfurth 2011, 63), if they see the purpose of the activity.

2. Task complexity: Tasks that are supposed to prepare learners for **real-life communication** have to integrate different linguistic skills rather than isolate, for example, just speaking or listening activities. They have to take a wide concept of competences into account that considers attitudes, skills and knowledge and includes communicative, methodological and intercultural competences. In the task example, learners use four skills, they develop communication strategies and techniques for learning vocabulary and structures. Intercultural competence is involved when politeness conventions (greetings and saying goodbye) are discussed.

Tasks that model real-life problems are necessarily complex. They involve **problem-solving activities** and should prepare learners for **social and cultural participation** (cf. the concept of the complex task in Hallet 2011, 143 ff.). They provide a framework that allows for learners' individual choices in terms of language and content and can lead to different outcomes (cf. Müller-Hartmann et al. 2013, 42 ff.), giving the possibility to cater to heterogeneous needs. In the sample task, complexity also depends on the degree of spontaneity that the students display. The student playing the alien can come up with previously rehearsed questions or ask for spontaneous answers, which increases the demands on his/her partners. Outcomes, for example presentations, role-plays, posters, interviews, surveys and so on should be agreed upon with the learners and might change in the process of working on the tasks.

3. Focus on form: Research has shown that learners benefit from a focus on form to support their language production (cf. Samuda/Bygate 2008, 208). It is helpful at different points in the process to direct learners' attention towards specific structures of the language or provide them with chunks to support their language production (cf. Müller-Hartmann et al. 2013, 45). The focus on form is therefore used as a task support to help students to better express their communicative needs. If students, for example, invent their own monster, adverbs of frequency can help them to write about its daily routine (cf. Kolb 2016).

4. Interaction: Based on the assumption that language is learned by using it, interaction between students during tasks offers these opportunities (cf. Müller-Hartmann/Schocker-v. Ditfurth 2011, 67). **Group** and **pair work** allow learners to try out communication strategies and promote their willingness to take risks, that is experiment with language without being afraid of making mistakes. The sample task allows students to both challenge their partner by asking tricky questions and support him/her through the collaborative development of the dialogue.

5. Task demand and task support: Demands that tasks pose on learners can be cognitive, linguistic or interactional (cf. Cameron 2001, 25). Depending on their individual group of learners, teachers have to provide appropriate support that can be adapted while working on the tasks. The **sequencing of activities** is also necessary to guide learners towards the intended outcome. From the start, students have to know what the **target task** and the different steps towards this target are and what function they have in the process. In the example, students first activate their prior knowledge on the topic and collect vocabulary and structures. The model text shows the product and provides further linguistic support. Learners start developing their own dream house first by drawing a picture and then by developing the presentation. They practise the role-play with a partner before they finally present it to the whole class.

Example   **Task: Present your dream house to an alien**

The students draw and label a picture of their dream house and develop a guided tour through the house for an alien who can ask all kinds of silly questions (for example, »What's a TV?«).

Task steps:
- The students describe pictures of different unusual houses, they develop a word web.
- The teacher presents a model text of a guided tour through his/her dream house.
- The students draw a picture of their dream house and label it (task support: dictionary, word web).

- In pairs, the students develop a guided tour (task support: pictures, model text, chunks, for example »Would you like to see my house? Come in.«, »This is ... I like ...«, »Thanks for coming.«, »Thanks for having me.«, »What's this?«, »What do you do with ...?«).
- The students present their guided tour in front of the class.

11.5 | Conclusion

Based on the communicative turn in foreign language teaching two fundamental claims of how to teach a language have been put forward: language teaching should be oriented around **authentic situations** of language use and learners should have **opportunities to interact with others** in the foreign language. Rather than outlining a coherent set of different language teaching methods, the current complexity and heterogeneity of teaching contexts was reflected in the discussion of language teaching principles in three categories: focus on content, focus on learners and focus on tasks. These principles are important points of references for teachers: Who are my learners? What is relevant content for them? And what tasks should they be able to complete with language? These are important questions for every teaching context. Examining one's own practice in the light of these principles can help to answer the central question when thinking about methodology: *why* do we do certain activities in the classroom?

Further Reading

Hallet, Wolfgang (2011): *Lernen fördern Englisch. Kompetenzorientierter Unterricht*. Seelze-Velber.

Larsen-Freeman, Diane/Anderson, Mati (2011): *Techniques and Principles in Language Teaching*. Oxford.

Müller-Hartmann, Andreas/Schocker-v. Ditfurth, Marita (2011): *Task Supported Language Learning*. Stuttgart.

Richards, Jack/Rogers, Theodore ([3]2014): *Approaches and Methods in Language Teaching* [2001]. Cambridge.

Annika Kolb / Thomas Raith

12 Media-Assisted Foreign Language Learning—Concepts and Functions

Whether media for entertainment, communication or distribution, analogue or digital learning materials, textbooks and digital multimedia that accompany textbooks or textbook-independent educational applications (apps) for smartphones—materials and media are an essential part of a contemporary communicative foreign language classroom. They offer diverse opportunities to enrich foreign language teaching and learning processes. Keywords like e-learning and blended learning, digital game-based learning, mobile-assisted language learning, big data and learning analytics are current media developments and trends. On the one hand, one often finds pedagogic-normative statements concerning the value, chances and risks of media; empirical research into details and interrelationships of their use, on the other hand, often fall short.

The goal of this chapter is to highlight the functions, quality criteria, applications and effects of different media in diverse foreign language teaching and learning processes and, ultimately, to allow insights into processes of mediating and constructing knowledge, as well as competence acquisition, in media-supported foreign language learning scenarios.

After an introductory analysis of central concepts in the context of teaching with media and a discussion of various concepts of literacy, the central part of this chapter focuses on the roles and functions, as well as the concrete applications of different media in the modern foreign language classroom. In order to understand the curricular and pedagogic implications of media-assisted foreign language teaching, basic definitions of types of media and their functions, including a historical overview of media development, will be presented. Particular attention will be given to the textbook as a central medium within a multimedia system of both analogue and digital media. A number of practical coursebook scenarios are presented in order to exemplify blended learning. The final subchapter deals with current technological and pedagogical trends and developments, focussing mainly on mobile-assisted language learning, big data, learning analytics and digital gamification. The subchapter on mobile learning reflects on how smartphones and tablets have changed the way we learn a language, discussing the communicative and interactive functions of apps. The learning analytics subchapter tries to find answers to numerous questions concerning privacy, profiling, information-sharing, data ownership and the improvement of the learning experience. Finally, the digital gamification subchapter presents a brief historical overview of learning games, presenting the stages of gaming development up to the 21st century gaming industry.

12.1 | Basic definitions

12.1.1 | Media in foreign language pedagogy

Definition

Media can be defined as the means by which information is conveyed from one place to another. »The most obvious characteristic of a medium is its technology: the mechanical and electronic aspects that determine its function and, to some extent, its shape and other physical features. These are the characteristics that are commonly used to classify a medium as a television, a radio, and so on« (Kozma 1991, 180).

In the past centuries, various forms of media have been used to convey instruction and support learning. In the area of foreign language learning, the use of media as a method for the acquisition of knowledge and foreign language skills has an equally long tradition. Depending on the technical capabilities and their relation to the dominant learning-theoretical approaches of the time, the use of media and the related goals have historically been integrated in different ways (cf. also chapter 1 in this volume). While textbooks and the chalkboard have a several centuries-long tradition as central media in the foreign language classroom, foreign language teaching and learning processes have undergone an enormous medial expansion, especially subsequent to the heyday of the audiolingual method in the 1950s and 1960s (cf. De Cillia/Klippel 2016).

The audiolingual method focused on bringing native speakers as role models into the classroom through **auditory media** like records and tape recordings (for example radio reports, communicative situations) and the ability of those media to offer input unlimited to learners. Dominant activities consisted of pattern drills based on imitation and repetition; and technologically elaborate environments of language labs were created for learners to train **listening comprehension** and **speaking**. Besides realia, typical **visual media** in the audiolingual framework were paintings (with keywords or line-drawings), flashcards, pinboards, murals, pictures, slides, later transparencies for overhead projectors (OHPs), film and television. The underlying teaching principle called for connecting language to visual material whenever possible. The technical cost and effort of providing and combining numerous audio and visual media and devices in the foreign language classroom were extremely high. While individual media had to be used additively in this **analogue multimedia system**, digital technology has created new opportunities to reduce the number of needed devices over time.

Technological shifts: With computers, smartphones or tablets, individuals today have control over multimedia devices, which, as media of presentation, information, communication, practice and entertainment, combine different functions that are especially relevant for foreign language learning. In this context, Grimm et al. (2015, 204) point to a »three layered function [of media] as teaching and learning aids, as communicative tools, and as subjects of reflection«. As a result of the rapid technological developments, an increasingly **digital multimedia system** has emerged out of the analogue multimedia system—a shift which should contribute to a competence-oriented, communicative and more motivating English learning environment. Next to print textbooks as the central medium (available also as e-books), in some cases up to 30 accompanying media are offered as educational packages for formal instructional settings, from classical workbooks to vocabulary apps, learning software on CD-ROM, digital lesson planners, Internet exercise platforms and slides for the interactive whiteboard. In addition to this are materials and media that are independent from textbooks, such as foreign language newspaper websites or news portals, blogs, social media sites, messengers (e. g. WhatsApp) or utility apps (for example for creating animations or film), all of which extend today's foreign language classroom medially (cf. Funk 2016). Questions concerning the appropriate digital infrastructure of the classroom to support learning—from laptop-classes to bring-your-own-device solutions (cf. Heinen 2015)—should be examined carefully and different approaches should be researched to determine whether and how media can increase learning quality.

Multimedia: In general, foreign language learning today has been greatly enriched by multimedia. However, the concept of multimedia is increasingly becoming an overstretched buzzword and umbrella term for every form of integration of media. For a differentiated description of the technological characteristics of multimedia in the fields of information and learning, for example foreign language learning apps, certain categories are needed (cf. e. g. Engelkamp/Zimmer 1990; Dick 2000, 90; Weidenmann 2002, 45). In this context, Weidenmann (2002, 61) recommends the description of media according to three dimensions:

- the **technological medium in-use**: e. g. book, DVD, computer, smartphone, tablet
- the **coding forms for information** in different symbol systems: monocodal (e. g. for only text or only audio) or multicodal (e. g. for text combined with images, animations or audio files)
- the **required sensory modalities**: monomodal (e. g. only visual or only auditory) or also multimodal (especially audiovisual)

Interactivity: Next to multicodality and multimodality, interactivity represents a further, if not the most important component of educational multimedia use. Media are labelled as interactive when there is a possibility of a reciprocal, dynamic exchange between the user and the media. Here it is important to differentiate between navigational interaction and didactic interaction (cf. Haack 2002):

Definition

> Navigational interaction describes the possibility of intervention, navigation and adjustment that the user can carry out (e. g. the choice and adjustment of content, choice of the order of activities). Didactic interaction comprises aspects such as the analysis of user-behaviour and the corresponding programme reaction (e. g. feedback, adaptivity).

12.1.2 | Multiliteracies and digital literacy

The term ›literacies‹ has been intensively discussed among language teaching experts, and the literature offers a myriad of various conceptualisations. However, a certain consensus can be identified. Literacy, or literacy education, implies the process of learning in different contexts (homes and communities) and an acknowledgement of the screen as a dominant text structure (cf. Rosswell/Walsh 2011, 53). As a result, a discussion about new literacies has emerged. New literacies are multiple and demand various modes. Among these, the multiliteracies pedagogy developed by the New London Group (1996) claims that »[...] the screen governs our understanding of the world and curricula need to reflect this dramatic shift in our ideological and interpretative frame« (quoted in Rosswell/Walsh 2011, 56). It is obvious that the screen and—to a certain extent—digital environments are recurring conceptual patterns within the academic and practical discourse of multiliteracies. Therefore, the focus here is on digital literacies, especially within an ELT-context. Although both teachers and learners should be digitally-literate, considering the target group of this book (mainly student teachers), the main focus in this chapter will be on **digital literacy teaching skills** and their potentials. The use of digital technologies for educational purposes has initiated a discussion among experts and practitioners on what digital skills actually are. While there is a wide range of various definitions, coinages and contexts, the focus here is on digital literacy skills for teachers as defined by the *Virtuelle PH* (2006):

Digital literacy skills for teachers: Before their studies begin, pre-service teachers should already have digital skills from section:

A **Digital literacy skills and IT-knowledge:** This knowledge includes knowledge about IT, humans and society, IT-systems and applied IT.

During and after their studies (in the first five years of teaching), pre-service teachers should be taught the following sections:

B **Digital life:** teaching with digital tools, questions of digital ethics, digital inclusion, etc.

C **Designing digital materials:** design, adapt, publish digital teaching material, copyright issues, creative commons, OERs, etc.

D **Teaching and learning with digital media:** plan, implement and evaluate teaching and learning processes with digital media and digital learning environments; digital assessment, feedback, safer Internet

E **Teaching and learning with digital media in the subject:** subject-related/specific use of contents, software, media and tools

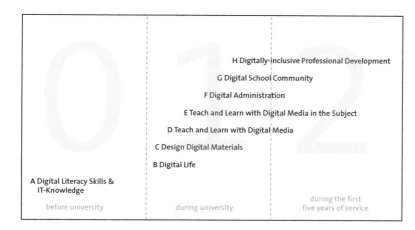

Illustration 12.1:
digikomp: digital
literacy skills for
teachers (VPH)
http://www.
virtuelle-ph.at/
digikomp/

F **Digital administration:** efficient and responsible use of pupils' data, digital registers, digital pupil administration

G **Digital school community:** communication and collaboration within the school's community and beyond

H **Digitally-inclusive professional development:** continuing professional development in the field of digital literacy

This model shows that digital literacy skills for teachers are more than simply IT-skills, like working with text-processing software or competently selecting hardware and software. The approach considers the acquisition of various general, interdisciplinary and subject-related digital skills as a continuous process in the career of a pre-service and early-career teacher. The following chart provides practical examples of digital literacy skills for an EFL (pre-service) teacher:

Section	Description	Activity
A	digital literacy skills and IT-knowledge	e.g. how to use laptop/tablet and projector to show L2-videos
B	digital life	e.g. discuss questions of data privacy (as a topic in the EFL classroom)
C	design digital materials	e.g. create interactive quizzes for the EFL classroom (crossword, cloze, millionaire game, etc.); design digital handouts with Evernote
D	teach and learn with digital media	e.g. create a lesson plan with cloud-based applications like Evernote, Google Drive, etc. in order to have ubiquitous access to materials
E	teach and learn with digital media in your subject	e.g. use interactive EFL websites, like http://www.lessonstream.org
F	digital administration	e.g. use digital grade sheets for your students (automatic algorithms, formulas, scoreboards, etc.) with Evernote, Google Drive, etc.
G	digital school community	e.g. use a learning management system like Moodle to communicate with pupils and parents

Table 12.1: Digital literacy skills in the EFL classroom

12.2 | From textbooks to multimedia learning environments

12.2.1 | The historical development of media-assisted foreign language learning

Media have always been an essential part of foreign language teaching and learning. Whether it is a magazine article, a short video, an audio snippet or a passage from the textbook, one purpose of incorporating media in the EFL classroom is to exploit the full potential of multisensory methods. Furthermore, Chan (2011, 132) observes that »media are essentially realia to be brought into a classroom from the outside world in an attempt to make language activities appear more realistic, more interactive, and therefore, more meaningful«. Since the 15th century, the following developments have taken place in the context of media-assisted (language) teaching and learning:

Media type	Media category	Since
textbook	visual	15th century
blackboard	visual	16th century
picture/photography	visual	around 1800
overhead projector (OHP)	visual	1870s
radio	auditory	end of 19th century
TV	audiovisual	1950s
CD	auditory	1980s
CD ROM	audiovisual and interactive	1980s
DVD	audiovisual and interactive	1990s
multimedia projector	visual	1990s
computer	audiovisual and interactive	1980s
MP3	auditory	1990s
smartphone	audiovisual and interactive	2000s
tablet	audiovisual and interactive	2010s

Table 12.2: Technical development of media types in the ELT classroom

The chart above shows that media systems (*Medienverbünde*) have existed for a long period of time. Up to the early 2000s, the focus has been on using analogue media in classroom teaching. Since then, more and more digital technology has been incorporated into the foreign language classroom. The use of the computer in the language classroom has initiated digital teaching scenarios: **computer-assisted language learning** (CALL). The development of CALL can be divided into three phases: behavioural, communicative and integrative CALL (cf. Akcaoglu 2008).

Stages of CALL: The first CALL scenarios (1980 to mid-1990s) typically consisted of grammar handouts performed on the computer (kill and drill handouts). The second wave (from mid-1990s to 2000s) of computer use »has gained power with the help of the World Wide Web« (Akcaoglu 2008, 1). Due to the large amount of accessible information, teachers were able to create more contextualised, authentic and meaningful tasks, such as e-mail projects or webquests, that increased interactive performance (e. g. online research, curation of digital content) and authentic interaction with learners from around the world, including the multi-faceted implications of intercultural competence (cf. O'Dowd 2007; cf. also chapter 9 in this volume). The latest CALL stage (starting from the 2000s) focuses on integrating the four skills ›reading‹, ›listening‹, ›speaking‹ and ›writing‹ (cf. chapters 6 and 7 in this volume) within an explicitly interactive and collaborative context by using multisensory Web 2.0-tools and educational applications, such as mind mapping, brainstorming or collaborative text writing tools.

CALL stage		Example
behavioural	1980–mid 1990s	e. g. drill grammar exercises with Word
communicative	1990s–2000s	e. g. webquests, e-mail projects
integrative	from 2000s	e. g. collaborative storytelling with cartoon applications

Table 12.3: CALL-development

Regardless of the technical development, whether analogue or digital, the benefits of media in the EFL classroom can be summarised as follows (cf. Knill 2007, 2) and will be discussed in more detail in the next subchapter:

Substantial benefits	Example
shaking up old paradigms	reducing frontal lessons by using collaborative media like digital mind mapping applications (http://www.padlet.com, http://www.bubbl.us, etc.).
explaining things better	using visualisations in order to understand lexical items (OHP, multimedia projector)
tackling real life problems	using newspaper articles with currents topics, teenage topics, etc.
adding a discovery component	using the Internet to do some research about a certain topic; extend topical knowledge
breaking the monotony of a lesson	using motivational and highly dynamic digital tools, like Kahoot (http://www.create.kahoot.it), in order to leave the sometimes monotonous learning space of the textbook
using audiovisual channels	using songs and videos about a certain topic (e. g. Jay-Z' and Alicia Keys' »Empire State of Mind«: topic New York) in order to teach intercultural and listening/viewing skills
sharing teaching tools with other teachers	using Evernote, Dropbox or OneNote to share handouts, exercises and useful links with teacher colleagues
better organising a lesson	using text processing software or note software to organise a lesson more effectively (embed links, handouts, downloads, timing, etc.); using bookmarking apps to save/archive/curate useful teaching material
increasing students' engagement	learning stations with CD/mp3 islands (*Offenes Lernen*)

Table 12.4: Substantial benefits of media in the EFL classroom

12.2.2 | Media pedagogy and media didactics in the EFL classroom

Getting rid of technological determinism: The media-assisted language classroom has developed from teaching with books, images, audio and videos to teaching that adopts a multisensory approach by additionally incorporating digital technology. However, in the contemporary EFL classroom, the emphasis should not be solely on the tool itself, but rather on how these tools can be methodologically exploited in order to achieve a learning goal (cf. Strasser 2012a; 2012b; 2015). Therefore, a closer look at the rather recent concept of media pedagogy is required (cf. Grimm et al. 2015, 199).

Media pedagogy consists of four subcategories:

- **Media education** is concerned with ways of using media sensibly. It is centred on enabling individuals to reflect critically on their use of media.
- **Media didactics** is concerned with the functions, effects and forms of utilising media in teaching and learning scenarios. It aims at improving and optimising teaching and learning processes and the facilitation of self-directed acquisition of knowledge and competences.
- **Media studies** imparts knowledge about all media across the media repertoire and basic technological competences. Foci include historical developments relating to media, legal issues (e.g. data protection), media monopolies, the power of the media, etc.
- **Media research** entails the analysis and exploration of issues pertinent to media education as well as to media socialisation across all age groups. Foci include media use in everyday life, the impact of different media, reception habits, media and gender, etc.

The emphasis in this subchapter will be on media didactics, more specifically, on digital media, since the latest developments address the use of digital technology within the context of the EFL classroom (cf. Strasser 2012b; Stanley 2013; Martín 2015). In order to provide a smooth conceptual and applicative transition from analogue teaching to the additional, symbiotic use of digital media in the foreign language classroom, Puentedura's (2010) SAMR model is briefly discussed.

The SAMR model aims at convincing teachers in favour of analogue teaching of the benefits of digital technology.

Illustration 12.2:
SAMR model
(Puentedura 2010)

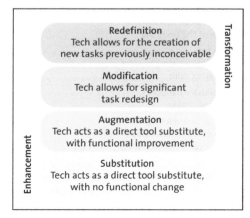

Redefinition
Tech allows for the creation of new tasks previously inconceivable

Modification
Tech allows for significant task redesign

Augmentation
Tech acts as a direct tool substitute, with functional improvement

Substitution
Tech acts as a direct tool substitute, with no functional change

Transformation

Enhancement

- The **substitution level** addresses the possibility of digital technology replacing analogue media (e.g. the use of computers instead of typewriters, etc.). The simple replacement does not automatically imply an improvement; however, it refers to the change of the medium due to societal changes (cf. Golumbia 2014).
- At the **augmentation level**, an improve-

ment of teaching and learning performances due to digital media is discussed, where digital facilitators such as spellcheck, hyperlinking or sharing of digital artefacts are listed.

- The **modification level** implies the potential of continuous development of digital artefacts, i. e. that certain digital texts (blog entries), etc. can be given feedback to, commented on and changed by the teacher and learner.
- Tasks that would not be possible without technological support are part of the **redefinition level**: instead of writing essays, learners pick digital storytelling tools (cartoon apps, etc.). One obvious advantage is the visualisation of complex contents.

To sum it up, this model serves as a rather simple but coherent approach developed in order to implement certain **blended learning** scenarios in a relatively techno-critical lesson. The teacher can start at a very low level (e. g. substitution) and gradually increase the degree of technology integration when creating specific tasks for the EFL classroom:

Level	ELT Scenario	Tools
Redefinition	Teacher lets students create cartoons or digital stories (instead of written texts on paper).	http://www.makebeliefcomix.com, http://www.animoto.com
Modification	Teacher uses a learning management system like Moodle forum or Wiki, so that students can interact with their peers.	http://www.wikispaces.com, http://www.moodle.org
Augmentation	Teacher shares grammar handouts or online newspaper articles with URL-shorteners instead of handing out copies or writing down links on the blackboard.	http://www.bit.do, http://www.tiny.url
Substitution	Teacher uses multimedia projector instead of OHP.	YouTube, mind mapping applications, etc.

Table 12.5:
The SAMR-approach within an ELT context

12.2.3 | Using modern coursebooks effectively

When speaking of media-assisted language learning and teaching, one has to consider that digital technology has played a dominant role within the last years. This, however, does not mean that analogue media should be avoided altogether because, in reality, the analogue textbook is still a vital part of the EFL classroom (cf. Harmer 2015; Ur 2012). Therefore, the approach here focuses on how the analogue medium of the textbook can be supported with media-enriched content within a symbiotic framework, so that digital media *per se* is not perceived as the motivational ›treat‹ but a methodologically-enhanced part of the whole lesson (inside and outside the classroom). In order to understand how analogue and digital media can be applied in a classic textbook-oriented EFL lesson, the following evaluation criteria for teachers using an EFL textbook should be considered (cf. White 2013):

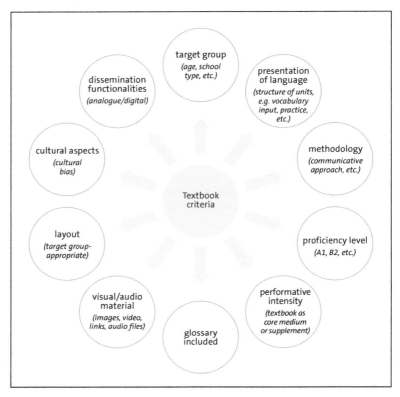

Textbook criteria: Illustration 12.3 shows how a textbook responds to versatile demands. In the EFL classroom, coursebooks are a relevant aspect of the curriculum and can act as a teacher's GPS through mandatory topics. O'Neill (1982, 111) presents four justifications for using coursebooks:

- A great amount of the coursebook's material meets the students' curricular needs.
- Students have the chance to »look ahead« or »refresh their knowledge with past lessons«.
- Coursebooks imply the »practical aspect of providing material which is well-presented in inexpensive form«.
- Well-designed coursebooks »allow for improvisation and adaptation by the teacher, as well as empowering students to create spontaneous interaction in the class«.

Adaptive learning with EFL coursebooks: These beneficial aspects of a coursebook have to be seen in the light of how teaching professionals use the coursebook in their classroom. O'Neill (1982, 111) emphasises that

»coursebooks should be accessible to a variety of students, regardless of their learning goals, as well as being adaptable to the diversity of teachers and teaching styles«. Coursebooks, however, should not only be adaptable to the teacher's, but also the learner's, needs. Therefore, adaptive learning, which is often embedded within an additional digital context, plays a considerable role for textbook design, especially for teachers who like to design additional material (cf. Sercu 2000 qtd. in Grimm et al. 2015, 249). Learners and teachers should also be able to pick elements of a unit, adapted to their personal performative needs. This is rarely possible with printed textbooks but would be possible with methodologically well-developed digital components. Experts (Swales 1980; Nunan 1991; Medgyes 1994 qtd. in White 2013) agree that »heavy dependence on a single [printed] coursebook is detrimental to students' needs, and that adaptability and supplemental materials are supportive additions« (Medgyes 1994 qtd. in White 2013, 1). The potential of digital technology as an essential multisensory extension to the textbook can be exploited in particular when considering the following disadvantages of a printed textbook (cf. Cunningsworth 1984, 3):

- There can be a lack of variety in teaching procedures.
- Innovations toward individual student's needs are reduced.
- Spontaneity and flexibility are diminished.
- There can be a lack of creativity in teaching techniques and language use.

Especially in the fields of variety of teaching procedures, individual students' needs, as well as flexibility and creativity, there is a large number of digital tools and materials that makes these flaws seem inconsequential. Furthermore, »digital technologies and applications may also help to make materials more appealing or to design and work on motivation tasks online« (Grimm et al. 2015, 257).

12.2.4 | From textbook exercises to digital learning

The following scenario illustrates how a printed textbook and digital tools can be meaningfully integrated in the EFL classroom.

In this unit (5th year of English, B1 level), students are asked to match words with pictures. This activity is supposed to be a lexical warm-up task, enabling students to review or acquire topic-related vocabulary, including contextualised sentences (cf. illustration 12.4).

However, the lexical competence of students may vary. The textbook offers neither individualisation nor flexibility, and the author assumes a certain homogeneous lexical repertoire amongst students. In this case, digital technology can enhance the learning experience and remedial or initial lexical acquisition performance.

Illustration 12.4:
Example from *TOP SPOT: English for PTS*, an Austrian textbook (vocational school, 5th year of English).
Topic: Travelling (Puchta/Strasser 2016, 52)

Illustration 12.5:
Using vocabulary with contextualised sentences (Puchta/Strasser 2016, 52)

② Fill in the missing words from the box. There is one word that you should not use.

train   bus   plane   bikes   taxi   cabs   motorcycle   subway   boats   ships   helicopters

Stuart and Mildred always wanted to visit America. They finally decided to take a weekend trip to New York City. Getting to the airport by road would take too long, so they ordered a ¹.. to take them to the local ².. station at 6:45 a.m. on Friday morning. They arrived at Heathrow Airport two hours later. The ³.. to JFK New York took off on time and eight hours later they were on the 40-seater ⁴.. taking them directly from the airport through the streets of Manhattan to their hotel. They thought it was amazing to see so many yellow taxi ⁵.. amongst the city traffic with courier riders on their ⁶.. speeding between the cars. Above them they could see several ⁷.. landing on the tops of skyscrapers. The next day

Example

Vocabulary learning

By using **multisensory flashcards** (with audio and images) and motivating quizzes, the learners can improve their lexical knowledge. The application **Quizlet** (http://www.quizlet.com), which works on PC, smartphone and tablet, helps learners create digital flashcards for personal use, where students can add additional topic-related vocabulary that is not included in the textbook. One of the main advantages of Quizlet is that new words that are learned in the classroom can immediately be added in the app. Compared to the traditional vocabulary notebook, Quizlet is mobile and, furthermore, the teacher can create a lexical unit inventory and let students participate in collaborative quizzes.

In the next example, a classic textbook matching exercise is supplemented with collaborative, individual and creative methodological design:

In this exercise, students become acquainted with frequent travel-related vocabulary (here: airports) by matching symbols and signs with the correct words or by filling in adequate words in a contextualised sentence (cf. illustration 12.7).

b) Match some of the signs with the sentences they refer to.

1 [d] Our plane leaves at 3 o'clock in the afternoon. The gate opens at 1:30 p.m.

2 [ ] The plane is expected to land at 2:15 p.m. We will wait for Aunt Suzie and surprise her.

3 [ ] We got through passport control quite quickly, but we had to wait for our bags for more than half an hour.

4 [ ] Wow, this store has a lot of cheap products without tax.

5 [ ] There's a café over there where you can go online for free.

6 [ ] This is where you can find out all about the airport (gates, shops, public transport, etc.).

Digital collaboration: In order to extend the airport vocabulary and practise contextualised sentences, the digital application **Padlet** (http://www.padlet.com) can be used. Padlet is a digital collaboration surface, which works on all kinds of devices. On this virtual wall, students can collaboratively add airport images and related vocabulary, and build contextualised sentences to strengthen the unit's required vocabulary. The advantages compared to the analogue medium are obvious: students and teachers can easily add various related media and collaboratively build adequate discursive elements during the lesson or outside the classroom. The fact that the medium is accessible wherever the students are is of great value to the lesson design outside the classroom. In case the activity is not finished during the lesson, the teacher can tell the students to continue with their ideas as homework.

Edu-App criteria: Based on the sample e-mail in illustration 12.8, students are asked to write a hotel enquiry as homework. In order to intensify the experience of collective intelligence, the application **Edupad** (http://www.edupad.ch) can be used. This app allows students to collaboratively create a hotel enquiry using the words, phrases and grammar learned in class. One of the major advantages is that students can benefit from the expertise of others, increasing the chance of creating a structurally coherent and lexically adequate text. Moreover, the teacher can give

immediate feedback within the text or via messenger. The text can be written as homework and be compared in the classroom with the timeslider function (the process of writing can be recapped step by step and the teacher can give feedback). This application does not replace the process of writing a unit-specific text type alone, but serves as a collective and collaborative basis to acquire new expertise by benefitting from the lexical inputs of the whole class and the valuable, ubiquitous feedback by the teacher.

On the one hand, all the examples mentioned show that the printed coursebook itself often serves as a reliable navigation system for the teacher and learner in order to acquire syllabus-related knowledge and skills. On the other hand, certain scenarios reveal the severe limitation of coursebooks. Because learning can also take place outside the classroom (cf. chapter 13 in this volume), a methodologically coherent use of digital tools adapted to the coursebook's needs should be supported to open a temporally and spatially delimited dimension of multisensory learning. The following qualitative and performative aspects should be considered when working with digital tools in the EFL classroom (cf. Strasser/Pachler 2014; Schmidt/Strasser 2016):

1. **Reflection:** Tools like Edupad (cf. above) help pupils and teachers reflect on a certain working process (e. g. collaboratively writing a hotel room enquiry).
2. **Modification:** Tools like Quizlet make it possible for learners and teachers to produce digital artefacts (e. g. flashcards) and adapt them to their own learning needs (e. g. extend unit vocabulary, public transport).
3. **Communication:** Communication about the learning progress is possible with tools like Edupad (e. g. learners can ask questions, their peers can answer).
4. **Multiplication:** The learning outcomes or products (e. g. airport vocabulary collage with Padlet) can easily be shared with peers or teachers (e. g. Facebook share button/link generator, etc.).
5. **Creation:** Students and teachers can easily create learning and teaching materials themselves (e. g. Padlet collage, Quizlet flashcards, etc.). They are active producers of the learning process.
6. **Collaboration:** Teacher and students actively collaborate within a digital framework in order to do unit-specific tasks (write an email enquiry together, mutually design a collage/picture dictionary related to the unit vocabulary, etc.).

12.2.5 | The digital coursebook

In comparison to the approach discussed above (i. e. the use of a printed textbook in combination with additional digital tools), the approach of the fully digital textbook is different. Due to the emergence of mobile devices and the growing implementation of tablets in classroom teaching, the concept of a multisensory, interactive digital coursebook has become more prominent. The digital textbook is more than just a simple digital pdf-version of the printed textbook. It includes **multi-media elements** (videos, interactive quizzes, hyperlinks, additional unit information, feedback elements, etc.) and **adaptive learning elements**, so that the learners can choose their favourite learning scenarios in order to do exercises or enhance the learning process based on their personal learning needs. When it comes to digital coursebooks in ELT, a lot of research work still needs to be done.

Digital coursebook monotony: The reason why the digital coursebook development within the context of ELT has not been extremely innovative so far is obvious: publishers want to jump on the bandwagon and are under pressure to produce digital material for schools. The result is a lack of innovation. The following chapter addresses the societal developments towards smartphone and tablet use in the classroom. The next generations of learners will grow up with digital media, and smartphones will be used for digital and mobile knowledge acquisition processes. In order to develop an authentic and methodologically-adequate e-textbook design, the idea of digitally replicating print versions must be abandoned.

12.3 | Current technological and pedagogical trends and developments

12.3.1 | Mobile-assisted language learning

By far the leading trend in media-supported foreign language learning is mobile-assisted language learning (MALL). Whether with smartphone, tablet, netbook or e-reader, our behaviour surrounding information, communication, entertainment and learning is increasingly shaped today by mobile digital devices. This applies to our free time, our work lives and our education. The number of software applications (apps) available for smartphones and tablets, for diverse purposes and target groups, is increasing rapidly. Especially smartphones, with their user-friendly interfaces and ubiquitous access, function as our personal digital control centres and assistants in many life situations. In total, there are over five million apps available to users in both the Google Play and the Apple App Store; educational apps comprise 8.48 % of this total (cf. Statista Inc. 2017).

Mobile technology   The field of foreign language learning is increasingly associated with mobile technology. Whether programmes for vocabulary and grammar training, dictionaries or tool programmes for mind mapping and designing learning plans, electronic dictionaries, podcast software and video platforms, programmes for images, audio and video recording, editing and animation, blogs, social network sites or augmented reality apps with multimedia content as supplementary to print textbooks—smartphones offer almost infinite opportunities for a diverse, location-independent, receptive and productive use of a foreign language.

Mobile-assisted language learning: The acronym MALL has been used since the mid-1990s as a subcategory of CALL and has been, in foreign language pedagogy, closely coupled with specific emerging technologies and popular forms of media usage. Since 2008, a rapid increase in MALL studies can be observed, coinciding with the emergence of smartphone technology (cf. survey studies from Burston 2013; Duman et al. 2015). While early MALL studies focused mostly on the single main function that the individual device provided, »we are starting to see more and more studies that can capitalise on the full range of multimedia tools, communication and social networking tools, and Internet capabilities that these devices possess« (Stockwell 2016, 297).

Quo vadis, MALL? It remains to be seen which digital applications and functions will change mobile foreign language learning in the future. Currently, the increasingly popular and rapidly developing functions like augmented reality, virtual reality, speech recognition, adaptivity and gamification—all concepts and application types closely related to smartphones as a central medium of access and interaction—serve as megatrends and focal points of innovation. In the future, these mobile technologies will allow for new opportunities for foreign language learning, especially through immersion in virtual foreign language worlds and cultures and through an intensification of foreign language use in diverse authentic discourses. For all types of use there remains the necessity to test exactly how these applications can lead to a personalised, differentiated, creative and, in terms of content, diverse acquisition of different foreign language competences.

12.3.2 | Big data, learning analytics and personalised learning

In the field of digital foreign language teaching and learning, the buzz-words ›big data‹ (cf. Yu 2015) and ›learning analytics‹ (cf. Kerr 2016) are potentially the most meaningful areas of future research and development. In fact, the analysis of user input and characteristics of user behaviour (e.g. the number of correct or incorrect answers, the selection of tasks, the frequency and usage of help features), the availability of feedback and also software adjustments to learning paths have, for many years, been the typical characteristics of quality CALL production. In the past, however, the adaptivity of such programmes has been based on decision trees developed by programmers. User decisions, their input and selection behaviours were anticipated and furnished with corresponding software reactions (for instance, when a cloze text exercise anticipates false answers and has a supply of pre-made, corresponding feedback). In this approach, the adaptivity occurs within a limited framework and in reaction to the input of an individual user. Through technological advances in the area of online-based practice, specifically big data and learning analytics, modern applications with adaptive systems are capable of much more. Such advances can serve as potentially important building blocks in creating personalised contexts for practice. The term ›big data‹ can be characterised by the 3 Vs: the extreme volume of data, the wide variety of types of data and the velocity at which the data must be processed (cf. Ward/Barker 2013).

Learning analytics is the measurement, collection and analysis of the big data of learners using educational software (e.g. learning apps) or digital materials (e.g. electronic textbooks) in order to understand and optimize learning processes. Variables such as learner history (e.g. time spent on learning, number of repetitions, discontinuations, comparisons to previous results), outcomes, learning steps, chosen topics, frequency and types of mistakes in relation to certain activities, reactions to specific forms of feedback, etc., can be analysed in correlation to the data of users worldwide or even selected subsets (for instance the classmates of an English class or students who previously took a course). In the ideal case, improved adaptive systems are now in the position of customising individual learning paths, to select activities and topics that better fit individual learning needs and that have a suitable level of difficulty, to offer appropriate feedback and assistance and thus to create the conditions for more effective practice.

Big data and learning success: However, the danger of over-interpretation and overestimation of big data and learning analytics does exist, especially in relation to the discussion of data-driven school improvement largely going on in the USA (cf. Mandinach/Honey 2008). Learning success is a multifaceted, multidimensional construct, which manifests itself not only through processing behaviour and the success of digital activities and tasks. Learning analytics supplement this with an informative and, for the development of quality, necessary (yet very limited) picture of the learner and learning processes that occur. At the level of the individual learner (cf. chapter 4 in this volume), a far more differentiated, holistic perspective from the teacher—one that is supported by the data collected by the system—is necessary to meet the quality expectations of adaptive, personalised learning and to choose tailored learning and support. Kruse and Pongsajapan (2013, 1) therefore call for a strong learning-centred approach to learning analytics (instead of one based on intervention) to serve (the students') learning and development, »[and] empower [...] [the students] as metacognitive agents of their own learning«. Especially when considering big data and learning analytics for foreign language learning, it should be closely observed which exercise processes are meaningfully supported, which competency developments are even measurable with which formats and whether and how, if measurable, the results can be transferred to the classroom.

Data privacy? Big data, learning analytics and ›transparent learning‹ offer, in theory, improved quality to learning and teaching processes in school, to the development of tasks, as well as to the development of educational institutions. However, despite all these opportunities, the ethical and moral dimensions of collecting and analysing digital learner data should be given serious consideration (cf. Slade/Prinsloo 2013; Schmidt 2016). Numerous questions concerning privacy, profiling, information-sharing and data ownership exist concerning how analytics relate to existing organisational systems. With respect to legal issues, it must be clearly determined and communicated which data, for which purposes and from which pre-determined users can be reviewed and analysed, which measures will be taken to protect user identity, how long the data will be stored in coordination with the established legal framework and standards and which opportunities a system offers the user to request the deletion of personal data. The opportunities and risks of data storage and analysis should be carefully balanced.

12.3.3 | Digital game-based language learning

In addition to the megatrends of mobile learning, big data and learning analytics, the field of digital game-based language learning (DGBLL) offers a third field of rapid product innovation destined to play a significant role in the development of media for the teaching and learning of foreign languages, as well as for the design of motivational learning environments in the future. The use of learning games, or playful approaches in general, in the foreign language classroom already has a long tradition (for an overview cf. Klippel 1980; cf. also chapter 11 in this volume). Games in the foreign language classroom, from simple vocabulary games to role-playing games, contribute to the increase of learning motivation, facilitate action-oriented practice of language skills and also allow for the pursuit of social and affective goals through the interaction in the game. Whilst the use of digital game formats to support foreign language learning processes has been addressed in a select handful of studies in the past (cf. e. g. Hubbard 1991), foreign language pedagogy has been intensifying its work in this area over the last five years, as evidenced by new edited volumes (cf. e. g. Reinders 2012), monographs (cf. e. g. Sykes/Reinhardt 2012; Peterson 2013) and research projects (cf. e. g. Sylven/Sundqvist 2012; Schmidt et al. 2016). The establishment of this new field of research and development in foreign language learning has run parallel to a strong and growing interest in digital games, which has been observable from around 2010 onwards, coupled with rapid technological advancements:

The globalisation of the digital gaming industry, the diversification of games into new and culturally hybrid genres, a global increase in access to broadband, and increasing numbers of non-traditional game players have precipitated a notable expansion of digital game and play activity into new contexts and applications. (Reinhardt/Sykes 2014, 2)

Categories of digital game-based language learning: It is important to draw a terminological distinction between different categories and/or approaches. **Gamification**, as one of the most frequently used labels, refers to a process which according to Deterding et al. (2011, 13) understands »the use of game design elements in non-game contexts« as part of the »socio-cultural trend of ludification«. Elements and mechanisms which are familiar to students from games, such as levels and progress bars, missions, competition (leader boards), discovery (e. g. hidden treasure), rewards systems (e. g. badges, bonus levels, virtual goods), are used outside the gaming context, in this case in the field of foreign language learning.

A cursory perusal of foreign language learning software, in the form of smartphone apps, websites or multimedia practice CDs accompanying workbooks, clearly reveals the increased use of such game mechanics. One example of gamification is the use of a digital learning management system such as Classcraft, in which everyday classroom activities are embedded in role-play scenarios and where students are rewarded for good classroom participation in the accompanying game. Whilst gamification as a process serves to describe the application of playful techniques and concepts in fields in which these methods are usually not found, **serious game** refers to the integration of educational content into a gaming context itself.

Mission US: City of Immigrants
Example

One example of a **serious game** is the social studies game *Mission US: City of Immigrants*, in which students playing the game assume the role of Lena Brodsky, a Jewish immigrant from Minsk, Russia who arrives in the United States in 1907. As Lena, students navigate New York City at the turn of the 20th Century, work to help support her family and witness changes in the way factories operate. Originally intended to teach students about tenement life in turn of the century New York, the game also reflects principles of Content and Language Integrated Learning. The game is designed to encourage students to empathise with the game's characters, make connections to their own experiences and ultimately learn more about American history.

A third subcategory of DGBLL is the so-called **commercial off-the-shelf game**. Whilst this type of game was designed for entertainment purposes rather than language learning, the foreign language versions of such games have significant potential as foreign language learning aids. Simulation programmes in particular, such as *SimCity* or massively multiplayer online games such as *World of Warcraft*, have been used in foreign language learning contexts to develop students' reading, writing, listening and speaking skills and have increasingly been the subject of research.

It is important to note that the development of good DGBLL applications and learning scenarios that provide opportunities for high levels of learner agency and engagement and that promote ›learning to play‹ rather than ›playing to learn‹ (cf. Arnseth 2006) is an extremely challenging task that can only be achieved effectively by game designers, educational researchers and foreign language learning specialists collaborating on an interdisciplinary basis. Only when this has been achieved will it become possible to make good use of the trend in gaming and its associated technical innovations in foreign language learner environments and to generate adaptive learning contexts, in which learning motivation is fostered and where learning and play serve to complement each other.

12.4 | Conclusion

In general, it can be stated that media-assisted foreign language learning and teaching is a terminologically and conceptually versatile topic. The concept of digital literacy skills does not focus on a certain technological determinism, but rather on the teacher's and learner's pedagogical application skills (e. g. teaching the four skills in the EFL classroom, improvement of the learner's discursive competence in turn-taking sequences, etc.).

Learning artefacts (e. g. handouts, brainstorming sequences, etc.) have become digital. Therefore, the role of coursebooks also needs to be reconsidered by embedding more multisensory digital content (e. g. augmented reality features). Mobile devices like smartphones or tablets can be effective catalysts to promote data-driven ubiquitous and/or digital game-based learning scenarios. Technology-enhanced foreign language teaching and learning has changed the way we learn a foreign language and the role of the teacher.

Further Reading

Burston, Jack (2015): »Twenty Years of MALL Project Implementation. A Meta-analysis of Learning Outcomes«. In: *ReCALL* 27/1, 4–20.

Funk, Hermann [6]2016: »Lehr-/Lernmaterialien und Medien im Überblick«. In: Burwitz-Melzer, Eva/Mehlhorn, Grit/Riemer, Claudia/Bausch, Karl-Richard/Krumm, Hans-Jürgen (eds.): *Handbuch Fremdsprachenunterricht* [1989]. Tübingen, 625–631.

Rosswell, Jennifer/Walsh, Maureen (2011): »Rethinking Literacy Education in New Times. Multimodality, Multiliteracies, & New Literacies«, https://blogs.otago.ac.nz/multiliteracies/files/2014/11/Roswell_2011.pdf (15.11.2017).

Stanley, Graham (2013): *Language Learning with Technology. Ideas for Integrating Technology in the Language Classroom*. Cambridge.

Stockwell, Glenn (2016): »Mobile Language Learning«. In: Farr, Fiona/Murray, Liam (eds.): *The Routledge Handbook of Language Learning and Technology*. New York, 296–307.

Torben Schmidt/Thomas Strasser

13 Settings—Teaching in and beyond the English Language Classroom

Setting is a multifarious term in the context of English language education. In a very general sense it refers to the overall **context and framework** of foreign language learning and teaching. As such, it has many further synonyms which are likely to be used in other publications on English language teaching, for example background, environment, classroom, *Lernumgebung* or *Lernort*. When remembering past experiences of English language learning, many people will probably think of settings such as the classrooms of their schools, perhaps a school exchange to an English speaking country or an English speaking visitor at their school. However, from an academic point of view the settings of foreign language education are much more versatile and complex. They can be roughly divided into the following four dimensions:

- the political framework of foreign language education: e. g. the school system, curricula or educational reforms
- the approach to teaching foreign languages: e. g. communicative, task-based or structure-based teaching (focusing on grammar and vocabulary teaching)
- the English language classroom: e. g. the classroom as a physical space, as an interpersonal meeting place or even out-of-school sites beyond the physical classroom (e. g. cinemas, theatres etc.)
- the role of the Internet in foreign language education: e. g. online English language resources or online communication in the English language

Questions of terminology

Four dimensions: It is important to understand that these four dimensions do not have clear boundaries and overlap in many instances. For example, the curricula of all German federal states determine communicative competence as one of the overarching objectives of modern foreign language education in German schools. This element of the political setting of English language teaching thus impacts on the approaches to English language teaching to be found in German schools. Because of this, teachers are obliged to pursue the communicative approach to English language teaching and cannot, for instance, adopt a structure-based approach. Another example for the overlapping of these four dimensions is the potential of the Internet as a communication tool in foreign language education. If teachers plan to exploit this communicative potential of the

Internet, their English language classrooms need to have the respective facilities, for example a notebook class or a computer room they could go to with their pupils.

Physical and virtual spaces

However, it is worthwhile to separately consider these different dimensions because it will help to develop a thorough understanding of the complex nature of the settings of English language teaching while at the same time gaining insights into the intricate relationship between them. Therefore, in this chapter the different dimensions of ›settings‹ of English language education will be discussed, focusing in particular on these aspects: (1) the English language classroom as a physical space, (2) English language learning beyond the classroom, (3) the English language classroom as a social meeting place and (4) the role of the Internet in English language education. The chapter concludes with a summary of the most salient empirical findings regarding the impact of settings on foreign language learning. The other dimensions—the political context and approaches to foreign language education—are being discussed in greater detail in other chapters of this book (cf. e. g. chapters 2 and 6).

13.1 | Inside the English language classroom

Classroom design

First and foremost, the English language classroom is a **physical space**. It is usually a room with walls, tables, chairs, very often with further media and materials such as books, posters, audio and audiovisual resources, wall decorations, hand puppets, realia, sometimes with computers or tablets. In Germany, probably a majority of classrooms is still equipped with chalkboards whereas in other parts of the world these have been replaced by white boards and interactive white boards. Given that the classroom is the pivotal site of institutional foreign language education it is surprising that in the discourse on teaching and learning foreign languages there is rather little explicit reference to the classroom as a physical space. This is except for Legutke (1998; 2006; 2013) who already in 1998 highlighted the significance and implications of classroom design in the wake of the communicative turn. According to him, the classroom is in the epicentre of communicative foreign language education since it is the very place where learners can experience participating in social discourses and co-constructive meaning-making in the foreign language (cf. Legutke 2013, 91).

In this context, he also points out a subtle, but interesting difference in the terminology commonly used in schools: Whereas the English term ›classroom‹ denotes both the processes of teaching and learning as well as the space in which they occur, the German term *Unterricht* relates to only the processes of education, thus disregarding the physical space in which it happens (cf. Legutke 1998, 93). However, ironically the physical characteristics of classrooms are often only scrutinised and reflected upon when actually leaving the school building in the context of out-of-school projects (cf. 13.2).

Classroom design: Yet the physical setting of foreign language learning deserves more attention and classroom design is far from being trivial. In fact, many teachers carefully plan how to set up their individual classrooms (cf. Dreßler 2012) as can, for instance, be seen in many primary schools. This is first of all based on the knowledge that in order to learn most successfully, humans need to feel safe and comfortable. Just like in private homes the design of school buildings and classrooms is one way of creating such an atmosphere. For example, since noise can cause stress in many modern school buildings, steps were taken to reduce noise levels. Another example are the sofas and cushions in one corner of a classroom or in a small extra room right next to the classroom. These are often used as a ›quiet corner‹ where pupils can retreat if they feel they need a little break. A third example is the personal decoration of many classrooms at primary or lower secondary level. By putting up for instance their own photos or creative products learners and teachers can develop a sense of ownership and feeling of home in this particular classroom. Some primary schools take this a step further and have pupils bring comfortable slippers, which they only wear inside the classroom. English language teachers often contribute to classroom design by, for example, putting up maps of target language countries, English language film posters, information leaflets on English theatre groups or portraits of authors.

A second reason for paying attention to physical classroom design is the knowledge that body movement and **physical activity** are significant for successful learning. Integrating different forms of physical activity in school education has a very long tradition which is usually related to concepts such as holistic and action-oriented learning (*Ganzheitlichkeit* and *Handlungsorientierung*; cf. e. g. Bach/Timm 2013b, 16; Mayer 2013, 76; chapter 6 in this volume). More recently Sambanis (2013, 89) has explored the results of neuroscientific research and their implications for foreign language education and in doing so dedicates a whole chapter to the relationship of movement and learning. She highlights that aside from anthropological, health and motivational reasons humans essentially need physical activity and body movements. These are healthy and motivating, in fact being physically active actually is significant for the learning process as such. Body movement is a means of processing new information and at the same time it activates different parts of the brain. Thus, in order to exploit the potential of body movements for learning, classrooms need to be designed accordingly and especially provide enough space. For example, for young learners there needs to be enough extra space between tables and chairs for pupils to partake in physical activities such as activity songs or games. Primary classrooms also need to provide enough space to set up a circle of chairs or the so-called ›cinema seat‹ (*Kinositz*), where all children closely sit together in rows on the ground, on chairs or tables right in front of the board. Secondary level classrooms ideally provide the space to move around tables during a lesson, for instance for group work, rotation learning (*Stationsarbeit*), project work, role playing or other drama methods.

In primary English language education, teachers typically employ a variety of action-oriented activities such as songs and games that allow their learners to move their bodies, sing songs or play games. For exam-

Physical activity and body movements

ple, the following is a popular chant often used as a routine to start the English lesson:

Chant

It's up and down and turn around.
It's up and down and touch the ground.
It's up and down and snap, snap, snap.
It's up and down and clap, clap, clap.
It's up and down and touch your knees.
It's up and down and freeze!

On chanting ›up‹ and ›down‹, teacher and children raise and lower their hands. This is followed by the movement described in the chant, for example turning around, touching the ground and three times snapping the fingers or clapping the hands. On chanting the final word, everybody freezes in their current movement and many children like to make a funny face at this moment.

Another popular song in primary English language classrooms is »Head, shoulders, knees and toes«, which also allows for constant body movement. Examples of popular games that all need some space include »Simon says…« or »Four corners« (*Eckenraten*) and »Double Circle« (*Kugellager*) for practising vocabulary (for further activities cf. Gegier 2006; Grieser-Kindel et al. 2016; Schmidt 2014).

Rich learning environment: It has thus become clear that the design of a classroom has a direct impact on the learning processes in English language education. As such the physical setting of a classroom may contain both affordances and limitations for foreign language learning. Ideally, it provides a multitude of **affordances** (cf. Singleton/Aronin 2007; van Lier 2000), i. e. a **rich learning environment** with

- a variety of non-linguistic and linguistic input, the latter containing both comprehensible and authentic elements,
- motivating and challenging resources and tasks allowing for autonomous learning and
- multiple opportunities to use the foreign language for interactions and negotiations of meaning.

In the context of English language learning the term affordances denotes the permanent linguistic and non-linguistic opportunities for language learning (to afford s. th.: *etw. ermöglichen, bieten* or *erlauben*) in a given educational setting. In the English language classroom this could be anything from a table, a sheet of paper or a bag of fruits (non-linguistic) to a poster, a textbook or a dictionary (linguistic). As such, affordances offer learners the possibility for interaction and learning, they do not force learners to use them. Affordances only become meaningful if learners perceive them as useful and possibly utilise them. The term was first coined by Gibson (1979) and later adapted for foreign language education by van Lier (2000). The theory of affordances is based on a constructivist approach to learning. This approach maintains that learners construct knowledge on their own in social contexts, while the teacher mainly operates as a facilitator.

One classical example for input in rich learning environments are small **classroom libraries** with various text types appropriate for the specific target group. In a primary classroom, it might contain authentic children's books, easy foreign language readers, audio resources, children's journals, picture and word cards or picture dictionaries. In a secondary classroom, it might contain young adult novels, graphic novels, journals, dictionaries or audiobooks. Furthermore, there are various software products and online resources available for both age groups. Very often these materials can be used by the children when they have time to spare, for example when they have completed another task earlier than the others. In case the teacher is pursuing a more **autonomous approach**, the classroom libraries are usually part and parcel of the lesson plan, for example as one stop in rotation learning or as a research phase in task-based teaching. Activities like these usually then give learners the opportunity to actively use and experiment with their new language skills in communicative situations, for instance they report to the class what they have learned about a certain topic from a journal they read or what they have learned about a certain character in a story.

Limitations: However, the classroom design and equipment can also prove to be a limitation for teaching and learning a foreign language. The most common examples seem to be the following:

- The **classroom is too small**, thus tables cannot be moved and pupils do not have enough space to move around freely or, for instance, meet in a separate corner for group work.
- There is **no subject-specific classroom** (*Fachraum*) as, for instance, for the sciences, the arts or food technology. Thus, the foreign language teachers cannot design one particular classroom according to their subject-specific needs. Especially at secondary level they move from classroom to classroom instead and therefore have to carry the necessary resources around. Quite understandably, this limits the quantity and type of resources teachers can provide for their foreign language learners.
- Because **money is scarce**, some schools do not have the funds to acquire a great variety of media or foreign language resources. The Internet overflows with useful audiovisuals, but they are of no use to teachers who cannot access a projector or an interactive white board. Similarly, schools sometimes lack the funds to purchase up-to-date resources for classroom libraries or even new textbooks.

Effects of classroom design: As this overview has shown, there is a close relationship between the **physical characteristics** of foreign language classrooms and the learning and teaching processes going on in these rooms. As Legutke (1998, 94) points out, any methodological approach to teaching indirectly implies particular claims to the physical setting of the classroom. For example, the autonomous language classroom is going to look very different from a structure-based classroom. Vice versa, the architecture of a classroom communicates the underlying understanding of education and learning. This can easily be seen in the remnant language labs or lecture halls still occasionally to be found in German schools which are testimonies of audiolingual or instructivist approaches.

13.2 | Beyond the English language classroom

Discovery learning

Leaving the actual school building to learn the English language outside ›in the world‹ has a rather long tradition even though in foreign language education it does not happen as often as it does in other school subjects such as the sciences or social studies. This form of school education outside the school premises is usually called **extra-curricular learning** or **out-of-school learning** (*außerschulisches Lernen*). Sometimes other terms are used in this context as well, such as discovery learning or situated learning (*forschendes Lernen*, cf. Gehring 2010b, 13). Historically, out-of-school learning originated in the **progressive educational movement** (*Reformpädagogik*) and as such was deeply rooted in a criticism of bookish and formal school education (cf. Gehring 2010b, 8; Thaler 2010b, 5 f.). The latter was criticised as failing to teach learners the knowledge and skills they can actually use in their future life after school (*Anwendungsbezug*; cf. Legutke 2013, 91). In contrast to this, the progressive educational movement aimed at allowing learners to better understand the real-life purpose of the things they learn at school. Thus, leaving the school building and having learners try out, experiment with and use their knowledge and skills in the world beyond the classroom was seen as a better way of achieving this objective. In this sense, extra-curricular learning is closely connected to concepts such as holistic and action-oriented learning because it usually integrates the cognitive, practical, affective and meta-cognitive dimension of learning.

The role of media: Furthermore, proponents of out-of-school learning often argue that current **social and media developments** call for teachers to provide learning opportunities for their pupils outside the school building. The JIM study 2016 (cf. MPFS 2016, 9 ff.), an annual study investigating the use of media among 12 to 19-year-olds in Germany, showed that a large proportion of teenagers state they regularly meet friends in their free time (73 %), do sports (69 %) or spend time with their family (35 %). However, at the same time many state to use their mobile phones (92 %) or the Internet (87 %) on a daily basis, thus indicating the significance of mediatised information and communication. These survey results can be seen as one indicator that young learners increasingly use media to explore and interact with the world rather than gaining primary, multi-sensory experiences. Also in this sense, preparing and equipping learners for an active and autonomous life in society is the very objective of school education (cf. KMK 2003, 6) and out-of-school learning is often pursued as one form of achieving this goal (cf. Gehring 2010a; Thaler 2010b; Legutke 2013).

Authenticity: Looking more closely at out-of-school foreign language learning, the most important benefit is usually considered the opportunity to use the target language for its true purpose, as a means of **authentic communication**. In this context, the adjective ›authentic‹ means that learners are pursuing a genuine communicative purpose (*kommunikative Ernstfälle*, Legutke 1998, 103) as opposed to the mock conversations (*Scheinkommunikation*, Gerngross/Puchta 1988, 52) often exercised in the foreign language classroom in order to practise certain language items. Through partaking in authentic communicative situations, learners can experience both how the target language is useful for their own purposes and how they can achieve a goal through using the language as a communicative tool (*Sprachhandlung*).

Since the communicative turn in the 1970s two distinct notions of authenticity have been established (cf. Leitzke-Ungerer 2017; van Lier 1996, 137 ff.):

Authentic resources include those materials which originally were designed for a target culture audience (e. g. newspapers, literature, movies) and not for the foreign language classroom. This form of authenticity is particularly important when aiming at inter- or transcultural learning objectives.

Authentication relates to the learners' perception of an educational setting. According to this notion, an educational setting can only be considered as ›authentic‹ if learners perceive it as relevant, meaningful and motivating: »the people [...], each and everyone individually for himself or herself, as well as in negotiation with one another, authenticate the setting and the actions in it« (van Lier 1996, 128).

Definition

Linguistic landscapes: Another equally important benefit of out-of-school foreign language learning is the fact that it can further raise learners' **awareness** for the role the English language plays in their everyday lives. Learners will probably be aware that they encounter the English language on a daily basis in various media such as the radio or the Internet. Some will probably be able to name nearby places where they overheard other people speaking English. They are less likely to be fully aware of the entire scope of the multilingual »linguistic landscape« surrounding them, i. e. the »language of public road signs, advertising billboards, street names, place names, commercial shop signs, and public signs on government buildings« (Landry/Bourhis 1997, 25). Becoming aware of their **multilingual environment** affords learners the opportunity to understand that they can find resources for learning and using foreign languages almost everywhere and that this is not restricted to their immediate school context.

Primary and secondary sites: Gehring (2010b, 10) uses a rough distinction between primary and secondary sites for out-of-school foreign language learning in order to categorise various examples. Even though he stresses that there is not a clear-cut demarcation line between the two, it is a helpful orientation in trying to understand the nature of learning beyond the English language classroom.

Primary out-of-school sites were specifically created and designed to initiate foreign language learning. These can be museums or art exhibitions offering, for instance, English language or bilingual tours for school classes. Further examples are the special school screenings in cinemas or English theatres touring from one town to another (cf. Lütge 2010; Surkamp/Feuchert 2010). More recently, so-called university-based outreach labs (*Schülerlabore*) have been created which also offer bilingual science or English language labs (cf. Duczak 2013; Vanderbeke/Wilden 2017).

Secondary sites for out-of-school foreign language learning were in the first place designed for very different purposes than language learning; however, they can be exploited for this very purpose because of certain international and multilingual traits they possess. These can, for instance, be airports, train stations, ferry terminals, outlet centres or restaurants attracting international customers. Following the idea of linguistic landscapes, almost any commercial or public space can nowadays be used as a foreign language learning site, such as supermarkets, clothes shops or market squares.

Structure for out-of-school projects: Importantly, teachers planning on using such a site need to carefully plan how to structure the project and guide their learners in order to exploit the full potential of this out-of-school site. Thaler (2010b, 6) suggests a general **three steps method** for out-of-school activities:

1. preparing the out-of-school project at school,
2. using and exploring the foreign language in the out-of-school learning site and
3. analysing and evaluating the out-of-school experience back at school.

Without the careful planning of these steps by teachers there is danger of frustration, distraction or disorientation among the learners. The following examples may serve as models for setting up such projects at both primary and secondary sites for out-of-school English language learning.

Example · **Outreach labs**

One example of primary out-of-school English language learning sites are the Humanities outreach labs based at, for example, the Ruhr-University Bochum (*Alfried Krupp-Schülerlabor*) or the University of Göttingen (YLAB). For example, the Bochum lab entitled *Shakespeare or ›Shakesfear‹? Ein literarischer Riese im Zwergenkostüm* (cf. Duczak 2013) focuses on classical matter of upper secondary English language education. However, this all day project away from the regular school classroom affords the opportunity to deal with this curriculum relevant topic without the pupils' work being marked. Thus, the lab aims at sparking learners' interest in Shakespeare through giving them more freedom of choice and pursuing creative methods alongside more traditional text-analytical methods when working with both original texts and modern adaptations (e. g. films). A further aim of outreach labs is to familiarise learners in upper secondary school with the context, methods and personnel of university-based science and research in order to motivate them to become university students themselves. Thus, pupils can experience the English language being used as a tool of communication in the academic and scientific discourse.

Since Humanities outreach labs are still rare, teachers mostly rely on other out-of-school sites to enable their students to experience the English language outside of their classroom. Watching a screening in the original English language at a nearby cinema (cf. Lütge 2010) or visiting an English language theatre (cf. Surkamp/Feuchert 2010) are frequently deployed activities by foreign language teachers, especially at upper secondary level.

The Airport Project

Example

One of the most famous secondary language learning site projects in the German English language teaching community is the so-called Airport Project (cf. Legutke 2006; original film documentation available online: Legutke/Thiel 1983) first implemented in 1982 which since has been repeated and adapted in numerous ways. In the initial Airport Project, a year 6 English class planned a day trip to the nearby international Frankfurt airport to try out and experiment with their communicative English skills after a year and a half of English learning. The class planned in small groups to complete the following tasks at the airport: investigate and collect English language texts, such as sign posts, restaurant menus, announcements, information leaflets; interview English-speaking travellers about where they are from and where they are travelling to.

After the visit to the airport each group chose the most interesting audio-recorded interviews, transcribed them and presented them to the whole class. Obviously, a class project like this needs careful planning both by teachers and pupils. For example, pupils need to prepare and practise useful language chunks, interview questions as well as strategies of how to react in case they do not understand what a traveller has been saying. Aside from linguistic preparation they also need to practise collecting data, discuss cooperative strategies and make sure they can orientate themselves at the airport (for a more detailed description of the different steps taken in the Airport Project cf. Legutke 2013, 104 ff.; 1998, 96 ff.).

Supermarket Rally

A final example for out-of-school English language learning at a secondary site is the Supermarket Rally (cf. Froese 2010, 33), a small-scale adaptation of the Airport Project, in which learners explore the linguistic landscape of a modern grocery store. It can be implemented in approximately 60 minutes during which groups of learners go to the nearest supermarket, explore and list all products imported from English-speaking countries and list English words they find at the shop. Back at the school the groups analyse and report their findings. Time permitting, this rally can also be extended through investigating more information about the countries of origin of the products, their process of production (e.g. fair-trade, organic farming methods) and their ways of being imported (e.g. by ship, by plane etc.). In this way, the rally could also be one element of cross-curricular bilingual education, for example with the social sciences or geography (for bilingual out-of-school learning cf. Gehring 2011; Gehring/Michler 2011).

Independent learning at school: These are but three examples illustrating the diverse forms English language learning beyond the classroom can take. There are numerous further examples to be found in the publications referred to in this section giving credit to teachers for using their imagination and creativity in designing out-of-school projects in order to provide their learners with stimulating, motivating and hands-on English language learning opportunities. Interestingly, the idea of teachers leaving the school premises with their pupils has reverberated to what is happening within the school building. In a way, the **principles of out-of-school learning** have thus been adapted to classroom learning, when schools (1) furnish areas for independent learning (*freie Lernorte*, Gehring 2010b, 12) within the school grounds such as reading or study corners or (2) invite external guests such as international visitors, people from the immediate neighbourhood, former pupils, local entrepreneurs, theatre groups etc.

13.3 | The classroom as a social meeting place

Aside from being a physical space, a classroom is always a social meeting place, where humans meet others and communicate as well as interact with one another. Legutke (1998, 2013) has repeatedly pointed out that as a consequence of the **communicative turn** there was a necessity to extend the notion of what constitutes a ›classroom‹ and consider its **interpersonal dimension**. In contrast to earlier structure-based and teacher-centred approaches (cf. Lightbown/Spada 2013, 126 f.), which were based on the assumption that communicative skills virtually develop automatically if learners have internalised the structures of language, in communicative language teaching learners ideally become agents of their own learning process, have their say in negotiating meanings and taking decisions on tasks and group processes (*Handlungsraum Klassenzimmer*; cf. Legutke 2013, 110). As a consequence, the **relationship between teachers and pupils** can become very dynamic in the communicative English language classroom. When teachers let go of control and give their learners a voice, for example have them bring in their own ideas, topics and materials, the outcome is uncertain. Both teachers and learners thus need to be flexible, willing to take risks and occasionally even overcome fears. For example, novice teachers sometimes report being afraid of losing control and feeling responsible for virtually everything happening in their classrooms. Thus, these young teachers often need to make a conscious effort to overcome this fear and take the risk of providing their learners with more autonomy. Very often they report afterwards how this has been a very positive learning experience in their professional development—yet, taking the first step can be difficult.

Further school staff: Besides the teacher-pupil relationship, the classroom as an interpersonal space can also involve other school staff such as teaching assistants, social workers or special educational needs (SEN) teachers (*Förderschullehrkräfte*). Especially, since **inclusion** has become an overarching goal of global educational policy (cf. Bongartz/Rohde 2015; Haß 2013; UNESCO 2009) schools are required to provide equal educational opportunities for *all* children and standard schools increasingly include children with SEN. Even though the practical implementation of inclusion in everyday schooling is far from being complete and many teachers feel overwhelmed by this task, there are numerous local and regional initiatives addressing this political innovation. For example, in many contexts teachers now have the chance to cooperate in **multiprofessional teams** with other (SEN) teachers, psychologists, social workers, teaching assistants and so on. In fact this teamwork seems to be a key in making inclusion work and take the pressure off individual teachers in the inclusive classroom (cf. Mays/Grotemeyer 2014). This form of team teaching also impacts on teacher-pupil relationships: learners will accustom themselves to having several adults in the classroom at the same time, sharing the teaching responsibilities and supporting *all* children.

13.4 | The Internet and English language education

It is commonly known that the Internet has transformed many aspects of life and one of them is foreign language education. Since approximately the mid-1990s, the Internet has been recognised and explored for its potential as an **educational tool** (cf. van Lier 2006, 758 f.) and educational Internet pioneers for some time enthusiastically claimed:

[...] the ›two-by-four-by-six‹ constraints of classroom instruction have been broken. This phrase [...] indicated how the Internet had managed to supersede the two covers of the textbook, the four walls of the classroom, and the six daily hours of (high school) instruction. (ibid., 758)

Even though to this day, textbooks, classrooms and school timetables still strongly feature in school education, there is a grain of truth in this eager and optimistic claim (for more critical arguments cf. Grünewald 2016). Especially regarding English language education, the Internet has amended and enriched traditional resources, teaching approaches and opportunities for foreign language communication (cf. chapter 12 in this volume). Thus, the Internet has impacted on the setting of foreign language education in that it has expanded the traditional classroom and its rather limited opportunities for exploring, researching and communicating in the English language. Thus, in the following the three different dimensions of how the Internet is most commonly used in foreign language education are sketched out (for further examples of alternative implementations cf. e. g. Biebighäuser et al. 2012b; Becker et al. 2016): the Internet as a (1) resource, (2) communicative tool and (3) creative tool.

The internet as resource, communicative tool, creative tool

Resources: The Internet provides a multitude of resources for English language education and a challenge for teachers usually is to select those resources that match the intended learning objectives and the age as well as language level of their target group. On the one hand, there are those Internet resources which teachers—similar to traditional text book material—explore for their **lesson planning** and bring to class, such as for example reading texts, audiovisuals, animated or still images. On the other hand, there are those resources which teachers pre-select and then design **research tasks** for their pupils to independently explore on the Internet, such as for example websites on a given topic, online dictionaries, online museums or the Internet profile of a political activist. The benefit of the Internet in this sense is that is has multiplied the sheer quantity of resources easily accessible for both English language learners and teachers.

Communicative tools: Similarly, the Internet has increased the number of communicative channels readily available for communicative foreign language education. Based on the knowledge that learning a foreign language is particularly successful when learners have the chance to use the target language for interaction and negotiations of meaning foreign language teachers have cherished and explored this particular potential of the Internet (cf. e. g. Zibelius 2012, 213 ff.)—in spite of the technological equipment of German schools not always being up to date.

One example are the so-called **correspondence projects** in which two classes located in different parts of the world communicate via Web 2.0 tools (or via e-mail before that) and very often collaborate on a given topic. In these projects the target language usually functions as a lingua franca thus giving learners the chance to experiment using it for authentic communicative purposes. Alongside their online correspondence both classes usually also meet according to their regular school timetable, thus the teachers on both ›sides‹ have the chance to monitor and guide the task process.

A further example are the **Facebook posts** which some teachers and their pupils prepare and ask their friends to share with their friends and so on in order to track how quickly information can travel across the globe via the Internet. Very often, they ask people to name their location in the world and then mark these on a map in the classroom. One final example of exploring the Internet for online communication in foreign language learning are the interview projects which some teachers have set up with their class. For example, when exploring career choices a class does a **Skype interview** with a professional from a certain vocational domain. Similarly to other encounter projects (cf. e. g. the Airport project in 13.2) the teacher and his/her pupils need to prepare the interview situation well in order to prevent frustration and boost the learners' self-confidence.

Creative tools: Finally, the Internet has been used as a creative and productive tool in English language education. With the Web 2.0 many tools have become available to foreign language learners for creating and publishing their own multi-media based texts, including, for example, written texts, images, video clips or podcasts. Bruns (2008) coined the term ›**produsers**‹ to illustrate that in the age of the Web 2.0, users of the Internet are at the same time producers of online content and many teachers have embraced this opportunity for their pupils to engage in creating new forms of foreign language output. One example is the digital storytelling approach (cf. Ohler 2013), which has been adapted in various ways and with very diverse target groups.

New forms of language output

Wilden/Matz (2015), for example, implemented several projects in which short stories were transformed into **digital stories**, i. e. short video clips published on YouTube. Aside from developing and practicing their English language skills learners in these projects also developed their multiliteracy skills enabling them to critically participate in multimodal discourses (cf. Kalantzis/Cope 2012; Elsner/Viebrock 2013).

Another example of using the Internet as a creative tool in foreign language education is the **podcast project** by Schmidt (2009) in which year 11 pupils launched a school podcast channel for which they created and published various contributions, for example a report on a local band or on a school exchange, a film review or a talk show about junk food. Such creative Internet projects give learners the opportunity to produce foreign language texts and publish them for a much bigger audience than in the normal school classroom. For example, the podcast project showed that the individual contributions were viewed from different parts of the world, an aspect that seemed to motivate learners just like the opportunity to stage themselves online and then show the results to their friends and family. It is thus clear that the Internet has had a major impact on the immediate setting of foreign language education in the traditional school classroom.

13.5 | Conclusion: the impact of settings on English language learning opportunities

In this section the evidence of selected empirical studies will be summarised which relate to the settings of English language learning. The guiding question in this respect will be what evidence there is regarding the

impact of settings on (foreign language) learning opportunities. In order to identify relevant studies a **database research** (*FIS Bildung, IFS Marburg, ERIC, Datenbank Grundschulenglisch*) was conducted in May 2016 using the term ›settings‹ as well as related synonyms and compounds such as classroom setting, educational setting, learning environment, *Unterrichtssetting, Lernumgebung, Unterrichtsarrangement, Lernkontext, Lernort*, classroom space, educational environment, *Lernsetting*, classroom context. An interesting result of this research was the fact that most empirical studies in this field focus on either teaching beyond the foreign language classroom or on how principles of out-of-school learning can be integrated into the classroom context. To this day, Legutke's (1998) reminder that the classroom is the central site of communicative foreign language education and thus ought to be carefully scrutinised and designed does not yet reverberate in empirical research on English language learning.

Teacher impact   The impact of teachers: Hattie (2009) published one of the most influential educational studies in recent years, which is a synthesis of more than 800 meta-studies identifying those factors which influence learners' achievements. In concluding his findings Hattie highlights—among others—an aspect which directly relates to the interpersonal dimension of classroom-based learning (cf. 13.3): »Teachers are among the most powerful influences in learning« (Hattie 2009, 238). Even though Hattie's study does not distinguish between different school subjects this major finding from his study is interesting in the light of other studies based in foreign language education. For example findings from the **DESI study** (cf. Klieme 2006), a major nationwide study in Germany researching English language learning achievements of more than 11,000 ninth graders in the school year 2003/2004, highlighted the importance of the English language teacher, thus matching Hattie's conclusion: those EFL teachers who actively participate in continuing professional development (*Lehrerfortbildung*) and maintain contacts to English-speaking countries manage to motivate their learners more through their teaching than others (cf. Klieme 2006, 7).

Errors as learning opportunities: Aside from highlighting the role of teachers as a significant factor in the school setting, Hattie also flagged up the importance of a positive and supportive **atmosphere** as another element of the interpersonal dimension of school classrooms:

School leaders and teachers need to create school, staffroom, and classroom environments where error is welcomed as a learning opportunity, where discarding incorrect knowledge and understanding is welcomed, and where participants can feel safe to learn, re-learn, and explore knowledge and understanding. (Hattie 2009, 239)

This aspect seems to be of particular importance in the context of foreign language learning since **errors and mistakes** have been recognised as an integral part of any language learning process (cf. Lightbown/Spada 2013). Thus, in the communicative English language classroom, teachers are called upon to follow the principle ›**message before accuracy**‹ and treat learners' target language mistake as opportunities for further developing their language skills.

Class size: Another finding from the DESI study is in contrast to Hattie's meta study and thus emphasizes the difference between foreign languages as communicative school subjects and other subjects: Whereas Hattie (2009, 239) does not identify class size as a factor in learning achievements, the earlier DESI study identified lower teaching quality in bigger-sized classes. Thus, class size indirectly impacted on learners' achievements in listening comprehension: smaller learning groups appear to be a beneficial factor in foreign language teaching with its strong focus on communication in the target language (cf. Klieme 2006, 7).

Home-school-connections: In exploring empirical findings relating to out-of-school factors in learning achievement both Hattie's meta-study and the DESI study highlight the importance of home-school-connections, i. e. **parental involvement** in what is going on in school, occasional **home visits** by school staff and so on. In those schools, in which the school management reports on close cooperation between parental homes, learners demonstrate higher learning achievements than elsewhere. These results are independent of school type or socio-economic background of the parents (cf. Klieme 2006, 5). Furthermore, in English language education the parents' English skills and attitudes towards the language seem to impact on their children's English language learning achievements as was found in the DESI study (cf. ibid.).

Size and atmosphere of learning groups

Further reading

Dreßler, Constanze (2012): »Where I Work Well. Lernumgebungen gestalten und ausschöpfen«. In: *Grundschulmagazin Englisch* 12/3, 7–8.

Gehring, Wolfgang (ed.) (2010a): *Außerschulische Lernorte des Fremdsprachenunterrichts*. Braunschweig.

Legutke, Michael K. (⁵2013): »Lernwelt Klassenzimmer. Szenarien für einen handlungsorientierten Fremdsprachenunterricht«. In Bach, Gerhard/Timm, Johannes-Peter (eds.): *Englischunterricht. Grundlagen und Methoden einer handlungsorientierten Unterrichtspraxis* [1998]. Tübingen/Basel, 91–120.

Eva Wilden

14 Assessment—What, Why and How?

Experienced foreign language teachers make use of a variety of approaches for evaluating their learners' competence development. These approaches range from appraisal of a learner's answer in the classroom to fully-fledged formal tests. In this chapter, some basic issues of language assessment will be outlined and discussed with a focus on **classroom-based language assessment** because this is what foreign language teachers spend much time and effort on. In fact, it is estimated that regular teachers can spend as much as a third to one half of their time on assessment-related activities (cf. Coombe et al. 2012c). And indeed, assessment can be seen as the extrinsic engine that drives learning—in any case, assessment and learning should be seen as inseparable in the foreign language classroom. As such, it is vital that teachers are in a position to integrate assessment with instruction so that they use appropriate forms of teaching. The capacity for this has come to be called **language assessment literacy.**

> Language assessment literacy is the ability to critically evaluate language tests, compile, design and monitor language assessment procedures in foreign language contexts, grade and score them on the basis of theoretical knowledge.

Definition

The chapter will address the what, why and how of foreign language assessment and thus try to develop language assessment literacy with a focus on the theoretical knowledge mentioned in the definition above. The ›what‹ refers to terms like testing, assessment, evaluation and the difference between them. It also refers to what good assessment is like, i. e. the quality criteria of assessment. The ›why‹ is concerned with purposes of assessment and the ›how‹ refers to the assessment cycle, which will be illustrated with an example from classroom-based language assessment. Alternatives in assessment will finally be discussed.

14.1 | Assessment: what is it and what is important about it?

First of all, it is important to determine what assessment actually is. Defining it is not that easy as there are different terms that involve the collection of evidence on learner performance.

Testing always involves **measurement** and is placed in a formal context. A test is an instrument that is used to elicit the performance of a test taker. Subsequently, this performance is measured, in other words quantified according to explicit rules or procedures, so that there is an outcome, e. g. a score. A test also observes an individual's performance in order to deduce the test taker's competence degree or level. This performance is usually linked to a certain domain, e. g. vocabulary tests on a specific word field.

Assessment is the term that is most widely accepted in the language testing and assessment community now. It connotes a broader concept than testing.

Definition

> Language assessment »involves obtaining evidence to inform inferences about a person's language-related knowledge, skills, or abilities« (Green 2014, 5).

Green explains this definition further by suggesting that the evidence is gathered from the **performance** of tasks that involve the use of language while the inferences are the interpretations of that very performance based on our beliefs both about the nature of language and the role that the language will play or is playing in the lives of the assessee. This is a definition related to language assessment only. For the EFL classroom, however, such an interpretation would involve additional aspects such as intercultural competence, language learning awareness or task achievement.

Evaluation, by contrast, is not necessarily the same as testing—it is involved when decisions are made on the basis of the results of an assessment procedure. Hence evaluation is the broadest term of the three.

Assessment for Learning: Most of what is happening in the EFL classroom can be considered as assessment since many procedures do not necessarily comprise measurement, for example of feedback that the teacher gives on a group presentation: the assessment ideally feeds back into teaching. In fact, the relationship between assessment and learning has been highlighted in the last two decades, which is also reflected in terminology. In the 1990s, Black and Wiliam (1998) and their UK-based Assessment Reform Group coined the term ›Assessment *for* Learning‹ that aims at bringing assessment and learning together and that can be contrasted with ›**Assessment *of* Learning**‹. Assessment of Learning focuses on the outcome, the products of learning only while Assessment for Learning takes a process-oriented perspective. Generally, the term ›assessment‹ accommodates far more procedures for collecting evidence on learner performance than testing. Assessment involves, among other things, diagnostic assessment, which aims at identifying strengths and weaknesses of the learner in order to help them move on from their current level of learning. According to Lee (2015), **diagnostic assessment** has three components, namely diagnosis, diagnostic feedback and remedial learning. In other words, the diagnosis is made, then feedback is given to the learner and adapted learning arrangements are designed so that learners' progress is ensured.

Quality criteria of assessment: How to know if a test is a ›good‹ test (or assessment for that matter) is one of the major questions to be asked. Whether this is called testing, assessment or evaluation, they have the same major principles in common. They are **reliability**, **validity** and **practicality** (some add fairness or authenticity as other criteria), which are to be applied to formal tests and all other types of assessment as well.

Reliability: A useful assessment is reliable, that means consistent in its measurement, and dependable. When the same test is given to the same learners at different points in time, it should yield the same results. A reliable test has clear instructions for evaluation or scoring, and the rubrics for these (i. e. an assessment sheet with the assessment criteria) are used consistently. For the learner who takes the test or assessment, the tasks are unambiguous so that s/he is able to perform to the best of his/her abilities. Threats to reliability can come from different sources, such as

- students being temporarily ill (**learner-related reliability**)
- subjective or biased raters who come up with different results (**inter-rater reliability**)
- construction noise that hinders the learners from hearing the listening comprehension text (**test administration reliability**)
- tests that have too many items so that learners become fatigued and do not have the time to think about answers in later items (**test reliability**)

Rules for increasing reliability in assessment
- Make sure the tasks are clear and unambiguous.
- Assess often or include more tasks in your assessment (but not too many!).
- Limit the scope of what you assess (e. g. listening only).
- Make sure the assessment conditions are the same for everyone.
- Make sure the way you evaluate the assessment is transparent, clear and is consistently used by raters.
- If possible, use several raters to assess the performance.

Key points

Validity: The most complicated aspect of test usefulness that is sometimes considered the most important one as well, is validity. In earlier views on this aspect, a test was considered to be valid when it measured what it was supposed to measure, that means that e. g. a listening comprehension test really only relates to listening comprehension and does not involve reading comprehension because the answers in the true/false task are too long. A valid assessment, from an earlier viewpoint, has a close correspondence between test results and the skills needed in real life. While these connections are still central in discussions of validity, this is no longer thought of as a quality inherent in an assessment. Rather, it is seen as a quality of the interpretations that are drawn from assessment results. In other words, how useful (or valid) are the assessment results of, say, a spelling test for an 8th grader in deciding whether s/he needs extra tuition in the foreign language? Assessment that has valid interpretations of test results does not measure irrelevant variables. It relies as much as possible on performance, which in turn is judged by way of assessment criteria. The assessment typically offers useful and meaningful information about a learner's ability in real life.

There are two threats to validity:

Construct irrelevance and construct under-representation

- The first is **construct irrelevance**, meaning the integration of elements in an assessment that are not connected to the competence we would like to measure. As an example, a vocabulary test that asks learners to translate isolated words from a textbook unit into the foreign language is construct irrelevant if the test is thought to be an indicator of communicative competence in the foreign language. The wrong elements have been included in the assessment.
- The second threat to validity is **construct underrepresentation**. Construct underrepresentation means that not enough elements that are relevant to the competence we would like to measure are included in the assessment (cf. Green 2014, 77). As an example, an achievement test that focuses on listening, reading and writing but has no speaking component in it cannot claim to test overall linguistic proficiency. The construct of overall linguistic proficiency, encompassing all four skills, is underrepresented.

In the context of standardised tests, the collection of evidence on the validity of the interpretations that test results are used for is called **validation**. For classroom-based assessment contexts, the quality criterion of validity is still important but tends to differ a little from standardised procedures. McKay (2006) maintains that validity rests in the construct held in the teacher's mind and is supported by teaching experience and evidence. This idea is closely related to the concept of **teacher cognition,** i. e. teachers' beliefs, attitudes and knowledge, which is virtually unexplored in the field of language testing and assessment but is supposed to have a major impact on how teachers perceive and practise assessment.

Practicality is related to the aspect of **feasibility** of a language assessment, e. g. regarding the time, cost or effort that has to be invested in an assessment.

14.2 | The why: purposes of assessment

For what purposes do we assess learners in the foreign language class-room? The previous distinction between Assessment of Learning and Assessment for Learning is suggestive of the relationship between assessment and learning.

Summative assessment: Assessment of Learning is closely associated with summative assessment, which typically occurs **at the end** of a course, a unit of instruction etc. It aims at summarising what a learner has learned, taking stock of his or her achievements. A classroom test after a textbook unit or Abitur examinations can be seen as a summative assessment.

Formative assessment: In contrast, Assessment for Learning is closely associated with formative assessment. And indeed, most of our class-room-based assessment is formative in nature with the aim of ›forming‹ learners' competences in the process of assessment. In other words, one major characteristic of formative assessment is that it feeds back into teaching and learning, giving the teacher and the learner insights into strengths and weaknesses of the learner performance. Formative assessment is **informal** and **ongoing**. It is typically embedded in classroom tasks. A teacher might ask the learners, for example, to present their dream school. S/he might then evaluate the performance of the learners in terms of their presentation skills, the originality of the content, the communicative achievement of the task at hand and the learners' range of vocabulary and structures used, giving them feedback on their strong points and room for improvement.

Achievement tests: When thinking about assessment in the classroom, classroom tests or vocabulary tests after a textbook unit or part of it often come to mind. The teacher would like to check what the learners have learned within a classroom lesson, unit or even the whole curriculum. To find out what the learners have achieved in terms of their competence development, achievement tests are used. Their primary function is to determine whether learners have achieved the **objectives** that were set in the course or curriculum. Achievement tests, at the same time, can be used for diagnostic purposes in order to see what might have to be covered again in future lessons. They are often, but not always, summative because they often come into play at the end of a unit or course. There is a large variety of achievement test types and formats, ranging from ten-minute quizzes to final exams that take several hours. At the same time, achievement tests can be formative in nature when the results point the teacher (and learner!) towards aspects that need attention and improvement.

Proficiency tests, on the other hand, are not based on or limited to a course or curriculum for that matter. The purpose of these (or assessment) is to gauge whether a learner has the necessary skills in the foreign language to carry out a task, study at a university in the target language country, do a job and so on. The focus is not on what the learner has been taught but on his or her **current ability**. Therefore, proficiency tests are almost always summative and are usually standardised tests, with stand-

Types of assessment

Types of tests

ardised conditions, a single score and a percentile rank as an outcome. They often have a gate-keeping function, e. g. when the result in a language test decides on whether the candidate is allowed to apply for citizenship or whether an academic certificate is awarded. Teachers themselves tend not to be involved in the design of proficiency tests but it is important that they are in a position to critically evaluate them, an ability that is part of assessment literacy on the part of teachers.

Diagnostic tests are about eliciting information on learners' learning needs, in other words their results determine the areas that learners have difficulties in and are to put a focus on in a course or unit of instruction. Contrary to achievement tests that analyse to what extent the learners have successfully engaged with the learning material, diagnostic tests will yield more detailed information on what they will need to engage with in the **future**. This form of assessment is related to formative assessment because it is about the development of learner competences as well.

Placement tests: When learners are to start a course and when the groups are rather heterogeneous, a placement test places them in a particular course at a particular level or section of a language curriculum. Ideally a placement test also has a diagnostic function and can gather valuable information on the learner that can be exploited for teaching. In that sense, a placement test has a formative role to play although this is not always the case. Placement tests are varied in their contents (e. g. the ability to use past tenses for a narration) and formats (open-ended responses, multiple choice formats etc.), depending on the programme in question and the needs of the institution.

14.3 | Effective assessment design

The previous two sections have dealt with rather theoretical ideas and conceptions of assessment. They have provided several definitions of assessment and related terms, information about the quality criteria of assessment and examples of different types of assessment that are used for certain distinctive purposes. In this rather comprehensive section, theory will be linked to practice by suggesting how to design an effective assessment for classroom-based language assessment purposes without losing track of the theoretical aspects previously discussed. The aim of this procedure is to improve the quality of the assessment, which is just as important in standardised testing as in classroom-based assessment.

Classroom-based language assessment: Following a systematic approach based on Brown and Abeywickrama (2010), the stages in developing and implementing a classroom-based language assessment will be outlined. To illustrate this approach, a 6th year classroom test will be taken as an example at the different stages.

Key points

> **Stages in developing and implementing an assessment (cf. Brown/Abeywickrama 2010)**
> - determine the purpose of the assessment
> - state the objectives relating to the assessment
> - draw up test specifications
> - devise assessment items
> - administer the assessment
> - develop a system of scoring, provide relevant feedback

The assessment scenario: The classroom context is a year 6 in Germany. The class works with a textbook and the group has just covered a textbook unit consisting of a short text on a British city (Bristol), on functions that include giving and following instructions using a map, on the word field ›sights, tourist activities and things to do‹ and on structures such as imperatives and the present perfect. The learner group has been engaged in listening, reading, speaking and writing activities, and at the end of the textbook unit they worked on a mini project during which they designed and presented a flyer, poster or a brief video clip on things that can be done in their home town and how to get there.

The teacher is now planning a **classroom test** as an achievement test. It is scheduled at the end of the textbook unit and it is part of a series of assessments. The test consists of several blocks that are supposed to cover the main linguistic competences and it is a pencil and paper test that is handed in, graded by the teacher and returned to the learners a few days later.

14.3.1 | Determining the purpose of the assessment

The first step to be taken when planning an assessment is to consider its purpose. It might be required by the educational authorities to administer a number of written assessments, for example at the end of a unit or period of time. While this might be a formal requirement, it should not be the only purpose of an assessment. The significance of the assessment relevant to the course also needs to be considered. Is it an important course where the stakes are high, that ›counts‹ a lot (high-stakes assessment)?

Overall purpose of assessment: What is its overall purpose for the teachers and for the learners? In the case of the classroom test for this year 6, it is an achievement test for the teacher, learners and other stakeholders such as parents to see whether the learners have achieved the objectives of the course. In terms of stakes involved, its significance is minor but it is not unimportant either as it is a part of a series of assessments (continuous assessment) that yields a result as a number grade. The classroom test is **formative** in nature because it is part of an ongoing assessment and because the results are supposed to feed into teaching in the weeks to follow the assessment. It is also **summative** in nature because it is scheduled at the end of a textbook unit. Once the major purpose of the assessment has been established, the objectives of the assessment have to be specified.

14.3.2 | Stating the objectives relating to the assessment

While the major purpose of the assessment provides a broad picture, determining the specific objectives of the assessment makes it a lot more refined. What exactly are you trying to find out by administering the assessment? Answering this question involves thinking about what competences are to be assessed (the **construct** of the assessment), about which instructional objectives are central to the assessment and which are less so, and how course objectives translate into observable descriptions of performance that can be used for assessment purposes.

Central instructional objectives: Therefore, the objectives to be used for the assessment have to be as explicit as possible. An objective like »pupils will learn to give directions« is not testable because it is not precise enough: Are learners supposed to give directions in writing or in spoken discourse? What is the context going to be—the learners giving directions to a friend, a tourist? What language (phrases etc.) is going to be used?

In the given example, the textbook will provide objectives at the beginning of the unit (for the learners) and in the teacher's manual:

Learners will
- recognise oral and written forms related to giving and following directions (»turn right«/»straight ahead«/»it's on the right hand side«, etc.) and be able to follow them,
- correctly produce phrases for giving directions orally and in writing,
- learn important words for the word fields ›sights‹, ›activities‹, ›places of interest‹ and be able to describe them for their own home town and for a British city,
- learn about famous sights of Bristol as an example of a British city and
- be able to communicate in speaking and writing about things they have (not) done, using the present perfect.

These objectives will be very useful for the next step, drawing up the **test specifications**, which will form the basis of the test. Since the learners have been using all skills throughout the unit, these are reflected in the objectives. But at the same time, it is clear that all the objectives of the course cannot possibly form part of the eventual test. Therefore, teachers will need to prioritise objectives that will in the next step be included in the test design.

14.3.3 | Drawing up test specifications

Test specifications are vital for test developers because they offer all the relevant information on the test: A description of its content, item types (e. g. multiple choice items), task types (e. g. reading tasks, writing an e-mail), skills that are included in the test, the way the test will be scored and the way the results of the test will be communicated to the learners.

For standardised testing, test specifications are much more detailed than they have to be for classroom-based language assessment purposes. Foreign language teachers might actually not be very used to doing this as part of their assessment preparations. However, being as specific as possible with test specifications has considerable advantages. First, they provide an instrument that helps ensuring desired **quality criteria** of assessment, in particular validity. They also maximise **transparency** of the assessment, helping to communicate the assessment principles and procedures to stakeholders like learners and parents, thereby helping learners to perform well on assessments.

Test specifications

Example

The learners are eleven to twelve years old and are assessed by way of a classroom test. It is an achievement test which is supposed to check whether the instructional objectives of the unit have been met. The linguistic skills to be assessed comprise listening, reading and writing competences but also intercultural competence involving e. g. cultural knowledge about tourist attractions in Bristol. Task types will include a matching task, a listening task during which learners are supposed to follow taped directions on a map and circle the destination, a picture-cued production task in which learners are supposed to write about their experiences (»Have you ever done bungee-jumping?«) using the present perfect and an open-ended production task in which they are supposed to write an e-mail using a template which scaffolds the structure of the e-mail (skeleton e-mail). The resources required are space in the classroom, copies of the test and the CD with the taped directions on it. Scoring is done by awarding points for correct items. Reporting will be done by number grades along with verbal feedback for learners.

This type of blueprint serves as an outline of any classroom-based language assessment that aspires to be comprehensive and transparent. Of course, a close consideration of test specifications requires some work, but they can be used and adjusted for different learner groups. It is then only a small step to the next stage, designing appropriate tasks and items.

Parameter/Aspect	Detailed Information
learners	year 6 (11–12 years old)
type of assessment	classroom test
purpose of assessment	achievement of instructional objectives of textbook unit (following directions, using correct words from word field ›places of interest/sights‹, describing activities related to places of interest; use of present perfect to describe activities in home town; knowing/recognising and naming famous sights of Bristol; (revision:) writing an informal message to a friend) to identify problem areas for review (class or individual)
skills and competences, language to be assessed	listening comprehension: following directions reading comprehension: places of interest in Bristol reading/writing: present perfect to express experience (»Have you ever ...?«) writing: activities and sights in Bristol
task types/item types	matching, following taped directions on the map and circling destination, picture-cued production on sentence level, open-ended response (skeleton e-mail)
resources required	space: classroom time: one lesson (45 minutes) copies: copies of the test; learner exercise books for classroom test (collect in advance) other: taped directions from teacher pack, CD, track 8
scoring plan	▪ listening comprehension part: 2 points each for correct destination circled (4 destinations: 8 points) ▪ reading comprehension part: 2 points each for correct matching of description and Bristol sight (5 sights: 10 points) ▪ reading/writing: 3 points each for correctly described activity (5 activities: 15 points) ▪ writing: 3 points for every appropriately formulated sentence (5 sentences: 15 points) ▪ total: 48 points
reporting	scores/number grades with verbal feedback to learners that includes their strengths and weaknesses plus areas for further work to be done

Table 14.1:
Test specifications
of the year 6
class test

14.3.4 | Devising assessment items

Describing and discussing all potential assessment items and explaining how to design them to assess the various competences would certainly be beyond the scope of the present chapter. As a very broad distinction, however, it suffices to differentiate between the part of the task that elicits some kind of linguistic performance, the **prompt**, and the part that actually comprises the desired performance, the **response**.

Response formats: In terms of responses, we usually differentiate between **closed-ended responses** or answers and **open-ended answers**.

Prompts can be verbal (e. g. a question) or nonverbal (e. g. a picture) or a combination of both (e. g. a graph and a factsheet with supplementary information). Closed-ended responses can be non-verbal (e. g. ordering the pictures in a story) or verbal (e. g. multiple choice format, true/false, cloze). Open-ended responses can vary from short answers, e. g. two to three sentences, to a 500-word essay or more. While closed-ended response formats might be more reliable and practical, they might lack validity and might be less authentic compared to communicative learning tasks. Open-ended responses might seem more valid because they potentially encompass and reflect more comprehensive competence profiles and they might enable more authentic responses to a task, e. g. in an argumentative essay or with creative writing tasks. The downside of open-ended responses is their potential threat to reliability if the scoring procedure is not transparent enough. For a sufficient reliability with closed-ended answers, however, the construction of the items must be flawless.

Contextual factors: These preliminary thoughts indicate that the process of designing assessment items is not so straightforward. It also depends on other contextual factors, e. g. the level of proficiency of the learner group (at level A1 of the CEFR, it is hardly possible to have anything else than closed-ended response formats), the instructional objectives, the related assessment priorities of the teachers, practical issues etc. (cf. chapter 2 in this volume).

Choice of assessment items: For the year 6 example, some choices had to be made as well. First of all, in the light of institutional constraints, e. g. lack of resources such as a second invigilator or other organisational aspects, not all competences could be included in the test. The speaking part of the assessment had to be separated and is administered as part of a formative assessment activity embedded in teaching. The skills covered are now reading, listening and writing. In order for the tasks to have some claim to content validity, they should mirror the tasks learners know from coursework and in that be authentic and/or close to real life situations learners might encounter in the future.

Arranging blocks: In order to align communicative tasks done during coursework, curricular objectives and test specifications, the first block of the short classroom test is devoted to directions. Since it is not possible to include a speaking component in the test for practical reasons, giving directions cannot be part of the task types, and the focus is on the receptive part of following directions.

1. Learners are given a map of Bristol that they know from the textbook. They listen to different short texts that give directions to several points of interest in Bristol. Learners need to understand the relevant phrases for directions by following directions on the map with a pencil, arriving at the correct destination, which they then circle as a non-verbal response (»You will hear three people. They give directions from Market Square. Follow the directions on the map with a pencil. Where do the people want to go? Circle the place on the map.«). For every correct itinerary and destination they will score two points, one point for the destination and one for the itinerary. For practical reasons this item comes first because the listening text has to be played for all learners

at once. The order of the rest of the blocks in the test can be chosen by the learners individually.

2. The next item is a matching exercise and focuses on reading comprehension. The sights of Bristol are taken up again and the learners have to read the descriptions of selected sights and match them with the names that they can see on the map. The learners can earn two points for every correctly matched sight. If they do not match correctly, zero points will be awarded.

3. The next item is a reading/writing task that is picture-cued and requires the learners to write short answers in which they use the present perfect. They use the verbs from the word field ›activities‹ that fit the pictures (»Have you ever...«?). The pictures show activities that learners know from coursework and that they can do in a city like Bristol. The learners are supposed to write short answers in one sentence. For every correctly described activity, learners score three points.

Example

Scores of reading/writing task

3 points: picture correctly described (correct verb used); no grammatical or orthographical mistakes
2 points: picture correctly described (correct verb used); minor grammatical or orthographical mistakes
1 point: picture correctly described (correct verb used); major grammatical or orthographical mistakes
0 points: picture not described, structure not used or major mistakes

4. The last item concerns writing and is an open-ended response format in the form of a skeleton e-mail. Learners are to activate their vocabulary on sights of Bristol and apply their knowledge on text types (e-mail messages to friends) to the context, the message to a friend in Bristol who has invited them. Learners are to write to their friend what type of activities they want to do and what sights they are interested in. Year 6 learners are supposed to be at A1/A2 level so that they are not yet able to produce free discourse in most cases. As help, they receive a skeleton text with greetings, complimentary close and sentence beginnings in order to structure the text. Learners are supposed to complete the sentences and fill in gaps with their own ideas so that the task can be called a **guided production task**. The entire message consists of five sentences. The learners can score 3 points for every correctly and appropriately completed sentence.

Example

Scores of writing task

3 points: sentence correctly and appropriately completed
2 points: sentence appropriately completed with minor mistakes
1 point: sentence completed but mistakes inhibit comprehension
0 points: sentence not completed or sentence not comprehensible

Once the assessment items themselves have been designed, the test can be administered. However, some practical aspects need to be considered here, which are the object of the next phase.

14.3.5 | Administering the assessment

To enhance transparency and help learners perform to the best of their abilities, they need to be informed in advance of the conditions of the test (e. g. time available, access to dictionaries), the kinds of items that will be on the test, evaluation criteria and test taking strategies for optimal performance (e. g. time for proofreading or the best possible ordering of tasks in different scenarios) in advance.

To prepare optimal conditions for the administration of the classroom test, enough copies of the test need to be provided, any necessary technology for the test and the seating arrangement of the room need to be checked in advance. Any opportunity to cheat on the test should be avoided by, for example, collecting mobile phones and smart watches or providing two versions of the same test. Other important considerations are time, such as starting and ending on time, warning the learners when the time is about to run out, quietly collecting the answer sheets or exercise books when the allotted time has run out and thinking of an assignment for learners who finish early.

14.3.6 | Developing a system of scoring, providing relevant feedback

Scoring and weighting: Once the answer sheets have been collected, decisions on scoring have to be taken before reading and marking the tests. The classroom test has four sections, each with a number of scorable items. One could put equal weight on the sections and assign equal points to each section. However, in the example more importance has been given to (and more points awarded to) more complex tasks and/or productive tasks, which are assumed to be more challenging. This procedure is called weighting.

Rating scales: For open-ended response formats like essay tasks discrete-point scoring, i. e. scoring item by item as isolated linguistic elements, is not an option. Instead, a system of **assessment criteria** can be employed with descriptors of observable performance that can be scaled. Several types of rating scales can be used for this or, in a simplified manner, checklists where teachers tick off criteria in a yes/no decision (e. g. »Does the story have a beginning, a middle part and an ending«?). The criteria included are a matter of priority (unless a preconceived scale needs to be used, e. g. for a centralised final exam) which is decided by the teacher. Criteria might include a range of vocabulary or structures, accuracy, cohesion and coherence or communicative appropriateness but also criteria that are not strictly language-related such as originality, task achievement or appropriateness e. g. relating to genres. The **error quo-**

tient, i. e. the number of mistakes divided by the total number of words, is not used in Germany anymore because it is indicative of one category only (accuracy) and is not a precise indicator and therefore not helpful. After administering a test, it is of course possible to revise the scoring system the next time a similar learner group is taught.

The score then needs to be ›translated‹ into a numerical grade according to the German system. In some contexts, additional feedback in the sense of a diagnostic analysis is required by the educational authorities and/or by the school. In any case, pointing out which tasks learners did well in and in which they did poorly with a view to improve their performance is a vital part of assessment, particularly if the feedback is supposed to become **positive washback**, which is a beneficial effect of assessment on teaching and learning. Feedback can be written or oral and can range from brief comments to teacher-learner conferences. The choice of the type of feedback depends on many factors such as time resources, the impact of the assessment and the ways that the assessment results are supposed to feed into teaching. It should commonly include positive comments about the performance. What is important about feedback, however, is its timing. It ought to immediately follow the assessment; otherwise it has less impact because learners are not interested in it anymore.

Definition	Washback is a (negative or positive) effect that a test can have on classroom practices.

14.4 | Beyond testing: alternatives in assessment

When thinking of assessment, many teachers have formal, planned, high-stakes testing in mind. However, a considerable part of assessment that takes place in the EFL classroom is beyond testing. In fact, there are some competences, such as intercultural competence, that do not really lend themselves to testing. Although alternative assessment has emerged as a counterweight to standardised testing, a lot of it has always been done in the EFL classroom.

Definition	Alternative assessment is the »ongoing process involving the student and teacher in making judgments about the students' progress in language using nonconventional strategies« (Coombe et al. 2012b, 147).

Alternatives in assessment: The aim of alternative assessment is to gain a dynamic picture of learners' competence development and to gather data to document this ongoing process. However, the term ›alternative assessment‹ is a little counterproductive because it suggests that it is something new. Instead, the term ›**alternatives in assessment**‹ will be used because it is seen as a part of assessment with tests as a subset of assessment, as discussed above.

The characteristics of alternatives in assessment can be summarised as follows:

Characteristics of alternative assessment
- ongoing, informal, formative in nature, non-intrusive
- interested in learner development over time rather than in the comparison of learners with one another
- focus on learner strengths rather than weaknesses
- authentic because tasks are based on activities that reflect typical classroom tasks and real-life settings
- usually related to some performance assessment

Teacher observations: Teachers constantly observe their learners in the classroom—they notice responses given, blank looks, questions asked. All the impressionistic data stemming from observations are stored in teachers' minds and form an impression of a learner's ability in the foreign language. Although these impressions are sometimes surprisingly accurate, their reliability should be increased by systematising teacher observations.

Planned, systematic observation as an assessment tool can take the stress from an assessment situation because the learners are not aware of the fact that they are assessed. In addition, it increases the relevance of teacher feedback to learners. Observations can be recorded with the help of e. g. observation sheets, checklists or rating scales. Teachers need to determine the objectives of the observation and limit the number of learners to be observed at one time. They also have to decide what to do with the observation results, e. g. conduct a teacher-learner conference. Observations can be made on a wide range of classroom tasks, from the length of utterances in class participation to learners' use of communication strategies in a role play. One example that takes up the topic of directions would be for learners to work in pairs and give each other directions, using relevant phrases in the process. Criteria for assessment would be e. g. pronunciation, turn-taking (›Does the performance resemble a real conversation?‹), the correct use of phrases for giving directions and task achievement (›Does the interlocutor arrive at the correct destination?‹). These are put down on a checklist the teacher uses for individual pairs who perform in front of the class. Regardless of what system for recording observations is used, the reliability of this tool will be increased by making it as systematic as possible.

Self-assessment: In self-assessment, learners reflect on their own performance and act as assessors of it, usually using a set of criteria or checklists for the self-assessment. This means involving the learners in the assessment process and helps to attain an additional perspective on the learner performance to be assessed. Moreover, self-assessment can raise the learners' **awareness** of (and possibly motivation for) their learning process. Thus, it might make them more autonomous, particularly if the self-assessment is firmly embedded in teaching and if results of the self-assessment result in setting new learning objectives for themselves. Self-assessment can be used for a wide range of activities. In order to avoid learners over- or underestimating their performance, it is helpful to establish **criteria** for the self-assessment together and to discuss them so that learners get a realistic picture of a good/medium/poor performance. The same criteria can then be used for subsequent teacher assessment.

Peer-assessment: In peer-assessment, learners evaluate and assess each other's performance, ideally on the basis of criteria and/or checklists. As with self-assessment, some of the aims of peer-assessment are involving the learner in the assessment process, enhancing **learner autonomy** but also **collaboration** in order to improve the quality of learners' work, possibly resulting in increased motivation. Peer-assessment can be used (and complemented by teacher assessment) with a range of activities, an example of which might be peer-assessment of writing. Learners are assigned to write e. g. an alternative ending to a short story they have read. On the basis of assessment criteria discussed in plenary before (›Is the ending original?‹, ›Are the protagonists involved?‹, ›Does the ending correspond with the previous plot of the short story?‹), learners work in pairs and assess each other's writing products in draft form. They give each other comments to improve their drafts and then produce a final version individually, which is then graded by the teacher. This is also an example of how peer-assessment and teacher assessment can work hand in hand to improve the quality of learning.

Portfolio assessment: ›Portfolio‹ might be a term familiar from art that designates a collection of the best works of an artist.

Definition

> A portfolio is »a purposeful collection of students' work that demonstrates [...] their efforts, progress, and achievements in given areas« (Genesee/Upshur 1996, 99).

Portfolios can include materials such as written homework, audio files, creative writing, essays, presentation outlines and much more, depending on the course objectives. These materials directly stem from activities and thus represent a strong **link between learning and assessment** when the collections of work are assessed. Furthermore, portfolios have the potential to enhance ownership of learning because learners decide what goes into the portfolios and is assessed. When conferencing on what materials to include, teacher-learner interaction is encouraged and learning is individualised. For portfolio assessment to be taken seriously, however, it is vital that portfolios are firmly embedded in the curriculum and that time be made for the selection of materials, their review and conferencing with the teacher. Guidelines for the selection of materials must be given and the assessment criteria must be clear in advance (e. g. for pattern poetry: ›What makes this a good poem?‹, ›What does the poem show you can do?‹ ›Do you like the pattern of your poem?‹, ›Why (not)?‹, ›Write down what you did well.‹). Portfolio assessment can be time-consuming, therefore it is vital that working with the tool becomes a natural part of teaching and assessment.

Journals: This piece of reflective writing can be an account (or a log) of a learner's thoughts, feelings, impressions, ideas etc. Journals can have a variety of functions such as focusing on language learning processes, responses to literature, thoughts on intercultural experiences, learning strategies-based logs, to name but a few. The increase in electronic communication entails the opportunity to use email, blogs or podcasts to have more or less interactive journals with the teacher being able to respond to the learner's thoughts in a timely manner (cf. chapter 12 in this volume). This way the learning experience is individualised and **assessment is personalised**. Learners must be introduced to the concept of journal writing and its objectives. Once the objectives are clearly stated and guidelines have been given on what topics to include, the criteria for assessment (less focus on grammatical accuracy and more on cohesion/coherence, fluency, communicative appropriateness) have to be specified. Feedback is vital and will take considerable time but is clearly valuable for the learners' competence development.

> In the context of the foreign language classroom, a journal is a piece of reflective writing.

Definition

Of course there are more alternatives in assessment that are predominantly used in classroom-based language assessment, such as informal **interviews**, writing conferences, teacher-learner **conferences** and many more. To conclude this part, a principled evaluation of the alternatives to assessment that have been discussed above will be given in the grid below.

Principle / Quality Criterion	Observation	Self-assessment	Peer-assessment	Portfolio Assessment	Conferences	Journals
Reliability	moderate	low	low	moderate	low	moderate
(Content) Validity	high	high	high	high	high	high
Practicality	moderate	moderate	moderate	low	low	low
Authenticity	high	high	high	high	high	high
Washback	moderate	high	high	high	high	high

Table 14.2: Principled evaluation of alternative assessment based on Brown/Abeywickrama (2010, 153)

14.5 | Conclusion and outlook: current trends in classroom-based language assessment

Challenges for teachers in language assessment: This chapter has delineated some basic issues in classroom-based language assessment relating to the what, the why and the how of assessment. The field of language assessment is dynamic and the requirements for classroom-based language assessment are changing constantly. Current trends in assessment in the German context include the implementation of **task-based language assessment** as a logical consequence to task-based language learning as a popular teaching approach. Furthermore, standardised tests have been introduced that ensure that educational standards are met. This, in turn, has led to an increased presence of **standardised, large-scale assessment** that sometimes stands in contrast to more formative, classroom-based forms of assessment. The reality of heterogeneous learner groups in all school types due to the promotion of inclusive education, increased migration movements and other factors calls for individualised teaching but also **differentiated assessment**.

For all these requirements and challenges, teachers need to have sufficient levels of language assessment literacy so that they can respond to these appropriately and guarantee good quality assessments that serve the purpose of good quality learning in the foreign language classroom.

Further reading

Brown, H. Douglas/Abeywickrama, Priyanvada (²2010): *Language Assessment. Principles and Classroom Practices* [2003]. White Plains, NY.

Coombe, Christine/Davidson, Peter/O'Sullivan, Barry/Stoynoff, Stephen (eds.) (2012): *The Cambridge Guide to Second Language Assessment.* Cambridge. (= Coombe et al. 2012a)

Green, Anthony (2014): *Exploring Language Assessment and Testing.* London/New York.

Tsagari, Dina/Banerjee, Jayanti (eds.) (2016): *Handbook of Second Language Assessment.* Boston/Berlin.

Karin Vogt

15 Authors

Prof. Dr. Andreas Bonnet, University of Hamburg
Prof. Dr. Sabine Doff, University of Bremen
Prof. Dr. Daniela Elsner, University of Frankfurt/Main
Prof. Dr. Britta Freitag-Hild, University of Potsdam
Prof. Dr. Matthias Hutz, University of Education Freiburg
Prof. Dr. Jörg-U. Keßler, University of Education Ludwigsburg
Prof. Dr. Petra Kirchhoff, University of Erfurt
Prof. Dr. Annika Kolb, University of Education Freiburg
Prof. Dr. Christiane Lütge, University of Munich
Prof. Dr. Thomas Raith, University of Education Freiburg
Prof. Dr. Torben Schmidt, Leuphana University of Lüneburg
Prof. Dr. Thomas Strasser, University College of Teacher Education Vienna
Prof. Dr. Carola Surkamp, University of Göttingen
Prof. Dr. Britta Viebrock, University of Frankfurt/Main
Prof. Dr. Karin Vogt, University of Education Heidelberg
Prof. Dr. Eva Wilden, University of Duisburg-Essen
Dr. Tanyasha Yearwood, University of Göttingen

16 Bibliography

Ahrens, Rüdiger/Eisenmann, Maria/Merkl, Matthias (eds.) (2008): *Moderne Dramendidaktik für den Englischunterricht der Sekundarstufe I und II*. Heidelberg.

Aitchison, Jean ([2]1994): *Words in the Mind. An Introduction to the Mental Lexicon* [1987]. Cambridge, MA.

Akcaoglu, Mete (2008): »History of CALL«, https://msu.edu/~akcaoglu/rdp.history.html (14.12.2017).

ALA (n. d.): »About«, http://www.lexically.net/ala/la_defined.htm (14.12.2017).

Alexie, Sherman (2009): *The Absolutely True Diary of a Part-Time Indian*. Berlin.

Allwright, Richard L. (1984): »Why Don't Learners Learn What Teachers Teach? The Interaction Hypothesis«. In: Singleton, David M./Little, David G. (eds.): *Language Learning in Formal and Informal Contexts*. Dublin, 3–18.

Alter, Grit (2016): »›I Am the Captain of My Soul‹. *Invictus* in the EFL Classroom«. In: Viebrock 2016, 129–141.

Altrichter, Herbert/Posch, Peter ([4]2007): *Lehrerinnen und Lehrer erforschen ihren Unterricht* [1990]. Bad Heilbrunn.

Antor, Heinz (ed.) (2006): *Inter- und transkulturelle Studien. Theoretische Grundlagen und interdisziplinäre Praxis*. Heidelberg.

Appel, Joachim (2000): *Erfahrungswissen und Fremdsprachendidaktik*. München.

Arnseth, Hans Christian (2006): »Learning to Play or Playing to Learn. A Critical Account of the Models of Communication Informing Educational Research on Computer Gameplay«. In: *Game Studies. The International Journal of Computer Game Research* 6/1, http://gamestudies.org/0601/articles/arnseth (14.12.2017).

Aronin, Larissa/Hufeisen, Britta (eds.) (2009): *The Exploration of Multilingualism*. Amsterdam.

Bach, Gerhard ([5]2013): »Alltagswissen und Unterrichtspraxis. Der Weg zum *Reflective Practitioner*«. In: Bach/Timm [5]2013a, 304–320.

Bach, Gerhard (2015): »Globalization from Below. Teachers as Agents of Change in the Everyday Challenges of EFL Teaching«. Lecture at Goethe-University Frankfurt a. M.

Bach, Gerhard/Timm, Johannes-Peter (eds.) ([5]2013a): *Englischunterricht. Grundlagen und Methoden einer handlungsorientierten Unterrichtspraxis* [1989]. Tübingen/Basel.

Bach, Gerhard/Timm, Johannes-Peter ([5]2013b): »Handlungsorientierung als Ziel und Methode«. In: Bach/Timm 2013a, 1–22.

Bachman, Lyle F./Palmer, Adrian S. (1996): *Language Testing in Practice. Designing and Developing Useful Language Tests*. Oxford.

Bachmann-Medick, Doris ([2]2004): *Kultur als Text. Die anthropologische Wende in der Literaturwissenschaft* [1996]. Tübingen/Basel.

Bailey, Kathleen M. (2006): *Language Teacher Supervision. A Case-Based Approach*. New York.

Baker, Will (2012): »From Cultural Awareness to Intercultural Awareness. Culture in ELT«. In: *ELT Journal* 66/1, 62–70.

Bandura, Albert (1997): *Self-Efficacy. The Exercise of Control*. New York.

Baten, Kristof/Keßler, Jörg-U. (2018): »Research Time Line. The Role of Instruction. Teachability and Processability«. In: Arntzen, Ragnar/Hakansson, Gisela/Hjelde, Arnstein/Keßler, Jörg-U. (eds.): *Teachability and Learnability Across Languages*. Amsterdam.

Batstone, Rob (1994): *Grammar*. Oxford.

Bauer, Viktoria (2015): *Englischlernen – Sinnkonstruktion – Identität*. Opladen/Berlin/Toronto.

Baumert, Jürgen/Kunter, Mareike (2006): »Stichwort: Professionelle Kompetenz von Lehrkräften«. In: *Zeitschrift für Erziehungswissenschaften* 9/4, 469–520.

Bausch Karl-Richard/Christ, Herbert/Hüllen, Werner/Krumm, Hans-Jürgen (eds.) (1989): *Handbuch Fremdsprachenunterricht*. Tübingen/Basel.

Becker, Carmen/Blell, Gabriele/Rössler, Andrea (eds.) (2016): *Web 2.0 und komplexe Kompetenzaufgaben im Fremdsprachenunterricht*. Frankfurt a. M. et al.

Benson, Phil ([2]2011): *Teaching and Researching Autonomy in Language Learning* [2001]. Harlow.

Berggren, Jessica (2015): »Learning from Giving Feedback. A Study of Secondary-Level Students«. In: *ELT Journal* 69/1, 58–70.

Bertschi-Kaufmann, Andrea (ed.) (2007): *Lesekompetenz, Leseleistung, Leseförderung. Grundlagen, Modelle und Materialien*. Seelze-Velber.

Bhabha, Homi (1994): *The Location of Culture*. London.

Biebighäuser, Katrin/Zibelius, Marja/Schmidt, Torben (eds.) (2012a): *Aufgaben 2.0. Konzepte, Materialien und Methoden für das Fremdsprachenlehren und -lernen mit digitalen Medien*. Tübingen.

Biebighäuser, Katrin/Zibelius, Marja/Schmidt, Torben (2012b): »Aufgaben 2.0. Aufgabenorientierung beim Fremdsprachenlernen mit digitalen Medien«. In: Biebighäuser/Zibelius/Schmidt 2012a, 11–56.

BIG-Kreis (ed.) (2015): *Der Lernstand im Englischunterricht am Ende von Klasse 4. Ergebnisse der BIG-Studie*. München.

Bitchener, John/Storch, Neomy (eds.) (2016): *Written Corrective Feedback for L2 Development*. London.

Black, Paul/Wiliam, Dylan (1998): »Assessment and Classroom Learning«. In: *Assessment in Education. Principles, Policy and Practice* 5/1, 7–71.

Bland, Janice (2015): »Pictures, Images and Deep Reading«. In: *CLELE Journal* 3/2, 24–36.

Bland, Janice/Lütge, Christiane (eds.) (2013): *Children's Literature in Second Language Education*. London et al.

Blell, Gabriele ([2]2017): »Audio Literacy«. In: Surkamp [2]2017, 7–8.

Bongartz, Christiane M./Rohde, Andreas (eds.) (2015): *Inklusion im Englischunterricht*. Frankfurt a. M.

Bonnet, Andreas/Breidbach, Stefan (2013): »Blut ist im Schuh. Wie gut kleidet der Kompetenzbegriff die literarisch-ästhetische Bildung beim Tanz auf dem Hofball der Standardisierung?«. In: Grünewald, Andreas/Plikat, Jochen/Wieland, Katharina (eds.): *Bildung, Kompetenz, Literalität. Fremdsprachenunterricht zwischen Standardisierung und Bildungsanspruch*. Stuttgart, 20–35.

Bonnet, Andreas/Hericks, Uwe (2014): »›...kam grad am Anfang an die Grenzen‹. Potenziale und Probleme von Kooperativem Lernen für die Professionalisierung von Englischlehrer/innen«. In: *Zeitschrift für interpretative Schul- und Unterrichtsforschung* 3/1, 86–100.

Borg, Simon (2006): *Teacher Cognition and Language Education. Research and Practice*. London.

Börner, Otfried/Lohmann, Christa (2015): *Heterogenität und Inklusion. Lernaufgaben im Englischunterricht*. Braunschweig.

Börner, Otfried/Engel, Gaby/Groot-Wilken, Bernd (eds.) (2013): *Hörverstehen – Leseverstehen – Sprechen. Diagnose und Förderung von sprachlichen Kompetenzen im Englischunterricht der Primarstufe*. Münster.

Bourdieu, Pierre (1986): »The Forms of Capital«. In: Richardson, John G. (ed.): *Handbook of Theory and Research for the Sociology of Education*. New York, 241–258.

British Council (ed.) (2017): »IELTS«, https://www.britishcouncil.de/en/exam/ielts (14.12.2017).

Bredella, Lothar (2002): *Literarisches und interkulturelles Verstehen*. Tübingen.

Bredella, Lothar (2012): *Narratives und interkulturelles Verstehen. Zur Entwicklung von Empathie-, Urteils- und Kooperationsfähigkeit*. Tübingen.

Bredella, Lothar/Burwitz-Melzer, Eva (2004): *Rezeptionsästhetische Literaturdidaktik mit Beispielen aus dem Fremdsprachenunterricht Englisch.* Tübingen.

Bredella, Lothar/Christ, Herbert (eds.) (1995): *Didaktik des Fremdverstehens.* Tübingen.

Bredella, Lothar/Christ, Herbert (eds.) (2007): *Fremdverstehen und interkulturelle Kompetenz.* Tübingen.

Bredella, Lothar/Delanoy, Werner (eds.) (1999): *Interkultureller Fremdsprachenunterricht.* Tübingen.

Breen, Michael P./Candlin, Christopher N. (1980): »The Essentials of a Communicative Curriculum in Language Teaching«. In: *Applied Linguistics* I/2, 89–112.

Breidbach, Stephan/Viebrock, Britta (2012): »CLIL in Germany. Results from Recent Research in a Contested Field of Education«. In: *International CLIL Journal* 1/4, 5–16.

Brown, H. Douglas/Abeywickrama, Priyanvada ([2]2010): *Language Assessment. Principles and Classroom Practices* [2003]. White Plains, NY.

Brown, George/Yule, George (1983): *Discourse Analysis.* Cambridge.

Bruner, Jerome (1978): »The Role of Dialogue in Language Acquisition«. In: Sinclair, Anne/Jarvella, Robert/Levelt, Willem (eds.): *The Child's Concept of Language.* Berlin/Heidelberg, 241–255.

Bruns, Axel (2008): *Blogs, Wikipedia, Second Life, and Beyond. From Production to Produsage.* New York.

Burmeister, Petra/Massler, Ute (2010): *CLIL und Immersion. Fremdsprachlicher Sachfachunterricht in der Grundschule.* Braunschweig.

Burston, Jack (2013): »Mobile-Assisted Language Learning. A Selected Annotated Bibliography of Implementation Studies 1994–2012«. In: *Language Learning & Technology* 17/3, 157–224.

Burston, Jack (2015): »Twenty Years of MALL Project Implementation. A Meta-Analysis of Learning Outcomes«. In: *ReCALL* 27/1, 4–20.

Burton, Jill (2009): »Reflective Practice«. In: Burns, Anne/Richards, Jack C. (eds.): *The Cambridge Guide to Second Language Teacher Education.* Cambridge, 298–308.

Burwitz-Melzer, Eva (2003): *Allmähliche Annäherungen. Fiktionale Texte im interkulturellen Fremdsprachenunterricht der Sekundarstufe I.* Tübingen.

Burwitz-Melzer, Eva (2007): »Ein Lesekompetenzmodell für den fremdsprachlichen Literaturunterricht«. In: Bredella, Lothar/Hallet, Wolfgang (eds.): *Literaturunterricht, Kompetenzen und Bildung.* Trier, 127–157.

Burwitz-Melzer, Eva/Mehlhorn, Grit/Riemer, Claudia/Bausch, Karl-Richard/Krumm, Hans-Jürgen (eds.) ([6]2016): *Handbuch Fremdsprachenunterricht* [1989]. Tübingen.

Butzkamm, Wolfgang ([2]2013): »The Monolingual Principle«. In: Byram/Hu [2]2013, 471–473.

Butzkamm, Wolfgang/Cladwell, John A. W. (2009): *The Bilingual Reform. A Paradigm Shift in Foreign Language Teaching.* Tübingen.

Byram, Michael (1997): *Teaching and Assessing Intercultural Communicative Competence.* Clevedon.

Byram, Michael (2008): *From Foreign Language Education to Education for Intercultural Citizenship. Essays and Reflections.* Bristol.

Byram, Michael/Hu, Adelheid (eds.) ([2]2013): *Routledge Encyclopedia of Language Teaching and Learning* [2000]. London/New York.

Cameron, Lynne (2001): *Teaching Languages to Young Learners.* Cambridge.

Canagarajah, Suresh (2013): *Translingual Practice. Global Englishes and Cosmopolitan Relations.* New York.

Canale, Michael/Swain, Merrill (1980): »Theoretical Bases of Communicative Approaches to Second Language Teaching and Testing«. In: *Applied Linguistics* 1/1, 1–47.

Cates, Kip (2000):»Global Education«. In: Byram, Michael (ed.): *Routledge Encyclopedia of Language Teaching and Learning*. London/New York, 241–243.

Cenoz, Jasone/Jeffner, Ulrike (eds.) (2000): *English in Europe. The Acquisition of a Third Language*. Clevedon.

Chan, Wai Meng (2011): *Media in Foreign Language Teaching and Learning*. Boston.

Channell, Joanna (1999):»Psycholinguistic Considerations in the Study of L2 Vocabulary Acquisition«. In: Carter, Ronald/McCarthy, Michael (eds.): *Vocabulary and Language Teaching*. London, 83–96.

Cherrington, Ruth (2000):»Interlanguage«. In: Byram, Michael (ed.): *Routledge Encyclopedia of Language Teaching and Learning*. London, 307–309.

Christ, Herbert/Hüllen, Werner (³1995):»Fremdsprachendidaktik«. In: Bausch Karl-Richard/Christ, Herbert/Krumm, Hans-Jürgen (eds.): *Handbuch Fremdsprachenunterricht* [1989]. Tübingen/Basel, 1–7.

Cohen, Andrew (2010):»Focus on the Language Learner. Styles, Strategies and Motivation«. In: Schmitt, Norbert (ed.): *An Introduction to Applied Linguistics*. London, 161–178.

Coombe, Christine/Davidson, Peter/O'Sullivan, Barry/Stoynoff, Stephen (eds.) (2012): *The Cambridge Guide to Second Language Assessment*. Cambridge. (=Coombe et al. 2012a)

Coombe, Christine/Purmensky, Kerry/Davidson, Peter (2012):»Alternative Assessment in Language Education«. In: Coombe et al. 2012a, 147–155. (=Coombe et al. 2012b)

Coombe, Christine/Troudi, Salah/Al-Hamly, Mashael (2012):»Foreign and Second Language Teacher Assessment Literacy. Issues, Challenges, and Recommendations«. In: Coombe et al. 2012a, 20–29. (=Coombe et al. 2012c)

Cope, Bill/Kalantzis, Mary (2013):»New Media, New Learning and New Assessments«. In: *E-Learning and Digital Media* 10/4, 328–331.

Council of Europe (2001):»Common European Framework of Reference for Languages. Learning, Teaching, Assessment«, http://www.coe.int/t/dg4/linguistic/Source/Framework_EN.pdf (14.12.2017).

Council of Europe (2017):»Common European Framework of Reference for Languages. Learning, Teaching, Assessment (CEFR)«, https://www.coe.int/en/web/common-european-framework-reference-languages/home (14.12.2017).

Coyle, Do/Hood, Philip/Marsh, David (2010): *CLIL. Content and Language Integrated Learning*. Cambridge.

Crystal, David (2003): *English as a Global Language*. Cambridge.

Crystal, David/Fletcher, Paul/Garman, Michael (1976): *The Grammatical Analysis of Language Disability*. London.

Cummins, Jim/Bismilla, Vicki/Chow, Patricia/Cohen, Sarah/Giampapa, Frances/Leoni, Lisa/Sandhu, Perminder/Sastri, Padma (2005):»ELL Students Speak for Themselves. Identity Texts and Literacy Engagement in Multilingual Classrooms«, http://citeseerx.ist.psu.edu/viewdoc/download?doi=10.1.1.569.8971&rep=rep1&type=pdf (14.12.2017).

Cunningsworth, Alan (1984): *Evaluating and Selecting ELT Materials*. London.

Cushing-Weigle, Sara (2002): *Assessing Writing*. Cambridge.

Dam, Leni (1994):»How Do We Recognize an Autonomous Classroom?« In: *Die Neueren Sprachen* 93/5, 503–527.

Darvin, Ron/Norton, Bonny (2015):»Identity and a Model of Investment in Applied Linguistics«. In: *Annual Review of Applied Linguistics* 35, 36–56.

Deci, Edward L./Ryan, Richard M. (1985): *Intrinsic Motivation and Self Determination in Human Behaviour*. New York.

De Cillia, Rudolf/Klippel, Friederike (⁶2016):»Geschichte des Fremdsprachenunterrichts in deutschsprachigen Ländern seit 1945«. In: Burwitz-Melzer et al. ⁶2016, 625–631.

Decke-Cornill, Helene (1994):»Intertextualität als literaturdidaktische Dimension.

Zur Frage der Textzusammenstellung bei literarischen Lektürereihen«. In: *Die Neueren Sprachen* 93/3, 272–287.

Delanoy, Werner (2006): »Transculturality and (Inter-)Cultural Learning in the EFL Classroom«. In: Delanoy/Volkmann 2006, 233–248.

Delanoy, Werner (2015): »Literature Teaching and Learning. Theory and Practice«. In: Delanoy/Eisenmann/Matz 2015, 19–48.

Delanoy, Werner/Volkmann, Laurenz (eds.) (2006): *Cultural Studies in the EFL Classroom*. Heidelberg.

Delanoy, Werner/Eisenmann, Maria/Matz, Frauke (eds.) (2015): *Learning with Literature in the EFL Classroom*. Frankfurt a.M. et al.

de Oliveira, Luciana C./Schleppegrell, Mary J. (2015): *Focus on Grammar and Meaning*. Oxford.

DESI-Konsortium (ed.) (2006): »Unterricht und Kompetenzerwerb in Deutsch und Englisch. Zentrale Befunde der Studie Deutsch Englisch Schülerleistungen International (DESI)«, http://www.dipf.de/de/forschung/projekte/pdf/biqua/desi-zentrale-befunde (14.12.2017).

DESI-Konsortium (ed.) (2008): *Unterricht und Kompetenzerwerb in Deutsch und Englisch. Ergebnisse der DESI-Studie*. Weinheim.

Deterding, Sebastian/Dixon, Dan/Khaled, Rilla/Nacke, Lennart (2011): »From Game Design Elements to Gamefulness. Defining ›Gamification‹«. In: *MindTrek '11. Proceedings of the 15th International Academic MindTrek Conference*. Tampere, 9–15.

Dick, Egon (2000): *Multimediale Lernprogramme und telematische Lernarrangements*. Nürnberg.

Diehr, Bärbel/Surkamp, Carola (2015): »Die Entwicklung literaturbezogener Kompetenzen in der Sekundarstufe I. Modellierung, Abschlussprofil und Evaluation«. In: Hallet, Wolfgang/Surkamp, Carola/Krämer, Ulrich (eds.): *Literaturkompetenzen Englisch. Modellierung, Curriculum, Unterrichtsbeispiele*. Seelze-Velber, 21–40.

Dirks, Una (2007): »The Professional Development of ESL/CLIL Teachers in Relation to their Biographical and Gender-Specific Resources«. In: Decke-Cornill, Helene/Volkmann, Laurenz (eds.): *Gender Studies and Foreign Language Teaching*. Tübingen, 103–119.

Doff, Sabine (2002): *Englischlernen zwischen Tradition und Innovation. Fremdsprachenunterricht für Mädchen im 19. Jahrhundert*. München.

Doff, Sabine (2008): *Englischdidaktik in der BRD 1949–1989*. München.

Doff, Sabine (ed.) (2010): *Bilingualer Sachfachunterricht in der Sekundarstufe. Eine Einführung*. Tübingen.

Doff, Sabine/Klippel, Friederike (2007): *Englischdidaktik. Praxishandbuch für die Sekundarstufe I und II*. Berlin.

Donnerstag, Jürgen/Bosenius, Petra (2000): »Die Funktion der Emotionen in der Konstruktion von Bedeutung zu englischen literarischen Texten«. In: Wendt, Michael (ed.): *Konstruktion statt Instruktion*. Frankfurt a.M., 153–162.

Dörnyei, Zoltán (2001): *Motivational Strategies in the Language Classroom*. Cambridge.

Dörnyei, Zoltán (2005): *The Psychology of the Language Learner. Individual Differences in Second Language Acquisition*. Mahwah, NJ.

Dörnyei, Zoltán/Ryan, Stephan (2015): *The Psychology of the Language Learner Revisited*. New York.

Doughty, Catherine J./Williams, Jessica (1998): »Issues and Terminology«. In: Doughty, Catherine J./Williams, Jessica (eds.): *Focus on Form in Classroom Second Language Acquisition*. Cambridge, 1–11.

Dreher, Eva/Dreher, Michael (1985): »Wahrnehmung und Bewältigung von Entwicklungsaufgaben im Jugendalter. Fragen, Ergebnisse und Hypothesen zum Konzept einer Entwicklungs- und Pädagogischen Psychologie des Jugendalters«. In: Oerter, Rolf (ed.): *Lebensbewältigung im Jugendalter*. Weinheim, 30–60.

Dreßler, Constanze (2012): »Where I Work Well. Lernumgebungen gestalten und ausschöpfen«. In: *Grundschulmagazin Englisch* 12/3, 7–8.

Duczak, Tobias (2013): »Shakespeare im Schülerlabor. Verständnis und Interesse statt Frust und ›Shakesfear‹«. In: *Praxis Fremdsprachenunterricht Englisch* 10/5, 9–13.

Duman, Guler/Orhon, Gunseli/Gedik, Nuray (2015): »Research Trends in Mobile Assisted Language Learning from 2000 to 2012«. In: *ReCALL* 27/2, 197–216.

Eckerth, Johannes/Wendt, Michael (eds.) (2003): *Interkulturelles und transkulturelles Lernen im Fremdsprachenunterricht.* Frankfurt a. M.

Eisenmann, Maria (2015): »Postcolonial Literature and Transcultural Learning«. In: Delanoy/Eisenmann/Matz 2015, 217–236.

Eisenmann, Maria (2016): »Kulturelles Sehverstehen am Beispiel der Cartoons in Sherman Alexies *The Absolutely True Diary of a Part-time Indian* (2007)«. In: Michler, Christine/Reimann, Daniel (eds.): *Sehverstehen im Fremdsprachenunterricht.* Tübingen, 396–409.

Eisenmann, Maria/Summer, Theresa (eds.) (³2017): *Basic Issues in EFL Teaching and Learning* [2012]. Heidelberg.

Elley, Warwick B. (ed.) (1994): *The IEA Study of Reading Literacy. Achievement and Instruction in Thirty-two School Systems.* Oxford.

Ellis, Rod (2003): *Task-Based Language Learning and Teaching.* Oxford.

Ellis, Rod (2005): »Principles of Instructed Language Learning«. In: *System* 33/2, 209–224.

Ellis, Rod (2009): »A Typology of Written Corrective Feedback Types«. In: *ELT Journal* 63/2, 97–107.

Ellis, Rod (⁴2014): »Principles of Instructed Second Language Learning«. In: Celce-Murcia, Marianne/Brinton, Donna/Snow, Marguerite Ann/Bohlke, David (eds.): *Teaching English as a Second or Foreign Language* [1979]. Boston, 31–45.

Elsner, Daniela (2014): *Kompetenzorientiert unterrichten in der Grundschule. Englisch 1–4.* München.

Elsner, Daniela (⁶2016): »Lehrwerke«. In: Burwitz-Melzer et al. ⁶2016, 41–44.

Elsner, Daniela/Keßler, Jörg-U. (eds.) (2013a): *Bilingual Education in Primary School. Aspects of Immersion, CLIL and Bilingual Modules.* Tübingen.

Elsner, Daniela/Keßler Jörg-U. (2013b): »Aspects of Immersion, CLIL and Bilingual Modules. Bilingual Education in Primary School«. In: Elsner/Keßler 2013a, 1–6.

Elsner, Daniela/Viebrock, Britta (2013): »Developing Multiliteracies in the 21st Century. Motives for New Approaches of Teaching and Learning Foreign Languages«. In: Elsner, Daniela/Helff, Sissy/Viebrock, Britta (eds.): *Films, Graphic Novels & Visuals. Developing Multiliteracies in Foreign Language Education. An Interdisciplinary Approach.* Münster, 17–32.

Elsner, Daniela/Bündgens-Kosten, Judith/Hardy, Ilonca (2015): »Affordanzen und Nutzung mehrsprachiger Lernumgebungen. Erste Ergebnisse aus der Pilotierung zum Forschungsprojekt LIKE«. In: Kötter, Markus/Rymarczyk, Jutta (eds.): *Englischunterricht auf der Primarstufe. Neue Forschungen, weitere Entwicklungen.* Frankfurt a. M., 35–57.

Enever, Janet (ed.) (2011): *ELLiE. Early Language Learning in Europe.* London.

Engel, Gaby/Groot-Wilken, Bernd/Thürmann, Eike (eds.) (2009): *Englisch in der Primarstufe. Chancen und Herausforderungen. Evaluation und Erfahrungen aus der Praxis.* Berlin.

Engelkamp, Johannes/Zimmer, Hubert D. (1990): »Unterschiede in der Repräsentation und Verarbeitung von Wissen in Abhängigkeit von Kanal, Reizmodalitäten und Aufgabenstellung«. In: Böhme-Dürr, Karin/Emig, Jürgen/Seel, Norbert M. (eds.): *Wissensveränderung durch Medien.* München, 84–97.

European Commission (ed.) (2014): »Languages in Education and Training. Final

Country Comparative Analysis«, http://ec.europa.eu/dgs/education_culture/repository/languages/library/studies/lang-eat_en.pdf (14.12.2017).

Eurostat (ed.) (2016): »Foreign Language Learning Statistics«, http://ec.europa.eu/eurostat/statistics-explained/index.php/Foreign_language_learning_statistics (14.12.2017).

EURYDICE (ed.) (2006): *Content and Language Integrated Learning (CLIL) at School in Europe.* Brussels.

Fäcke, Christiane (2006): *Transkulturalität und fremdsprachliche Literatur. Eine empirische Studie zu mentalen Prozessen von primär mono- oder bikulturell sozialisierten Jugendlichen.* Frankfurt a. M.

Fairclough, Norman (1999):»Global Capitalism and Critical Awareness of Language«. In: *Language Awareness* 8/2, 71–83.

Flower, Linda/Hayes, John (1981): »The Cognitive Process Theory of Writing«. In: *College Composition and Communication* 32/4, 365–387.

FMKS (ed.) (n. d.): »Bilinguale Schulen«, http://www.fmks-online.de/bilischools.html (14.12.2017).

Freitag-Hild, Britta (2010): *Theorie, Aufgabentypologie und Unterrichtspraxis inter- und transkultureller Literaturdidaktik. British Fictions of Migration im Fremdsprachenunterricht.* Trier.

Freitag-Hild, Britta (2014): »Lernaufgaben im genre-basierten Englischunterricht. Kompetenzen zum monologischen und dialogischen Sprechen entwickeln«. In: Fäcke, Christiane/Rost-Roth, Martina/Thaler, Engelbert (eds.): *Sprachenausbildung, Sprachen bilden aus, Bildung aus Sprachen. Dokumentation zum 25. Kongress für Fremdsprachendidaktik der Deutschen Gesellschaft für Fremdsprachenforschung.* Baltmannsweiler, 77–89.

Froese, Wolfgang (2010): »Lernrallyes in der Sekundarstufe I«. In: Gehring 2010a, 27–35.

Funk, Hermann ([6]2016): »Lehr-/Lernmaterialien und Medien im Überblick«. In: Burwitz-Melzer et al. [6]2016, 625–631.

Gaile, Dorothée/Gold, Andreas/Souvignier, Elmar (2007): *Text Detectives.* Göttingen.

Garcia, Ofelia/Wei, Li (2014): *Translanguaging. Language, Bilingualism and Education.* New York.

Gardner, Dee (2013): *Exploring Vocabulary. Language in Action.* Abingdon/Oxon.

Gardner, Howard (1983): *Frames of Mind. The Theory of Multiple Intelligences.* New York.

Gardner, Howard (1993): *Multiple Intelligences. New Horizons.* New York.

Gardner, Robert C./Lambert, Wallace E. (1972): *Attitudes and Motivation in Second Language Learning.* Rowley, MA.

Garman, Michael (1990): *Psycholinguistics.* Cambridge.

Gass, Susan M./Mackey, Alison (2007): »Input, Interaction and Output in Second Language Acquisition«. In: VanPatten/Williams 2007, 175–199.

Gass, Susan M./Mackey, Alison (eds.) (2012): *The Routledge Handbook of Second Language Acquisition.* Abingdon.

Gegier, Birgit (2006): *Let's Get Moving! Bewegungsspiele in Englisch ab 2. Lernjahr.* Mülheim a. d. Ruhr.

Gehring, Wolfgang (ed.) (2010a): *Außerschulische Lernorte des Fremdsprachenunterrichts.* Braunschweig.

Gehring, Wolfgang (2010b): »Zur Einleitung. Lernort, Lernstandort, Lernumgebung. Warum ein Fremdsprachenunterricht auch außerhalb des Klassenzimmers ertragreich ist«. In: Gehring 2010a, 7–16.

Gehring, Wolfgang (2011): »Bilinguale Lernorterkundungen. Authentisch, inhaltsbasiert, kommunikationsorientiert«. In: Gehring/Michler 2011, 11–31.

Gehring, Wolfgang/Michler, Andreas (ed.) (2011): *Außerschulische Lernorte bilingual.* Göttingen.

Genesee, Fred/Upshur, John A. (1996): *Classroom-Based Evaluation in Second Language Education*. Cambridge, MA.

Gerngross, Günter/Puchta, Herbert (1988): »Warum reden die bloß nicht? Die Persönlichkeit des Lehrers und ihre Einflüsse auf die Interaktion im Fremdsprachenunterricht«. In: *Unser Weg* 43/2, 51–55.

Gerngross, Günter/Puchta, Herbert/Thornbury, Scott (2006): *Teaching Grammar Creatively*. Cambridge.

Gibbons, Pauline (2009): *English Learners, Academic Literacy, and Thinking*. Portsmouth, NH.

Gibbons, Pauline (²2015): *Scaffolding Language, Scaffolding Learning. Teaching Second Language Learners in the Mainstream Classroom* [2002]. Portsmouth, NH.

Gibson, James J. (1979): *The Ecological Approach to Visual Perception*. Boston.

Gilroy, Marie/Parkinson, Brian (1996): »Teaching Literature in a Foreign Language«. In: *Language Teaching* 29/4, 213–225.

Gnutzmann, Claus (1995): »Sprachbewusstsein (›Language Awareness‹) und integrativer Grammatikunterricht«. In: Gnutzmann, Claus/Königs, Frank G. (eds.): *Perspektiven des Grammatikunterrichts*. Tübingen, 267–284.

Gogolin, Ingrid (²2008): *Der monolinguale Habitus der multilingualen Schule* [1994]. Münster/New York.

Goh, Christine/Burns, Anne (eds.) (2012): *Teaching Speaking. A Holistic Approach*. Cambridge.

Golumbia, David (2014): »Characteristics of Digital Media«. In: Ryan, Marie-Laure/Emerson, Lori/Robertson, Benjamin J. (eds.): *The John Hopkins Guide to Digital Media*. Baltimore, 54–59.

Graham, Steven/Harris, Karen (2009): *Writing Better. Effective Strategies for Teaching Students with Learning Difficulties*. Baltimore, MD.

Graham, Steven/Perin, Dolores (2007): *Writing Next. Effective Strategies to Improve Writing of Adolescents in Middle School. A Report to Carnegie Corporation of New York*. Washington, DC.

Green, Anthony (2014): *Exploring Language Assessment and Testing*. London/New York.

Grieser-Kindel, Christin/Henseler, Roswitha/Möller, Stefan (eds.) (2016): *Method Guide 2. Methoden für den Englischunterricht Klasse 5–13*. Paderborn.

Grimm, Nancy/Hammer, Julia (2015): »Performative Approaches and Innovative Methods«. In: Delanoy/Eisenmann/Matz 2015, 321–340.

Grimm, Nancy/Meyer, Michael/Volkmann, Laurenz (2015): *Teaching English*. Tübingen.

Groot-Wilken, Bernd/Engel, Gaby/Thürmann, Eike (2007): »Learning to Speak English«. In: *forum schule. Magazin für Lehrerinnen und Lehrer* 2, 32.

Grünewald, Andreas (⁶2016): »Digitale Medien und soziale Netzwerke im Kontext des Lernens und Lehrens von Sprachen«. In: Burwitz-Melzer et al. ⁶2016, 463–466.

Gruschka, Andreas (2013): *Unterrichten. Eine pädagogische Theorie auf empirischer Basis*. Opladen.

Haack, Johannes (³2002): »Interaktivität als Kennzeichen von Multimedia und Hypermedia«. In: Issing, Ludwig J./Klimsa, Paul (eds.): *Information und Lernen mit Multimedia* [1995]. Weinheim,127–136.

Habermas, Jürgen (1981): *Theorie des Kommunikativen Handelns*. Vol. 1: *Handlungsrationalität und gesellschaftliche Rationalisierung*. Frankfurt a. M.

Haenni Hoti, Andrea (2007): »Leistungsvielfalt als Herausforderung für den Englischunterricht in der Primarstufe«. In: *Beiträge zur Lehrerbildung* 25/2, 205–213.

Hall, Graham/Cook, Guy (2012): »Own-Language Use in Language Teaching and Learning«. In: *Language Teaching* 45/3, 271–308.

Hall, Stuart (ed.) (1997): *Representation. Cultural Representations and Signifying Practices*. London.

Hallet, Wolfgang (2002): *Fremdsprachenunterricht als Spiel der Texte und Kulturen. Intertextualität als Paradigma einer kulturwissenschaftlichen Didaktik*. Trier.

Hallet, Wolfgang (2007): »Literatur und Kultur im Unterricht. Ein kulturwissenschaftlicher didaktischer Ansatz«. In: Hallet, Wolfgang/Nünning, Ansgar (eds.): *Neue Ansätze und Konzepte der Literatur- und Kulturdidaktik*. Trier, 31–47.

Hallet, Wolfgang (2008): »Literarisches Verstehen und Kognition. Mentale Modelle und Visualisierungsaufgaben im Literaturunterricht«. In: Bosenius, Petra/ Rohde, Andreas/Wolff, Martina (eds.): *Verstehen und Verständigung*. Trier, 137–170.

Hallet, Wolfgang (2010): »Didaktische Kompetenzen von Fremdsprachenlehrern«. In: Hallet/Königs 2010, 350–353.

Hallet, Wolfgang (2011): *Lernen fördern. Englisch. Kompetenzorientierter Unterricht in der Sekundarstufe I*. Seelze-Velber.

Hallet, Wolfgang (2015): »Teaching Multimodal Novels«. In: Delanoy/Eisenmann/ Matz 2015, 283–298.

Hallet, Wolfgang (2016): *Genres im fremdsprachlichen und bilingualen Unterricht. Formen und Muster der sprachlichen Interaktion*. Seelze-Velber.

Hallet, Wolfgang/Königs, Frank (eds.) (2010): *Handbuch Fremdsprachendidaktik*. Seelze-Velber.

Hallet Wolfgang/Königs, Frank (eds.) (2013): *Handbuch Bilingualer Unterricht. Content and Language Integrated Learning*. Seelze-Velber.

Hallet, Wolfgang/Nünning, Ansgar (eds.) (2007): *Neue Ansätze und Konzepte der Literatur- und Kulturdidaktik*. Trier.

Hallet, Wolfgang/Surkamp, Carola/Krämer, Ulrich (eds.) (2015): *Literaturkompetenzen Englisch. Modellierung, Curriculum, Unterrichtsbeispiele*. Seelze-Velber.

Hamers, Josiane F./Blanc, Michel H.A. (^{2}2000): *Bilinguality and Bilingualism* [1989]. New York.

Hammond, Adam (2016): *Literature in the Digital Age. An Introduction*. Cambridge.

Han, Zhao Hong/Selinker, Larry (2005): »Fossilization in L2 Learners«. In: Hinkel, Eli (ed.): *Handbook of Research in Second Language Teaching and Learning*. Mahwah, NJ., 455–470.

Harmer, Jeremy (^{5}2015): *The Practice of English Language Teaching* [1983]. London.

Haß, Frank (2013): »Inklusion im Englischunterricht – oder: Lernerorientierung endlich ernst nehmen. Wie kann der Englischunterricht Kindern mit ganz unterschiedlichen Förderbedarfen gerecht werden?«. In: *Englisch 5 bis 10* 22/2, 28–32.

Haß, Frank (ed.) (^{2}2016): *Fachdidaktik Englisch. Tradition, Innovation, Praxis* [2006]. Stuttgart.

Hattie, John A. C. (2009): *Visible Learning. A Synthesis of Over 800 Meta-Analyses Relating to Achievement*. New York.

Hattie, John A. C. (2011): *Visible Learning for Teachers. Maximising Impact on Learning*. London/New York.

Havighurst, Robert (1953): *Human Development and Education*. New York.

Hecke, Carola (^{2}2017): »Visuelle Kompetenz«. In: Surkamp ^{2}2017, 372–373.

Hecke, Carola/Surkamp, Carola (eds.) (^{2}2015): *Bilder im Fremdsprachenunterricht. Neue Ansätze, Kompetenzen und Methoden* [2010]. Tübingen.

Hedge, Tricia (2000): *Teaching and Learning in the Language Classroom*. Oxford.

Heinen, Richard (2015): »BYOD. Bring Your Own Device. Digitale Medien. Bedingungen und Folgen kennen und reflektieren«. In: *Pädagogische Führung. Zeitschrift für Schulleitung und Schulberatung* 26/5, 174–177.

Heinz, Susanne/Hesse, Mechthild (2012): »Literatur unterrichten«. In: Lütge 2012b, 84–105.

Heinz, Susanne/Hesse, Mechthild (2014): »Write Your Own Poems that Deal with Fire. Kurzeinheit zu kreativem Schreiben für alle Jahrgänge«. *Praxis Englisch* 1, 8–10.

Helbig, Beate (1998): »Texterschließungstechniken und -strategien bei der Arbeit mit authentischen Textmaterialien im Anfangsunterricht der dritten Schulfremdsprache«. In: Bausch, Karl-Richard (ed.): *Auf der Suche nach dem Sprachlernabenteuer*. Bönen, 131–146.

Helmke, Andreas ([6]2015): *Unterrichtsqualität und Lehrerprofessionalität. Diagnose, Evaluation und Verbesserung des Unterrichts* [2009]. Seelze-Velber.

Henseler, Roswitha/Möller, Stefan/Surkamp, Carola (2011): *Filme im Englischunterricht. Grundlagen, Methoden, Genres*. Seelze-Velber.

Henseler, Roswitha/Surkamp, Carola (eds.) (2007): Special Issue »Lesemotivation. Jugendliteratur«. *Der Fremdsprachliche Unterricht Englisch* 89.

Henseler, Roswitha/Surkamp, Carola (eds.) (2009): Special Issue »Lesekompetenz«. *Der Fremdsprachliche Unterricht Englisch* 100/101.

Hericks, Uwe/Keller-Schneider, Manuela/Bonnet, Andreas (2018): »Herausforderung. Lehrerprofessionalität in berufsbiographischer Perspektive«. In: Gläser-Zikuda, Michaela/Rohlfs, Carsten/Harring, Marius (eds.): *Handbuch Schulpädagogik*. Münster, 111–121.

Hericks, Uwe/Spörlein, Eva (2001): »Entwicklungsaufgaben in Fachunterricht und Lehrerbildung. Eine Auseinandersetzung mit einem Zentralbegriff der Bildungsgangdidaktik«. In: Hericks, Uwe/Keuffer, Josef/Kräft, Hans Christof/ Kunze, Ingrid (eds.): *Bildungsgangdidaktik. Perspektiven für Fachunterricht und Lehrerbildung*. Opladen, 33–50.

Hermes, Liesel ([2]2017a): »Leseverstehen«. In: Surkamp [2]2017, 228–232.

Hermes, Liesel ([2]2017b): »Lektüren«. In: Surkamp [2]2017, 214–215.

Hesse, Mechtild ([2]2016): *The English Teacher's Handbook of Youth Literature. Why, What and How to Read in the Classroom* [2009]. Stuttgart.

Holec, Henri (1981): *Autonomy and Foreign Language Learning*. Oxford.

Horwitz, Elaine K. (2010): »Foreign and Second Language Anxiety«. In: *Language Teaching* 43/2, 154–167.

Howatt, Antony P. R./Smith, Richard (eds.) (2002): *Modern Language Teaching. The Reform Movement. Vol. III: Germany and France*. London/New York.

Hu, Adelheid (2003): *Schulischer Fremdsprachenunterricht und migrationsbedingte Mehrsprachigkeit*. Tübingen.

Hu, Adelheid/Byram, Michael (eds.) (2009): *Interkulturelle Kompetenz und fremdsprachliches Lernen. Modelle, Empirie, Evaluation*. Tübingen.

Hubbard, Philip (1991): »Evaluating Computer Games for Language Learning«. In: *Simulation and Gaming* 22/2, 220–223.

Hudson, Thom (2007): *Teaching Second Language Reading*. Oxford.

Hughes, Rebecca ([2]2011): *Teaching and Researching Speaking* [2002]. Harlow.

Hüllen, Werner (2000): »Ein Plädoyer für das Studium der Geschichte des Fremdsprachenunterrichts«. In: *Zeitschrift für Fremdsprachenforschung* 11/1, 31–39.

Hüllen, Werner (2004): »Linguistik und Didaktik *revisited*«. In: Appel, Joachim (ed.): *Aufschwung im Rückblick*. München, 87–98.

Hüllen, Werner (2005): *Kleine Geschichte des Fremdsprachenlernens*. Berlin.

Hurrelmann, Bettina (2003): »Lesen. Lesen als Basiskompetenz in der Mediengesellschaft«. In: Special Issue »Lesen und Schreiben«. *Friedrich Jahresheft*, 4–10.

Hurst, Beth/Reding, Ginny (2000): *Professionalism in Teaching*. Upper Saddle River, NJ.

Hutz, Matthias (2006): »Lemonade for Sale! Grammatik im aufgabenorientierten Unterricht«. In: *Der fremdsprachliche Unterricht Englisch* 84/40, 22–26.

Hutz, Matthias (2014): »Baptisms of Fire. Vom Umgang mit Idiomatik«. In: *Praxis Englisch* 1, 47–48.

Hutz, Matthias (2016): »Definite Must-Haves for Beautiful Men. Kollokationen mit Textkorpora überprüfen, eine Reportage erstellen«. In: *Der Fremdsprachliche Unterricht Englisch* 140, 38–45.

Hutz, Matthias (³2017): »Storing Words in the Mind. The Mental Lexicon and Vocabulary Learning«. In: Eisenmann/Summer ³2017, 105–117.

Hutz, Matthias/Kolb, Annika (2010): »Am Anfang war das Wort. Prinzipien der Wortschatzvermittlung«. In: *Grundschulmagazin Englisch* 1, 6–8.

Hyland, Ken (²2009): *Teaching and Researching Writing* [2002]. Harlow.

Ivey, Gay/Fisher, Douglas (2006): »Learning From What Doesn't Work«. In: *Best of Educational Leadership 2005–2006* 63, 7–12.

Jakisch, Jenny (2014): *Mehrsprachigkeit und Englischunterricht*. Frankfurt a. M.

Jenkins, Jennifer (2000): *The Phonology of English as an International Language. New Models, New Norms, New Goals*. Oxford.

Kalantzis, Mary/Cope, Bill (2012): *Literacies*. Cambridge.

Kelly, Michael/Grenfell, Michael (2004): »European Profile for Language Teacher Education. A Frame of Reference«, http://www.lang.soton.ac.uk/profile/report/MainReport.pdf (14.12.2017).

Kerr, Philip (2014): *Translation and Own-Language Activities*. Cambridge.

Kerr, Philip (2016): »Adaptive Learning«. In: *ELT Journal* 70/1, 88–93.

Keßler, Jörg-U. (2005): »Fachdidaktik meets Psycholinguistik. Heterogenität im Englischunterricht erkennen, verstehen und als Chance nutzen«. In: Bräu, Karin/Schwerdt, Ulrich (eds.): *Heterogenität als Chance. Vom produktiven Umgang mit Gleichheit und Differenz in der Schule*. Münster, 263–284.

Keßler, Jörg-U. (2006): *Englischerwerb im Anfangsunterricht diagnostizieren. Linguistische Profilanalysen am Übergang von der Primarstufe in die Sekundarstufe I*. Tübingen.

Keßler, Jörg-U. (2007): »Assessing EFL-Development Online. A Feasibility Study of Rapid Profile«. In: Mansouri, Fethi (ed.): *Second Language Acquisition Research. Theory Construction and Testing*. Newcastle, 119–144.

Keßler, Jörg-U. (2008): »Communicative Tasks and Second Language Profiling. Linguistic and Pedagogical Implications«. In: Eckerth, Johannes/Siekmann, Sabine (eds.): *Research on Task-Based Language Learning and Teaching. Theoretical, Methodological and Pedagogical Perspectives*. Frankfurt a. M./New York, 291–310.

Keßler, Jörg-U. (2009): »Englischdidaktik in Erklärungsnot? Implizites und explizites Wissen und die Rolle der Bewusstmachung im schulischen Englischerwerb«. In: Vogt, Rüdiger (ed.): *Erklären. Gesprächsanalytische und fachdidaktische Perspektiven*. Tübingen, 93–107.

Keßler, Jörg-U./Lenzing, Anke (2008): »›The dog is grabing‹. Englischunterricht in der Grundschule und den Übergang neu denken«. In: Heggen, Tanja/Götze, Daniela (eds.): *Grundschule neu denken*. Münster, 97–109.

Keßler, Jörg-U./Liebner, Mathias (2011): »Diagnosing L2 Development«. In: Pienemann/Keßler 2011, 133–148.

Keßler, Jörg-U./Plesser, Anja (2011): *Teaching Grammar*. Paderborn.

Keßler, Jörg-U./Liebner, Mathias/Mansouri, Fethi (2011): »Teaching«. In: Pienemann/Keßler 2011, 149–156.

Kielhöfer, Bernd (1994): »Wörter lernen, behalten, erinnern«. In: *Neusprachliche Mitteilungen* 47/4, 211–220.

Kimes-Link, Ann (2013): *Aufgaben, Methoden und Verstehensprozesse im englischen Literaturunterricht der gymnasialen Oberstufe. Eine qualitativ-empirische Studie*. Tübingen.

Klieme, Eckhard (2006): »Zusammenfassung zentraler Ergebnisse der DESI-Studie«, https://www.dipf.de/de/forschung/aktuelle-projekte/pdf/biqua/DESI_Ausgewaehlte_Ergebnisse.pdf (14.12.2017).

Klippel, Friederike (1980): *Spieltheoretische und pädagogische Grundlagen des Lernspieleinsatzes im Fremdsprachenunterricht*. Bern/Frankfurt a. M.

Klippel, Friederike (1994): *Englischlernen im 18. und 19. Jahrhundert. Die Geschichte der Lehrbücher und Unterrichtsmethoden.* Münster.

Klippel, Frederike (1995): »Wörternetze«. In: Bausch, Karl-Richard/Christ, Herbert/Königs, Frank G./Krumm, Hans-Jürgen (eds.): *Erwerb und Vermittlung von Wortschatz im Fremdsprachenunterricht.* Tübingen, 101–107.

Klippel, Friederike (2012): *Keep Talking. Communicative Fluency Activities for Language Teaching.* Cambridge.

Klippel, Friederike ([6]2016): »Didaktische und methodische Prinzipien der Vermittlung«. In: Burwitz-Melzer et al. [6]2016, 315–320.

KMK (ed.) (n. d.): »KMK Fremdsprachenzertifikat«, https://www.kmk.org/themen/berufliche-schulen/duale-berufsausbildung/kmk-fremdsprachen zertifikat.html (14.12.2017).

KMK (ed.) (2003): »Bildungsstandards für die erste Fremdsprache (Englisch/Französisch) für den Mittleren Schulabschluss. Beschluss vom 4.12.2003«, http://www.kmk.org/fileadmin/Dateien/veroeffentlichungen_beschluesse/2003/2003_12_04-BS-erste-Fremdsprache.pdf (14.12.2017).

KMK (ed.) (2004): »Bildungsstandards für die erste Fremdsprache (Englisch/Französisch) für den Hauptschulabschluss. Beschluss vom 15.10.2004«, http://www.kmk.org/fileadmin/Dateien/veroeffentlichungen_beschluesse/2004/2004_10_15-Bildungsstandards-ersteFS-Haupt.pdf (14.12.2017).

KMK (ed.) (2012a): »Ländergemeinsame Anforderungen für die Ausgestaltung des Vorbereitungsdienstes und die abschließende Staatsprüfung. Beschluss der Kultusministerkonferenz vom 06.12.2012«, https://www.kmk.org/fileadmin/Dateien/veroeffentlichungen_beschluesse/2012/2012_12_06-Vorbereitungs dienst.pdf (14.12.2017).

KMK (ed.) (2012b): »Bildungsstandards für die fortgeführte Fremdsprache (Englisch/Französisch) für die Allgemeine Hochschulreife. Beschluss der Kultusministerkonferenz 18.10.2012«, http://www.kmk.org/fileadmin/Dateien/veroeffentlichungen_beschluesse/2012/2012_10_18-Bildungsstandards-Fortgef-FS-Abi.pdf (14.12.2017).

KMK (ed.) (2013): »Bericht ›Fremdsprachen in der Grundschule. Sachstand und Konzeptionen 2013‹. Beschluss der Kultusministerkonferenz vom 17.10.2013«, http://www.kmk.org/fileadmin/Dateien/veroeffentlichungen_beschluesse/2013/2013_10_17-Fremdsprachen-in-der-Grundschule.pdf (14.12.2017).

KMK (ed.) (2014): »Standards für die Lehrerbildung. Bildungswissenschaften. Beschluss der Kultusministerkonferenz vom 16.12.2004 i. d. F. vom 12.06.2014«, https://www.kmk.org/fileadmin/Dateien/veroeffentlichungen_beschluesse/2004/2004_12_16-Standards-Lehrerbildung-Bildungswissenschaf ten.pdf (14.12.2017).

KMK (ed.) (2015): »Ländergemeinsame inhaltliche Anforderungen für die Fachwissenschaften und Fachdidaktiken in der Lehrerbildung. Beschluss der Kultusministerkonferenz vom 16.10.2008 i. d. F. vom 10.09.2015«, http://www.kmk.org/fileadmin/Dateien/veroeffentlichungen_beschluesse/2008/2008_10_16-Fachprofile-Lehrerbildung.pdf (14.12.2017).

Knill, Oliver (2007): »Benefits and Risks of Media and Technology in the Classroom«, http://abel.math.harvard.edu/~knill/pedagogy/benefits/paper.pdf (14.12.2007).

Koehler, Matthew J./Mishra, Punya (2009): »What is Technological Pedagogical Content Knowledge?«. In: *Contemporary Issues in Technology and Teacher Education, 9/1,* 60–70.

Kolb, Annika (2016): »The World's Next Top Monster«. In: *Der Fremdsprachliche Unterricht Englisch* 140, 14–19.

Kolb, Elisabeth (2009): »Finite Resources – Infinite Communication. Sprachmittlung im Englischunterricht der Unterstufe«. In: *Forum Sprache* 1, 69–86.

Kolb, Elisabeth (2016): *Sprachmittlung. Studien zur Modellierung einer komplexen Kompetenz.* Münster.

Kormos, Judit/Smith, Anne Margaret (2012): *Teaching Languages to Students with Specific Learning Differences.* Bristol et al.

Kozma, Robert B. (1991): »Learning with Media«. In: *Review of Educational Research* 61/2, 179–212.

Kramsch, Claire (1993): *Context and Culture in Language Teaching.* Oxford.

Kramsch, Claire (2009): *The Multilingual Subject.* Oxford.

Krashen, Stephen D. (1981): *Second Language Acquisition and Second Language Learning.* Oxford.

Krashen, Stephen D. (1982a): »Acquiring a Second Language«. In: *World Englishes* 1/3, 97–101.

Krashen, Stephen D. (1982b): *Principles and Practice in Second Language Acquisition.* Oxford.

Krashen, Stephen D. (2004): *The Power of Reading. Insights from Research.* Portsmouth, NH.

Krumm, Hans-Jürgen (2011): »Die Lernerperspektive bei der Erforschung des Fremdsprachenunterrichts. Ein Rück- und Ausblick aus Anlass von 30 Jahren Frühjahrskonferenz zur Erforschung des Fremdsprachenunterrichts«. In: Bausch, Karl-Richard/Burwitz-Melzer, Eva/Königs, Frank G./Krumm, Hans-Jürgen (eds.): *Fremdsprachen lehren und lernen. Rück- und Ausblick.* Tübingen, 75–83.

Krumm, Hans-Jürgen/Reich, Hans ([6]2016): »Ansätze zum Mehrsprachigkeitsunterricht«. In: Burwitz-Melzer et al. [6]2016, 230–233.

Kruse, Anna/Pongsajapan, Rob (2013): »Student-Centered Learning Analytics«, https://cndls.georgetown.edu/m/documents/thoughtpaper-krusepongsajapan. pdf (14.12.2017).

Kumaravadivelu, Balasubramanian (2001): »Toward a Postmethod Pedagogy«. In: *TESOL Quarterly* 35/4, 537–560.

Kumaravadivelu, Balasubramanian (2003): *Beyond Methods. Macrostrategies for Language Teaching.* New Haven/London.

Kumaravadivelu, Balasubramanian (2006a): *Understanding Language Teaching. From Method to Post-Method.* Mahwah, NJ/London.

Kumaravadivelu, Balasubramanian (2006b): »TESOL Methods. Changing Tracks, Challenging Trends«. In: *TESOL Quarterly* 40/1, 59–81.

Kumaravadivelu, Balasubramanian (2012): *Language Teacher Education for a Global Society. A Modular Model for Knowing, Analyzing, Recognizing, Doing, and Seeing.* New York/London.

Küster, Lutz (2005): »Kulturverständnisse in Kulturwissenschaft und Fremdsprachendidaktik«. In: Schumann, Adelheid (ed.): *Kulturwissenschaften und Fremdsprachendidaktik im Dialog. Perspektiven eines interkulturellen Fremdsprachenunterrichts.* Frankfurt a. M., 59–70.

Küster, Lutz (2014): »Multiliteralität. Zur Einführung in den Themenschwerpunkt«. In: *Fremdsprachen Lehren und Lernen* 43/2, 3–11.

Lado, Robert (1967): *Moderner Sprachunterricht. Eine Einführung auf wissenschaftlicher Grundlage.* Aus dem Amerikan. übertr. von Reinhold Freudenstein. München.

Landry, Rodrigue/Bourhis, Richard Y. (1997): »Linguistic Landscape and Ethnolinguistic Vitality. An Empirical Study«. In: *Journal of Language and Social Psychology* 16/1, 23–49.

Larsen-Freeman, Diane ([2]2000): *Techniques and Principles in Language Teaching* [1986]. Oxford.

Larsen-Freeman, Diane/Anderson, Marti ([3]2011): *Techniques and Principles in Language Teaching* [1986]. Oxford.

Lave, Jean/Wenger, Etienne (1991): *Situated Learning. Legitimate Peripheral Participation.* Cambridge.

Leavis, Frank R. (1943): *Education and the University.* London.

Lee, Yong-Won (2015): »Diagnosing Diagnostic Language Assessment«. In: *Language Testing* 32/3, 299–316.

Legutke, Michael K. (1998): »Handlungsraum Klassenzimmer and beyond«. In: Timm 1998, 93–109.

Legutke, Michael K. (2006): »Projekt Airport Revisited«. In: Küppers, Almut/ Quetz, Jürgen (eds.): *Motivation revisited. Festschrift für Gert Solmecke.* Berlin, 71–80.

Legutke, Michael K. (⁵2013): »Lernwelt Klassenzimmer. Szenarien für einen handlungsorientierten Fremdsprachenunterricht«. In: Bach/Timm ⁵2013a, 91–120.

Legutke, Michael K./Thiel, Wolfgang (1983): »Airport. Ein Projekt für den Englischunterricht in Klasse 6«, https://www.youtube.com/watch?v=4N1U2sqdU1M (14.12.2017).

Legutke, Michael/Müller-Hartmann, Andreas/Schocker-v. Ditfurth, Marita (³2014): *Teaching English in the Primary School* [2009]. Stuttgart.

Lehberger, Rainer (1986): *Englischunterricht im Nationalsozialismus.* Tübingen.

Leitzke-Ungerer, Eva (²2017): »Authentizität«. In: Surkamp ²2017, 12–13.

Lenzing, Anke (2016): »Modelling and Assessing Second Language Acquisition. 30 Years Onwards«. In: Keßler, Jörg-U./Lenzing, Anke/Liebner, Mathias (eds.): *Developing, Modelling and Assessing Second Languages.* Amsterdam, ix–xiv.

Leung, Constant (2009): »Second Language Teacher Professionalism«. In: Burns, Anne/Richards, Jack C. (eds.): *The Cambridge Guide to Second Language Teacher Education.* Cambridge, 49–58.

Levelt, Willem (1989): *Speaking. From Intention to Articulation.* Cambridge, MA.

Levy, Mike (2009): »Technologies in Use for Second Language Learning«. In: *The Modern Language Journal* 93/3, 769–782.

Lewis, Michael (1993): *The Lexical Approach. The State of ELT and a Way Forward.* Hove.

Lewis, Michael (1997): *Implementing the Lexical Approach. Putting Theory into Practice.* Andover/Hampshire.

Liebner, Mathias/Pienemann, Manfred (2011): »Explaining Learner Variation«. In: Pienemann/Keßler 2011, 64–74.

Lightbown, Patsy (1998): »The Importance of Timing in Focus on Form«. In: Doughty, Catherine/Williams, Jessica (eds.): *Focus on Form in Classroom Second Language Acquisition.* Cambridge, 177–196.

Lightbown, Patsy (2000): »Anniversary Article. Classroom SLA Research and Second Language Teaching«. In: *Applied Linguistics* 21/4, 431–462.

Lightbown, Patsy (2014): *Focus on Content-Based Language Teaching.* Oxford.

Lightbown, Patsy/Spada, Nina (⁴2013): *How Languages Are Learned* [1993]. Oxford.

Lindstromberg, Seth/Boers, Frank (2008): *Teaching Chunks of Language. From Noticing to Remembering.* London.

Little, David (1994): »Learner Autonomy. A Theoretical Construct and its Practical Application«. In: *Die Neueren Sprachen* 93/5, 430–442.

Little, David (²2013): »Autonomy and Autonomous Learners«. In: Byram/Hu ²2013, 72–74.

Littlewood, William (1981): *Communicative Language Teaching. An Introduction.* New York/Cambridge.

Littlewood, William (2007): »Communicative and Task-Based Language Teaching in East Asian Classrooms«. In: *Language Teaching* 40/3, 243–249.

Liu, Jun/Hansen, Jette G. (2002): *Peer Response in Second Language Writing Classrooms.* Ann Arbor, MI.

Lohe, Viviane/Elsner, Daniela (2014): »Developing Language Awareness in Primary School Children with Multilingual Virtual Talking Books. First Results of the Pilot Study«. *International Journal of Computer-Assisted Language Learning and Teaching* (IJCALLT) 4/4, 30–47.

Long, Michael H. (1991): »Focus on Form. A Design Feature in Language Teaching Methodology«. In: de Bot, Kees/Ginsberg, Raph/Kramsch, Claire (eds.): *Foreign Language Research in Cross-Cultural Perspective*. Amsterdam, 39–52.

Long, Michael H. (1996): »The Role of the Linguistic Environment in Second Language Acquisition«. In: Ritchie, William C./Bathia, Tej K. (eds): *Handbook of Second Language Acquisition*. San Diego, 413–468.

Long, Michael H. (2003): »Stabilization and Fossilization in Interlanguage Development«. In: Doughty, Catherine J./Long, Michael H. (eds.): *The Handbook of Second Language Acquisition*. Malden, 487–535.

Long, Michael H./Robinson, Peter (1998): »Focus-on-Form. Theory, Research, and Practice«. In: Doughty Catherine/Williams, Jessica (eds.): *Focus on Form in Classroom Second Language Acquisition*. Cambridge, 15–41.

Ludwig, Christian/Pointer, Frank Erik (eds.) (2013): *Teaching Comics in the Foreign Language Classroom*. Trier.

Lütge, Christiane (2007): »›And Lose the Name of Action‹? Überlegungen zur Schüleraktivierung mit Drama und Film im Shakespeare-Unterricht«. In: *Scenario* 1, 126–141.

Lütge, Christiane (2010): »Kinowelten erkunden. Fremdsprachliche Begegnungen im audiovisuellen Lernraum«. In: Gehring 2010a, 113–124.

Lütge, Christiane (2012a): *Mit Filmen Englisch unterrichten*. Berlin.

Lütge, Christiane (ed.) (2012b): *Englisch Methodik. Handbuch für die Sekundarstufe I und II*. Berlin.

Lütge, Christiane (2012c): »Developing ›Literary Literacy‹. Towards a Progression of Literary Learning in the EFL Classroom«. In: Eisenmann/Summer (2012), 191–202.

Lütge, Christiane (2012d): »A Speaking Image, with this End to Teach and to Delight. Lyrik im Englischunterricht«. In: *Praxis Englisch* 5/12, 6–8.

Lütge, Christiane (2012e): »Hörverstehen und Hörsehverstehen«. In: Lütge 2012b, 51–63.

Lütge, Christiane (ed.) (2015a): *Global Education. Global Perspectives for English Language Teaching*. Münster.

Lütge, Christiane (2015b): »Handlungs- und Produktionsorientierung im Dramenunterricht. Perspektiven für die fremdsprachliche Literatur- und Kulturdidaktik«. In: Hallet, Wolfgang/Surkamp, Carola (eds.): *Dramendidaktik und Dramapädagogik im Fremdsprachenunterricht*. Trier, 189–201.

Lütge, Christiane (2017): »Postcolonial Literature and Transcultural Learning in the EFL Classroom. Crossovers, Trodden Paths or Winding Roads?«. In: Lütge, Christiane/Stein, Mark (eds.): *Crossovers. Postcolonial Studies and Transcultural Learning*. Münster, 159–176.

Maley, Alan (1989): »A Comeback for Literature?«. In: *Practical English Teaching* 10/1, 59.

Manchón, Rosa/Roca de Larios, Julio/Murphy, Liz (2007): »A Review of Writing Strategies. Focus on Conceptualization and Impact of First Language«. In: Cohen, Andrew/Macaro, Ernesto (eds.): *Language Learner Strategies. 30 Years of Research and Practice*. Oxford, 229–250.

Mandinach, Ellen B./Honey, Margaret (2008): *Data-Driven School Improvement*. New York.

Mansouri, Fethi/Duffy, Loretta (2005): »The Pedagogic Effectiveness of Developmental Readiness in ESL Grammar Instruction«. In: *Australian Review of Applied Linguistics* 28/1, 81–99.

Martín, Daniel (2015): *From Whiteboards to Web 2.0. Activating Languages Skills with New Technologies*. Rum.

Mayer, Nikola ([5]2013): »Wo Fremdsprachenlernen beginnt. Grundlagen und Arbeitsformen des Englischunterrichts in der Primarstufe«. In: Bach/Timm [5]2013a, 61–90.

Mays, Daniel/Grotemeyer, Marita (2014): »Teamarbeit in der inklusiven Schule. Den Einzelnen entlasten, das Team stärken«. In: *Praxis Schule* 2, 4–8.

McArthur, Tom (1991): *A Foundation Course for Language Teachers*. Cambridge.

McCarthy, Michael/Dell, Felicity (2005): *English Collocations in Use. How Words Work Together for Fluent and Natural English*. Cambridge.

McCarthy, Michael/O'Keeffe, Anne/Walsh, Steven (2010): *Vocabulary Matrix. Understanding, Learning, Teaching*. Andover/Hampshire.

McKay, Penny (2006): *Assessing Young Language Learners*. Cambridge.

McKay, Sandra Lee (2012): »English as an International Language«. In: Burns, Anne/Richards, Jack C. (eds.): *The Cambridge Guide to Pedagogy and Practice in Second Language Teaching*. Cambridge, 15–22.

Meier, Gabriela (2014): »Our Mother Tongue is Plurilingualism. A Framework of Orientations for Integrated Multilingual Curricula«. In: Conteh, Jean/Meier, Gabriela (eds.): *The Multilingual Turn in Languages Education. Opportunities and Challenges*. Bristol, 132–157.

Meißner, Franz-Josef ([6]2016): »Interkomprehension«. In: Burwitz-Melzer et al. [6]2016, 234–239.

Merse, Thorsten/Schmidt, Jochen (2012): »Internet-Medien und Web 2.0«. In: Lütge 2012b, 155–176.

Meyer, Hilbert (2004): *Was ist guter Unterricht?*. Berlin.

Möller, Stefan/Netz, Gabi (2009): »Gezielt durch Texte surfen. Strategien für das Lesen von Hypertexten vermitteln«. In: *Der fremdsprachliche Unterricht Englisch* 100/101, 42–45.

Morrow, Kristine (1977): »Teaching the Functions of Language«. In: *ELT Journal* XXXII/1, 9–15.

Moskowitz, Gertrude (1976): »The Classroom Interaction of Outstanding Foreign Language Teachers«. In: *Foreign Language Annals* 9/2, 135–157.

MPFS (ed.) (2016): »JIM-Studie 2016. Jugend, Information, (Multi-)Media. Basisuntersuchung zum Medienumgang 12- bis 19-Jähriger«, https://www.mpfs.de/fileadmin/files/Studien/JIM/2016/JIM_Studie_2016.pdf (14.12.2017).

Mukherjee, Joybrato (2005): »The Native Speaker Is Alive and Kicking. Linguistic and Language-Pedagogical Perspectives«. In: *Anglistik* 16/2, 7–23.

Müller, Richard-Matthias (1979): »Das Wissenschaftsverständnis der Fremdsprachendidaktik«. In: Heuer, Helmut/Sauer, Helmut/Kleineidam, Hartmut (eds.): *Dortmunder Diskussionen zur Fremdsprachendidaktik*. Dortmund, 132–148.

Müller-Hartmann, Andreas/Schocker-v. Ditfurth, Marita ([2]2014): *Introduction to English Language Teaching* [2004]. Stuttgart.

Müller-Hartmann, Andreas/Schocker-v. Ditfurth, Marita (2011): *Teaching English. Task-Supported Language Learning*. Heidelberg.

Müller, Hartmann, Andreas/Schocker, Marita/Pant, Hans Anand (2013): *Lernaufgaben Englisch aus der Praxis*. Frankfurt a. M.

Murray, Denise E./McPherson, Pam (2006): »Scaffolding Instruction for Reading the Web«. In: *Language Teaching Research* 10/2, 131–156.

Myskow, Gordon/Gordon, Kana (2010): »A Focus on Purpose. Using a Genre Approach in an EFL Writing Class«. In: *ELT Journal* 64/3, 283–292.

Nation, Ian S. P. (2001): *Learning Vocabulary in Another Language*. Cambridge.

Norton, Bonny ([2]2013): *Identity and Language Learning. Extending the Conversation* [2000]. Bristol et al.

Nunan, David (1991): *Language Teaching Methodology. A Textbook for Teachers*. New York.

O'Dowd, Robert (2007): *Online Intercultural Exchange. An Introduction for Foreign Language Teachers*. Clevedon.

Ohler, Jason (2013): *Digital Storytelling in the Classroom. New Media Pathways to Literacy, Learning, and Creativity*. Thousand Oaks, CA.

O'Neill, Robert (1982): »Why Use Textbooks?«. In: *English Language Teaching Journal* 36/2, 104–111.

Ortega, Lourdes (2009): *Understanding Second Language Acquisition*. London.

O'Sullivan, Barry (2012): »The Assessment Development Process«. In: Coombe et al. 2012a, 47–58.

O'Sullivan, Emer/Rösler, Dietmar (2013): *Kinder- und Jugendliteratur im Fremdsprachenunterricht.* Tübingen.

Oxford, Rebecca (1990): *Language Learning Strategies. What Every Teacher Should Know.* New York.

Oxford, Rebecca/Anderson Neil (1995): »A Crosscultural View of Learning Styles«. In: *Language Teaching* 28/4, 201–215.

Paran, Amos (2010): »Between Scylla and Charybdis. The Dilemmas of Testing Language and Literature«. In: Paran, Amos/Sercu, Lies (eds.): *Testing the Untestable in Language Education. New Perspectives on Language and Education.* Bristol, 143–164.

Paran, Amos/Robinson, Pauline (2016): *Literature.* Oxford.

Pennycook, Alastair (1989): »The Concept of Methods, Interested Knowledge, and the Politics of Language Teaching«. In: *TESOL Quarterly* 23/4, 589–618.

Peterson, Mark (2013): *Computer Games and Language Learning.* New York.

Pienemann, Manfred (1984): »Psychological Constraints on the Teachability of Languages«. In: *Studies in Second Language Acquisition* 6/2, 186–214.

Pienemann, Manfred (1989): »Is Language Teachable? Psycholinguistic Experiments and Hypotheses«. In: *Applied Linguistics* 10/1, 52–79.

Pienemann, Manfred (1998): *Language Processing and Second Language Development.* Amsterdam.

Pienemann, Manfred (2005): »An Introduction to Processability Theory«. In: Pienemann, Manfred (ed.): *Cross-Linguistic Aspects of Processability Theory.* Amsterdam, 1–60.

Pienemann, Manfred (2011): »Developmental Schedules«. In: Pienemann/Keßler 2011, 3–11.

Pienemann, Manfred/Keßler, Jörg-U. (eds.) (2011): *Studying Processability Theory.* Amsterdam.

Pienemann, Manfred/Keßler, Jörg-U. (2012): »Processability Theory«. In: Gass, Susan M./Mackey, Alison (eds.): *Handbook of Second Language Acquisition.* New York, 228–246.

Piepho, Hans-Eberhard (1974): *Kommunikative Kompetenz als übergeordnetes Lernziel im Englischunterricht.* Limburg.

Piepho, Hans-Eberhard (1979): *Kommunikative Didaktik des Englischunterrichts Sekundarstufe I. Theoretische Begründung und Wege zur praktischen Einlösung eines fachdidaktischen Konzepts.* Limburg.

Polio, Charlene (2017): »Second Language Writing Development. A Research Agenda«. In: *Language Teaching* 50/2, 261–275.

Posner, Roland (2003): »Kultursemiotik«. In: Nünning, Ansgar/Nünning, Vera (eds.): *Konzepte der Kulturwissenschaften. Theoretische Grundlagen, Ansätze, Perspektiven.* Stuttgart, 39–72.

Prabhu, N. S. (1990): »There Is No Best Method – Why?«. In: *TESOL Quarterly* 24/2, 161–176.

Puchta, Herbert/Strasser, Thomas (2016): *Top Spot. English for PTS.* Rum.

Puentedura, Ruben R. (2010): »SAMR and TPCK. Intro to Advanced Practice«, http://hippasus.com/resources/sweden2010/SAMR_TPCK_IntroToAdvanced Practice.pdf (14.12.2017).

Reinders, Hayo (ed.) (2012): *Digital Games in Language Learning and Teaching.* Basingstoke.

Reinhardt, Jonathan/Sykes, Julie M. (2014): »Special Issue Commentary. Game and Play Activity in Technology-Mediated L2 Teaching and Learning«. In: *Language Learning & Technology* 18/2, 2–8.

Reppen, Randi (2010): *Using Corpora in the Language Classroom.* Cambridge.

Richards, Jack C. (2006): *Communicative Language Teaching Today.* Cambridge.

Richards, Jack C. (2010): »Competence and Performance in Language Teaching«. In: *RELC Journal* 41/2, 101–122.

Richards, Jack C. (2012): »Competence and Performance in Language Teaching«. In: Burns, Anne/Richards, Jack C. (eds.): *The Cambridge Guide to Pedagogy and Practice in Second Language Teaching*. Cambridge, 46–56.

Richards, Jack C./Farrell, Thomas S. C. (2005): *Professional Development for Language Teachers*. New York.

Richards, Jack C./Rodgers, Theodore S. (³2014): *Approaches and Methods in Language Teaching* [1986]. Cambridge.

Richards, Jack C./Platt, John/Weber, Heidi (1985): *Longman Dictionary of Applied Linguistics*. London.

Riemer, Claudia (1997): *Individuelle Unterschiede im Fremdsprachenerwerb*. Baltmannsweiler.

Riemer, Claudia (²2013): »Successful Language Learner«. In: Byram/Hu ²2013, 671–674.

Ringbom, Håkan (1987): *The Role of the First Language in Foreign Language Learning*. Clevedon.

Risager, Karen (2006): *Language and Culture. Global Flows and Local Complexity*. Clevedon.

Risager, Karen (2007): *Language and Culture Pedagogy. From a National to a Transnational Paradigm*. Clevedon.

Rosebrock, Cornelia/Nix, Daniel (2006): »Forschungsüberblick. Leseflüssigkeit (Fluency) in der amerikanischen Leseforschung und -didaktik«. In: *Didaktik Deutsch* 20, 90–112.

Rosswell, Jennifer/Walsh, Maureen (2011): »Rethinking Literacy Education in New Times. Multimodality, Multiliteracies, & New Literacies«, https://blogs.otago.ac.nz/multiliteracies/files/2014/11/Roswell_2011.pdf (14.12.2017).

Sächsisches Staatsministerium für Kultus (ed.) (2012): »Musteraufgaben für das Fach Englisch zur Vorbereitung der Einführung länderübergreifender gemeinsamer Aufgabenteile in den Abiturprüfungen ab dem Schuljahr 2013/14«, https://www.sba.smk.sachsen.de/ppdf/2012_04_Englisch_Muster.pdf (14.12.2017).

Sambanis, Michaela (2013): *Fremdsprachenunterricht und Neurowissenschaften*. Tübingen.

Samuda, Virginia/Bygate, Martin (2008): *Tasks in Second Language Learning*. Basingstoke.

Sara, Kira/Elis, Franziska (eds.) (2017): Special Issue »Creative Writing«. *Der fremdsprachliche Unterricht Englisch* 150.

Schmenk, Barbara (2008): *Lernerautonomie. Karriere und Sloganisierung des Autonomiebegriffs*. Tübingen.

Schmenk, Barbara (⁶2016): »Lernerautonomie und selbst gesteuertes Sprachenlernen«. In: Burwitz-Melzer et al. ⁶2016, 367–372.

Schmidt, Claudia (2010): »Lesen und neue Medien«. In: Lutjeharms, Madeline/Schmidt, Claudia (eds.): *Lesekompetenz in Erst-, Zweit- und Fremdsprache*. Tübingen, 27–38.

Schmidt, Jochen (³2014): *Rituale im Englischunterricht der Grundschule. 1.–4. Klasse* [2011]. Hamburg.

Schmidt, Torben (2009): »Mündliche Lernertexte auf der 2.0-Bühne. Mediale Inszenierung im Englischunterricht am Beispiel eines Schulpodcast-Projekts«. In: *Forum Sprache* 1, 24–42.

Schmidt, Torben (2016): »Chocolate-Covered Drill & Practice? Möglichkeiten und Grenzen des ›gamifizierten‹, adaptiven Übens mit Fremdsprachenlern-Apps«. In: Burwitz-Melzer, Eva/Königs, Frank G./Riemer, Claudia/Schmelter, Lars (eds.): *Üben und Übungen beim Fremdsprachenlernen. Perspektiven und Konzepte für Unterricht und Forschung. Arbeitspapiere der 36. Frühjahrskonferenz zur Erforschung des Fremdsprachenunterrichts*. Tübingen, 200–210.

Schmidt, Torben/Strasser, Thomas (2016): »Digital Classrooms. Basisartikel«. In: *Der fremdsprachliche Unterricht Englisch* 144, 2–7.

Schmidt, Torben/Schmidt, Inke/Schmidt, Philipp René (2016): »Digitales Spielen und Lernen – A Perfect Match? Pädagogische Betrachtungen vom kindlichen Spiel zum digitalen Lernspiel«. In: Dadacynski, Kevin/Schiemann, Stephan/Paulus, Peter (eds.): *Gesundheit spielend fördern. Potenziale und Herausforderungen von digitalen Spielanwendungen für die Gesundheitsförderung und Prävention.* Weinheim/Basel, 18–49.

Schmitt, Norbert (2000): *Vocabulary in Language Teaching.* Cambridge.

Schneider, Edgar W. (2011): *English Around the World. An Introduction.* Cambridge.

Schocker, Marita (2016): »Auf die Lerner kommt es an!«. In: *Der fremdsprachliche Unterricht Englisch* 143, 2–7.

Schön, Donald (1983): *The Reflective Practitioner. How Professionals Think in Action.* London.

Schumann, Adelheid (2008): »Transkulturalität in der Romanistischen Literaturdidaktik. Kulturwissenschaftliche Grundlagen und didaktische Konzepte am Beispiel der *littérature beur*«. In: *Fremdsprachen Lehren und Lernen* 37, 81–94.

Schwab, Götz/Keßler, Jörg-U./Hollm, Jan (2014): »CLIL goes Hauptschule. Chancen und Herausforderungen bilingualen Unterrichts an einer Hauptschule. Zentrale Ergebnisse einer Longitudinalstudie«. In: *Zeitschrift für Fremdsprachenforschung* 25/1, 3–37.

Schwerdt, Thomas (2010): *PISA und die Folgen. Wozu ist die Schule da? Ein Modell einer ökonomisch orientierten Bürger- und Lebensschule.* Bad Heilbrunn.

Schwerdtfeger, Inge C. (1989): *Sehen und Verstehen. Arbeit mit Filmen im Unterricht Deutsch als Fremdsprache.* Berlin.

Scrivener, Jim (³2011): *Learning Teaching. The Essential Guide to English Language Teaching* [1994]. Oxford.

Selinker, Larry (1972): »Interlanguage«. In: *International Review of Applied Linguistics in Language Teaching* 10/3, 209–232.

Setter, Jane/Jenkins, Jennifer (2005): »Pronunciation. State-of-the-Art Review Article«. In: *Language Teaching* 38/1, 1–17.

Shulman, Lee S. (1986): »Those Who Understand. Knowledge Growth in Teaching«. In: *Educational Researcher* 15/2, 4–14.

Shulman, Lee S. (1987): »Knowledge and Teaching. Foundations of the New Reform«. In: *The Harvard Educational Review* 57/1, 1–23.

Singleton, David/Aronin, Larissa (2007): »Multiple Language Learning in the Light of the Theory of Affordance«. In: *Innovation in Language Learning and Teaching* 1/1, 83–96.

Skehan, Peter (1986): »Cluster Analysis and the Identification of Learner Types«. In: Cook, Vivian (ed.): *Experimental Approaches to Second Language Acquisition.* Oxford, 81–94.

Slade, Sharon/Prinsloo, Paul (2013): »Learning Analytics. Ethical Issues and Dilemmas«. In: *American Behavioral Scientist* 57/10, 1509–1528, http://oro.open.ac.uk/36594/2/ECE12B6B.pdf (14.12.2017).

Sommer, Roy (2003): *Grundkurs Cultural Studies/Kulturwissenschaft Großbritannien.* Stuttgart.

Spada, Nina/Lightbown, Patsy (2013): »Instructed Second Language Acquisition«. In: Robinson, Peter (ed.): *Routledge Encyclopedia of SLA.* London, 319–327.

Spiro, Jane (2004): *Creative Poetry Writing.* Oxford.

Stanley, Graham (2013): *Language Learning with Technology. Ideas for Integrating Technology in the Language Classroom.* Cambridge.

Stathopoulou, Maria (2015): *Cross-Language Mediation in Foreign Language Teaching and Testing.* Clevedon.

Statista Inc. (ed.) (2017): »Number of Apps Available in Leading App Stores as of

March 2017«, http://www.statista.com/statistics/276623/number-of-apps-available-in-leading-app-stores/ (14.12.2017).

Steele, Claude M./Aronson, Joshua (1995): »Stereotype Threat and the Intellectual Test Performance of African-Americans«. In: *Journal of Personality and Social Psychology* 69/5, 797–811.

Stockwell, Glenn (2016): »Mobile Language Learning«. In: Farr, Fiona/Murray, Liam (eds.): *The Routledge Handbook of Language Learning and Technology*. New York, 296–307.

Strasser, Thomas (2012a): *Mind the App. Inspiring Internet Tools and Activities to Engage Your Students*. Rum.

Strasser, Thomas (2012b): »A Change of Paradigm with Web 2.0? Why Educational Apps Might Be Worth a Try«. In: Exteberria, Ana Landeta (ed.): *Global E-Learning*. Madrid, 135–144.

Strasser, Thomas (2015): »Using Edu Apps 2.0«. In: Schwetlick, Alison (ed.): *IATEFL VOICES. The Bi-Monthly Newsletter of the International Association of Teachers of English as a Foreign Language* 247, 12–13.

Strasser, Thomas/Pachler, Norbert (2014): »Digital Technologies in Modern Foreign Language Teaching and Learning«. In: Pachler, Norbert (ed.): *Teaching Foreign Languages in the Secondary School. A Practical Guide*. London, 94–110.

Sudhoff, Julian (2010): »CLIL and Intercultural Communicative Competence. Foundations and Approaches Towards a Fusion«. In: *International CLIL Research Journal* 1/3, 30–37.

Summer, Theresa (2011): *An Evaluation of Methodological Options for Grammar Instruction in EFL Textbooks. Are Methods Dead?*. Heidelberg.

Surkamp, Carola (2012): »Teaching Literature«. In: Middeke, Martin/Müller, Timo/Wald, Christina/Zapf, Hubert (eds.): *English and American Studies. Theory and Practice*. Stuttgart/Weimar, 488–495.

Surkamp, Carola (2013): »Geschichte der Kanones englischsprachiger Literatur an deutschen Schulen«. In: Rippl, Gabriele/Winko, Simone (eds.): *Handbuch Kanon und Wertung. Theorien, Instanzen, Geschichte*. Stuttgart/Weimar, 193–200.

Surkamp, Carola (2015): »Playful Learning with Short Plays«. In: Delanoy/Eisenmann/Matz 2015, 141–158.

Surkamp, Carola (²2017) (ed.): *Metzler Lexikon Fremdsprachendidaktik. Ansätze, Methoden, Grundbegriffe* [2010]. Stuttgart/Weimar.

Surkamp, Carola/Feuchert, Sascha (2010): »Lernort Theater. Potentiale, Methoden und Anregungen für den fremdsprachlichen Dramenunterricht«. In: Gehring 2010a, 78–94.

Surkamp, Carola/Nünning, Ansgar (⁴2016): *Englische Literatur unterrichten 1. Grundlagen und Methoden* [2006]. Seelze-Velber.

Surkamp, Carola/Nünning, Ansgar (²2014): *Englische Literatur unterrichten 2. Unterrichtsmodelle und Materialien* [2009]. Seelze-Velber.

Swain, Merrill (1985): »Communicative Competence. Some Roles of Comprehensible Input and Comprehensible Output in its Development«. In: Gass, Susan/Madden, Carolyn (eds.): *Input in Second Language Acquisition. Issues in Second Language Research*. Rowley, MA, 235–253.

Swain, Merrill (2000): »French Immersion Research in Canada. Recent Contributions to SLA and Applied Linguistics«. In: *Annual Review of Applied Linguistics* 20, 199–212.

Swain, Merrill (2005): »The Output Hypothesis. Theory and Research«. In: Hinkel, Eli (ed.): *Handbook on Research in Second Language Learning and Teaching*. Mahwah, 471–483.

Swan, Michael (2005): *Grammar*. Oxford.

Swales, John (1980): »ESP. The Textbook Problem«. In: *ESP Journal* 1/1, 11–23.

Sykes, Julie E./Reinhardt, Jonathon (2012): *Language at Play. Digital Games in Second and Foreign Language Teaching and Learning*. New York.

Sylven, Liss K./Sundqvist, Pia (2012): »Gaming as Extramural English L2 Learning and L2 Proficiency Among Young Learners«. In: *ReCALL* 24/3, 302–321.

Teng, Lin Sophie/Zhang, Lawrence Jun (2016): »A Questionnaire-Based Validation of Multidimensional Models of Self-Regulated Learning Strategies«. In: *The Modern Language Journal* 100/3, 674–701.

Terhart, Ewald ([4]2005): *Lehr-Lernmethoden. Eine Einführung in Probleme der methodischen Organisation von Lehren und Lernen* [1989]. Weinheim/ München.

Tesch, Bernd/Leupold, Eynar/Köller, Olaf (eds.) (2008): *Bildungsstandards Französisch konkret. Sekundarstufe I. Grundlagen, Aufgabenbeispiele und Unterrichtsanregungen*. Berlin.

Thaler, Engelbert (2010a): *Lernerfolg durch Balanced Teaching. Offene Lernarrangements – aufgabenorientiert, spielorientiert, medienorientiert*. Berlin.

Thaler, Engelbert (2010b): »Außerschulische Lernorte«. In: *Praxis Fremdsprachenunterricht* 7/3, 5–7.

Thaler, Engelbert (2012): *Englisch unterrichten. Grundlagen, Kompetenzen, Methoden*. Berlin.

Thaler, Engelbert (2014): *Teaching English with Films*. Paderborn.

Thomson, Ron/Derwing, Tracy (2015): »The Effectiveness of L2 Pronunciation Instruction. A Narrative Review«. In: *Applied Linguistics* 36/3, 326–344.

Thornbury, Scott (2002): *How to Teach Grammar*. Harlow.

Thornbury, Scott (2005a): *How to Teach Speaking*. Harlow.

Thornbury, Scott (2005b): *Uncovering Grammar*. Oxford.

Thornbury, Scott (2011): »Language Teaching Methodology«. In: Simpson, James (ed.): *The Routledge Handbook of Applied Linguistics*. Abingdon/New York, 185–199.

Thürmann, Eike (2010): »Zur Konstruktion von Sprachgerüsten im bilingualen Sachfachunterricht«. In: Doff 2010, 137–153.

Timm, Johannes-Peter (ed.) (1998): *Englisch lernen und lehren. Didaktik des Englischunterrichts*. Berlin.

Timmis, Ivor ([3]2017): »Teaching Grammar«. In: Eisenmann/Summer [3]2017, 119–129.

Tsagari, Dina/Banerjee, Jayanti (eds.) (2016): *Handbook of Second Language Assessment*. Boston/Berlin.

UCLES (ed.) (2015): »IELTS Guide for Teachers«, https://www.ielts.org/-/media/ publications/guide-for-teachers/ielts-guide-for-teachers-2015-uk.ashx (14.12.2017).

UNESCO (ed.) (2009): »Policy Guidelines on Inclusion in Education«, http:// unesdoc.unesco.org/images/0017/001778/177849e.pdf (14.12.2017).

Ur, Penny (2012): *A Course in English Language Teaching*. Cambridge.

Ur, Penny ([2]2015): *Discussions and More. Oral Fluency Practice in the Classroom* [1981]. Cambridge.

Van den Branden, Kris (ed.) (2006a): *Task-Based Language Education. From Theory to Practice*. Cambridge

Van den Branden, Kris (2006b): »Introduction. Task-Based Language Teaching in a Nutshell«. In: Van den Branden 2006a, 1–16.

Vanderbeke, Marie/Wilden, Eva (2017): »Sachfachliche Diskursfähigkeit durch fremdsprachliche *affordances* in bilingualen Schülerlaborprojekten«. In: *Zeitschrift für Fremdsprachenforschung* 28/1, 3–27.

Van Gorp, Koen/Bogaert, Nora (2006): »Developing Language Tasks for Primary and Secondary Education«. In: Van den Branden 2006a, 76–105.

Van Lier, Leo (1995): *Introducing Language Awareness*. London.

Van Lier, Leo (1996): *Interaction in the Language Curriculum. Awareness, Autonomy, and Authenticity*. London/New York.

Van Lier, Leo (2000): »From Input to Affordance. Social Interactive Learning from an Ecological Perspective«. In: Lantolf, James P. (ed.): *Sociocultural Theory and Second Language Learning*. Oxford, 155–177.

Van Lier, Leo (²2006): »Internet and Language Education«. In: Brown, Keith (ed.): *Encyclopedia of Language & Linguistics* [1993]. Oxford, 758–764.

Van Lier, Leo (2007): »Action-Based Teaching, Autonomy and Identity«. In: *Innovation in Language Learning & Teaching* 1/1, 46–65.

VanPatten, Bill/Williams, Jessica (eds.) (²2015): *Theories in Second Language Acquisition* [2007]. New York.

Viebrock, Britta (2010): »Alltagstheorien, methodisches Wissen und unterrichtliches Handeln«. In: Doff 2010, 107–123.

Viebrock, Britta (2014): »Zur Professionalisierung von Lehrkräften im bilingualen Erdkundeunterricht«. In: *Zeitschrift für interpretative Schul- und Unterrichtsforschung* 3/1, 72–85.

Viebrock, Britta (ed.) (2016): *Feature Films in English Language Teaching*. Tübingen.

VOICE (ed.) (2013): »The Vienna-Oxford International Corpus of English (Version 2.0 online)«, http://www.univie.ac.at/voice/ (14.12.2017).

Volkmann, Laurenz (2010): *Fachdidaktik Englisch. Kultur und Sprache*. Tübingen.

Volkmann, Laurenz (2015): »Opportunities and Challenges for Transcultural Learning and Global Education via Literature«. In: Delanoy/Eisenmann/Matz 2015, 237–262.

Vygotsky, Lev (1978): *Mind in Society*. Cambridge, MA.

Wallace, B./Oxford, Rebecca (1992): »Disparity in Learning Styles and Teaching Styles in the ESL Classroom. Does This Mean War?«. In: *AMTESOL Journal* 1, 45–68.

Wallace, Michael J. (1991): *Training Foreign Language Teachers. A Reflective Approach*. Cambridge.

Wanders, Annika (2006): »Die Rolle des Transfers«. In: Pienemann, Manfred/Keßler, Jörg-U./Roos, Eckhard (eds.): *Englischerwerb in der Grundschule*. Paderborn, 97–109.

Ward, Jonathan Stuart/Barker, Adam (2013): »Undefined By Data. A Survey of Big Data Definitions«, http://arxiv.org/pdf/1309.5821.pdf (14.12.2017).

Weidenmann, Bernd (2002): »Multicodierung und Multimodalität im Lernprozeß«. In: Issing, Ludwig J./Klimsa, Paul (eds.): *Informationen und Lernen mit Multimedia und Internet*. Weinheim, 45–62.

Weinert, Franz-Emanuel (ed.) (2001a): *Leistungsmessungen in Schulen*. Weinheim/Basel.

Weinert, Franz-Emanuel (2001b): »Vergleichende Leistungsmessung in Schulen. Eine umstrittene Selbstverständlichkeit«. In: Weinert 2001a, 17–31.

Welsch, Wolfgang (1999): »Transculturality. The Puzzling Form of Cultures Today«. In: Featherstone, Mike/Lash, Scott (eds.): *Spaces of Culture. City, Nation, World*. London, 194–213.

White, Andrew (2013): »Evaluation of an ELT Coursebook Based on Criteria Designed by McDonough and Shaw«, https://www.birmingham.ac.uk/Documents/college-artslaw/cels/essays/sylabusandmaterials/AWhiteCOURSE BOOKEVALUATIONsyllmat.pdf (14.12.2017).

White, Goodith (1998): *Listening*. Oxford.

White, Lydia (2007): »Linguistic Theory, Universal Grammar, and Second Language Acquisition«. In: VanPatten/Williams 2007, 37–55.

Widdowson, Henry G. (1972): »The Teaching of English as Communication«. In: *ELT Journal* XXVII/1, 15–19.

Wilden, Eva/Matz, Frauke (2015): »How to Tell Digital Stories with Handcrafted Video Clips. A (Multi-)Literacies Approach to Foreign Language Teaching«. In: Sanz, Ana M.G./Levy, Michael/Blin, Françoise/Barr, David (eds.): *WorldCALL. Sustainability and Computer-Assisted Language Learning*. London, 511–529.

Willis, Dave (2003): *Rules, Patterns and Words. Grammar and Lexis in ELT.* Cambridge.

Willis, Dave/Willis, Jane (2007): *Doing Task-Based Teaching.* Oxford.

Wolff, Dieter (2010a): »Individuelle Lernermerkmale und institutionalisierter Fremdsprachenunterricht. Ein unlösbarer Konflikt?«. In: Berndt, Annette/Kleppin, Karin (eds.): *Sprachlehrforschung. Theorie und Empirie. Festschrift für Rüdiger Grotjahn.* Frankfurt a. M., 291–306.

Wolff, Dieter (2010b): »Bilingualer Sachfachunterricht/CLIL«. In: Hallet/Königs 2010, 298–302.

Wright, Andrew/Hill, David (2009): *Writing Stories.* Innsbruck.

Wright, Toni (2013): *Professionalism and English Language Teaching.* Lecture at 6th. International English Language Teaching Conference, Georgetown, Penang, Malaysia.

Yu, Quinglan (2015): »Learning Analytics. The Next Frontier for Computer-Assisted Language Learning in Big Data Age«. In: *SHS Web of Conferences* 17, https://www.shs-conferences.org/articles/shsconf/pdf/2015/04/shsconf_icmetm2015_02013.pdf (14.12.2017).

Yu, Shulin/Lee, Icy (2016): »Peer Feedback in Second Language Writing (2005–2014)«. In: *Language Teaching* 49/4, 461–493.

Zibelius, Marja (2012): »Theorie und Realität. Task-as-workplan und Task-in-process in einer Aufgabensequenz für virtuelle Kooperation«. In: Biebighäuser/Zibelius/Schmidt 2012a, 213–248.

Zeichner, Kenneth. M./Liston, Daniel P. (1996): *Reflective Teaching. An Introduction.* Mahwah, NJ.

Zimmermann, Barry (2011): »Motivational Sources and Outcome of Self-Regulated Learning and Performance«. In: Zimmerman, Bary J./Schunk, Dale H. (eds.): *Handbook of Self-Regulation of Learning and Performance.* New York, 49–69.

Zydatiß, Wolfgang (1988): »Fremdsprachendidaktik und Linguistik. Plädoyer für eine fremdsprachendidaktisch orientierte Linguistik«. In: Doyé, Peter/Heuermann, Hartmut/Zimmermann, Günther (eds.): *Die Beziehung der Fremdsprachendidaktik zu ihren Referenzwissenschaften.* Tübingen, 107–123.

17 Index

Printed by Printforce, the Netherlands